Debugging Perl

Troubleshooting for Programmers

Martin Brown

Osborne/**McGraw-Hill**

Berkeley / New York / St. Louis / San Francisco / Auckland / Bogotá
Hamburg / London / Madrid / Mexico City / Milan / Montreal / New Delhi
Panama City / Paris / São Paulo / Singapore / Sydney / Tokyo / Toronto

Osborne/**McGraw-Hill**
2600 Tenth Street
Berkeley, California 94710
U.S.A.

For information on translations or book distributors outside the U.S.A., or to arrange bulk purchase discounts for sales promotions, premiums, or fund-raisers, please contact Osborne/**McGraw-Hill** at the above address.

Debugging Perl: Troubleshooting for Programmers

1234567890 2CUS-2CUS 01987654321

ISBN 0-07-212676-0

Publisher	Brandon A. Nordin
Vice President & Associate Publisher	Scott Rogers
Editorial Director	Wendy Rinaldi
Acquisitions Editor	Ann Sellers
Project Editor	Pamela Woolf
Acquisitions Coordinator	Timothy Madrid
Technical Editor	Ann-Marie Mallon
Copy Editor	Carl Wikander
Proofreader	Rachel Lopez
Indexer	Karin Arrigoni
Computer Designers	Lauren McCarthy, Dick Schwartz
Illustrators	Michael Mueller, Lyssa Wald, Beth E. Young
Series Design	Peter F. Hancik
Cover Design	Dodie Shoemaker, Dian Aziza-Ooka
Cover Illustration	Mark Cable

This book was composed with Corel VENTURA™ Publisher.

Debugging Perl

Troubleshooting for Programmers

About the Author

Martin Brown is the author of *OMG's Perl Annotated Archives*, *Perl: The Complete Reference*, *Perl: Programmer's Reference*, *Python Programming from the Ground Up*, and *ActivePerl Developer's Guide*. A programmer for more than 15 years, he is formally the IT director of a large advertising agency dealing with blue-chip clients such as Hewlett-Packard, Oracle, and Cable & Wireless.

For practicality and speed he writes most of the application and management software he uses everyday in either Perl or shellscript. As part of his Perl work, he wrote the first ever online configuration tool for the Internet, in the form of the *HP Computer Systems Buyers Guide* (www.hp.com/hpwebcat). This system is written entirely in Perl and has been a huge success with Hewlett-Packard. His most recent programming endeavor is a complete network management toolkit with performance monitoring.

You can reach Martin via email at books@mcwords.com.

To Oscar, who provided comfort when I wanted it and
useful distractions to the vet when I didn't.

Contents at a Glance

Table of Contents

Acknowledgements

Once again, the primary thanks go to Wendy Rinaldi who tempted me with Bug Candy and my own custom bug, just so I could write about a topic I know way too much about.

Next, I'd like to thank Ann Sellers who was very patient with me, whilst at the same time keeping me on my toes. Thanks as well to Monika Faltiss, and later Timothy Madrid, who kept all the files in order, and to Pamela Woolf and the rest of the editorial and production team for getting the book edited and produced, and for managing to work through all the mistakes I made.

Ann-Marie Mallon deserves thanks for reading through the entire manuscript and telling me where I'd made a technical error. Extra special thanks go to Jon Piers and the rest of the team on Cix for providing some inspiration and technical help whilst I was working on the book.

Neil Salkind, my agent, deserves a mention for his negotiating skills. He also deserves a slap on the back for continually finding me new things to do. Whilst I'm at it, I also need to thank the rest of the team at StudioB, that's Kristen, Tara, Stacey and Sherry.

Finally, a big thanks to the people who develop Perl—a language that is simultaneously easy to use, prone to bugs, and easy to debug. Without those three components this book would never have been a possibility, and nor would it have been any fun to write!

If there's anybody I've forgotten to acknowledge, I apologize unreservedly in advance. I have done my best to check and verify all sources and contact all parties involved but it's perfectly possible for me to make a mistake.

Introduction

It might surprise you to know that this book is all about debugging Perl scripts and applications. Just like the bug on the front cover, Perl bugs can be annoying and difficult to get rid of and in some cases, just like our little friend, they can sting you. This book will tell all about how to avoid bugs through better programming, how to trap bugs, and how to debug your program when all the other methods have failed.

About this Book

How much time did you spend debugging your last application? 10% of the total development time? 20%? 40%? It might surprise you to know that the general rule of thumb is that you should spend 80% of your time testing and debugging. The obvious solution is not to introduce bugs in the first place, but there we have a problem.

You're going to hear me saying this a lot, but Perl is a very easy and freeform language that just breeds bugs. Perl's power lies in the way that you can write quite complex applications in only a few lines. Even complex projects like text processing and database management can be handled with relative ease in Perl. However, that power comes at a price. A simple typing error can cause a whole heap of problems in Perl that can be difficult to trace. Turn that into a logic error and you've got a bigger problem.

Whether they are simple typographical errors or more significant problems with your code's logic is largely irrelevant; they're bugs and they need to be resolved.

It's this debugging process that we cover in this book. In fact, we go a little bit further. I'm a firm believer in good software design, and that means obtaining a better understanding of how the text that you use for a script is translated by the language into a working program. As part of that process, it's also worth understanding where mistakes can be made during that parsing stage.

There are of course problems in your program that can be tracked and caught as part of the program itself—for example when you **open** a file, you should be testing the return value to make sure it was successful. Knowing when and where to use these is a valuable part of the debugging process that can take place during your programs design. You can also use warnings and pragmas to get Perl to do the work for you. If you've still got bugs once the program has been completed, you'll need to know how to use a debugger to find problems.

An often forgotten type of bug can be resolved through the use of different optimization techniques. Some things you can spot and resolve manually, but others require the use of special tools to enable the problem functions and program areas to be identified. We can even use the Perl compiler for more than just compiling Perl programs. With a little work and creative thought, we can use the compiler to give us in depth information about a script and provide us with useful starting points for isolating problems.

This book covers all these areas and more, giving you a detailed look at how best to approach the problems of writing less error-prone Perl scripts, and at how to resolve and identify bugs after your script has been completed.

Who Is the Book For?

The book is not targeted at a specific group of Perl users. If you use Perl, you should be able to use this book. It obviously relies on some knowledge of how to program in Perl, but even beginners can benefit from the tips on better program design and error trapping. In fact, I'd recommend it as a good read for beginners; it should help you to write less bug prone applications!

For the more advanced users, or those looking to gain an edge in Perl programming, the sections on optimizing Perl and testing your code are required reading. There's a lot more to optimization than just reducing the number of times that you call a subroutine, and you'd be amazed at how many external influences can cause problems in your script when you're not looking.

How to Use This Book

Debugging Perl: Troubleshooting for Programmers is not a reference manual but a guide on better Perl programming and the tools and features available for debugging Perl. This means that for most Perl programmers, the best approach is to read the first three sections and use the remainder for reference purposes. These will give you a good grounding in how best to write Perl programs with fewer bugs, and how to use the built-in trapping features to isolate possible problems before they become reality.

The last two sections should only be used once you are comfortable and familiar with both Perl and the topics introduced earlier in the book. Part IV in particular is highly focussed on the optimization of scripts and not a high priority for most programmers

Appendix A is the main reference section. It contains a list of error messages, with sample code that will raise the error, and solutions to the problem where appropriate. It also provides a cross-reference to other parts of the book where relevant.

Chapter Breakdown

The book is split into six parts. Part I is an introduction and looks at the types of bugs and problems that the book aims to resolve. Part II is a guide to better programming practices when using Perl. Part III covers the art of debugging, from simple error trapping, right up to the tools and facilities provided by Perl for debugging your scripts. Part IV centers on optimization of Perl code. Part V looks at testing and breaking your code once it's been completed to make sure that your program is bug free. Part VI contains Appendix A.

The chapter-specific contents are as follows:

Chapter 1—Introduction, looks at the types of bugs, the mechanics of how bugs are introduced, and some of the ways in which you can ease the development process through the use of good editors and version management systems like RCS and CVS.

Chapter 2—Basic Perl Parsing Rules and Traps gives a detailed look at how Perl takes raw text and parses it into the language statements that make up a Perl program.

Chapter 3—Common Variable Traps is a guide to some of the more popular problems associated with using variables that make it into many Perl programs.

Chapter 4—Statement and Function Traps follows on from the previous chapter and looks instead at problems to do with using functions and statements. This includes a good to some of the function specific bugs that can creep into your applications.

Chapter 5—Program Design is a guide to better program design, from the basics of abstraction, through to better design of functions, modules and objects and classes.

Chapter 6—Language/Platform Migration Guide looks at the common problems associated with moving Perl scripts from platform to platform and at the common mistakes made by programmers who are migrating to Perl from another language.

Chapter 7—Basic Error Trapping is a fundamental look at how to trap and report errors in your scripts.

Chapter 8—Using Pragmas and Warnings gives information on how to use the built-in Perl systems to report possible problems.

Chapter 9—Manual Debugging Techniques is a guide to some of the simpler alternatives to a full blown debugger that you can use to trace and report information so that you can identify and locate a particular bug.

Chapter 10—The Perl Debuggers gives information on the both the standard and ActivePerl debuggers and on the embedded debugging systems that can optionally be included in the Perl interpreter.

Chapter 11— Manual Optimization looks at some of the ways in which you can improve performance, or memory usage, just be looking at the code you are producing.

Chapter 12—Automatic Optimization gives detailed information on the Perl profiler and compiler and how to use the information they provide to identify areas of code that can be optimized.

Chapter 13—Testing Methods is a guide to writing test routines and scripts that check the limits and covers the debugging tool available with the Perl Development kit.

Chapter 14—Breaking Your Code offers some insight into the external factors, and how to manipulate them, so that you can test your code in extreme conditions. This should help you to consider making changes to your code to handle situations you might not have considered during development.

Appendix A—Error Message Quick Reference is a complete guide to the error messages produced by Perl.

Conventions Used in This Book

All Perl keywords are highlighted in **bold**, but functions are listed without parentheses. This is because the C functions on which the Perl versions may be based are shown like **this**().

```
Examples and code are displayed using a fixed-width font.
```

Function descriptions are formatted using the same fixed-width font.

| Note | Notes are formatted like this and include additional information about a particular topic. |

Error Watch *This indicates statements or processes that are likely to trip you up.*

24x7

The 24x7 element is used to indicate good programming styles that should be adopted if you want your code to be robust and stable enough to keeping running 24 hours a day, 7 days a week.

Design Tip *This highlights an item that promotes better programming practice and usually identify a better way of approaching an existing piece of code.*

Contacting the Author

I'm always willing to help you out if you are having problems with any of the scripts and solutions offered in this book. Despite the best efforts of me, my tech editor and the team at Osborne/McGraw-Hill, errors do sometimes occur. Sometimes they can be blamed on a lack of sleep, other times, we've just slipped up! If you are having problems, please check the web site (details below) which will always contain the latest information on any errors and bugs found in the book and it's code.

I also welcome comments and suggestions on my work. Despite programming in Perl for more than six years, there's still a lot to learn. In particular, if you think you've got a better way of doing things, let me know, and I'll try to incorporate it into the next book and post a summary on my web site.

If you do need to get in touch, I prefer to be contacted by email. You can use either books@mcwords.com (preferred) or mc@whoever.com. Alternatively, visit my web site, http://www.mcwords.com, which contains resources and updated information about the scripts and contents of this book. I'll also be updating the examples of common errors on the site too, so keep checking the homepage for more information.

## PART I

Introduction to Perl Debugging

## CHAPTER 1

Introduction

Perl is an exceedingly practical and useful language. You can be as structured or as unstructured as you like and still achieve the same result. Perhaps its most endearing and significant achievement, though, is its use of fairly simple constructs that enable you to solve a variety of problems with only a few lines of actual code. The language is so easy to use, especially for Unix programs, that dropping into an editor to write a quick Perl program to solve a problem has become a way of life for many programmers.

Unfortunately, Perl's free and easy format means that it is easy to introduce errors into your program without realizing what you've done. Perl doesn't enforce error checking—if you decide not to check the return value of a function Perl won't complain. It's even possible to write code that shouldn't really pass the interpreter and still have your program execute, even though it probably won't work.

Identifying and removing bugs is an art. You need to know what you are looking for, and you need to know where the problem occurs. Even within a simple application the root of a problem can be located one or two function calls from where the real problem lies. There are of course different techniques to finding bugs. You can use **print** statements, the built-in debugging functions, or an external debugger. All have their merits and drawbacks.

No matter how you debug your programs, there is actually more to the debugging process than merely picking out those bugs that cause your program to display the wrong result, call the wrong procedure, or fall over completely. It's a fallacy that debugging is just about solving problems in your program after it has been written; you need to think about how the program was written in the first place.

By following some simple practices while writing the code, you can eliminate most bugs before they occur. From the outset, you should be thinking holistically about your program and designing it in such a way that errors are either trapped before the user is aware of them or handled in such a way that they don't affect the user. Basic error trapping should be a part of all your programs—even the simple ones.

You can also use *abstraction*—the division of a program into functions and modules—to split your program up. By dividing your application into functions and modules you increase its reliability and ease of maintenance and, most importantly, make it easier to trace and fix bugs when they do occur.

Design Tip *Even simple things like the use of a good programmer-friendly editor can make a difference. A good editor can help to highlight typographical errors and display your program in a way that makes it easier to understand without having to trace your finger across each component of the statement.*

Irrespective of how you debug your code and what tools and methods you use to make that process easier, an important step in the debugging process is to take a closer look at your code and what it's doing. Many programmers write a piece of code that works, rather than code that works well. For 90 percent of the time the execution does not cause a problem, but it is the 10 percent that counts. If you ask users about their experiences with a program, they are more likely to remember its failures than its successes.

You can use all sorts of techniques to take a closer look at your code. By employing debuggers you can follow the execution of your code in minute detail. For finding individual bugs, this approach is perfect, but when you want to improve on the execution of your code, you need to use a profiler to monitor how much time each section of your code takes. You can also employ some unexpected features of the Perl compiler to provide you with some useful background information on your script. Identifying all these different effects and solutions to those problems is what this book is about. We'll be looking at how Perl parses a statement and how easy it is to introduce a bug just from typical programming techniques. We'll also look at the methods available for tracing and tracking bugs, both in the code and in the logic and execution of the code. The final part of the book looks at methods of testing your code to ensure that you trap all of the bugs that might appear.

As an introduction, let's look at the basic bug types and briefly go over some of the general issues that you need to address when debugging your code.

Bug Types

You can think about the process of program development as a sort of hierarchical tree. At the top are the input values and at the bottom is the output value, or result of the program. It is a sad fact that a lot of application development is treated from the bottom up, rather than the top down. The *top-down* approach forces the developer into thinking about all of the steps to reach the result. The *bottom-up* approach means trying different techniques until you reach a result that works from the top to the bottom.

The bottom-up approach is slower, but often more practical from a programmer's point of view because it helps to gel ideas and form methods and processes in the programmer's mind that will ultimately be reflected in the final application.

The approach chosen has some effect on the bugs that you can introduce into the program. With the bottom-up approach you do not consider all of the factors before developing a new component and are, therefore, likely to introduce more errors than with the more pragmatic, top-down approach.

A mistake often made by developers is to ignore the effects of a bug or to fail to classify the bug and its effect. Although not normally seen as a major problem—a bug is a bug—it can affect the way bug problems are solved (which may have "knock on" effects to other bugs) and can also cause other bugs to be ignored entirely.

Personally, I've always considered that there are essentially three types of bugs when programming: the typographical, the logic, and the execution bugs.

The Typographical Bug

The *typographical bug* is one introduced through a typographical error, either through bad typing or a momentary lapse in concentration that causes you to forget the semantics of the language. In Perl this can be as easy as using $ instead of @ when referring to a variable, or forgetting to place parentheses around a statement to ensure list, rather than scalar, context on a function.

Some of these errors will of course be picked up by the Perl interpreter during the compilation process, as they will break the basic rules of the parsing engine for Perl. Other errors will be compiled okay, and they might even pass the usual warning and **strict** pragmas without raising any sort of indication of the problem. As a typical example, look at this code:

```
$string = "The cat sat on the mat";
$animal = ($string =~ m/The (.*) sat/);
print $animal;
```

If you knew that there was a bug in there, what would you do? Reading it probably doesn't highlight the problem immediately, even to the hardened programmers. Asking Perl to check code through the parser with warnings switched on will not raise any errors. Run the script though and the error is obvious—we get a value of 1, instead of the expected "cat" response.

Other typographical bugs can be more obscure. On a recent web project the login process suddenly stopped working. The login system worked by checking the user name and password against a database, and, assuming both were approved, the script would generate a unique session ID, which was also placed into the database. The problem was that the ID would be approved and the session ID created, but the user couldn't connect using the new session ID.

It took a little time, but by comparing the session ID returned to the user and the session ID in the database it was obvious that the 27-digit session ID would exceed the 26-digit field width. For 50 percent of the time the session ID system worked fine, for the other 50 percent the session ID would exceed the field width and fail. This is another type of typographical error: entering the wrong width into the database creation script.

You can generally resolve typographical bugs through a combination of careful code reading and a sound understanding of how Perl parses statements. We'll be looking at the specifics of how Perl approaches the problem of parsing individual statements in Chapter 2.

The Logic Bug

Logic bugs occur when the programmer has failed to spot a flaw in the logical flow of the program. Like typographical bugs, these can be very obvious—for example, failing to identify one of the possible return values from a function or incorrectly specifying a test or other operation. These are not typographical errors—the programmer really thought he or she was doing the right thing at the time.

As an example, and as an extension of the typographical error earlier, the same login system suddenly started returning bad logins after some optimization of the login code. The login function returned a negative number on error, a zero if the session or login had expired, and a positive number on success. After tracing the bug for hours it finally became apparent that the problem was because the **if** statement checking the return value tested for a strict zero response as failure, with any other response taken as valid.

Another example is the use of references in your code. When using a reference you must *dereference* the variable before the variable contents can be accessed. For example, when accessing a reference to a hash, you don't use

```
$hash{$key}
```

but instead use

```
$hash->{$key}
```

This is not a typographical error, but a logic error; the programmer completely ignored the fact that the access was to a reference to a hash, not a real hash.

Logic bugs are generally easier to identify than typographical errors. With typographical errors you can generally track the problem to a possible location, but without aid from the Perl parser it can be hard to see the woods for the trees. With logic bugs, you can trace and track the logic and execution sequence until you find the specific line that causes the problem.

Logic bugs can be approached from a number of directions. The most obvious is for the programmer to understand the logic of the Perl interpreter, from the basics of variables and how to access them to the uses of operators, functions, and regular expressions. Logic bugs are all related to how you access and use the information stored within your script—if you can understand and identify how Perl approaches the problem, tracing the problem should be straightforward. Chapters 3 and 4 concentrate on how to identify logic bugs in your programs.

Other ways of tracing logic bugs include the use of abstraction—turning components of your program into subroutines, modules, packages, even objects. By separating out the individual elements, you can eliminate the source of the problem section by section. Abstraction also makes your code more portable and more manageable. We'll look at abstraction in Chapter 5, and we'll see how it can improve the portability of your code in Chapter 6.

The Execution Bug

The *execution bug* is one of the hardest to find, and there are many who probably do not consider it to be a bug at all. The execution bug is one that affects the execution process of a program; not because of a typo or a logic problem, but because the application has been designed in a way that allows a certain chain of events to slow or halt the application's execution.

Execution bugs do slow your application but might not actually generate a bad result or manifest themselves in any other way. For example, imagine a database application that pulls records out of a database. A typical search returns 200 records, and the script works within a few seconds, well within the limits you might expect for extracting information from the database. When a search returns 1,000 records, however, the script takes almost a minute to execute.

The problem is not logic—the script works and behaves exactly as it should—and it's not a typographical error—the information is formatted correctly and there really are 1,000 records in the database to be displayed. So how come it takes so long?

The problem here is one of execution—either the programmer needs to introduce a limiter to reduce the effect of accessing and displaying that many records, or there's a portion of the application that takes an excessive amount of time to parse the information. This is an execution bug—there's nothing wrong with the application, it just doesn't execute at the level you would expect.

Execution bugs are difficult to trace, but once found and resolved they have some benefits. An application that has been cleansed of its execution bugs will be more robust than a normal application, and it's likely to be more stable in use. Because execution bugs frequently affect the performance, eliminating those bugs will help to optimize your application.

The easiest way to find an execution bug is to execute your program, but to isolate the location of that bug you'll need some tools and techniques. The last sections of the book—from Chapter 7 through 14—will look at bug trapping and application optimization and testing.

Basic Perl Debugging Rules

Whatever tricks or methods you use to try to trace and track the bugs in your code, there are some fairly basic rules that you should always follow, irrespective of your approach.

- **Always check the obvious**—If you were to give the average programmer a piece of code to debug, he or she would almost certainly start looking in the wrong place. Some of the examples given earlier in this chapter should demonstrate that it's often the obvious things that cause the most difficulty.

- **Always check from the outside in**—You should always follow the execution path from the outside of the code to the inside. Unless you've got an exact reference of where the bug occurs, you should look at the function in which the bug appears and then trace the bug through from that function to other nested functions until you find the root.

  Tracing from the inside out causes problems because you don't know what other processes have occurred that might have led to the bug. For example, a function that returns the wrong value may have been supplied the wrong value—checking the function and finding nothing wrong is a pointless exercise.

- **Always start from the top when dealing with a typographical error**—You should start looking at the code from the top and work down; don't work backward. Typographical errors have a nasty habit of causing run-on effects. In order to demonstrate this, try placing an additional opening parenthesis into a script—Perl will return all sorts of errors that have nothing to do with actual problem.

- **Always start from the bottom when solving parser errors**—Perl outputs a probable line number for the problem. If you work from the top and upset the line numbering you'll need to re-parse the script to identify the new line numbers. If you work from the bottom your line changes will not affect the earlier line numbers, and you can solve many more bugs before you need to re-parse the script.

- **Always switch on warnings**—Warnings give you much more information about the possible bugs that you may have overlooked than just allowing the parser to work normally. Warnings highlight potential problems, such as unused variables (which highlight typos), misused variable types (which highlight logic errors), and code that might never be reached.

> • **Always work with the strict pragma**—The **strict** pragma enforces many Perl parsing rules to a much higher standard than normal. It causes Perl to check the syntax of certain operations—variables, references and subroutines—to a much greater degree than normal and, like warnings, can highlight problems during the parsing process.
>
> We'll look at many of these issues in closer detail elsewhere in this guide.

Bug Prevention

It should be obvious that trying to prevent the introduction of bugs before they occur is the best way to approach the problem—prevention is always better than cure. The problem is that prevention is sometimes more time-consuming than the curing process and gives the appearance of slowing down the development process. In truth, by preventing the bugs instead of curing them, you improve the chances of making the deadlines, because you'll be spending less time searching for them after the event.

But how do you prevent bugs from occurring in the first place? Many of the techniques are beyond the scope of this book because they rely on the fundamental approach toward the programming goal rather than Perl language, but they are worth mentioning.

Program Design

When developing an application, having a good idea about what it is going to produce is vital, and having a good idea about how to achieve that goal is a good way of ensuring that bugs are not introduced into the software. Even just writing down a quick list of functions and what you expect them to do is better than making it up as you go along.

It's also worth coming up with a system or style and sticking to it. When programming a database, for example, you could exchange information by supplying an array, or a reference to a hash, or an object. Using all three is bound to lead to problems; first when you try to remember what a particular function does, and second when you try to convert between the two methods.

At the other end of the equation are programs that are designed and developed to the *nth* degree from start to finish and end up with design manuals that run to more lines than code you are producing. Program design to this level has its place—I would hope that Nuclear Power station software and the fly-by-wire computers built into most modern planes use this. On the other hand, developing this kind of documentation for quick script to convert data file formats is wholly unnecessary.

Editors

A good editor should be a vital component of any programmer's armory. Most modern editors will match parentheses and help you indent your code to make it more readable. Emacs, probably the most popular programmer's editor, does this automatically and almost enforces the option for scripts that it identifies as Perl-based. More advanced editors, such as BBEdit (for Mac), EditPlus (for Windows), and the modified xemacs (for Unix), can also color the code according to the individual language.

Using an editor that performs these simple checks will help to eliminate many of the simple typographic errors that cause many bugs and compilation failures. They can also provide visual cues for identifying problems.

Formatting

Choose a formatting standard and stick to it. You don't have to look at much of the code written by programmers to see that, in general, it's clean and tidy and easy to read. Perl helps this process along, and using a good editor will also help, but there's still some flexibility in choosing your own style. Don't mix and match styles, as it will be more difficult for you to identify bugs when you do go back in to read your code.

For example, when you create a new code block there are two basic formats:

```
if ($condition) {
...
} else {
...
}
```

or

```
if ($condition)
{
...
}
else
{
...
}
```

The former is shorter and more compact, but it can become fussy when you introduce **elsif** statements. The second style is longer, but generally easier to follow because you can match up braces vertically within the code.

Larry Wall, the original instigator of Perl, suggests the following guidelines:

- Four-column indent
- Opening curly on same line as keyword, if possible; otherwise line up
- Space before the opening curly of a multiline BLOCK
- One-line BLOCK may be put on one line, including curlies
- No space before the semicolon
- Semicolon omitted in "short" one-line BLOCK
- Space around most operators
- Space around a "complex" subscript (inside brackets)
- Blank lines between chunks that do different things
- Uncuddled **elses**
- No space between function name and its opening parenthesis
- Space after each comma
- Long lines broken after an operator (except **and** and **or**)
- Space after last parenthesis matching on current line
- Line up corresponding items vertically
- Omit redundant punctuation as long as clarity doesn't suffer

There are also other style issues you should consider; check the **perlstyle** man page for information

Comments

Have you ever read a piece of code just a few weeks after you've written it and wondered exactly what it was you were doing?

Imagine trying to debug that same bit of code—it might work okay, but without a comment to that effect there is no way for the programmer to know for certain that the technique achieves the desired result. Tools such as bug-tracking systems and code revision monitors will help; we'll take a quick look at those later in this chapter. If it doesn't work correctly, you might still need a quick guide as to how the function or code fragment works so that you can follow the execution when it comes to debugging the code.

Some other issues to keep in mind when writing comments:

- Don't repeat what the line does—saying "while loop" on a line that contains the **while** keyword is not helpful. Say "iterate through the source file" or something similar.
- Don't list the arguments—a good programmer will be able to spot what arguments are being extracted.

- Do list the types of input variable (for example, classify array or reference to array).

- Do specify the return values and expectations of when they should be returned.

- Do document the error/failure conditions and return values.

Remember that comments are there to jog your memory and highlight the execution sequence to other programmers, not to provide an English language running commentary or vent for your frustrations. We'll look in more detail at comments and documentation in Chapter 5.

Code Revisions

The Revision Code System (RCS) and Concurrent Versioning System (CVS) both provide ways for you to track the differences between the versions of the your code. The general mode of operation is to write a piece of code and have it working, but perhaps not necessarily debugged, and then "check in" the revision to the revision system. When you make changes to the code and it fails, you can then always go back to a previous version.

24x7   Bug Tracking

Finding bugs is one thing, but remembering where they all are is another matter. At the very least you should be keeping a textual record of the bugs that have occurred and whether they have been fixed. Including information about what the bug was and how it was fixed is also a good idea, because doing so might help you to identify and trace subsequent bugs.

When you discover a bug you should be recording:

- Location—give the line number and file name if known or, at the very least, a possible function culprit.

- Description of the bug that occurs, including what you expect to happen and what actually did happen.

- Date and time the bug was discovered and name of user who reported the bug.

- Any other relevant information, such as the platform, environment variables, and any factors that may have led to the bug.

If you want to be more professional about your bug tracking, consider using tracking software such as BugZilla, which is part of the Mozilla project. The system is actually written in Perl and is available as a Web interface to an underlying MySQL database. You can download BugZilla from http://bugzilla.mozilla.org.

RCS (which is actually used by CVS) allows you to store comments with each revision and to automatically track version numbers of each file that you check in. You should use those opportunities to give a status report, both on what you achieved in the new revision and an indication of the bugs or issues that you addressed. The version numbers can be useful when tracking bugs as well as when receiving bug reports from your end users—it's quite possible that the bug they are reporting has already been fixed in a new revision.

The difference between CVS and RCS is that RCS allows only a single user to be editing an individual source file at any one time, whereas CVS allows for true concurrent development by a number of programmers. CVS also includes additional features, such as the capability to export its tree over the Internet and the ability to automatically create a new package based on the "current" version numbers of the source files, even if they are still in production.

If you are the only programmer, RCS will more than likely serve your needs. You can get more information and download RCS from http://www.gnu.org/software/rcs/rcs.html. If you think you need CVS, check out the CVS Bubbles page at http://www.loria.fr/~molli/cvs-index.html.

## PART II

Perl Logic and Syntax

## CHAPTER 2

Basic Perl Parsing Rules and Traps

Many problems with applications that manifest themselves as bugs are really just faults in the simple logic and syntax used to parse the language. The problems can range from those that are introduced through a typographical error to those that violate the more esoteric parsing rules employed by Perl. Unfortunately, Perl has many basic rules and also exceptions to those rules, even at the fundamental level of the parsing engine (see the section later in the chapter entitled "Terms and List Operators").

The obvious approach to this problem is to make sure that you write the code correctly in the first place. It's also a good idea to at least "sanity check" your code manually before you try executing it—often you'll pick up errors just by rereading what you just typed. It's quite possible to waste hours of time fixing individual bugs and then re-trying the code, when a simple read-through would have revealed a number of problems in a single pass.

We'll be looking at debugging techniques later in this book, and many of the tricks we'll examine will help you isolate problems and identify their location. Prevention is always better than cure. A better understanding of how Perl takes a raw script, compiles it, and then executes each line should help you to make fewer mistakes and introduce fewer of those accidental bugs. Over time, it'll also help you to automatically write cleaner code, so that you won't have to go back and fix bugs that you've introduced.

In this chapter we'll start by looking at the basic Perl syntax rules, at precedence rules, at how different operators and expressions are evaluated, and at how Perl treats string and numerical constants. The intention here is not really to teach you Perl—you should already know it!—but to give you a better understanding of the rules and logic that govern the Perl language.

These rules cover statements and lines in Perl, naming conventions, operators, precedence, and the evaluation of values into their logical equivalents. The chapter also serves as the basis for understanding how and why Perl highlights statements and sequences with particular problems and will include examples of how some of the more basic bugs can occur at a statement level. We will look at specific problems with variables, constants, compound statements, and functions in future chapters.

The Execution Process

The first step in understanding how Perl parses a script is to take a top-level look at how Perl takes the source text and executes. Perl works in a similar fashion to many other script-based languages—it takes raw input, parses each statement, and converts it into a series of *opcodes* (the smallest executable component within a Perl program). Next, it builds a suitable opcode tree and then executes the opcodes within a Perl "virtual machine." This technique is used by Perl, Python, and Java, and it's one of the most significant reasons that Perl is as quick as it is—the code is optimized into very small executable chunks, just like a program compiled for a specific standard hardware processor.

To summarize, the basic sequence works as follows:

1. Read the source code and identify any basic problems, such as an inability to open a required module.

2. Compile the source into a series of opcodes. Doing this involves the use of a parser that translates the Perl source into the opcode structures. It is actually here that the majority of source errors are identified and raised.

3. Execute the opcode tree.

I'd like to take a detour for a moment and actually take a look at how Perl parses the individual statements and converts them into the opcodes used by the Perl virtual machine to actually execute the script. It's not vital to understand, and if you want to skip this section, feel free—I won't be referring back to this. If you're not sure whether you should read this, read it anyway—it provides a useful, if largely trivial for this instance, look at Perl from the inside.

If you really want to get to the details of Perl, the obvious solution is to start reading the source code. Perl has an advantage over many other languages in that the source code is readily available for you to read. However, it's not for those with a weak heart. Perl's core interpreter consists of over 78,000 lines of code. Despite the fact that it is so large, and relatively uncommented, this fact shouldn't dissuade you from at least having a peek.

The best way to read the code is to download the latest sources and start by examining the source code for the different variable types. The most important is obviously the *SV*, or *scalar value*, this will tell the basics of how Perl stores most types of information. The definition for an SV is in the **sv.c** file. The **av.c** and **hv.c** files contain information on array and hash values, respectively. Once you are comfortable with the concepts there, you should move on to the **op.c** and **doop.c** files, which handle the opcode definitions (see "Opcodes" later in this chapter), before finally examining the execution process in **run.c**, preferably with a debugger such as **gdb** (available from GNU, http://www.gnu.org) or the debugger that comes with Microsoft's Developer Studio Product. If you want to skip the technical details and examine the lexical process of converting the written Perl script into the internal structures and opcodes, look at **perly.y**. This is a **yacc** definition file that outlines the main components and structures for the Perl language. It's this file that contains the precedence rules and governs the entire parsing process. It's also at this point that most of the warnings and parsing errors are first discovered and then raised.

Some of the more complex lexical analysis is hand-coded within the other source files, most notably **toke.c**. For regular expressions, Perl uses a modified standard regular expression library, although all the functionality has actually been rewritten from scratch. The regular expression compiler and executor are in the **regcomp.c** and **regexec.c** files, respectively.

If you want to avoid the source code, or perhaps just cannot follow it, three tools are available on CPAN that provide access to the internal structures within Perl. The **Devel::Peek** module allows you to dump the internal information associated with a variable, while **Devel::Symdump** will dump the symbol table. The **Devel::RegExp** module can examine and monitor regular expressions.

Architecture

You can see from Figure 2-1 the basic architecture for the entire Perl interpreter. The shaded blocks show the internal components of the Perl interpreter, including the internal data structures and the execution components. The unshaded blocks on the diagram are the compiled C source code.

Some of you will recognize the diagram as being somewhat similar to the virtual machine diagram often used to describe the operation of the Java language. There *are* some similarities between the two languages: Perl uses the optimized opcodes in combination with the Executor component to actually run the Perl script. We'll look at these similarities more closely as we examine the execution process.

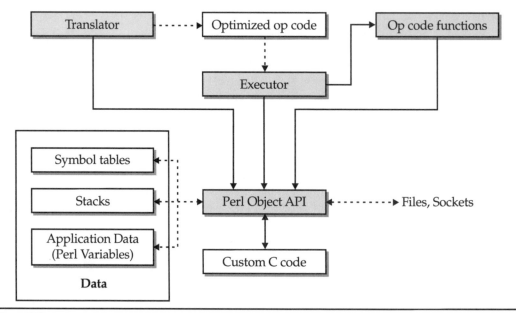

Figure 2.1 The Perl architecture

Internal Objects

The Perl Object API in Figure 2-1 represents the functions and structures used to support the four main internal data structures for any Perl program: variables, symbol tables, stacks, and external data streams.

The data formats supported by Perl are a core part of the language; they enable you to program the language, of course, but they are also used to hold a significant amount of internal information used by the interpreter. For example, the symbol tables for individual packages are stored within a hash variable, with the values as pointers to *glob values* of the real variable stored within the interpreter. Each variable is known by its two-letter abbreviation, which are listed in Table 2-1.

The scalar value can also be further subclassed as an IV (*integer value*), PV (*string value*), and DV (*double value* or *floating point value*). Other internal data structures, such as the symbol tables and

Acronym	Full Name
SV	Scalar value
AV	Array value
HV	Hash value
CV	Code value
GV	Glob value (typeglobs)
RV	Reference value

Table 2.1 Internal Perl Data Type Acronyms

stacks, are also represented by these core value types, which are strictly managed and controlled with efficient memory management.

Temporary information such as that passed to functions as arguments, the current location within a script, and the variables used to store temporary data are all held on stacks. For example, when function **foo** wants to call function **bar** with arguments, the arguments are pushed onto the argument stack and **bar** is called. The first operation performed by **bar** internally is to pop the arguments off the stack and populate the function's @_ array. Other individual stacks are used to hold the other temporary variables, such as local variables, loop iterators, and control information for the Perl interpreter. Incidentally, *external* data streams are handled by a separate I/O abstraction API. This API is a suite of functions that provides a thin porting layer for the standard **stdio** and **sfio** libraries and the necessary hooks to the interpreter to allow **print**, the **<FILEHANDLE>,** and similar operators and functions with connectivity to the outside world. A similar system is used for sockets.

Translator

The translator converts the Perl script into a series of opcodes, which we'll take a closer look at shortly. The opcodes are listed in a tree format to allow for branching, argument passing, and structured logical progression through the original script. The translator is made up of a combination of the **yacc**-based parser file, a hand-coded lexical analyzer, and the actual opcode generator. This point is also where regular expressions are compiled (assuming they can be compiled at compilation time) using a customized regular expression engine.

Opcodes

An opcode is the smallest executable component within a Perl program. There are opcodes for all of the built-in functions and operators in the Perl language. During the execution stage it is the opcodes, and the functions on which they rely, that are executed by the Perl interpreter. It is at this point that Perl begins to resemble the Java-style virtual machine.

Within Java, all operations are resolved down a machine-code–like format, not vastly dissimilar to the assembly language for a RISC (reduced instruction set computer) processor. RISC processors use a small number of instructions, with more complex operations being based on collections of the reduced set of instructions. When you execute a Java program, you are effectively emulating a RISC processor and all the baggage that goes with it. This process has some advantages, since it makes building a hardware-based Java processor as easy as building any other processor. However, this is where the similarities between Java and Perl end.

In Perl, the level of abstraction is much higher. Many of the functions in Perl that you use at a scripting level are in fact entire opcodes. Even functions as seemingly complex as the **grep** function are handled by a single opcode. Perl 5.6 includes 351 opcodes, a slight increase over the previous version. The source code for many of the opcodes is entirely hand- rather than compiler-optimized, which explains why much of the Perl code executes so fast. When you "interpret" a Perl script, you are running almost native C code, just written (translated) from Perl.

The use of such high-level opcode abstraction and the hand-coded and hand-optimized C source code that executes it explains why it is so easy to build a Perl compiler that creates very fast stand-alone executables. It also explains why the speed difference between interpreted Perl scripts and Perl-based executables generated by the Perl compiler is often minimal. In fact, I've even seen an interpreted version of an application working faster than the compiled version. The unexpected comparative speed in this instance could be due to the effects of loading the wrapper that sits around the opcodes in order to make them run, or it could just be a complete fluke.

An opcode is defined by a C structure called **op** in the **op.h** header file. The important fields for any opcode are defined as follows:

```
OP*         op_next;
OP*         (*op_ppaddr)();
OPCODE      op_type;
```

The **op_next** field is a pointer to the next opcode to be executed when the current opcode has completed. The **op_type** field defines the type of opcode that will be executed. Different opcodes require different additional fields in order to define their execution. The list of opcode types can be determined from the **opcodes.pl** script, which is itself executed during the compilation of the interpreter. This file also conveniently lists all of the opcodes.

The **op_ppaddr** field contains the pointer to the function that will actually be executed. The functions are defined in the **pp.c**, **pp_ctl.c**, **pp_sys.c**, and **pp_hot.c** source files in the distribution tree. The first three define a range of opcode functions that support the standard operators and functions, while the last is the most important from a speed point of view.

The **pp_hot.c** file contains all the opcode functions that are hand-optimized and are expected to be executed a number of times in a typical Perl script. The opcodes defined in this file include those related to assignments, regular expressions, conditional operators, and functions related to handling and converting scalar and list values.

It's also worth noting that there are opcodes for defining and obtaining different variables and constants. Even the definition of a static value within a Perl script is actually handled by an opcode. The significance of this aspect of Perl will become apparent very shortly.

Remember that I described the opcode sequence as being a tree? I made this analogy because certain opcode functions require calls to additional opcodes for their information. Consider the following Perl script:

```
$a = $b + 2;
```

There are four opcodes in this statement. There are two operators—one is the assignment of the expression to the **$a** scalar, and the other is the addition of the **$b** scalar and the constant. There are also two values—one is the **$b** scalar, the other the constant value of 2. Each of these items, operators and values, is an opcode.

You can view the opcodes produced by the statement if your version of Perl has been built with the **–DDEBUGGING** option. The opcode tree is reproduced when you execute a Perl program using the **-Dx** command line option. For example, the command

```
perl -Dx -e '$a = $b +2;'
```

produces

```
{
8   TYPE = leave  ===> DONE
    FLAGS = (VOID,KIDS,PARENS)
    {
```

```
1         TYPE = enter   ===> 2
      }
      {
2         TYPE = nextstate   ===> 3
          FLAGS = (VOID)
          LINE = 1
      }
      {
7         TYPE = sassign   ===> 8
          FLAGS = (VOID,KIDS,STACKED)
          {
5             TYPE = add   ===> 6
              TARG = 1
              FLAGS = (SCALAR,KIDS)
              {
                  TYPE = null   ===> (4)
                    (was rv2sv)
                  FLAGS = (SCALAR,KIDS)
                  {
3                     TYPE = gvsv   ===> 4
                      FLAGS = (SCALAR)
                      GV = main::b
                  }
              }
              {
4                 TYPE = const   ===> 5
                  FLAGS = (SCALAR)
                  SV = IV(2)
              }
          }
          {
              TYPE = null   ===> (7)
                (was rv2sv)
              FLAGS = (SCALAR,KIDS,REF,MOD,SPECIAL)
              {
6                 TYPE = gvsv   ===> 7
                  FLAGS = (SCALAR)
                  GV = main::a
              }
          }
      }
   }
}
```

You can follow the execution through the opcode tree by following the opcode numbers, which are shown in the first column. Each pair of braces defines the information about a single opcode, and nested braces show the parent-child relation between the opcodes. Execution starts at opcode number one, which starts the execution of the script. Then it moves to opcode number two, which defines the line number (this is where line directive information is stored). Opcode number two hands off to the first executable opcode, which is number three. This third opcode gets the scalar value of the **main::b** scalar variable and places it onto the stack.

Execution is then passed to opcode number four, which places the static integer value of 2 onto the stack, which then passes execution to opcode number five, the "add" opcode. It takes the two arguments from the stack and adds them together, placing the result back on the stack for opcode six, which obtains the reference for the variable named **main::a** and places it on the stack. Then opcode seven assigns **main::a** the value of addition placed on the stack in opcode five. This is the end of the script.

The tree structure can be seen from this description. The assignation opcode has two siblings: the variable to which the value is to be assigned and the value. The value is calculated from the result of the addition, which as a binary operator has two children: the values it is adding together. You can see this opcode structure more clearly in Figure 2-2.

Obviously, the more complex the statement, the more complex the opcode tree. And once you examine the output from a multiline script, you'll begin to identify just how efficient and complex the Perl opcode system is. We'll actually be taking a look at the -D debugging option in Chapter 10 and Chapter 12, and at how you can use the Perl compiler to improve the execution speed of your script in Chapter 12.

Compilation

The actual compilation stage is a multipass process that first processes the basic Perl script using the **yacc** parser. Language parsed by **yacc** is actually processed from the bottom up—the most complex expressions within single statements are processed first. So the nodes at the deepest points (leaves) of an execution tree are populated first, before the higher opcodes (twigs and branches) are finally produced. After the statements have been passed, you can follow the execution line by line, by examining the trunk of the opcode tree.

After all the opcodes have been produced, the compiler then goes over a number of optimization processes. The first is called *constant folding* and identifies entries that can be executed at the point of compilation. For example, the statement

```
$a = 4 + 5;
```

can be reduced from four opcodes to three by instead creating a parent opcode that assigns a value of 9 to the **$a** variable:

```
$a = 9;
```

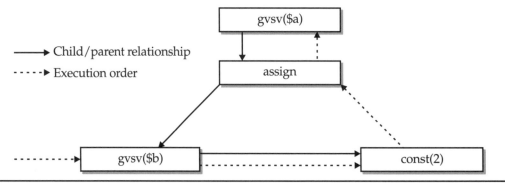

Figure 2.2   Opcode tree structure

You can see the effect of this by comparing the opcode tree above, which added a value to a variable and assigned it to a new variable, against the opcode tree for this more basic statement, which essentially just assigns the constant 9 to the **$a** variable:

```
{
6    TYPE = leave   ===> DONE
     FLAGS = (VOID,KIDS,PARENS)
     {
1        TYPE = enter   ===> 2
     }
     {
2        TYPE = nextstate   ===> 3
         FLAGS = (VOID)
         LINE = 1
     }
     {
5        TYPE = sassign   ===> 6
         FLAGS = (VOID,KIDS,STACKED)
         {
3            TYPE = const   ===> 4
             FLAGS = (SCALAR)
             SV = IV(9)
         }
         {
             TYPE = null   ===> (5)
                (was rv2sv)
             FLAGS = (SCALAR,KIDS,REF,MOD,SPECIAL)
             {
4                TYPE = gvsv   ===> 5
                 FLAGS = (SCALAR)
                 GV = main::a
             }
         }
     }
}
```

The next optimization process is *context propagation*, which is the act of defining the context to a specific opcode and its children. You are used to the terms "scalar" or "list" context when creating and using functions. Internally, Perl also supports contexts for void, Boolean, and lvalue statements. Context propagation works top down—that is, parent opcodes are examined first, and the context requirement is then propagated down to child opcodes.

The final optimization stage is a process of reduction and is handled by the peephole optimizer. This process effectively executes the opcode tree, but without actually doing anything. The purpose is to look ahead to future opcodes in the tree and reduce them as much as possible. In current versions of the interpreter the lookahead is only two statements, which means that a maximum of three statements could be reduced to just one statement.

Any larger figure would slow down the optimization process to the point that any gains made in optimizing the opcode tree would be lost in the optimization process itself. Remember that Perl is still essentially an interpreter, and unlike with C or Java, the opcode tree is regenerated each time a script is executed. When you execute a Perl script, Perl doesn't simply re-execute the previous optimized opcode tree. Perl assumes the source file has changed (probably a good idea).

Some schools of thought find the optimization and compilation of Perl scripts for each invocation to be a bad process, since all scripts must be compiled and interpreted every time. Even the modules in the standard library or those obtained from CPAN are compiled each time, despite the fact that the chances of them changing for each execution are small.

Python, one of Perl's biggest competitors, is also a scripted and compiled-at-runtime language, but it compiles modules once and incorporates the compiled versions at runtime, updating them only if the module source modification date is later than the compiled version. The Python language lends itself more readily to this process—being entirely object-based, it provides much more scope for importing an object definition and its methods in a solid block. Doing this would be difficult with Perl in its current form because Perl is not modular enough to support such blocked imports. There might be improvements in this area in the future.

There are solutions to the problem of using raw source instead of compiled opcodes each time. Perl will allow you, through the compiler extensions, to execute an opcode tree directly. There are also tools that follow this train of thought—the script is compiled and then held in memory in its opcode rather than source state, ready for immediate execution. Both the PerlEx extension for use with Microsoft's Internet Information Server product and the **mod_perl** extension for Apache use this model.

Ultimately, the use of the source script for each invocation makes individual executions slower than they might otherwise be. The current restriction of a two-statement lookahead for peephole optimization also has an effect, since it does not fully optimize the code. Truly compiled language such as C/C++ will, if required, optimize and reduce as far as possible, with a reasonable compilation overhead beforehand.

On the other hand, Perl's optimization pass ensures that every execution of a script is optimized to a reasonable point, even if you change just one character in the original script each time. Unfortunately, there is no way of controlling the peephole process. You cannot specify, for example, that when creating a stand-alone executable the peephole lookahead value will be greater than two, although this would be a great idea.

Execution

After all three stages of the optimization have taken place, it's time to execute the code. The actual path of execution is not as sequential as it may have appeared earlier. All opcodes are numbered, and it's the value of the **op_next** (from the **op** structure) that defines the actual execution path. Since Perl supports conditional statements like **if** and loops like **while**, some opcodes may never be executed or may be executed a significant number of times. Perl therefore relies on the value of **pp_next** returned by each opcode to decide which opcode to execute next.

For each opcode, Perl calls the corresponding opcode function. Each opcode is just a C function embedded into the interpreter, and the opcode is supplied with any suitable arguments and information, including any child opcodes, that are also required to call what the programmer recognizes as the original statement. Once all the opcodes in the desired execution path have been executed, with the entire tree having been followed, the Perl interpretation ends, and Perl quits.

Execution Summary

You can see from this, if you've been able to follow it through, that Perl has a number of locations and opportunities for highlighting and indicating a particular error. At every stage of the execution Perl could raise an error, right from the primary parsing to the execution stage. How Perl handles these errors and how you can trap, identify, and rectify them are really what this book is all about. You can actually classify errors according to where and when they occur. See the Appendix A for a comprehensive list of error messages and information on which stage of the execution process they are raised.

Syntax and Parsing Rules

The Perl parser has to consider a number of different items when it takes in a source script and attempts to execute the statements. The primary purpose is, of course, to identify the different elements within each line as operators, terms, and constants; the parser then evaluates each sequence to produce a particular result—this might include calling a function (which itself will need the same statement examination) or performing a calculation.

Even before Perl gets to these elements, however, the parser must examine the individual source lines for information. Comments need to be identified and removed and the basic layout of the line has to be validated (Does it have a trailing semicolon? Does it run on to the next line? and so on).

In fact, the Perl parser thinks about all the following when it looks at a source line:

- **Basic syntax**   The core layout, line termination, and so on.
- **Comments**   If a comment is included, ignore it.
- **Component identity**   Individual terms (variables, functions, and numerical and textual constants) are identified.
- **Barewords**   Character strings that are not identified as valid terms.
- **Precedence**   Once the individual items are identified, the parser processes the statements according the precedence rules, which apply to all operators and terms.
- **Context**   What is the context of the statement? Are we expecting a list or scalar, a number or a string, and so on. This process actually happens during the evaluation of individual elements of a line, which is why we can nest functions such as **sort, reverse**, and **keys** into a single statement line.
- **Logic Syntax**   For logic operations, the parser must treat different values, whether constant-or variable-based, as true or false values.

All these present some fairly basic and fundamental rules about how Perl looks at an entire script; from the basic Hello World to entire database applications, each line is executed in the same manner, using the same basic rules.

Basic Syntax

The basic syntax rules govern such things as line termination and the treatment of whitespace. These basic rules are as follows:

- Lines must start with a token that does not expect a left operand—for example,

```
= 99;
```

  is invalid, because the = operator expects to see a valid lvalue on the left-hand side of the expression. As a general rule, a function, keyword, or variable is the primary token in a line, with some exceptions.

- Lines must be terminated with a semicolon, except when it's the last line of a block, when the semicolon can be omitted. For example,

```
print "Hello\n"
```

  is perfectly legal as a single-line script; since it's the last line of a block, it doesn't require any semicolon. On the other hand,

```
print "Hello "
print "World\n"
```

  will cause a fault.

- If you split a line within a quoted string, the line termination becomes part of the string.
- Whitespace is required only between tokens that would otherwise be confusing, so spaces, tabs, newlines, and comments (which Perl treats as whitespace) are ignored. The line

```
sub menu{print"menu"}
```

  works as it would if it were more neatly spaced.

- Lines may be split at any point, providing the split is logically between two tokens. The following is perfectly legal:

```
print
"hello"

            "world";
```

 These are fairly basic rules, and if broken they'll cause an error during the initial parsing stage and halt the execution of the script.

Comments

Comments are treated by Perl as whitespace—the moment Perl sees a hash on a line outside of a quoted block, the remainder of the line is ignored. It does this even within multiline statements and regular expressions (when the **/x** modifier is used):

```
matched = /(\S+)      #Host
          \s+         #(space separator)
          (\S+)       #Identifier
          \s+         #(space separator)
          (\S+)       #Username
          \s+         #(space separator)
          \[(.*)\]    #Time
          \s+         #(space separator)
          "(.*)"      #Request
          \s+         #(space separator)
          (\S+)       #Result
          \s+         #(space separator)
          (\S+)       #Bytes sent
          /x;
```

Error Watch *Comments end when Perl sees a normal line termination, so the following is completely invalid:*

```
print("Hello world");  # Greet the user
                         and let them know we're here
```

There is also no way of indicating to Perl that you have a multiline comment to include, short of placing the hash symbol before each comment segment.

One exception to the ignore rule is if the comment includes a "line directive"; in such a case, the information is stored within the opcode tree and used to populate the **__LINE__** and **__FILE__** special tokens. These are available directly and are also used as the basis for error messages raised by **die** and **warn** when no trailing newline is supplied.

In order to introduce the directive, you must use the word "line," followed by a line number and an optional string. The match is actually made by a regular expression:

```
/^#\s*line\s+(\d+)\s*(?:\s"([^"]+)?\s*$/
```

The first group, **$1**, populates **__LINE__** ,and **$2** populates **__FILE__**.

For example,

```
# line 200 "Parsing engine"
die "Fatal";
```

produces

```
Fatal at Parsing engine line 200
```

Note that the line directive actually modifies the **__LINE__** token, which is normally automatically parsed and populated by the Perl interpreter based on the current line within the script. So the script

```
#line 200 "Parsing engine"
print "Busy\n";
print "Doing\n";
print "Nothing\n";
die 'Fatal';
```

actually reports

```
Busy
Doing
Nothing
Fatal at Parsing engine line 203.
```

It is reported as an error on line 203, not the real source line 4—the earlier line directive has permanently modified the line numbering counters. You can update the line directive with any number, such that

```
#line 200 "Parsing engine"
print "Busy doing nothing\n";
warn "Warning";
#line 100 "Post-process engine"
print "Working the whole day through\n";
die "Fatal";
```

generates

```
Busy doing nothing
Warning at Parsing engine line 201.
Working the whole day through
Fatal at Post-process engine line 101.
```

We'll be looking at the use of line directives in more detail in Chapter 7.

Component Identity

When Perl fails to identify an item as one of the predefined operators, it treats the character sequence as a *term*. Terms are core parts of the Perl language and include variables, functions, and quoted strings. The *term recognition system* uses these rules:

- Variables can start with a letter, number, or underscore, providing they follow a suitable variable character, such as $, @ or %.

- Variables that start with a letter or underscore can contain any further combination of letters, numbers, and underscore characters.

- Variables that start with a number can only consist of further numbers—be wary of using variable names starting with digits. The variables such as **$0** through to **$9** (and beyond) are used for group matches in regular expressions.

- Subroutines can start only with an underscore or letter, but can then contain any combination of letters, numbers, and underscore characters.

- Case is significant; **$VAR**, **$Var** and **$var** are all different variables.

- Each of the main variable types has its own name space; **$var**, **@var**, and **%var** are all separate variables.

- Filehandles should use all uppercase characters—this is only a convention, not a rule, but useful for identification purposes.

Once the term has been extracted using these rules, it's compared against Perl's internal symbol table and the symbol table of the current package. Quotes and constants are also identified and either resolved or tagged as being bare values at this stage. If, after all this, the item has still not been identified, it is treated as a bareword—see "Barewords" later in this chapter for more information on how these items are parsed. Quotes are also a special case; since their values may be interpolated, they are actually resolved at this stage—see Chapter 3 for details on how interpolation works.

Precedence

Like most languages, Perl's parsing rules are based on precedence—the order in which individual elements of a line are evaluated and then processed. As a general rule, Perl parses statements from left to right, except in situations where the rightmost value might affect the evaluation of a term on the left. A good example is the **+=** operator, which adds and assigns a value to a variable. If the right-hand side of this operator wasn't evaluated first, Perl would be incapable of determining what value should be added to the variable on the left-hand side.

The list of operators in Table 2-2 gives the individual operator precedence and overall precedence for all operators.

The operators in Table 2-2 are also listed in overall precedence, from top to bottom—the first items in the table, terms and list operators, have the highest precedence and will always be evaluated by Perl first when used within a compound statement. You can see here, for example, that * has a higher precedence than +. This means that the statement

```
$a = 5*6+4;
```

is evaluated as

```
$a = (5*6)+4;
```

and not as

```
$a = 5*(6+4);
```

and produces a result of 34, not 50.

Name	Precedence	Examples
Terms and List Operators	Left	
The Arrow (Dereference) Operator	Left	->
Auto-Increment and Auto-Decrement	Nonassoc	++ —
Exponential	Right	**
Symbolic Unary Operators	Right	! ~ \ and unary + and −
Regular Expression Bindings	Left	=~ !~
Multiplication	Left	* / % x
Addition and Subtraction	Left	+ - .
Shift Operators	Left	<< >>
Named Unary Operators	Nonassoc	-X file test, some functions
Relational Operators	Nonassoc	< > <= >= lt gt le ge
Equality Operators	Nonassoc	== != <=> eq ne cmp
Bitwise And	Left	&
Bitwise Or and Exclusive Or	Left	| ^
Symbolic Logical And	Left	&&
Symbolic Logical Or	Left	||
Range Operators	Nonassoc	.. ...
Conditional Operator	Right	?:
Assignment Operators	Right	= += -= *= etc.
List Operators	Left	, =>
List Operators	Nonassoc	
Logical Not	Right	not
Logical And	Left	and
Logical Or and Exclusive Or	Left	or xor

Table 2.2   Operators in Order of Precedence

If you want to check the precedence rules, you can use the Perl compiler **Deparse** backend. This takes a Perl script and regurgitates it after the precedence rules have been applied and optimization has taken place. The output is then reformatted according to the precedence rules, using parentheses to highlight the precedence rules; for example

```
$ perl -MO=Deparse,-p -e '$a + $b *$c / $d % $e'
-e syntax OK
($a + ((($b * $c) / $d) % $e));
```

You can see here that the statement has been grouped according to the precedence rules. Any statement or script can be run through the backend. However, because the output includes any optimization, passing in statements that include constant values will not yield what you want:

```
$ perl -MO=Deparse,-p -e '$a = 5*6+4;'
($a = 34);
-e syntax OK
```

The compiler and its backends, which can provide useful nuggets of information about your script, are discussed in more detail in Chapter 12.

Terms and List Operators

Terms have the highest precedence in Perl and include the following:

- Variables
- Quotes
- Any parenthesized expression
- Function calls with parentheses
- The **do {}** and **eval {}** constructs
- Subroutine and method calls
- Anonymous constructors for arrays, [], and hashes, {}

The basic effect can be seen with a simple calculation:

```
print 6*(5+4);
```

prints out 54; the **5+4** is evaluated first because it's in parentheses even though the precedence rules state that the * operator has a higher precedence.

However, if you embed a term within a list, the term is evaluated first because it's a term and therefore has a higher precedence:

```
sub add { print 'Result:' }
print(2,3,add);
```

As a general rule, the terms are evaluated from left to right, such that

```
sub first { print 'First' }
sub second { print 'Second' }
print(2,3,first,second);
```

generates

```
FirstSecond2311
```

The **first** and **second** functions are terms and therefore evaluated first, left to right, before the 2, 3 and return values are supplied to the **print** function. This order also affects embedded terms that accept further list operators:

```
print 2,3,sort 2+2, 1+1;
```

Here, the arguments on the right of the **sort** term are immediately gobbled up and then evaluated left to right, before the elements before **sort** are evaluated.

In general, this left-to-right term evaluation produces the behavior you expect when you embed calls to other functions within a statement:

```
print "Warning:", sort ('A','B','C'), "\nContinuing";
```

But it also has the effect of ignoring further arguments, or earlier arguments if the script or function returns

```
print "Warning:", die("Error"), "Exiting";
```

which outputs

```
Error.
File 'Untitled'; Line 1
```

or the script:

```
sub add
{
    print "Sum: ",return($_[0]+$_[1]);
}

print add(1,2);
```

which outputs "3," the return value of the function, but without the prefix string.

Finally, the statement

```
print(4+5) + 1, "\n";
```

does not do what you expect; the call to **print** will be evaluated—the enclosing parentheses force the 4+5 to be supplied as a single element to **print**. Then Perl will attempt to add the value, which is actually void, to 1, while the newline character is just discarded as a useless constant. If you switch on warnings, you get more information:

```
Useless use of integer addition (+) in void context at t.pl line 1.
Useless use of a constant in void context at t.pl line 1.
9
```

but the **Deparse** backend is more explicit:

```
((print(9) + 1), '???');
t.pl syntax OK
```

The first part shows the result of **print** and 1 being added together, but the newline argument is never properly evaluated or included in the statement. Note that Perl still treats the syntax as being okay—there is nothing invalid about the statement as far as the parser is concerned; it just doesn't make any sense.

The Arrow (Dereference) Operator

The arrow or infix dereference operator is used to access the properties and methods of an object or the data contained within hash or array references. Since this directly relates to variables, we'll look more closely at this operator in the next chapter.

Auto-Increment and Auto-Decrement

The increment and decrement operators have no significant precedence; they are listed in the table as non-associative because there are no left or right arguments—the operators work directly on the variable or string supplied. If the operator is placed before a variable, the variable's value is incremented or decremented before the variable's value is used. If placed after, the variable is incremented or decremented after the variable has been evaluated. This means that the statement

```
$a = 3;
print $a++ * $a
```

actually prints the result of the calculation 3*4—the increment is executed immediately after the value of the variable has been extracted.

The only other thing of note that can cause problems is the special use of the increment operator:

```
print ++($foo = 'aa');
```

You cannot use the increment on constant values, only variables; the statement

```
print ++('aa');
```

will fail.

You also cannot decrement a variable using the same technique.

Exponentiation

The exponential operator, **, evaluates the expression on the right before the one on the left, such that

```
$a = 2;
print $a**++$a;
```

prints 27, (that is, 3^3). Care should be taken to ensure you aren't executing nested exponential statements that exhibit this sort of behavior—if you're unsure, either use **Deparse** to check the entire syntax and sense of the statement or try to devolve the statement into a number of individual statements.

Symbolic Unary Operators

There are no special tricks or traps with the symbolic unary operators as a whole. However, the unary minus (-) performs an arithmetic negation if the argument to the right is numeric:

```
$a = -3;
```

On strings, the effects are slightly different:

```
print -minus;    # prints -minus, forces interpretation as string
print -'-minus'  # prints +minus
print -'+minus'  # prints -minus
```

The unary plus (+) has no effect, except to force Perl to interpret the following parenthesized element as an expression, and not as a list of arguments.

Regular Expression Bindings

Regular expressions are a special case—we'll look at regular expression problems in Chapter 4.

Multiplication

The *, /, and % operators are fairly straightforward, doing the normal numerical multiplication, division, and modulus on two numbers. The x repetition operator is useful when you want to repeat a string:

```
print 'Ma' x 8; # outputs MaMaMaMaMaMaMaMa
```

If you supply a numerical value on the left-hand side, the number is converted to a string:

```
print 123 x 2; # outputs 123123
```

You should be careful, however, when using it with lists and arrays. If the item on the left-hand side of the operator is a list, the entire list is repeated:

```
print (join(',',(1,2,3) x 2)); # outputs 1,2,3,1,2,3
```

As for arrays, you must enclose them in parentheses so they are treated as lists, not scalars. The fragment

```
@abc = ('a','b','c');
@abc = @abc x 5;
print join(',',@abc);
```

generates "33333;" the **@abc** array has been populated with a list, consisting of one element; the scalar value of **@abc** (its length) repeated five times.

To fix this, place parentheses around the source array:

```
@abc = ('a','b','c');
@abc = (@abc) x 5;
print join(',',@abc);
```

Finally, if you supply an array on the right and a list on the left, the result is a repetition based on the scalar value of the array, effectively setting each item of a non-empty array to the list you supply. If the array on the right is empty, an empty list is returned. For instance,

```
@abc = ();
@abc = (5) x @abc;
print "First: ",join(',',@abc),"\n";
@abc = ('a','b','c');
```

```
@abc = (5) x @abc;
print "Second: ",join(',',@abc),"\n";
```

generates

```
First:
Second: 5,5,5
```

Addition and Subtraction

There are no significant problems—errors and bugs related to addition and subtraction are usually caused by problems elsewhere within the statement or through the supply of the wrong figures and/or variables. See Chapter 4 for some examples.

Shift Operators

The shift operators shift the bits of an expression right or left, according to the number of bits supplied. For example,

```
2 << 8;
```

is 512. Be aware that, if supplied a floating point value, it is converted to an integer without rounding (that is, always rounded down), such that

```
2.9 << 7.9;
```

produces 256; 2 shifted to the left 7 times.

Named Unary Operators

Certain Perl functions are really named unary operators; that is, functions that take a single argument and return a value. The exact list of unary operators is difficult to determine manually, but as a guide the Perl source defines the following functions and operations as unary operators:

abs	getgrnam	lock	sethostent
alarm	gethostbyname	log	setnetent
caller	getnetbyname	oct	setprotoent
chdir	getpgrp	ord	setservent
chr	getprotobyname	pos	sin
chroot	getpwnam	quotemeta	sleep
cos	getpwuid	rand	sqrt
defined	gmtime	readlink	srand
delete	hex	ref	study
eval "string"	int	require	subroutine prototype
exists	lc	reset	Uc
exit	lcfirst	rmdir	Ucfirst
exp	length	scalar chomp	Umask
getgrgid	localtime	scalar chop	-X tests

If any of these are followed by an opening parenthesis, they automatically have highest precedence; however, if you use them without parentheses, their precedence is as listed here, lower than most calculations but higher than most of the relational and logical operations.

For example, the **rand** function has a lower precedence than the multiplication operator, so

```
rand 10 * 20;   # rand (10*20)
rand(10) * 20; # (rand 10)*20;
```

You can always check these functions with **Deparse** if necessary.

Also remember that a comma automatically terminates a named unary operator, such that

```
print rand 10, 2;
```

prints a random number up to 10, immediately followed by the character 2.

Relational and Equality Operators

The relational and equality operators are different based on what you want to compare. To logically compare numerical values you use the symbolic equality and relational operators; for example:

```
if ($a > 0)
```

For string comparisons, you must use the text operators:

```
if ($a gt 'a')
```

A common mistake is to use the wrong operator on the wrong type of value and to fail to notice it because for 99 percent of situations it would resolve true anyway. The statement

```
if ($a == $b)
```

will work fine if both values are numerical. If they are textual, Perl compares the logical value of the two strings, which is always true. This process might seem confusing, but even the undefined value resolves to true when comparing it numerically. For example, the following tests all return true:

```
undef == 'a'
undef == undef
'a' == 'a'
'a' == 'b'
```

The reverse is not true when using string comparisons on numerical values. The statement

```
0 eq 9
```

will return false, and

```
0 eq 0
```

will return true because Perl automatically converts the numerical values to strings, since that's what the operator is expecting, and then compares those values.

There is a very simple rule to follow here: If you are comparing numbers, use symbolic operators, and if you are comparing strings, use text operators.

See "Logical Values" at the end of this chapter for details on the logical value of different constant expressions.

Bitwise And, Or, and Exclusive Or

The bitwise **and** (**&**) returns the value of two numbers **AND**ed together on a bit level. If you supply two strings, then each character of the string is **AND**ed together. Bitwise **or**(|) and Exclusive **or** (**^**) work in the same fashion.

The most common mistake here is usually a typographical error, forgetting the double & or | symbol when you want a comparison, or using double when you want bitwise operation.

Symbolic Logical And

The Perl logical **and** (**&&**) works on a short-circuit basis. Consider this statement:

```
a || b;
```

If *a* returns a false value, *b* is never evaluated.

The return result will be the right operand in both scalar and list context, such that

```
@list = ('a','b');
@array = ('1','2');

print(@list && @array);

$a = 'a' && 'b';

print $a;
```

produces "12b".

See the "Symbolic Logical Or" section that follows for details on using the operator for comparisons and tests.

Symbolic Logical Or

The Perl logical **or** (||) works on a short-circuit basis. Consider this statement:

```
a || b;
```

If *a* returns a true value, *b* is never evaluated. However, be wary of using the operator with functions that return only a true value; for example,

```
select DATA || die;
```

will never call **die**, even if **DATA** has not been defined.

Also be careful when using it with functions and terms that accept list arguments; the statement

```
print DATA "The answer is ", 0 || warn "Can't write: $!";
```

actually performs a logical **or** between the argument **0** and the call to **warn**. The **warn** function will be called before the zero is evaluated and returned to **print**:

```
Can't write:  at t.pl line 1.
The answer is 1
```

The solution is to use the **or** operator, which has a much lower precedence:

```
print DATA "The answer is ", 0 or warn "Can't write: $!";
```

or enclose your statements in parentheses to give them higher precedence:

```
print DATA ("The answer is ", 0) || warn "Can't write: $!";
```

Range Operators

The range operators, **..** and **...**, allow you to create ranges on the fly and to operate as simple "flip-flop" operators. The value of each **..** operator is unique, with each operator maintaining its own state. The value returned by the operator is false as long as the left operand is false. When the operand changes to true, the operator returns true until the right operand is also true, then at the next execution the operator becomes false again.

If the operands are scalars or constant expressions, the operand is compared against the **$.** operator—the current input line number.

In a list context, the operator returns a list of values between the supplied ranges:

```
@hundred = (0 .. 100);
```

It also operates in a similar fashion to the increment operator when supplied string values:

```
@characters = ('a' .. 'z');
```

Conditional Operator

The conditional operator is like an embedded *if...else* statement. The format is

```
EXPR ? IFTRUE : IFFALSE
```

If **EXPR** is true, the **IFTRUE** expression is evaluated and returned; otherwise **IFFALSE** is evaluated and returned.

Scalar and list context is propagated according to the expression selected. At a basic level, it means, for instance, that the following expressions do what you want:

```
$value = $expr ? $true : $false;
@list  = $expr ? @lista : @listb;
```

while the following

```
$count = $expr ? @lista : @listb;
```

populates **$count** with the number of elements in each array. On the flip side, the following:

```
$result = $wantcount ? @list : join(',',@list);
```

returns the array size or merged array accordingly. The conditional operator is evaluated as a single element when used within a list, so don't confuse the interpreter by inserting additional list operators without qualifying them. Therefore, if you want to return more than one item based on a conditional operation, you'll need to parenthesize the expression you want to return. The script

```
$name = <STDIN>;
chomp $name;
print "Hello ",length($name) ? $name,', how are you today?'
                             : 'nobody',"\n";
```

should be written as

```
$name = <STDIN>;
chomp $name;
print "Hello ",length($name) ? ($name,', how are you today?')
                             : 'nobody',"\n";
```

You can also use the conditional operator for assignment, provided that the two options are valid lvalues (see the following section "Assignment Operators"). However, you'll need to qualify the entire expression:

```
($group ? $a : $b) = 'users';
```

To use the conditional operator for choosing an assignment value, use the conditional operator as the assignment value, rather than embed the assignment expression:

```
$a = $group ? 'is a group' : 'not a group';
```

Assignment Operators

The assignment operators assign a value to a valid lvalue expression—usually a variable, but it can be any valid lvalue. An *lvalue*, or left-hand value, is an expression to which you can assign a new value. Assignment happens with the = and associated operators. Valid lvalues include the following:

- Any recognizable variable, including object properties
- **vec** function (for setting integer values)
- **substr** function (for replacement strings)
- **keys** function (for setting bucket sizes)
- **pos** function (for setting the offset within a search)
- Any lvalue-defined function (Perl 5.6 only)
- **? :** conditional operator
- Any assignment expression

As well as the basic = operator, there are also combined expression assignments that translate into embedded expressions. For example,

```
$a += 10;
```

is equivalent to

```
$a = $a + 10;
```

Note that assigning a value to an assignment expression should be read from left to right, such that

```
($a += 10) *= 5;
```

reads as

```
$a += 10;
$a *= 5;
```

and

```
($match = $source) =~ tr/a-z/A-Z/;
```

resolves to

```
$match = $source;
$match =~ tr/a-z/A-Z/;
```

Finally, assignment works differently according to context when assigning lists. In a list context, a list assignment causes the lvalue to be resolved into a list of lvalues to be assigned to, so that

```
($a, $b) = (1,2);
```

is in effect

```
$a = 1;
$b = 2;
```

You'll be looking more closely at the traps when assigning values to variables in Chapter 3.

Comma Operator

The comma is the list operator, and arguments are evaluated in order from left to right. In a scalar context when used in an implied list, the left argument is evaluated, then thrown away, and the right-hand argument returned. For example,

```
$a = (1,4);
```

will assign a value of 4 to $a. In a list context, it causes all arguments to be evaluated from left to right, and then returns them as a list:

```
@a = (1,2);
```

Be careful when using the list operators in a scalar context without parentheses, because the first element of the list will bind tighter than the right hand arguments, since the list operator has a lower precedence than most other statement forms. For example,

```
$a = 1,2;
```

will populate **$a** with a value of 1, because it's interpreted as

```
($a = 1),2;
```

Its use with a named unary operator is similar; for example,

```
chdir 'tmp','etc';
```

will change the current directory to **tmp**, not **etc**.

The same is true of arrays; the line

```
@a = 1,2;
```

is interpreted as

```
(@a = 1),2;
```

The **=>** operator is just an alias to the **,** operator, best used when separating the key and value of a hash element:

```
%hash = ('key' => 'value');
```

Since Perl, the **=>** automatically implies that the left argument should be interpreted as a string, making

```
%hash = (key => 'value');
```

perfectly legal, even with warnings and the **strict** pragma in force.

List Operators (Rightward)

The right side of a list operator has a low precedence, with only the **and**, **or**, **xor** and **not** having a lower precedence. This low precedence is what causes the problems when using implied lists and the symbolic logical operators:

```
tie %oldhash, NDBM_File, $old, O_RDONLY, 0444
                    || die "$0: Error opening source $old: $!\n";
```

which is actually interpreted as the last list argument being logically compared with the **die** statement. Use the named logical operators, which have lower precedence, to solve the problem.

Named Logical Not

The logical **not** provides a logical negation for the item on the right of the operator; any term on the left will immediately raise an error, so the statement

```
$a = $b not $c;
```

is completely nonsensical. Use ‖ if you want to choose between two values.

Named Logical And

This operator works identically to the symbolic logical **and**, including the short-circuit execution. The only difference is that it has a lower precedence.

Named Logical Or and Exclusive Or

The named logical **or** works like the symbolic logical **or**, including the short-circuit execution. Its main benefit is that it operates at very low precedence—in the lowest precedence of all statements—and is therefore useful in control statements.

Care should be taken when using **or** in assignment statements; because it has the lowest precedence the assignment operator will bind tighter than the **or** operator, so that

```
$a = $b or $c;
```

is interpreted as

```
($a = $b) or $c;
```

It's better to write it as

```
$a = $b || $c;
```

The same is true of any other statement where you want to make comparisons—the **or** operator is really useful only when you want to check the return value of a function without affecting the value returned.

The **xor** operator returns the exclusive **or** of two expressions.

Barewords

Barewords within a script are essentially a bad idea. First, Perl tries to identify if the bareword is a proper value—if it can be resolved to a function within the symbol table, then the function is called, otherwise it's treated as a string. The following script demonstrates this process quite nicely:

```
sub hello
{
    return 'Hello user!';
}

$message = hello;
print "$message\n";

$message = goodbye;
print "$message\n";
```

The output is

```
Hello user!
goodbye
```

If you have warnings switched on, Perl will warn if it sees an all-lowercase bareword that it can't otherwise identify as a term:

```
Unquoted string "goodbye" may clash with future reserved word at t.pl line 10.
```

A mixed-case bareword is interpreted as a string in most instances and should raise a suitable error when warnings are switched on. However, there is one exception —where a bareword is used in a situation that requires a filehandle, the bareword is used as the filehandle name. For example, the code

```
print Tester;
```

prints the value of **$_** to the filehandle **Tester**, assuming it's open and writable. If you try

```
print Tester, "Hello World\n";
```

you'll get an error when warnings are switched on because Perl assumes that **Tester** is the name of a filehandle.

If you have the **subs** portion of the **strict** pragma invoked, execution will terminate because of the bareword:

```
Bareword "goodbye" not allowed while "strict subs" in use at t.pl line 10.
```

If you have both warnings and the **strict** pragma in effect, the **pragma** takes precedence. We'll be looking at pragmas and warnings in more detail in Chapter 8.

Contexts

Perl supports a number of different contexts that are identified for each operator or term during the parsing process. The exact effects vary according to the operator or term concerned. We'll be looking more closely at traps associated with context issues in Chapters 3 and 4. For now, we'll look at the basic premise of each context.

Scalar and List Context

There are two basic contexts that all programmers are aware of: *scalar* and *list*. These two contexts affect the operation of a function or operator by implying the accepted value, or value returned. For example,

```
$size = @list;
```

Here, the **$size** variable is a scalar, and therefore implies scalar context on the array, causing it to return the array size rather than the array values. Conversely, the statement

```
sort @list;
```

is evaluated in list context, since the **sort** function expects a list of values.

Within a function, you can identify the requested context using the **wantarray** function, which returns true if the caller is expecting a list (or array, or hash) to be returned instead of a scalar value.

Numerical and String Context

Some of the internal Perl functions also distinguish scalar context between numerical and string contexts. A classic example is the **$!** special variable. In a numerical context, this variable returns the numerical error number of the last error that occurred and, in a string context, the associated message. The interpreter uses this context as the basis for the conversion of values into the internal integer, floating point, or string values that the SV scalar value is divided into.

Unfortunately, there's no way of determining from within a script what the expected numerical or string context is—you must leave it up to Perl to make the decision for you, converting the value accordingly.

Boolean Context

Boolean context is where an expression is used solely to identify a true or false value. See the last section in this chapter, "Logical Values," to see how Perl treats individual values and constants in a logical context.

Void Context

Void context is a special case and is an extension of the scalar context. It identifies areas of the code where a constant has been introduced but never used. At its simplest point, the statement

```
99;
```

would be identified as a void context, since introducing a constant at this point does nothing. You'll be notified of this instance only if you have warnings switched on.

Other more common areas where void context applies includes the instance where the precedence rules would cause a portion of the statement to be ignored. For example,

```
$a = 1,2;
```

causes the 2 to be identified in a void context. Look at the earlier precedence rules for details on why this and similar statements cause void context warnings.

Interpolative Context

The Perl documentation identifies the interpolation of variables into interpolating quoted values as a separate context. This description is a good way of explaining why some quoted blocks interpolate—they are identified as interpolated context—but doesn't really do the process justice. We'll look more closely at the interpolation process in Chapter 3.

Logical Values

Perl's boolean logic relies on its ability to identify different variable and constant types as having a true or false value. As a general rule, anything that is undefined, empty, or zero is taken as a false value, while any other value is taken as true. You can see a more explicit list in Table 2-3.

Value	Logical Value
Negative number	True
Zero	False
Positive number	True
Empty string	False
Non-empty string	True
Undefined value	False
Empty list	False
List with at least one element	True

Table 2.3   Values and Their Logical Equivalents

To check for the undefined value, you can use the **defined** function, which returns a positive integer (true) if the variable contains a valid value, or zero (false) if the variable equals the **undef** value.

## CHAPTER 3

Common Variable Traps

Understanding the language is one thing, but getting used to a particular programming style takes time, and it is hard to avoid typographical errors and those brief memory lapses. The obvious solution when you find a problem is to use a debugger or one of the debugging techniques that we'll look at later in this book. What debuggers don't do is tell you why a problem occurred or how to fix it.

Giving specific information on why a particular bug is occurring is difficult, because the exact effects are entirely dependent on the script and other modules and systems you are using. What we can do is look at some of the problems and bugs that crop up and that can have potentially significant effects. These range from simple usage problems, like creating an array of array references, and not a simple array, to the more complex problems of changing the values of **$a** and **$b** during a sort.

For a good example of the individuality of bugs, consider this fragment, which was used to print out the expanded email address as returned by an SMTP server:

```
$realrecipient = $smtp->expand($email);
chomp $realrecipient;
print  "<BR>\n expand for $email ->  [" . $realrecipient . "]";
```

When run normally at the command line, the script worked fine, but when run as a CGI script, it seemed to return nothing. The email addresses were not being expanded. The problem was very simple, the value of **$realrecipient** was returned in the form "<mc@mcwords.com>." When parsed by the browser, the email address was interpreted as an unknown HTML tag and therefore just ignored!

You could easily spend the rest of your life giving examples of those sorts of errors, but it would be unproductive. Instead, as a precursor to the debugging process, we'll be looking at more generic errors, such as bad variable usage and hidden traps in compound statements and functions.

In this chapter we'll concentrate on the core of any script: variables and how they are created and used. In the next chapter we'll move on to some of the problems with statements, functions, and regular expressions.

If you are having problems with a particular error being reported by Perl during execution, check out Appendix A, which lists all of the error messages reported by Perl and provides examples of how to produce the error and how to resolve it.

Creating/Using Variables

The process of initially creating a variable, either with or without some initial values, is not as simple and straightforward as you might think.

There are some simple rules that you can follow when creating and using variables that should eliminate some of the more common problems:

- All scalars start with **$**, including those accessed from an array of hash, for example **$array[0]** or **$hash{key}**.
- All arrays start with **@**, including arrays or hashes accessed in slices, for example **@array[3..5,7,9]** or **@hash{'bob', 'alice'}**
- All hashes start with **%**

Just remembering those simple rules should help to eliminate a number of common problems.

Scalars

Beyond the issues of interpolation and quoting, which are covered later in this chapter, there are a few other major difficulties when creating and using scalars.

- You must be careful when creating and populating multiple variables; the following will not work:

```
$first, $second = 1,2;
$first, $second = (1,2);
($first, $second) = 1,2;
```

  You must use list operators on both sides:

```
($first, $second) = (1,2);
```

- Remember that assigning to a scalar automatically implies scalar context on the right-hand side of the assignment operator, such that

```
$size = @array;
```

  will populate **$size** with the number of elements of the array.

Arrays

The array is just an array of scalars, but you need to take care when creating an array to ensure that you don't create an array containing only a single reference and that when accessing information you use the correct notation to extract single elements and slices.

Creation

Array variables have a prefix of the @ sign and are populated using either parentheses or the **qw** operator, as, for example,

```
@array = (1, 2, 'Hello');
@array = qw/This is an array/;
```

don't use square brackets to create a normal array; the line

```
@array = [1, 2, 'Hello'];
```

initializes **@array** with only one element, a reference to the array contained in the square brackets.

Extracting Individual Indices

When extracting individual components, there are only a few things to remember:

- Array indices start at zero, not one, when working forward.
- Array indices start at -1 for the last element when working backward.

The use of $[, which changes the lowest index of an array, is heavily deprecated, so the rules above should always apply.

Be careful when extracting elements from an array using a calculated index. If you are supplying an integer, then there shouldn't be any problems with resolving that to an array index (providing the index exists). If it's a floating point value, be aware that Perl always truncates (rounds down) values as if the index were interpreted within the **int** function. If you want to round up, use **sprintf**—this is easily demonstrated; the following script:

```
@array = qw/a b c/;

print("Array 8/5 (int)   is: ", $array[8/5], "\n");
print("Array 8/5 (float) is: ",
      $array[sprintf("%1.0f",(8/5))],"\n");
```

generates

```
Array index 8/5 (int)   is: b
Array index 8/5 (float) is: c
```

The bare 8/5, which equates to 1.6, is interpreted as 1 in the former statement, but 2 in the latter.

Slices

When extracting a slice from an array, you must remember to use **@array**:

```
print join(', ',@array[3..5,7,9]);
```

If you try accessing multiple values using **$array** you'll get nothing, but an error is only reported if you switch warnings on:

```
$ perl -ew "print $ARGV[2,3];" Fred Bob Alice
Multidimensional syntax $ARGV[2,3] not supported at -e line 1.
Useless use of a constant in void context at -e line 1.
Use of uninitialized value in print at -e line 1.
```

Multidimensional Slices

Note that, unlike as with hashes, you cannot use the comma syntax to access an individual component of a multidimensional array. The following will not work:

```
@tictactoe = ([1, 2, 3],
              [4, 5, 6],
              [7, 8, 9]);
print $tictactoe[1,2];
```

With warnings, you'll get an error. Under any circumstance, what you'll actually get is the last element specified, in this case, a reference to the array "7, 8, 9."

Single Element Slices

Be careful when using single element slices; the statement

```
print @array[1];
```

is no different than

```
print $array[1];
```

but the affects when assigning information are more marked. The fragment

```
@array[1] = <DATA>;
```

actually reads in all the remaining information from the **DATA** filehandle, but assigns only the first record read from the filehandle to the second argument of the array.

Size

The size of an array can be determined using scalar context on the array—the returned value will be the number of elements in the array:

```
@array = (1,2,3);
print "Size: ",scalar @array,"\n";
```

The value returned will always be the physical size of the array, not the number of valid elements. You can demonstrate this, and the difference between **scalar @array** and **$#array**, using this fragment:

```
@array = (1,2,3);
$array[50] = 4;

print "Size: ",scalar @array,"\n";
print "Max Index: ", $#array,"\n";
```

This should return

```
Size: 51
Max Index: 50
```

There are only four elements in the array that contain information, but the array is 51 elements long, with a highest index of 50.

Arrays in List Context

When accessing an entire array or slice, arrays work as lists, that is

```
@array = (1,2);
($a, $b) = @array;
```

is equivalent to

```
($a, $b) = (1, 2);
```

Arrays and slices on the left hand side of an assignment operator always imply list context:

```
@fields = split /:/;
```

Hashes

Hashes are open to problems because of the freeform nature of the key string used to extract values. Most problems with creating and using hashes can be traced to problems associated with the key string you are using, or how Perl interprets it.

Creation

Hashes are created using list context—a list is converted by taking individual pairs from the list: the first is used as the key and the second as the value. For clarity, you should use **=>** as an alias for **,** to indicate the key/value pairs. For example,

```
%hash = ('Fred' , 'Flintstone', 'Barney', 'Rubble');
```

and

```
%hash = ('Fred' => 'Flintstone', 'Barney' => 'Rubble');
```

are interpreted identically, but the latter makes a much better visual distinction between the pairs and the relationship between the two values.

- Only even lists can be assigned to a hash; an odd list will raise an error.
- Don't use braces when initializing a real hash:

  ```
  %hash = {'Fred' => 'Flintstone', 'Barney' => 'Rubble'};
  ```

The braces return a reference to an anonymous hash, so the example above will first fail because you've tried to create a hash with an odd number of arguments. If when accessing the hash keys you get a value like

```
HASH(0x99d33e8)
```

it means you've created the hash badly.

- When creating hashes, Perl will automatically interpret a bareword used as a key as a string, even with the **strict** pragma in force:

  ```
  use strict;
  my %hash = (Fred => 'Flintstone', Barney => 'Rubble');
  ```

  But the same rule does not apply to values.
- You can also use the **-** operator in front of a word, although this makes the key include the leading **-** sign as part of the key:

```
%hash = (-Fred => 'Flintstone', -Barney => 'Rubble');
print $hash{-Fred};
```

However, for single letter strings this will raise a warning; use single quotes to explicitly define these arguments.

Extracting Individual Elements

You can extract individual elements from a hash by supplying the string within the braces:

```
print $hash{Fred};
```

The string within the braces is automatically quoted and interpreted as a string by Perl—even with the **strict** pragma in force and warnings enabled.

- Care needs to be taken when embedding strings and/or variables that are made up of multiple components. The following statements are identical, albeit with a slight performance tradeoff for the former method:

```
print $hash{$fred . $barney};
print $hash{"$fred$barney"};
```

- When using more complex hash keys, use **sprintf**:

```
print $hash{sprintf("%s-%s:%s",$a,$b,$c)};
```

- If you are using numerical data to build up your hash keys, then use **sprintf** to enforce a fixed format for the numbers to prevent minor differences from causing you problems. For example, when formatting time values, it's better to use:

```
$hash{sprintf("%02d%02d",$hours,$min)};
```

than

```
$hash{$hours . $min};
```

With the former, all times will be displayed in the form '0505' instead of '55'.

Extracting Slices

When extracting slices, you must use the @ prefix:

```
%hash = (-Fred => 'Flintstone', -Barney => 'Rubble');
print join("\n",@hash{-Fred,-Barney});
```

Using **$hash{-Fred, -Barney}** would return nothing.

Hashes in List Context

In the same way that hashes are essentially populated using a list, if you evaluate a hash in list context, then what you get is a list of key/value pairs. For example,

```
my %hash = (Fred => 'Flintstone', Barney => 'Rubble');
@list = %hash;
print join(', ',@list);
```

produces

```
Barney, Rubble, Fred, Flintstone
```

Care needs to be taken if you are supplying a hash directly as argument to a subroutine—you must extract @_ as hash. You can mix scalars and a single hash element into a subroutine call, but the hash should be last, and you must ensure that the number of arguments preceding the hash argument is identical to the number expected to prevent the "odd number of elements in hash assignment" error. If you want to supply a mixture of hashes and arrays, or multiple hashes, then you use references. See the tips for good function design in Chapter 5 for some examples and solutions.

Sorting/Ordering

There is no way to simply guarantee that the order in which a list of keys, values, or key/value pairs will always be the same. In fact, it's best not to even rely on the order between two sequential evaluations:

```
print(join(', ',keys %hash),"\n");
print(join(', ',keys %hash),"\n");
```

If you want to guarantee the order, use **sort**, as, for example,

```
print(join(', ',sort keys %hash),"\n");
```

If you're accessing a hash a number of times and want to use the same order, consider creating a single array to hold the sorted sequence, and then use the array (which will remain in sorted order) to iterate over the hash. For example:

```
my @sortorder = sort keys %hash;
foreach my $key (@sortorder)
```

This will be more efficient than continually calling **sort** and creating temporary lists, and it will also allow you to build your own custom order sequence that you can use any number of times.

Size

You get the size—that is, the number of elements—from a hash by using scalar context on either **keys** or **values**:

```
print "Hash size: ",scalar keys %hash,"\n";
```

Don't use **each**; as in a scalar context it returns the first key from the hash, not a count of the key/value pairs as you might expect.

If you evaluate a hash in scalar context, then the value returned is the number of used buckets compared to the number of allocated buckets. (see the section "Hash Dump" in Chapter 10 for a more detailed look at how hashes work).

Lists

Lists are merely a temporary array returned by a function when it's called, usually in list context. When extracting individual indices from a function that returns a list, you must use parentheses to imply list context on the function call. The following are wrong:

```
$hours = localtime()[2];
$hours,$minutes = localtime()[2..3];
($hours,$minutes) = localtime()[2..3];
```

The correct notation is

```
($hours,$minutes) = (localtime())[2..3];
```

Note that the parentheses go around the expression that returns the list.

Filehandles

The name of a filehandle is **DATA** or similar; it's not **<DATA>**. Using

```
print <DATA> "Hello\n";
```

won't do what you expect at all. The **<DATA>** construct is actually the angle operator, which does a line input operation on the handle.

Use of **defined**

The **defined** function can be used only to check the existence of specific variables or for a defined value in scalars. All scalars can hold the undefined value **undef**, but you cannot assign **undef** to an entire array. The fragment

```
@array = undef;
print "Defined" if defined(@array);
```

will always print "Defined" because the array has been defined, even though it's empty. Even if you populate the array properly with the undefined value, the result will be the same:

```
@array = (undef);
print "Defined" if defined(@array);
```

Again, the reason is that the array holds a list of scalars, and in this case the array size is one element—the fact that the one element is a scalar populated with **undef** doesn't modify the return value of **defined**.

However, if we try the same process on a scalar,

```
$scalar = undef;
print "Defined" if defined($scalar);
```

we don't get anything, because the value of **$scalar** is **undef**.

Note that the statement

```
%hash = undef;
```

will always fail, because we're assigning an odd number of elements to the hash.

Default Values

It's not necessary within Perl to initialize variables with some default values. Perl automatically creates all scalars as empty (with the **undefined** value). Lists and hashes are automatically created empty. That said, there is nothing wrong with setting the initial value of a variable—it won't make any difference to Perl—and sometimes it makes sense if only for sheer clarity, especially if you are using **my** to declare the variables beforehand.

Variable Scope

The **my**, **local**, and **our** declarations can cause problems if they are used incorrectly. Check the tips in this section if you are experiencing problems with variables having incorrect values.

Effects of **my**

The **my** keyword declares a variable to be scoped within the current block. For the duration of the block, the new variable will take precedence over any previously scoped variable. When the block ends, the variable goes out of scope. You can demonstrate this with:

```
my $string = "We are the world";
print "$string\n";
myfunction();
print "$string\n";

sub myfunction
{
    my $string = "We are the function";
    print "$string\n";
    mysub();
}

sub mysub
{
    print "$string\n";
}
```

This generates

```
We are the world
We are the function
```

```
We are the world
We are the world
```

The most common problem is to expect to access a variable declared with **my** within a subroutine or block outside of that subroutine—which you can't do. Note that even the call to **mysub** accesses the global **$string**.

- Variables declared with **my** within a module are not accessible outside of that module (since the module is a single block), even when called upon explicitly using **$MyModule::string** or similar. Either use the **vars** pragma or, with Perl 5.6 or later, use the **our** keyword to declare a global variable and then place the full name in **@EXPORT** or **@EXPORT_OK**.
- The **my** keyword is a list operator, so you must include parentheses when declaring multiple variables using **my**, for example,

```
my ($var,@array);
```

Effects of **local**

When using **local** on a global variable, the variable is given a temporary value each time the **local** statement is executed. The temporary value lasts only for the duration of the block. However, the use of **local** does not affect its accessibility—it's still a global variable; it just has a temporary value while it's being used within that block. For example,

```
{
    local $var = 'newvalue';
    myfunc();
}
```

can be thought of as

```
{
    $oldvalue = $var;
    $var = 'newvalue';
    my func();
}
continue
{
    $var = $oldvalue;
}
```

except that the **continue** block is executed however the block exits, including through a **return**.

- The value of a variable modified using **local** is consistent for all functions called from the block in which the variable has been localized. In our example, the **myfunc** function will access the temporary value of **$var** when called from within that block, but the normal value outside of it.
- Don't use **local** on an exported module variable—the value of the variable will never change.

Effects of **our**

The **our** keyword (introduced in Perl 5.6) declares a variable to be global, effectively making it the complete opposite of **my**. For example,

```
our $string = "We are the world";
print "$string\n";
myfunction();
print "$string\n";

sub myfunction
{
    our $string = "We are the function";
    print "$string\n";
}
```

produces

```
We are the world
We are the function
We are the function
```

Using **our** within a function or indeed any form of nesting within any block on the same variable has no effect; you are *always* referring to the same global variable. The use of **our** on a variable declared with **my** will have no effect.

Special Variables

A number of variables have special meaning in Perl and also imply special operations or values when used in certain circumstances. Some of the more regular traps are listed below.

The @_ Array

The @_ array holds the arguments passed to a function and exhibits the same problems as a standard array. In addition,

- The @_ array is populated only within a subroutine call or when **split** is called in a scalar context. The use of **split** in this way is now deprecated.

- The @_ variable is an array, so the statement

  ```
  $value = @_;
  ```

will result only in **$value** being populated with the count of the elements in @_, not the first value from the @_ array. Place parentheses around the argument list, even if there's only one, to imply list context:

```
($value) = @_;
```

- The variables **$_** and **$_[0]** are not the same—the first is the scalar used to hold certain scratchpad values, the second is the first element of the **@_** array.

- Arrays and hashes supplied to a function are converted to lists; there is no way of determining where compound array/hash arguments start and end. The call

```
myfunc(@array,%hash)
```

will result in @_ being populated with one long list of array values, followed by key/value pairs from the hash. Use references if you want to pass multiple arrays and/or hashes to a function. (See Chapter 5 for more details.)

The $_ Scalar

The **$_** variable is used as a default storage space by and for all sorts of functions and operators. Care should be taken to ensure that you don't inadvertently modify or use the value of **$_** unless you really want to.

- The **$_** scalar is shared by *all* packages, which means changing the value of the variable between subroutine calls may have unexpected consequences. For example:

```
$_ = "Hello World\n";

sub parse
{
    tr/[a-z]/[A-Z]/;
}
```

A call to **parse** will translate **$_** to uppercase.

- The **$_** variable is used as the default *source* variable for some functions, including **print**, **unlink**, **ord**, **pos**, **split**, and all file tests. For example, all of the following statement pairs are identical:

```
while(<FILE>)
while(defined($_ = <FILE>))

chomp;
chomp($_);

split /,/;
split /,/,$_;

print;
print $_;
```

If you're unsure of the possible effects, always supply the name of the variable you want to use with these functions.

- The **$_** variable is the default variable used in regular expressions when called without the **=~** operator, so,

```
s/a/b/;
```

and

```
$_ =~ s/a/b/;
```

are identical.

- The **$_** variable is used as the default iterator in a **for** or **foreach** loop, a common error is:

```
foreach (@array)
{
    foreach (split)
    {
    ...
    }
}
```

The first iteration of the inner loop will overwrite the value of the iterator for the outer loop. Although it won't affect the operation in this instance, you won't be able to use the values either.

The **$_** variable is the implicit operator in **map** and **grep**, and you cannot specify an alternative. Avoid using **$_** within loops that employ either of these two functions.

The **$_** variable is the default destination for the **<FH>**operator, **readline** function, or **glob** operator when the operation's result is tested by itself as part of a **while** loop.

The $a and $b Scalars

The **$a** and **$b** scalars are made available only to blocks and subroutines used in combination with the **sort** function.

- Avoid using variables with the same names to prevent confusion.

- The variables are treated by Perl as globals for individual packages, which means that individual packages have their own versions. In fact, **$a** and **$b** belong to the same package as the one that the **sort** operator was compiled into. This is not necessarily the same as the package in which the function that has been called by **sort** is located.

- **$a** and **$b** are in fact aliases to the actual array or hash *value* that you are sorting. You should therefore avoid changing the variables, as doing so will have the effect of changing the actual value within the array or hash. If you need to compare more complex values that need pre-processing, use a function and make copies; for example the code fragment below will compare and sort American style dates (Month/Day/Year):

```
sub sortdate
{
    my ($c,$d) = ($a,$b);

    $c =~ s{(\d+)/(\d+)/(\d+)}{sprintf("%04d%02d%02d",$3,$1,$2)}e;
```

```
$d =~ s{(\d+)/(\d+)/(\d+)}{sprintf("%04d%02d%02d",$3,$1,$2)}e;

    $c <=> $d;
}
```

The $1..$9 and other Regex Variables

The **$1..$9** variables (and beyond) are populated only during a regular expression match or substitution, and the values of these variables are reset during each regular expression match or substitution, whether you use groupings or not:

```
$string = "The cat sat on the mat";
$string =~ m/The (.*?) sat on the (.*)/;
my ($animal, $where) = ($1,$2);
$string =~ m/(.a.)/;
print "Animal: $animal, Where: $where\n";
print "Animal: $1, Where: $2\n";
```

The second **print** statement will fail, because **$2** has never been initialized. The same rule holds true for the **$'**, **$&** and **$'** variables as well. The solution is to assign the values immediately by evaluating the match in a list context:

```
my ($animal, $where) = ($string =~ m/The (.*?) sat on the (.*)/);
```

This negates the need for the **$1** and other variables entirely.

References

References confuse many programmers because of the change in the way information needs to be extracted from the variables.

Scalars

Scalar references cause few problems; just remember that you must de-reference a scalar using

```
print $$scalar;
```

Note that you can create a reference to a scalar using any of the following statements:

```
$ref = \$scalar;
$ref = \'Hello world';
$ref = \134_569.99;
```

However, be careful with three-digit numbers; the line

```
$ref = \012;
```

actually sets **$ref** to be a reference to a scalar holding the decimal value of 10—the sequence would have to be quoted in order for it to be interpreted as a newline.

Arrays

The most common problem with arrays is when creating or dereferencing them. Array references are created using square brackets, not parentheses. Array references can be created using square brackets:

```
$array = [1,2,3];
```

to convert an existing array

```
$array = \@array;
```

or

```
$hash{ = [1,2,3];
```

When de-referencing an individual element:

```
print $$array[0];
print $array->[0];
```

To access the entire array:

```
print join(', ', @$array);
print join(', ', @{$array});
```

Once de-referenced, an array implies array context, such that:

```
($first, $second) = @{$array}->[1,2];
```

Hashes

Hash references are the most common you will come across, and exhibit a number of regular traps.
    You create a reference to a new hash by using braces:

```
$hash = { Fred => 'Flintstone', Barney => 'Rubble'};
```

You can convert an existing hash using

```
$hash = \%hash;
```

You can create a nested hash using

```
$hash{fields} = { Fred => 'Flintstone', Barney => 'Rubble'};
```

To de-reference a hash element, you use either of these two formats:

```
print $hash->{Fred};
print $$hash{Fred};
```

using

```
print $hash;
```

will result in the object type and its address in memory instead of being printed.

To access the entire hash, use

```
print keys %$hash;
print keys %{$hash};
```

You must de-reference a hash reference when you want to use **keys**, **values**, or **each**. Simply trying

```
print keys $hash;
```

will not work.

Once de-referenced, a hash implies list context, just as if it were a normal hash. There is no special treatment for a list returned by a de-referenced hash compared to a normal hash.

Be careful when using braces to return hash references to ensure that Perl treats the braces as a hash reference, and not a block. For example,

```
sub new_hash
{
    { @_ };
}
```

doesn't work; what it actually does is return @_ as a list, because there is no qualification on those braces to tell Perl to interpret them as a hash reference. Instead, use

```
sub new_hash
{
    +{ @_ };
}
```

or

```
    sub new_hash
    {
        return { @_ };
    }
```

Functions

You should create references to functions using the **\&function** notation, for example:

```
$coderef = \&parse_text;
```

The following will not do what you expect and won't in fact make **$coderef** point to a code reference:

```
$coderef = \parse_text();
$coderef = \parse_text;
$coderef = \&parse_text();
```

When calling a function that is referred to by a code reference, use:

```
&$coderef(1,2,3);
&{$coderef}(1,2,3);
```

Note that in the second form, the arguments to the function go *after* the block, not within it. (See the section "Dispatch Tables" in Chapter 5 for details on using soft references for functions.)

You can also create a code reference using an anonymous subroutine:

```
$coderef = sub { print "Hello world\n" };
```

Remember to include the closing semicolon—you must include the semicolon to terminate the expression, since we are not creating a named subroutine.

Globs

Typeglobs should be referenced as:

```
$globref = \*STDOUT;
```

Note that typeglobs do not, as such, need to be de-referenced:

```
$globref = \*STDOUT;
$globin = \*STDIN;

$var = <$globin>;

print $globref 'Hello world',$var,"\n";
```

Nested Structures

When you create a nested reference, it's the *value* of the parent that is a reference to the new type. For example, in:

```
$hash{list}[0]='First';'
```

the **$hash{[0]** is the first argument of the array held in the *value* of the key **$hash{M}** within the hash **%hash**.

To access the entire array, you must de-reference the parent:

```
print join(', ',@$hash{list});
```

For clarity, you can use block notation to specify the value you want to de-reference:

```
print join(', ',@{list}$hash{);
```

You can omit the infix operator for nested structures, so that

```
$hash{list}->{numbers}->[0] = 'First';
```

can be rewritten as

```
$hash{list}{numbers}[0] = 'First';
```

But remember, the following statements are not the same

```
print $hash{list}[0];
print $hash->{list}->[0];
```

The first accesses the first argument of the array contained in the hash element of **%hash**, while the second accesses the first argument of the array contained in the hash reference pointed to by **$hash**.

You don't have to initialize a nested structure with a value for it to work. The first line in the following fragment isn't necessary:

```
$hash->{list} = 1;
$hash->{list}->[0] = 1;
```

The second line will populate **$hash->{M}** with a reference to the new array. Similarly, it's not necessary to set a default value when you need to use the increment or decrement operators. The following fragment

```
unless (exists ($hash->{list}->{$field})
{
    $hash->{list}->{$field} = 0;
}
else
{
    $hash->{list}->{$field}++;
}
```

can be shortened to

```
$hash->{list}->{$field}++;
```

Reference Types

You cannot guess the type of a reference, so make sure you use the **ref** function to determine the type. Remember that **ref** returns a string that relates to the reference type; it'll be one of:

```
REF
SCALAR
ARRAY
HASH
CODE
GLOB
```

The **ref** function defaults to using **$_** if you don't supply a type.

It's easier to convert an existing type to a reference and then use that throughout a section or function. For example, the code below will allow you to supply either a hash or a hash reference to the function:

```
sub db_new_user
{
    my ($info, $key);

    if (ref($_[0]) eq 'HASH')
    {
        ($info) = @_;
    }
    else
    {
        $info = {@_};
    }

    foreach my $key (sort keys %{$info})
    {
        $user->{$key} = $info->{$key};
    }

    return $user;
}
```

Objects

Aside from the rules governing references (and therefore objects) seen earlier in this chapter, the other potential problems with objects relate to the use of methods and/or inheritance. Make sure that, if you want to rely on inheritance, the **@ISA** array for the current package, or the parent class for the object you are creating, has been populated correctly. See Chapter 5 for some other tips.

Perl follows the sequence below when calling **method** on an object of the type **classname**:

1. Perl checks the object's own class (package) for a routine named **class::method**.

2. Perl checks the **parent** classes listed in **@class::ISA**, looking for **parent::method**.

3. Perl looks for a subroutine named **UNIVERSAL::method**.

4. Inheritance then moves to autoloaded methods, first by looking for the **class::AUTOLOAD** subroutine.

5. Perl searches all the **parent** classes listed in **@class::ISA**, looking for the **parent::AUTOLOAD** subroutine.

6. Finally, Perl looks for the **UNIVERSAL::AUTOLOAD** subroutine.

If the sequence fails, then you'll get the "Can't locate object method" error.

Constants, Quotes, and Interpolation

When introducing raw data into the Perl script, Perl will do its best to interpret and resolve the information during the compilation stage. The line

```
$var = 4 + 5;
```

will immediately resolve the calculation to its raw value. This will also affect how Perl approaches strings; the following

```
$message = "Hello " . 'user' . ", how are you today?";
```

will be resolved during compilation to:

```
$message = "Hello user, how are you today?";
```

There are three basic formats for introducing string constants: single quotes, double quotes, and 'here' documents. The single and double quotes work identically, except that single quotes are not interpolated.

Quoting Operators

The quoting operators are listed in Table 3-1. Note that only some operators interpolate and that single quotes used as delimiters always disable interpolation, even on those forms that normally interpolate.

Customary	Generic	Meaning	Interpolates
"	q//	Literal	No
""	qq//	Literal	Yes
``	qx//	Command	Yes, unless ' is used as delimiter
	qw//	Word list	No
//	m//	Pattern match	Yes, unless ' is used as delimiter
	qr//	Pattern	Yes, unless ' is used as delimiter
s///	s///	Substitution	Yes, unless ' is used as delimiter
y///	tr///	Translation	No

Table 3.1   Quote Operators and Interpolation

If you use characters for delimiters that are normally matched in pairs (parentheses, braces, and square or angle brackets) then you must use matching forms. For example, the fragment

```
$_ = 'hello';
s{hello{goodbye{;
print;
```

will raise an error; it should be written like this:

```
$_ = 'hello';
s{hello}{goodbye};
print;
```

'Here' Documents

When using a 'here' document, you must specify the termination string immediately after the << operator, for example,

```
print <<EOF;
This is a here document!
EOF
```

Using spaces after the << operator will require you to use the spaces in the real termination.

You must also use a semicolon to end the statement and avoid further arguments becoming part of the expression. Avoid using a blank termination string (which allows a blank line to be used for termination), as it's prone to minor problems.

Variable and String Interpolation

Variables and strings are evaluated and inserted into strings and other interpolated sequences such as regular expressions according to the rules outlined below.

Interpolating Scalars

The most common error for all interpolation operations is to use single quotes when using interpolation:

```
print 'Hello World\n';
```

You should also be careful when trying to interpolate multiple variables into a single string or variables into a string that contains valid variable name characters. None of the following will work:

```
$prefix = 'file.';
$suffix = 'ext';
print "Filename is $prefixdoc\n";
print "Filename is $prefix_doc\n";
print "Filename is $prefix_$suffix\n";
```

Interpolation is not nested; you cannot do

```
$string = 'Hello world\n';
print "$string";
```

And expect the output to be terminated with a newline—interpolation works strictly at the point at which the string has been quoted. Embedded variables are not re-evaluated.

Interpolating Arrays

You can interpolate arrays directly into a suitable quoted block—just place the variable name into the quote. The individual elements of the array will be separated by the value of the **$"** special variable, a space by default. Thus, you can display a comma-separated list of values:

```
@list = qw/Martin Wendy Sharon/;
$" = ',';
print "@list\n";
```

In general it's easier to use **join** than **$"**.

The exception to the rule is that Perl will raise an error if the name after the @ symbol does not resolve to a suitable variable within the symbol table. For example, the following:

```
print "mc@whoever.com";
```

will cause Perl to try to interpolate the **@whoever** array, which doesn't exist. Perl will raise an error during compilation to highlight this problem. To get around the problem, either escape the @ sign or use non-interpolating strings:

```
print "mc\@whoever.com";
print 'mc@whoever.com';
```

Interpolating Hashes

Perl entirely ignores entire hashes embedded into a string that interpolates; there are no tricks to embedding a hash into a string. Hash elements and slices work as the scalars and arrays described above.

If you want to output an entire hash, you'll have to use a loop:

```
foreach (keys %hash)
{
    print "$_ = $hash{$_}\n";
}
```

Alternatively, use **keys** or **values** in combination with the **join** function to output entire sequences.

Character Interpolation

The characters in Table 3-2 are interpreted only in strings that interpolate. Non-interpolating quotes will use these character sequences verbatim.

Escape Sequence	Description
\t	Specifies tab.
\n	Specifies newline.
\r	Specifies carriage return.
\f	Specifies form feed.
\a	Specifies alarm (bell).
\e	Specifies escape.
\b	Specifies backspace.
\033	Specifies octal character.
\x1B	Specifies hex character.
\c[	Specifies control character.
\l	Makes next character lowercase.
\u	Makes next character uppercase.
\L	Forces lowercase till \E.
\U	Forces uppercase till \E.
\Q	Quotes (disables) regexp metacharacters till \E.
\E	Ends case modification.

Table 3.2   Character Interpolation Supported by Perl

## CHAPTER 4

Statement and Function Traps

In Chapter 3 we looked at some of the variable-specific traps and errors that can creep into your Perl scripts. In this chapter we'll be looking at the general statements, statement sequences, and functions and the problems they can cause. Unfortunately, we don't have the space to go through all of the different possible combinations of all the scripts in the world that might cause problems and bugs, but the information in this and the last chapter may help you to identify and resolve a bug once you've identified a particular problem.

Tests and Comparisons

The most common problem with tests and comparisons is using the wrong comparison operator for the value type. You must use **==**, **!=**, and so on with numerical values, and **eq**, **ne**, and other text-based comparisons on text. In this example,

```
print "Same\n" if ('123.0' eq '123');
print "Same\n" if ('123.0' == '123');
```

the former case is false, because the two strings are not identical, but in the latter case the strings are translated by Perl into numbers and are equal.

When using **sort** you should use the **<=>** to compare numerical values and **cmp** to compare strings.

The **cmp** operator returns the comparison of two values if they are the same, the value returned by the operator is zero, not one. In the two lines below (which are logically opposite),

```
print "Same eq\n" if ('Martin' eq 'Martin');
print "Same cmp\n" if ('Martin' cmp 'Martin');
```

the first works as you expect, the second doesn't. The **cmp** operator is best used in a **sort** block.

Similarly, the **<=>** operator compares two numerical values, but isn't identical to **==**:

```
print "Same ==\n" if (1 == 1);
print "Same <=>\n" if (1 <=> 1);
```

The **<=>** operator is best used as part of **sort** block.

Loops

Most problems relating to loops can actually be traced back to the comparison operators you are using within the statements. Most of the remaining errors can be reduced to the special and nonstandard treatment of certain constructs—for example, the special handling of the **<FILEHANDLE>** operator within a **while** loop.

Using **while**

When using **while**, remember that the construct:

```
while(<FILE>)
```

is actually treated by Perl as

```
while(defined($_ = <FILE>))
```

The **<FILEHANDLE>** operator changes the **$_** variable *only* when it's used within the confines of a **while** loop test. The fragment

```
while(1)
{
    <FILE>;
    print "Line: $_";
    last unless(defined($_));
}
```

will be a continuous loop, because, **$_** is not being updated by the **<FILE>** statement.

The **do {} while** loop

The **do {} loop** is not really a loop at all—**do** executes statements while the statement is true. This means that you cannot use the loop control statements (**next**, **last**, an so on) within a **do** loop.

The **for** and **foreach** loops

Use **for** rather than **foreach** when using the three-argument form, just like C. For example,

```
for(my $i=0;$i<100;$i++)
```

is clearer than

```
foreach(my $i=0;$i<100;$i++)
```

Conversely, the statement

```
foreach (@array)
```

is clearer than

```
for (@array)
```

Remember the test operator logic when using **for** on an array. The following work correctly:

```
for(my $i=0;$i<@array;$i++)
for(my $i=0;$i<=$#array;$i++)
```

but

```
for(my $i=0;$i<=@array;$i++)
```

reads one element too many, and

```
for(my $i=0;$i<$#array;$i++)
```

never reaches the end of an array.

- Remember that **foreach** uses the **$_** variable if you don't supply the name of an alternative.
- The **foreach** statement accepts an array or list generated either dynamically or through the return result from **keys** or **values**. It's also non-destructive—you work through the elements of the list or array; elements are not removed using **pop** or **shift**.

Control Statements

When using the control statements, **next**, **last**, and **continue** care needs to be taken to ensure that you are correctly moving on to the next executable block. The guide below should help.

The **next** operator skips the remainder of the code block, forcing the loop to re-evaluate the next iteration of the loop. For example,

```
while (<DATA>)
{
    next if /^#/;
}
```

would skip lines from the file if they started with a hash symbol. This is the standard comment style under Unix. If there is a **continue** block, it is executed before execution proceeds to the next iteration of the loop.

The **last** keyword ends the loop entirely, skipping the remaining statements in the code block as well as dropping out of the loop. This is best used to escape a loop when an alternative condition has been reached within a loop that cannot otherwise be trapped. The **last** keyword is therefore identical to the **break** keyword in C and shellscript. For example,

```
while (<DATA>)
{
    last if ($found);
}
```

would exit the loop if the value of **$found** was true, regardless of whether the end of the file had actually been reached. The **continue** block is not executed.

The **redo** keyword re-executes the code block without reevaluating the conditional statement for the loop. This skips the remainder of the code block and also the **continue** block before the main code block is re-executed. For example, the code below would read the next line from a file if the current line terminates with a backslash.

```
while(<DATA>)
{
    if (s#\\$#)
    {
        $_ .= <DATA>;
        redo;
    }
}
```

Unless the name of the loop is specified, all loop control statements affect the current (innermost) loop. For example,

```
OUTER:
while(<DATA>)
{
    chomp;
    @linearray=split;
    foreach $word (@linearray)
    {
        next OUTER if ($word =~ /next/i)
    }
}
```

This would skip the current input line from the file if there was a word "next" in the input line while allowing the remainder of the words from the file to be processed. If we'd used an unqualified **next** statement, it would have just proceeded to the next word in the **foreach** loop.

Regular Expression Traps

Regular expressions are very prone to simple logic problems as part of the expression itself. Rather than list all the possible different combinations, I've instead listed the most common regular expression usage problems when employed as part of a statement.

The pattern binding operator for regular expressions is =~. The following lines do not do the same thing:

```
$string = /foo/;
$string =~ /foo/;
```

The first line matches **$_** against the characters "foo" and returns a true value to **$string** if the match succeeded. The second line matches **$string** against the characters "foo."

When you want to match multiple variables against groupings in a regular expression you should use

```
($first, $second) = ($var =~ m/(.*):(.*)/);
```

Note the parentheses around the match statement; the following example is wrong:

```
($first, $second) = $var =~ m/(.*):(.*)/;
```

and should raise an error, but the statement

```
$first = ($var =~ m/(.*):(.*)/);
```

will silently fail, and set **$first** to 1.

Beware of matching too much in a regular expression. The fragment

```
$string = 'The cat sat on the mat';
($match) = ($string =~ /The (.*) /);
```

sets **$match** to "cat sat on the," when you probably wanted only "cat." This happens because you've used a maximal match that includes everything up to the last space, tracking from the end of the string. Use a minimal match by appending a question mark to the qualifier:

```
($match) = ($string =~ /The (.*?) /);
```

This forces the regular expression engine to return the text matching to the next occurrence of the regex token, rather than to the last token.

Function Traps

Because of the way in which most of the Perl functions operate, it's difficult to give a strict or coherent meaning to all the functions. Most of functions and operators have their own special meaning and treatment, depending on the context in which they are used. It's also impossible to qualify functions according to what they return, since different functions return different information according to their context. For example, the **localtime** function returns a date/time string in scalar context, but the individual components in list context.

For a quick reference to some of the more popular problems and effects of the Perl built-in functions, see Table 4-1. This lists functions and the variables they use or modify, or the types of exceptions they raise. The column descriptions are given here:

- D   Uses **$_**, **@_**, or similar as a default value
- $!   Sets **$!** on an error
- $@   Raises an exception—use **$@** to get the error message from **eval**
- $?   Sets **$?** when a child process exits
- T   Taints data

- XA   Raises an exception when supplied an invalid argument
- XR   Raises an exception if you modify a read-only argument
- XT   Raises an exception if fed tainted data
- U   Raises an exception if unsupported on the current platform—support is only guaranteed on Unix

Function	$_	$!	$@	$?	T	XA	XR	XT	U
abs	X								
accept	X					X			X
alarm	X								X
atan2									
bind		X				X		X	X
binmode						X			
bless						X			
caller									
chdir		X					X		
chmod		X					X		
chomp	X						X		
chop	X						X		
chown		X					X		X
chr	X								
chroot	X	X					X		X
close		X		X		X			
closedir		X				X			X
connect		X				X		X	X
cos	X								
crypt									X
dbmclose		X							X
dbmopen		X							X
defined	X								
delete									
die			X						
do (block)									
do (file)	X			X			X		

Table 4.1   Attributes for Built-in Perl Functions

Function	$_	$!	$@	$?	T	XA	XR	XT	U
do (subroutine)			X						
dump									
each									
endgrent									X
endhostent									X
endnetent									X
endprotoent									X
endpwent									X
endservent									X
eof						X			
eval	X							X	
exec		X						X	
exists									
exit									
exp	X								
fcntl		X				X	X	X	X
fileno						X			
flock		X				X			X
fork		X							X
format									
formline									
getc					X	X			
getgrent									X
getgrgid									X
getgrnam									X
gethostbyaddr									X
gethostbyname									X
gethostent									X
getlogin									X
getnetbyaddr									X
getnetbyname									X
getnetent									X
getpeername		X				X			X

Table 4.1   Attributes for Built-in Perl Functions *(continued)*

Function	$_	$!	$@	$?	T	XA	XR	XT	U
getpgrp		X							X
getppid									X
getpriority		X							X
getprotobyname									X
getprotobynumber									X
getprotoent									X
getpwent					X				X
getpwnam					X				X
getpwuid					X				X
getservbyname									X
getservbyport									X
getservent									X
getsockname		X				X			X
getsockopt		X				X			X
glob	X		X		X			X	
gmtime									
goto			X						
grep									
hex	X								
import									
index									
int	X								
ioctl		X				X	X	X	X
join									
keys									
kill		X				X		X	X
last			X						
lc	X				X				
lcfirst	X				X				
length	X								
link		X						X	X
listen		X				X			X
local									

Table 4.1 Attributes for Built-in Perl Functions *(continued)*

Function	$_	$!	$@	$?	T	XA	XR	XT	U
localtime									
log	X		X						
lstat	X	X							X
m//					X			X	
map									
mkdir		X						X	
msgctl		X							X
msgget		X							X
msgrcv		X							X
msgsnd		X							X
my									
next			X						
no			X						
oct	X								
open		X				X		X	X
opendir		X				X		X	X
ord	X								
pack			X						
package									
pipe		X				X			X
pop									
pos	X								
print	X	X				X			
printf	X	X				X			
prototype						X			
push									
quotemeta	X								
rand									
read		X			X	X	X		
readdir		X			X	X			X
readline		X			X	X			
readlink	X	X			X				X
readpipe		X		X	X			X	X

Table 4.1   Attributes for Built-in Perl Functions *(continued)*

Function	$_	$!	$@	$?	T	XA	XR	XT	U
recv		X			X	X	X		X
redo			X						
ref	X								
rename		X						X	
require	X	X	X					X	
reset									
return			X						
reverse									
rewinddir		X				X			X
rindex	X	X						X	
rmdir									
s///					X		X	X	
scalar									
seek		X				X			
seekdir		X				X			X
select (filehandle)						X			
select (files)		X							X
semctl		X							X
semget		X							X
semop		X							X
send		X				X			X
setgrent									X
sethostent									X
setnetent									X
setpgrp		X						X	X
setpriority		X						X	X
setprotoent									X
setpwent									X
setservent									X
setsockopt		X				X			X
shift									
shmctl		X							X
shmget		X							X

Table 4.1 Attributes for Built-in Perl Functions *(continued)*

Function	$_	$!	$@	$?	T	XA	XR	XT	U
shmread		X							X
shmwrite		X							X
shutdown		X				X			X
sin	X								
sleep									
socket		X				X		X	X
socketpair		X				X		X	X
sort			X						
splice			X						
split	X				X				
sprintf									
sqrt	X		X						
srand									
stat	X	X				X			
study	X								
sub									
substr			X			X	X		
symlink		X						X	X
syscall		X						X	X
sysopen		X				X			
sysread		X	X	X		X	X		
sysseek		X				X			
system		X		X				X	
syswrite		X	X			X			
tell						X			
telldir						X			X
tie		X							
tied									
time									
times									
times									
tr///							X		
truncate		X				X		X	X

Table 4.1 Attributes for Built-in Perl Functions *(continued)*

Function	$_	$!	$@	$?	T	XA	XR	XT	U
uc	X				X				
ucfirst	X				X				
umask								X	X
undef							X		
unlink	X	X							X
unpack			X						
unshift									
untie									
use		X	X						
utime		X						X	X
values									
vec							X		
wait		X		X					X
waitpid		X		X					X
wantarray									
warn		X							
write		X	X			X			
y///							X		

Table 4.1   Attributes for Built-in Perl Functions *(continued)*

More specific problems and errors for certain functions are listed below.

alarm

You can have one only **alarm** active at any one time—the call to **alarm** overwrites or resets the previous call.

- Be wary of using **alarm** and **sleep** together—some systems use **alarm** to implement the **sleep** function.
- Don't use **alarm** for precise wait periods, since the actual delay may be up to one second more or less than you specify. A busy system may also delay the alarm call (see Chapter 14 for more details on the effects).

binmode

The **binmode** function has no effect on Unix or Mac implementations of Perl and is also safe to use if you want to support a cross-platform script.

Be wary of using scripts that access a file in raw and **binmode** forms on systems that require the function, especially if you are overwriting information or storing the values returned by **tell** to use a references to parts of the data. The difference in sizes and interpretation is likely to corrupt data.

 *It might be easier to use **open** for text files and the **sys*** functions for binary access, thereby negating the need for **binmode** entirely.*

chdir

Remember that when using **chdir** on a Windows machine, there are both current working drives and current working directories. This means that

```
chdir('D:\Demos');
chdir('C:\Windows');
chdir('D:');
```

actually puts you back in D:\Demos—either specify the directory explicitly each time or make sure you track and check the current directories on each machine before continuing.

chomp

The **chomp** function is the moderately safer version of **chop**, but its operation on arrays and when the **$/** is undefined is unsual.

- Remember that this takes the last character off the end of a variable, or each element of a list, *if* the last character matches the **$/** variable.
- If **$/** is empty, **chomp** removes all trailing newlines from a string or all elements of a list. Be careful using **chomp** if **$/** has been localized.
- The function returns the number of characters deleted, *not* the character deleted.

chop

Unlike **chomp**, **chop** deletes just the last character of the supplied string or all elements of a list. It returns the last character deleted (which may be a space)—make sure you check with **eq** or similar and not with the numerical test operators.

chown

The first two arguments *must* be numeric. Use **-1** to signify that the value should not be changed.

crypt

The **crypt** function cannot (easily) be decrypted, and there is no **decrypt** function—it's designed to be used one way only for password verification.

delete

The **delete** function deletes hash or array elements from *any* array or hash, so you must keep the following in mind:

- When deleting (or indeed modifying) the **%ENV** hash, be aware that this modifies the environment only for the current Perl interpreter and its children.

- Be careful when deleting values of a hash while you are iterating over it.

- When deleting hash or array entries from a tied database, you *are* modifying the file; a tie doesn't create an in-memory copy of the database for you to work with.

each

The **each** function returns key/value pairs from a hash.

You cannot use **each** within a **foreach** block; use **while** instead

```
while( ($key, $value) = each %hash)
```

use **each** in preference to **keys** or **values** on large hashes, especially those tied to external databases and files.

- Don't mix **each** and **keys** or **values** on the same hash within a loop—the iterator for these will be reset when **keys** or **values** is called, which may upset your loop.

eval

The **eval** keyword is a function and needs a closing semicolon even when using a code block. The fragment

```
eval
{
    local $SIG{ALRM} = sub { die "Timeout" };
    alarm 10;
    chomp($answer = <STDIN>);
    alarm 0;
}
```

will fail with a parser error. The same is also true for functions that take an inline block—that is, **map**, **grep**, and **sort**. They must have a terminating semicolon to define the end of the statement.

exec

The **exec** function normally *never* returns—it replaces the current instance of the interpreter with the program that you call. The only time it will return is if the command does not exist and the command was called directly instead of via a shell.

If the command is not found and you used **exec** in combination with a shell, normally the shell will replace Perl.

exists

This function returns true if the supplied element exists in the array or hash—the value of the element is irrelevant. This means that the values returned by **defined** and **exists** may well be different.

exit

Use **exit** to exit a script, not a function. You should use **return** to immediately return from a function call. Remember that **exit** calls any **END** blocks before finally quitting the interpreter.

fork

You should set **SIG{CHLD}** to IGNORE or alternatively to point to a child handler that calls **wait** to ensure that you don't accumulate zombie processes.

gmtime/localtime

When comparing different times, use **gmtime**, not **localtime**. The **localtime** function will always return the time according to the current locale. If you compare two time values, the value will be adjusted according to the local time zone. For example,

```
$newtime = time();
$oldtime = $newtime-((180*24*3600)+98764);
($secdiff,$mindiff,$hourdiff,$ydaydiff)
    = (localtime($newtime - $oldtime))[0..2,7];
print "$ydaydiff days, $hourdiff:$mindiff:$secdiff\n";
($secdiff,$mindiff,$hourdiff,$ydaydiff)
    = (gmtime($newtime - $oldtime))[0..2,7];
print "$ydaydiff days, $hourdiff:$mindiff:$secdiff\n";
```

Even with the time set to GMT, we get

```
181 days, 3:26:4
181 days, 2:26:4
```

This happens because of the effects of British Summer Time (which was in effect at the time this was executed). In another time zone, the differences would be more significant.

join

The **join** function accepts a string as a first argument, not a regular expression like **split**.

The contents of the first argument is interpolated between pairs of array elements, such that:

```
$string = join(':', qw/a b c/);
```

produces a:b:c, not :a:b:c or a:b:c:.

keys/values

The **keys/values** functions return an entire list of the keys or values from a hash in one go, unlike **each** which only returns one key/value pair for each call.

- Use **each** in preference to **keys** or **value** when dealing with large hashes.
- Using **keys** resets the iterator (used by all three functions) to iterate over the hash.
- In theory, providing the hash hasn't changed, two subsequent calls to any of the three functions should produce keys/values in the same order. But don't rely on it; use **sort** or a predefined array to hold the sequence instead.

map

map iterates over an array, running the supplied block, and returns the modified list—it *doesn't* return the list that was provided to the function.

The function doesn't, by default, modify the list contents. For example, the following

```
@array = qw/a b c/;
map { uc($_) } @array;
```

does nothing, while

```
@array = map {uc ($_) } @array;
```

and

```
map { $_ = uc($_) } @array;
```

actually modify the array.

Don't use the **$_** assign format on a temporary list—it may have unpredictable results. For example,

```
map { $_ = uc($_) } glob('*');
```

The **$_** variable is used to hold each element of the list, so don't mix **$_** loop variables with **map** functions.

open

Be careful when opening files: Make sure you use the right mode (see Table 4-2 for a quick guide).

Be especially careful with the **+>>FILE** mode; although it can be written to, you can only add, not overwrite, existing information.

print

The most common mistake with **print** is to place a comma after a filehandle:

```
print FILE, "Some data\n";
```

This should be written as

```
print FILE "Some data\n";
```

Perl will pick this up during compilation and raise an error. However, there are situations when using a scalar that mistakenly identifies the first argument as a filehandle when it isn't, and raises the error anyway. If there's any doubt, you should use parentheses around the argument list:

```
print ($notfile, ": Some data\n");
print $notfile ("Some data\n");
```

 I prefer to use parentheses around all function calls if I can because doing so solves so many problems. Although Perl allows you to ignore the parentheses, the interpretation can be problematic.

sprintf

The format of the **sprintf** function is

```
sprintf(FORMAT, LIST);
```

and not

```
sprintf(LIST);
```

Mode	Read	Write	Append	Create New	Delete Existing
<FILE	Y	N	N	N	N
>FILE	N	Y	N	Y	Y
>>FILE	Y	Y	N	Y	N
+<FILE	Y	Y	N	N	N
+>FILE	Y	Y	N	Y	Y
+>>FILE	Y	N	Y	Y	N

Table 4.2   Modes for open

Accordingly, the following code doesn't do what you expect with **sprintf**:

```
@args = ("%0.2f:%s\n",3.141,'PI');
print sprintf(@args);
```

Instead, scalar context is enforced on **@args**, and you get a count of the number elements in **@args** instead. With **printf**, it works correctly:

```
3.14:PI
```

ref

The **ref** function works only on references to data structure: You cannot use **ref** to identify a variable's type (you should know it already!). For example,

```
%hash = ('Fred' => 'Flintstone', 'Barney' => 'Rubble');
print ref(%hash);
```

prints nothing, because **%hash** is not a reference to anything. Remember that **ref** returns a string relating to the type of *ref*erence.

scalar

The **scalar** function is actually a unary operator, so supplying a list of arguments, such as

```
print scalar($first,$second);
```

will actually cause **$first** to be interpreted in a void context, and only **$second** to be evaluated in a scalar context.

seek

Don't use **seek** on filehandles opened with **open**: Use **sysseek** to avoid the buffering issues.

select (filehandle)

The **select** function returns the *previous* selected filehandle, not the new filehandle.

select (files)

Don't mix **select** with buffered I/O (**read** or **<FILEHANDLE>**). Switch buffering off or use **sysread** instead.

 *The **IO::Select** module is much easier to use than the **select** function and avoids making calls to **vec** on large filehandle lists.*

shift and unshift/pop and push

When not supplied an array on which to operate, **shift**, **unshift**, **pop**, and **push** operate on **@ARGV** when outside of a function (that is, within the **main::** package) or on the @_ argument variable when called within a function. A common mistake is

```
del_files();

sub del_files
{
    while($_ = shift)
    {
        unlink($_) or warn "Can't delete: $_, $!\n";
    }
}
```

Here **shift** will never do what the user expects—it'll try to take arguments off of @_, which is empty because **del_files** has never been supplied anything. It won't take arguments off of **@ARGV** either, because it's being called within a function. We could either change the way the function is called:

```
del_files(@ARGV);
```

or the way in which the **while** loop operates:

```
while ($_ = shift @ARGV)
```

If you're not sure of the effect, consider explicitly supplying the name of the array on which you want the functions to operate.

pop deletes and returns the *last* element of an array, and **shift** deletes and returns the *first* element of the array. These modify the array, and, if you're using the functions to iterate entirely through an array, the array will be empty when the loop completes. If you want a non-destructive effect, use a **for/foreach** loop:

```
foreach my $element (@array)
```

Similarly, **unshift** inserts a new element at the start of the array, effectively renumbering the remaining existing elements. The **push** function adds a new element to the array without modifying the existing numbering.

If you're using arrays as a way of processing a constantly changing list of arguments, use **shift** and **push** or **pop** and **unshift** so that you place and remove items from different ends.

You cannot use the functions on a list; they operate only on an array. The following will not work:

```
while($_ = pop keys %hash)
```

use **foreach** to loop through each key:

```
foreach (keys %hash)
```

or use **each** to get each element:

```
while($_ = each %hash)
```

or create a temporary array to hold the information:

```
@array = keys %hash;
while($_ = pop @array)
```

## CHAPTER 5

Program Design

Although it's not possible to ensure that all your programs are bug free the first time, there are some aspects of the development process that will make the process of finding and resolving bugs significantly easier. Tools like debuggers and profilers will only help you find and trace the source of a bug—actually eliminating a bug is a different matter.

There are a number of ways in which the design and methods employed in your program can serve to help the debugging process. The most obvious way is to divide your program up into a number of individual components—functions—which can then be debugged and optimized in isolation from the rest of the program. The same process can then also be extended to the modules that you create to support your desired function set. Producing a series of functions, debugging them, and then placing them in a "debugged" module should mean that any problem lies within the script that's calling the module, not the module itself.

This method doesn't always work or provide a perfect solution, but it does make the tracking easier—debugging a single subroutine either in a script or module is easier than trying to debug a huge multiline script.

There are also some tricks supported by Perl that can improve the chances of spotting a potential problem. Here we're not talking about pragmas or warnings (see Chapter 8), instead it's the algorithms language features that can make the difference. For example, defining a function prototype means that when a function is called, the arguments supplied are matched against what the function expects—a mismatch will raise an error.

The final step in developing good programming design skills that help to find bugs is the use of code comments and documentation. Comments are an often forgotten part of all program development, and most programmers, including myself, often fail to include even the most basic of comments. Documenting your code is another area which is often neglected by most programmers—with Perl, since we can embed the documentation directly into the source code, there are really no excuses.

Abstraction

Abstraction—the process of taking a program and splitting it into a number of component parts—is a natural process for all scripts. There will always be some scripts that lend themselves well to the process, and certainly a number that just can't be resolved that easily. You can abstract Perl programs into three basic levels. The first two levels are obvious, subroutines (or functions) and modules, but the last is the special form of the previous options, the object or class system. You can see a simplified diagram of the whole system in Figure 5-1.

Even at the simplest level, using subroutines will help to improve the reliability of your scripts. Once you've divided the program up into subroutines, you can debug each subroutine in isolation and introduce any necessary error checking and handling at the subroutine level. Once a subroutine has been tested and debugged you shouldn't ever need to fix it again—the only time you'll need to modify it is when modifying its capabilities.

When developing modules the same rule applies—each subroutine within the module can be debugged. Aside from the additional dressing required to turn the file into a proper module, the module should also be free of bugs. The act of turning a suite of functions and possibly modules into a series of classes is more complex, but again, if done correctly, it should help to eliminate

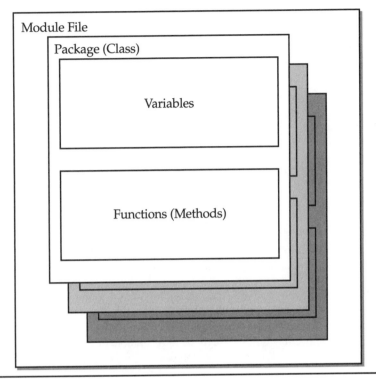

Figure 5.1   An overview of an abstracted Perl script

any bugs or potential bugs and, therefore, make the process of debugging the script that uses them much easier.

In this section we'll look at some of the techniques for developing good subroutines, modules, and classes that should highlight and help to prevent at least some of the problems you might experience.

Developing Good Subroutines

If you ignore the contents of a subroutine and what it does, you can resolve the operation of the subroutine into two basic components—the parsing of any supplied arguments and the return of new information. All subroutines will be combinations of at least one of these; subroutines will accept and return data, accept data without a return value, or return a value without any data.

Further, there will be subroutines that do a combination of these operations, but not likely all three. The **rand** function, for example, returns a number between zero and one, if you call it without arguments, or a number between zero and the supplied number. It's impossible in this instance to determine the situation when the subroutine shouldn't return any values.

We'll look at these two aspects of subroutine design—how to parse the arguments that have been supplied and the best methods for returning information to the caller.

Parsing Arguments

There are three things to consider when developing a subroutine with respect to the arguments that will be passed to the subroutine:

- Argument numbers
- Argument types
- Default values

We'll look at each of these in turn and see how their definition can be refined to reduce, rather than propagate, problems. We'll also look at a fourth instance, where the number and order of the supplied arguments is irrelevant.

> **Design Tip** *For information on reducing the load when exchanging arrays and hashes and on how to supply multiple arrays and hashes to a function without losing the distinction between each argument, see "References" later in this chapter.*

You might also want to examine the prototyping system for Perl subroutines, which allows you to pre-declare the number and type of arguments that are supported by the subroutine. This process forces errors to be raised if there is a mismatch during the compilation process, rather than during execution. It may not be practical for all situations and might be most suitable for simple subroutines with uncomplicated arguments (see the section on "Prototypes" later in this chapter for more information).

Counting Arguments

First and foremost you should think about the number of arguments that will be supplied to a subroutine. If the subroutine expects a specific number of arguments, then your function should check for the correct number. The most obvious way of doing this is to check the scalar value of the @_ array:

```
carp "Not enough/too many arguments in mysub" unless(@_ == 2);
```

Note here the use of **carp** to report a problem, rather than using **warn** or **die**—this is to ensure that the error is reported back with respect to the caller. (See Chapter 7 for more information on using **carp** and the rest of the **Carp** module.) By using **carp** we can indicate that the problem is related to how the subroutine was called, rather than a problem with the subroutine's operation. The same trick can be used for supporting multiple argument numbers—see the sidebar for more details.

Remember, no matter how you extract the individual arguments for the argument array, that hashes and arrays will always gobble up the remaining arguments to a function. Also remember that, when passing entire arrays or hashes to the function, it becomes impossible to modify how the arguments are extracted based on the number of supplied arguments. For example, the subroutine

```
sub sum
{
    my ($first, $second, @rest) = @_;
...
}
```

24x7   Supporting a Variety of Argument Numbers

You can also use the scalar value of the @_ array in subroutines that support a multiple number of arguments. For example,

```
if (@_ == 2)
{
    ($fname, $sname) = @_;
}
elsif (@_ == 3)
{
    ($fname, $sname, $title) = @_;
}
```

Alternatively, you can use **shift** to progressively take arguments from the stack.

If you're going to use the **shift** method, then it's a good idea to set default values for any arguments that you consider to be optional.

will accept 300 as easily as three—checking for a minimum of three arguments is valid, but checking for 300 is pointless.

Design Tip   *If you're going to support a function that accepts multiple arguments, remember to use* **my** *to declare the variables before the tests and assignation; otherwise the variables will go out of scope before they need to be used in the rest of the function.*

Argument Types

Although prototypes will help to identify the sort of datatype that should be supplied, you still need to determine how the individual arguments within the subroutine will be interpreted. The normal method for doing this is to verify each argument against either a known type—using the **ref** function if you're using references—or against a valid value. The latter depends entirely on the script, and a good example is a function that is expecting a numerical argument:

```
sub square
{
    carp "Not a number" unless($_[0] =~ /^[0-9]+$/);
    return($_[0] * $_[0]);
}
```

Again, we use **carp** (see Chapter 7) to report a problem. The benefit of testing the function at this point is that it doesn't matter where the incorrect data is introduced, the error will be trapped before it upsets the normal execution of the script. Checking the variable type in this instance would do nothing, we need to verify the data supplied. Merely checking the string returned by the **ref** function is only useful in situations where the data you are supplying is a reference to another object, but it can still be useful.

Additionally, it can be a good idea to develop a subroutine that is capable of accepting a number of different argument types based on where it might be called. The subroutine below accepts either a hash or reference to a hash when building the record for a new login group. If a hash is supplied, then the argument list is translated internally into a reference to a hash. If a hash reference is supplied, then the information is used verbatim.

```perl
sub db_new_group
{
    my $group = {
        'login' => '',
        'password' => '',
        'userlevel' => 0,
        'emails' => 0,
        'isbns' => 0,
    };
    my $info;

    if (ref($_[0]) eq 'HASH')
    {
        ($info) = @_;
    }
    else
    {
        $info = {@_};
    }

    foreach my $key (sort keys %{$info})
    {
        $group->{$key} = $info->{$key};
    }
    return $group;
}
```

Of course, the resulting value is the same—we return a reference to a hash that contains the group record—but you get the idea.

Default Values

For functions that accept a varying number and/or type of arguments, you should be setting the variable used within the subroutine to a default value. This will help to ensure that when an argument is not supplied, the variable still contains either valid data or a value that can be ignored or tested when it needs to be used. For example, the **power** function below raises the first argument to the power of the second argument or to 2 if there is no second argument:

```perl
sub power
{
    my $base = shift;
    my $power = shift || 2;
    return $base**$power;
}
```

Here I've used **shift** to take off the arguments and then used the || operator to set the power to a default value if **shift** fails. If called with a single argument, the function will return the square of the supplied value, and if supplied with two it'll return the first raised to the power of the second.

Dynamic Arguments

There are times when there is no set argument order for a function, but you still want to accept changes to the function's variables. The way to do this is to accept a hash, where each key of the hash is the variable that you want to accept, and the value is the data for that variable. This method has the advantage of allowing you to pass a variety of scalars, arrays, and hashes without directly worrying about the order of the references you supply.

For example, we could rewrite the function **power** seen earlier like this:

```
sub power
{
    my (%args) = @_;
    my $base = $args{base} || 2;
    my $power = $args{power} || 2;
    return $base**$power;
}
```

which means that we can now call the function in a number of different ways:

```
print power(base => 16, power => 3); # returns 16384
print power(base => 16)              # returns 256
print power(power => 8)              # returns 256
print power();                       # returns 4
```

The order or the arguments is no longer an issue, which makes supporting default values and/or multiple options within a single subroutine significantly easier.

Design Tip *If you want to use this option, consider using '-argument' as the argument string, that way you won't need to quote the hash key each time—the preceding hyphen translates the bareword to a string.*

Return Values

The values returned by your subroutine are as important as what the subroutine does with the arguments it's been supplied. It's probably best to approach the return values from the point of view of what happens when the subroutine fails, then work from there to the point of valid return values. But beware—don't be tempted to return a zero or empty string, as these may actually be real values.

For example, the simple **add** function we've seen before could legitimately return a zero if it's been supplied values that sum up accordingly. Instead, use an **undef** to indicate a failure. This is universally accepted as an indication of failure, and it will be correctly identified during a boolean test as a failure.

Developing Good Modules

The quality of a module depends entirely on the subroutines that you supply to it—if the subroutines are not up to scratch, it doesn't matter if they are part of a script, module, or class. You should be using the tricks described earlier in this section, as well as those in the "Prototypes" section later in this chapter, for developing subroutines.

Beyond the individual subroutines that make up your module, the only other component you need to worry about is the configuration of the **Exporter** module that you use to provide the **import** method used by the **use** statement when importing a module. When configuring the module you should think about:

- *Version number*   Essential for tracking the module version, especially if the module is going to be made public.

- *Functions you want to export*   For dealing with a non-object–based module, export functions or function sets appropriately. For classes, don't export anything—the methods defined by the class should be enough.

- *Variables that you want to export or publish*   Useful for debug variables or setting global options in modules that aren't supporting a class.

- *Extensibility*   Consider converting your module into a class. Doing this will make it easier to extend the functionality without having to modify the other elements or rely on messy "public" module variables.

- *Using the* **strict** *pragma*   Remember that **strict** is block scoped, so it must be defined in your module as well as the parent script to enable strict checking.

- *Using the* **warnings** *pragma*   Available from Perl 5.6 onward, it enforces warnings within your module, even if the parent script hasn't enabled them.

Version number

The version number is a vital way of tracking the version of module being used and therefore an important tool when debugging, as it provides a reference point for determining which version of a module is actually being used.

The easiest way to introduce a version number is

```
$VERSION = 1.01;
```

 Remember to use at least two digits after the decimal point in a version number. Remember that 1.9 is greater than 1.10, and 1.09 is less.

If you're using RCS or similar or you want to use a multi-point version number, then you'll need to define **$VERSION** in terms of a inline subroutine—most documentation recommends this:

```
$VERSION = do { my @r = (q$Revision: 2.21 $ =~ /\d+/g);
                sprintf "%d."."%02d" x $#r, @r };
```

Note, however, that this should be supplied on one line (not two as shown here) so that it's compatible with the **MakeMaker** module.

Exporting Functions/Variables

When deciding which objects should be exported, think about the namespace—objects that are exported by default will pollute the **main::*** namespace, which may conflict with the names used for global objects and functions. You can avoid exporting anything and then force users either to explicitly import the objects they require or to use the fully qualified name—for example **MyModule::process**. If you're creating a new class (see "Developing Good Classes" later in this chapter), then you shouldn't need to export anything—the inheritance rules and objects will have access to the methods they need.

The **Exporter** module will supply the **import** function required by the **use** statement to import functions. The absolute minimum required at the top of your module is

```
package ModuleName;
require Exporter;
@ISA = qw(Exporter);
```

The package name should reflect the module's file name—remember that the module **MyGroup::MyModule** equates to a file name of **MyGroup/MyModule.pm**. The remaining statements import the **Exporter** module, and the **@ISA** array defines the inheritance—it's a case of inheritance that allows the **import** module in **Exporter** to be inherited by the module you are creating.

The **Exporter** module then uses the values in **@EXPORT**, **@EXPORT_OK**, **@EXPORT_FAIL,** and **%EXPORT_TAGS** to determine which objects should or should not be exported from the module.

The **@EXPORT** array should be used to list the objects that should be exported by default from the module. The **@EXPORT_OK** array should list the objects that can be exported if they have been specifically requested. For example,

```
use MyModule qw/process regurgitate/;
```

would cause **MyModule** to only export the **process** and **regurgitate** subroutines.

The **%EXPORT_TAGS** is a hash that contains a series of import sets; for example, the definition

```
%EXPORT_TAGS = ('standard' => [process, regurgitate],
                'processing' => [process, parse]);
```

can be used from a caller with

```
use MyModule qw/:standard :processing/;
```

Finally, if you don't want any specific objects to be exported, then the naming convention is to use a preceding underscore; however this is not actually enforced—it's still possible to import an object with that prefix. You can disable this ability by defining those objects within the **@EXPORT_FAIL** array—the **Exporter** will **die** if any objects that appear in this array are explicitly requested.

24x7   Exporting Objects with the **strict** Pragma

There is an obvious problem with defining the **@EXPORT**, **@ISA**, and other variables used by the **Exporter** module when you are employing the **strict** pragma—the variables will not have been explicitly defined. Using **my** won't work, as this will hide the variables from the **import** method, which is not the effect we want. The easiest way to get around this is to use the **vars** pragma to declare the variables beforehand, as, for example:

```
use vars qw/@EXPORT @EXPORT_OK @ISA/;
```

Alternatively, if you are using Perl 5.6 or later, you can use the **our** keyword, which has the same effect:

```
our (@EXPORT, @EXPORT_OK);
```

Developing Good Classes

We don't have the time to look into the specifics of turning your modules into classes. Actually, it's not that complicated—you just have to create a suitable **new** method for creating a new object and returning a reference blessed to a particular class, and then convert your functions to accept the object reference as the first argument. And there are some things that you can do to ensure that your class has been created correctly:

- *Use the two-argument form of* **bless**   This will help to ensure that your objects are blessed explicitly to the right class. For example, use

  ```
  sub new
  {
      my $class = shift;
      return bless {}, $class;
  }
  ```

  Or, if you want to support both static and dynamic object creation, use the following:

  ```
  sub new
  {
      my $self = shift;
      my $class = ref($self) || $self;
      return bless {}, $class;
  }
  ```

- *Use class inheritance*   You can split a "mega" class into a number of smaller individual classes and then use inheritance. Using a class with a number of frequently used methods in combination with an inheritance tree is much more efficient.

- *Use @ISA*   The **@ISA** array is your inheritance table; use it whenever possible to inherit methods from other modules and to avoid messy **$object->Class::method**() constructs.

Using Prototypes

The prototype is used by Perl to make decisions about the number or type of arguments that are supplied to the function. The prototypes affect only function calls when called using the "new" form, that is, without a leading ampersand. If it looks like a built-in function, Perl will treat it as such. If you call a function using the "old" ampersand style, prototypes are ignored. In all cases, Perl checks only at compile time, so the function and calls must be visible at the time the functions are compiled. Because of this rule, the subroutine prototype declaration must have been parsed before any call to the function is made. Either the function should be placed before the **main** part of the script,

```
sub add($$)
{
    return $_[0]+$_[1];
}
add(3);
```

or you must make a "forward" declaration for the function prototype:

```
sub add($$);

print add(3);

sub add($$)
{
    return $_[0]+$_[1];
}
```

Note that the forward and actual subroutine declarations must match, just as in C.

When importing a subroutine from a module using **use** or **require**, the functions will have been parsed before the **main** section of the script executes. Beware, though, of functions that are loaded using the **AUTOLOAD** system and of those imported and generated dynamically using **do** and **eval**.

Prototype Definitions

You define the argument types the function accepts by using the same characters that precede variables. For example, dollar signs signify that scalar values are expected. The @ and % characters, as expected, specify arrays and hashes. However, except in the case noted below, unbackslashed @ or % characters will gobble up all the remaining arguments, regardless of the rest of the prototype definition. In addition, the $ implies a scalar context, and @ or % imply list context accordingly.

An ampersand requires an anonymous subroutine that can be specified without the **sub** keyword or the trailing comma if specified as the first argument. A * character specifies a typeglob, typically used to supply filehandles.

Any backslash quoted character signifies that the argument absolutely must start with that character— for example, \@ would require that the function call specify a list as the first argument. A semicolon separates required arguments (those before the semicolon) and optional arguments (those after the semicolon) in the prototype. Table 5-1 shows some examples taken from the **perlsub** man page.

Declaration	Example Call
sub mylink ($$)	mylink $old, $new
sub myvec ($$$)	myvec $var, $offset, 1
sub myindex ($$;$)	myindex &getstring, "substr"
sub mysyswrite ($$$;$)	mysyswrite $buf, 0, length($buf) - $off,
sub myreverse (@)	myreverse $a, $b, $c
sub myjoin ($@)	myjoin ":", $a, $b, $c
sub mypop (\@)	mypop @array
sub mysplice (\@$$@)	mysplice @array, @array, 0, @pushme
sub mykeys (\%)	mykeys %{$hashref}
sub myopen (*;$)	myopen HANDLE, $name
sub mypipe (**)	mypipe READHANDLE, WRITEHANDLE
sub mygrep (&@)	mygrep { /foo/ } $a, $b, $c
sub myrand ($)	myrand 42
sub mytime ()	mytime

Table 5.1   Sample Prototype Declarations

In the last three examples in Table 5-1, Perl treats the declarations slightly differently. The **mygrep** function is parsed as a true list operator, with the first argument interpreted as an anonymous subroutine, and the remaining arguments identified as elements of a list to the original **mygrep** function. For example, in the function

```
sub mygrep(&@)
{
    my ($func,@arg) = @_;
    @arg = grep &$func @arg;
}
```

the **$func** would be populated with a reference to an anonymous subroutine and **@arg** would contain the remaining arguments and imply a list context on the function, so a call to **wantarray** would return true.

The **myrand** function behaves like a true unary operator, and the **mytime** function is treated as a function with no arguments at all. This means you can get away with statements like this:

```
mytime +2
```

You'll end up with the return value of **mytime** added to the static value, instead of Perl calling **mytime** with an argument of **+2**.

You should be careful when specifying prototypes, since many of the options imply the context in which the function should return and, in turn, the function-specific utilities, such as **wantarray**. In general, therefore, you should use prototypes only on new functions, rather than retrofitting them to functions you have already written. Doing this will prevent the effects of imposing a scalar context on a function that is expecting to return in a list context. For example, consider a function with a single argument:

```
sub printmsg($)
{
    print "Message: ", shift, "\n";
}
```

Calling this function with an argument that returns a single element list wouldn't produce the same results. The call

```
printmsg(@message);
```

would actually print a value of 1, since the scalar prototype has imposed the condition that the list argument supplied be interpreted as a scalar.

In the case of a list, the scalar value of a list variable is the number of elements in the list. Using a function such as **split**, which uses the context in which it is called to determine where it puts its results, would cause a more serious problem. If used as the argument where a scalar was expected, **split** would execute in the scalar context, messing up your @_ argument list.

Dispatch Tables

For scripts and applications that support a number of different options, there are times when you need to be able to pick a function or subroutine from a list of predetermined options. The obvious solution is to use a simple **if** statement:

```
if ($command eq 'memory')
{
...
}
elsif ($command eq 'diskspace')
{
...
}
```

Although this is a perfectly acceptable solution, it becomes unworkable and difficult to manage as the size and complexity of the scripts and possible functions increase. Using **if** is also relatively inefficient, both from an execution point of view and from a programmer's point of view. Having to "manually" add each option presents a number of problems and situations where new errors can be introduced. Reference the wrong subroutine, or mistype an argument, and you'll have to find and fix the problem later.

There is a much easier way, and that's to use a dispatch table. Dispatch tables are simply hashes where the keys of the hash refer to a particular command, and the corresponding values refer to the name of a function to be called. For example, we might change the example above to

```
%commands = (memory    => \&memory_report,
             diskspace => \&diskspace_report
             load      => \&load_report );
```

The users supply the command they want to execute—either directly as part of a UI or web interface or through the use of a command line switch. You then match the command name to the function that you want to call.

To make the process safer and prevent the user from supplying the name of a function that doesn't exist, all you need to do is check the hash:

```
if (exists($commands{$command}))
```

To make doubly sure that you don't try to execute a function that hasn't yet been defined, we need to verify that the corresponding function actually exists. For this we need to resolve the function reference into a code reference, which we can then check using **defined**:

```
*code = \&{$commands{$command}};
die "Function does not exist: $command"
    unless (defined(&code));
```

Now the user can supply a command and get a useful "command not implemented" error if you haven't yet developed the function, rather than the script failing because the function being called does not exist. As you add new facilities just update the table.

You can also use the system for forward planning. When I'm developing a website that uses a script to access information, I invariably use a dispatch table. That way I can introduce commands into the HTML that I output without worrying about developing the function required to support it. Doing this reduces the development time, because I'm not going back and updating past HTML blocks with the new facilities that I'd always planned to include anyway.

Using Dispatch Tables Without the Table

Actually, we can afford to skip the hash used to hold the dispatch table and instead call the dispatch functions directly. Here's a snippet from a commercial website script that accepts an "action" and "subaction" command from the browser, and then builds the function name and checks the function before calling it. This example is an extract from an account management script:

```
my $func = sprintf("%s_%s",$action,$subaction);

*code = \&{$func};
if (defined(&code))
{
    &code($user,$group,$session);
}
else
{
    display_account($user,$group,$session);
}
```

Here we call the corresponding function, or just display the account information if the function doesn't exist. This way, the script doesn't fail but does provide the user with a way of continuing.

The benefits of using a dispatch table are listed here:

- Allows for multiple function calls based on user input without the need for a multi-option **if** statement.
- Allows you to "develop" functions and facilities into the rest of a script, even though the function may not have been created yet. You only need to supply a function definition for the script to work.
- You can extend and expand the script without having to manage that complex **if** statement.

There is really only one downside to using a dispatch table that I've come across: The functions you call must be supplied the same list of arguments—you cannot change the argument list based on the function/operation name without introducing another if statement. In a properly designed script this is unlikely to cause a problem, because you will probably be supplying the same information, just for different processing, in each case. There may be other disadvantages, but I've yet to come across any others in the years I've been using dispatch tables.

References

When using and distributing a lot of information around a script, and especially between a script and module, it's much better to use a reference than to use the variable directly. The reason is that when you pass a reference to a subroutine, what you are actually doing is only supplying the pointer to the information, not the information itself. This reduces the amount of time required by the Perl interpreter to copy values into the argument array before calling the subroutine, and then to copy them back out once you are in the subroutine.

Using references you can also supply more complex information than would normally be supported—for example, to supply a record that consists of both static information and a list of keywords, you could use

```
$record = { Name     => 'MCwords.com',
            Address  => 'http://www.mcwords.com',
            Keywords => ['Perl', 'Python', 'iMac']
          };
write_data($record);
```

Here the record itself is a reference to a hash, enabling us to name the individual fields within the record, and the Keywords field refers to an array of keyword strings.

Also, because we're dealing with references to information, rather than the variables directly, you can supply multiple arrays or hashes to a function without all the arguments getting merged into one big argument list. For example, to merge multiple hashes together, you might use

```
sub merge
{
    my ($from,%hash);

    foreach $from (@_)
    {
        foreach my $key (keys %{$from})
```

```
        {
            $hash{$key} = ${$from{$key}};
        }
    }
    return %hash;
}
%newhash = merge(\%hasha, \%hashb);
```

This is probably the biggest benefit of references—because a single scalar is used to refer to the information, it can be exchanged easily between functions, and you can find out with the **ref** function the type of structure that you have been supplied. It also makes for an easy path for converting a suite of functions into methods used for classes.

Design Tip *If you're going to use references, I recommend that you use them for all forms of complex information in your scripts. That way, you have consistency throughout the entire system, and you'll always know when accessing an array or hash which format you should be using to access a single element.*

24x7   Referring to References

I actually like to use references for most complex data structures, mostly because I find the individual elements easier to spot and extract, along with the other advantages already outlined. I also find that explicitly de-referencing using the block and the de-reference infix operator is much clearer than using the shortened and combined format. For example, consider this:

```
print $$record{'A158'}{'Keywords'}[0];
```

compared to this:

```
print $record->{'A158'}->{'Keywords'}->[0];
```

The latter makes it clear that we're referring to a nested structure, consisting first of a hash, then another hash, and finally an array.

And, when referring to entire nested structures,

```
print join(',',@$keywords);
```

is much more like line noise than

```
print join(',',@{$keywords});
```

The latter format makes it clear that what we're actually accessing is the array embedded in the reference **$keywords**.

Of course it's all down to personal preference, but if you are making code that ultimately needs to be readable, either by you at a later stage or by somebody else, then consider the longer, but clearer, format.

Comments and Documentation

When was the last time you went back and looked at a piece of code and thought "what was I doing here?" or "why did I choose this way of doing this?" Using comments is a great way of making your code readable by you and other people—although you might think you'll never forget a piece of code, the reality is that a month or more down the line you're going to need some sort of mental jogger.

The obvious solution is to use comments to annotate how the script works and what arguments and return values are handled by the different functions and methods used in the script or module. Writing good comments is an art, and we'll have a look at some good and some bad examples.

Once you've completed your project the next step should be to convert your comments into documentation so that other people can understand how to use your code without having to read the comments. Mind you, if you're going to document your script properly, why write comments and then documentation? You could just write the documentation as you go along.

Writing Comments

It's a well-known and unfortunate fact that most programmers either don't write comments or write them only after they have completed the software. This is a really bad habit—not using comments makes the code difficult to understand, and writing comments after the program is completed leads to bad comments being introduced, because you probably won't remember precisely the reason behind the design of a particular section. Instead, you should write the comments as you are programming to ensure that you don't write the wrong information.

Comments are an obvious way of documenting what you are doing without affecting the execution of a script. As we already know, you introduce comments using the # character, with everything after that character effectively being ignored by the interpreter (unless the comment includes a line directive—see "Comments" in Chapter 2 for more information).

There is a certain amount of style to writing a good comment. Including

```
print $message if ($message) # Prints a message if it exists
```

in your script isn't going to be very helpful to you or the person reading the code. Instead, you should write:

```
print $message if ($message) # Prints out the warning message from the
                             # get_message() function, assuming a valid
                             # value was returned.
```

When writing comments, think about annotating the following elements:

- *File Headers* should be used to outline the purpose and contents of the file and to include a copyright statement, if appropriate.

- *Variable Names* should be commented to explain what they are used for and the data you expect them to contain.

- *Subroutines* should be commented, at least to explain what the function expects and returns.

- *Classes* should be described so that the reader understands the whole scope of the class, but don't describe the object fields or methods.

- *In-line Comments* should be used to highlight particular lines or sections that are important, but don't label every line.

Finally, here are some things to avoid when writing comments:

- *Don't annotate every line*   It probably won't be helpful to the reader, and will probably confuse more than aid their understanding.

- *Don't just reiterate the line*   Saying "prints message message" against a print statement is not useful.

- *Don't "pretty print" your comments*   Adding a lot of window dressing and whitespace can often detract from the real meat of the comment, and it certainly won't make it easier to read if the user has to scroll down to read the comments in conjunction with the code.

Writing Documentation

Perl documentation is supplied in a simple format called POD, short for Plain Old Documentation. This is a text-based format designed to be processed simply by a Perl script into a variety of destination formats. Like HTML, the POD format uses tags to describe the individual features of the document; but POD documents have a stricter structure and are geared more specifically to the process of producing destination documentation formats.

Because POD is a very simple, textual format, it can be easily converted into other, more familiar formats. Thus, a POD document can be converted into man pages for easy use on Unix machines and HTML for any platform. The MacPerl toolkit includes an application called **Shuck** that reads and displays POD documentation directly. Translators are supplied with the Perl distributions for making HTML, man, TeX/LaTeX, and even plain text files.

POD documentation can also be embedded into Perl files (scripts, packages, and so on). The Perl interpreter will ignore the POD definitions, and POD readers/converters will ignore the Perl scripting elements. This provides a facility for supplying a single file that will be supported both as a script and as documentation, with all the flexibility of both.

Documentation Components

A POD document is made up of three different types of paragraph: verbatim, command, and ordinary text. Each type of paragraph is translated and handled differently, according to the output format of the translator.

In addition to these paragraph types, there are also escape sequences, which allow you to specify an alternative printed format for a word or sentence. This includes things like boldfacing and underlining text as well as references and links to other parts of the document. All of these elements are translated by the conversion scripts into suitable destination formats.

There is no standard format or layout for a POD document, but different translators place certain levels of significance on different elements within the source POD file. We'll examine a "standard" POD document later in this section, but be aware that many of the constructs we discuss here can be used, as with any normal word processing document, to create very simple documentation.

Command Paragraph   A command paragraph specifies that some special element or formatting should be applied to the supplied word, sentence, paragraph, or section. It is typically used to insert headings, subheadings, and lists into the document. All command paragraphs start with an equal sign (=) and a keyword that specifies the formatting to be applied. The paragraph may include an additional keyword or reference. For example, the paragraph

```
=head1 This is a main heading
```

creates a level-one heading, the text of which is "This is a main heading."

The full list of available command paragraphs is in Table 5-2.

Ordinary Text Paragraph   Ordinary paragraphs of text are converted by the translation program into justified and filled paragraphs, according to the destination format. How the justification takes place is entirely dependent on the translator and the reader of the file that it creates. For example, if the conversion is to HTML, then the browser handles paragraph formatting; so an ordinary text paragraph will simply be copied to the destination file.

Verbatim Paragraph   A verbatim paragraph will be reproduced within the final document exactly; you cannot use formatting escapes, and the translator won't make any assumptions about the contents of the paragraph. A verbatim paragraph is identified by indentation in the source text, either with spaces or tabs. Probably the best use for a verbatim paragraph is to reproduce code within the document to ensure that it appears as working code within the final document. Without this facility, the code would be justified and filled just like any other paragraph.

Command	Result
=head1 text	Applies first-level heading, using "text" as the description.
=head2 text	Applies second-level heading, using "text" as the description.
=over n	Starts a section for the generation of a list. The value of *n* specifies the number of characters to indent the paragraphs.
=item text	Specifies the title for an item in a list. The value of text will be interpreted differently, according to the translator.
=back	Ends a list/indentation.
=for format	Allows you to specify that the following paragraph should be inserted exactly as supplied, according to the specified format. For example, **=for html <font size=+1>Heading</font>** would be inserted into the translated file only by an HTML translator.
=begin format **=end format**	Acts similarly to **=for**, except that all the paragraphs between **=begin** and **=end** are included by the specified format translator as preformatted text.
=pod	Specifies the start of a POD document. It is best used when the documentation is included as part of a script. The **=pod** command paragraph tells the compiler to ignore the following text.
=cut	Specifies the end of a **=pod** section.

Table 5.2   POD Command Paragraphs

Escape Sequences   Escape sequences are recognized within both ordinary text and command paragraphs. The escape sequences allow you to specify that a block of text is to be displayed as italicized, boldfaced, underlined, and so on. An escape sequence consists of a single letter and a pair of angle brackets that contain the text to be modified. For example, the POD fragment

```
B<Hello World!>
```

specifies that the string should be boldfaced, producing

```
Hello World!
```

A note: The resulting format must support this sort of text formatting!

The full list of escape sequences supported by the POD standard is shown in Table 5-3. The sequences will not always be transferred correctly to the destination format and, in such cases, will be open to interpretation by the resulting file-viewing mechanism.

Sequence	Description
I<text>	Italic text
B<text>	Boldfaced text
S<text>	Text with nonbreaking spaces (spaces within text that will not be used to wrap or split lines)
C<code>	Literal code fragment (for example, the C **printf()** function)
L<name>	A link or cross-reference to another section, identified by name. Links are further subdivided as follows:
L<name>	Manual page
L<name/ident>	Item or section within a manual page
L<name/"sec">	Section in other manual page
L<"sec">	Section within the current manual page (quotes optional)
L</"sec">	Same as above
L<text|name> L<text|name/ident> L<text|name/"sec"> L<text|"sec"> L<text|/"sec">	Same as above, but destination is identified by *name* and displayed as *text*; the *text* element cannot contain | or >
F<file>	Used for file names
X<index>	An index entry
Z<>	A zero-width character
E<escape>	A named character (similar to HTML escapes):
E<lt>	A literal <
E<gt>	A literal >
E<n>	Character number (in ASCII)

Table 5.3   POD Escape Sequences

Suggested Elements

Different resulting formats have different requirements and restrictions on what can and can't be incorporated within a POD source document. At first glance, this would appear to have an effect on the cross-platform nature of the POD format, but in fact it helps to standardize the base POD documents.

The translated format that has the most stringent rules is the **man** format, because the Unix manual format places certain restrictions and requirements on a manual page so that the information can be indexed and displayed in standard format. Within the confines of POD documentation, this restriction aids in the formatting and layout of nearly all the documents that are produced.

The format of a manual page consists of the elements outlined in Table 5-4. Element titles are conventionally shown in uppercase, although this is not a requirement, and each should referenced with the **=head1** element. Subheadings can be included in **=head2** elements.

Embedding Documentation in Scripts and Modules

You can embed documentation into a Perl script simply by starting the POD section with **=head1** and ending it with **=cut**. The compiler ignores the POD documentation between the two command paragraphs. A POD translator ignores any code outside of the command paragraphs. In this way, you

Element	Description
NAME	Mandatory comma-separated list of the functions or programs documented by the man page
SYNOPSIS	Outline of the function's or program's purpose
DESCRIPTION	Longer description/discussion of the program's purpose
OPTIONS	The command line options or function arguments
RETURN VALUE	What the program returns if successful
ERRORS	Any return codes, errors, or exceptions that may be produced
EXAMPLES	Examples of the program's or function's use
ENVIRONMENT	The environment or variables used by and modified by the program
FILES	The files used
SEE ALSO	Other entries to refer to
NOTES	Any additional commentary
CAVEATS/WARNINGS	Anything to be aware of during the program's use
DIAGNOSTICS	Errors or messages produced by the program and what they mean
BUGS	Things that do not work as expected
RESTRICTIONS	Items that are built-in design features and limitations
AUTHOR	Who wrote the function or program
HISTORY	The source or origin of the program or function

Table 5.4   Elements of a POD Manual Page

can place both script and documentation within a single file, allowing the compiler and translator to interpret the corresponding sections. For example, the script

```
=head1 NAME

HelloWorld.pl

=cut

print "Hello World!";

=head1 SYNOPSIS

This program prints Hello World! on the screen.

=cut
```

when parsed with the compiler, produces

```
Hello World!
```

When parsed with a POD viewer, it will produce the documentation.

The process can be used when developing any script, and in most cases it can be used as a direct replacement for comments, especially if you use it to document the arguments and return values from a function.

## CHAPTER 6

Language/Platform
Migration Guide

People come to Perl from many different directions. Years of ingrained development in a particular language can cause problems when you migrate to a new one. Most people who learn to use Perl will have started to use the language when migrating from something else. For me, years of C/C++, shellscript, and **awk/gawk** programming meant that I felt right at home.

It also meant that I made loads of mistakes. Simple things like requiring all variables to have a suitable prefix character or using a semicolon at the end of almost every line tripped me up countless times. In fact, sometimes they still do today, especially if I've just been programming in Python or shellscript for some reason.

Most people will come to Perl from a language like Python, Visual Basic, or perhaps an embedded scripting language like JavaScript or even PHP. The first part of this chapter provides useful background information for the obvious traps that trip people up when moving to Perl from another language.

Other people are existing Perl programmers who migrate to a different platform, albeit still using Perl. Although Perl tries to hide most of the differences from the casual programmer, some of the built-in functions and modules that rely on the operating system, such as **getpwnam** and **fork**, can cause problems. There are specific guides for some of the major platforms, such as MacOS and Windows, but the remainder of this chapter will look at the more generic problems that you may encounter.

Language Migration Traps

Most of the traps listed in this section are the common things that trip up the majority of people. I've done my best to be as comprehensive as possible, but it's difficult to account for all situations. The errors or traps that are covered here will probably fix any remaining errors—the simple traps like missing quotes and termination generate more errors than are probably necessary.

Differences from awk/gawk

Most of the differences between Perl and **awk/gawk** relate to the built-in variables and regular expression systems in each language.

- The **English** module in Perl allows you to use the full variable names used by **awk** for variables as the record separator (**$RS** in **awk** is identical to **$RS** in the **English** module).

- Perl uses a semicolon to signify the end of a statement; the new line as used in **awk** is not sufficient.

- All blocks require braces, including those used with **if** and **while** statements.

- Variables in Perl begin with a prefix character—**$** for scalars, **@** for arrays (numeric indices), and **%** for hashes (string indices). Indices in arrays and subscripts begin at zero, as do references to specific characters within strings.

- Numeric and string comparisons are different in Perl. Numeric comparisons use special characters, such as **!=** for not equal to. String comparisons use letters; the equivalent of "not equal to" when comparing strings is **ne**.

- Input lines from files must be manually split using the **split** function. The results will go to the array you specify, or to the global @_ if you don't specify a destination (this also clobbers any function arguments). The current input line (or default pattern space) is $_ in Perl; if you want the newline stripped, you must use **chop** or **chomp** (better).

- Once the fields have been split, you cannot access them using the variables **$1**, **$2** (and so on) to extract each field. These variables are filled only on a match or substitution of a regular expression with grouping. To actually extract the fields from an input line, use **split**.

- The pattern binding operator is =~ in Perl, and the range operator is **..** not **,**. The exponential operator is ******.

- Field and record separators are not automatically added to arrays printed with **print**. Use the **$,** (or **$OFS**) for the field separator and **$** (**$ORS**) for the record separator. If you want to concatenate variables, the concatenation operator is the period.

- Files must be opened before you can print to them—use the **open** function to assign a filehandle to the open file and then use **print FILEHANDLE**.

- Within loop control, the keywords **next**, **exit**, and **continue** work differently. For **next**, Perl always proceeds to the next iteration of the enclosing loop, or the next iteration of the named loop if a name is supplied. The **exit** keyword in Perl terminates the entire script. The **continue** statement indicates a BLOCK of code that should be executed before the conditional test for the loop is reevaluated.

The variables in **awk** are equivalent to those in Perl, as shown in Table 6-1.

awk	Perl
ARGC	**$#ARGV** or **scalar @ARGV**
ARGV[0]	**$0**
FILENAME	**$ARGV**
FNR	**$.** is only valid for the current/last used filehandle.
FS	No equivalent; use **split** to split fields.
NF	No equivalent; you could count the number of fields returned by **split**.
NR	**$.**
OFMT	**$#**
OFS	**$,**
ORS	**$**
RLENGTH	**length($&)**
RS	**$/** can only be set to a string; regular expressions are not supported when using this variable. Use **split** if you need to separate by an expression.
RSTART	**length($`)**
SUBSEP	**$;**

Table 6.1   awk/Perl Variable Differences

C Traps

Within C, most of the traps relate to variable types and conversions. Perl does not support separate variable types for numbers and strings. Perl supports only a scalar type that can contain virtually any data:

```
$value = 99;
$value = "String";
```

Also, you cannot access the individual characters of a string using a subscript. The following will not work:

```
$char = $value[0];
```

What it will try to do is access the first element of the array **@value**, which is probably not defined. Use the **substr** function to access individual characters or slices, for example:

```
$char = substr($value,0,1);
```

Alternatively, if you need to iterate over the characters within an array, use **split**:

```
foreach $char (split //,$string)
```

This also highlights a performance issue. When working through the elements of an array, don't use indexing. For example, you might iterate over an array using

```
for($index=0;$index<scalar @array;$index++)
```

Instead, use **foreach**:

```
foreach $element (@array)
```

All code blocks require curly brackets, {}. The statement

```
if (1) print "Hello";
```

will fail in Perl. You can, however, do

```
print "Hello" if (1);
```

if the statement you want to execute fits on one line.

There is no **switch** statement in C, although you can emulate it in a number of different ways in Perl. The most obvious is a messy **if..elsif..else** conditional block. Note that the secondary test is **elsif** in Perl, not **else if**. A better alternative for the **switch** statement, and also one that will look familiar, is

```
SWITCH:
{
    ($date == $today) && do {
                            print "Happy Birthday!\n";
```

```
                                         last SWITCH;
                                };
        ($date != $today)  && do {
                                print "Happy Unbirthday!\n";
                                last SWITCH;
                                };
        ($date == $xmas)   && do {
                                print "Happy Christmas!\n";
                                last SWITCH;
                                };
}
```

Note from this example that the keyword to break out from the statement is **last**, not **break**. The **last** and **next** keywords are direct replacements for the C **break** and **continue** keywords. However, be aware that the Perl versions do not work within a **do { } while** loop.

Here are some other differences between C and Perl to watch out for:

- Perl uses special characters to identify a variable (and its type). Variables start with **$**, **@**, and **%** in Perl and relate to scalars (normal variables), arrays, and hashes.

- The **&** symbol in C takes the address of an object; this is not supported in Perl, although you can use \ to pass a reference to an object instead of the object itself.

- Arguments to a Perl script, which are accessed via **@ARGV**, start at zero. The first (zeroth) element refers to the first *argument* to the script, not the name of the script, which can instead be found in the **$0** special variable.

- The Perl **printf** function does not accept the * character in a format definition for inserting a variable field width. However, since Perl does support variable interpolation, you can insert the variable directly into the format and let Perl interpolate the value into the format string.

- Comments in Perl start with the hash sign and continue until the end of the line. They do not need to be terminated as in the C /*..*/ construct.

- The system call functions built into Perl (and indeed most functions) return non-zero for success and zero for failure. In cases where a zero would be a valid return result, the function returns **0 but true**, which evaluates to zero when interpreted as a number.

- When using a signal handler, Perl allows you to use the signal name (without the prefix **SIG**) instead of the signal numbers.

sed Traps

Much of the functionality for Perl, including a large bulk of the regular expression syntax, was inherited from **sed**. There are some minor differences that relate mostly to the way in which **sed** and Perl expect to take in and process data.

Logical groupings of regular expression elements are specified using unbackslashed brackets. The line

```
s/\([A-Z]+\)/\1/;
```

in **sed** should be written as

```
s/([A-Z]+)/$1/;
```

The same is true for the logical **or** operator, which is also unbackslashed. A backslashed bracket **or |** operator within a regular expression will be interpreted by Perl as a literal. Group references in substitutions should use **$1** instead of **\1**. Also note that in Perl the **$1**..**$xx** variables are populated generally—their values are present after the regular expression.

Finally, when specifying a range of values in Perl, the **...** operator should be used instead of the comma.

Note that a translator **(s2p)** is available to convert **sed** programs into Perl equivalents.

emacs Traps

The regular expression syntax in **emacs** is more or less identical to the **sed** syntax. Refer to the "**sed** Traps" section above for details on the differences.

Shellscript Traps

The most fundamental difference between any shell and the Perl interpreter is that Perl compiles the program into a series of opcodes before execution; whereas a shell interprets lines (and sometimes blocks) at once, ignoring the remainder of the code until it reaches it.

The interpolation of variables is different. Perl always interpolates variables into backticked and double-quoted strings and into angle brackets and search patterns, and the interpolation is done only once (not recursively).

Variables in Perl start with **$**, **@**, and **%**. You must always specify the prefix character in Perl. You cannot get away with

```
var = "Hello"
```

as you can in shellscript. To confuse matters, you can't do the reverse in shellscript either. The example

```
$var = "Hello"
```

will fail in most shells.

Three more differences are worth noting:

- All statements in Perl must end with a semicolon (except when the last statement is in a block).
- The command-line arguments in Perl are available via the **@ARGV** array, and not in the variables **$1**, **$2** (and so on) that the shell uses; Perl uses these for grouped regular expression matches.
- With particular reference to **csh**, return values from backticks in Perl are not parsed in any way.

Python Traps

Python and Perl are two very different languages, and since both are available on identical platforms, which one you use is likely to be driven by personal choice or the requirement of a client. However, necessity dictates all sorts of things, so here is a list of differences that may trip up a Python programmer trying to work in Perl. It's intended as a quick checklist of things you may have done wrong, not a list of all the differences, which would probably take up an entire book!

- All statements in Perl end in a semicolon, unlike in Python, which effectively doesn't have a statement terminator other than the newline, and even then it's only implied as the statement terminator.

- Variables in Python are free-form; there is no difference between creating a scalar, array, or hash. You must remember to specify your Perl variables by their type and to use the prefix of **$** for scalars (strings or numbers), **@** for arrays, and **%** for hashes (the Perl term for Python dictionaries).

- Accessing an element from an array or a hash changes the prefix character to a **$** within Perl. For example, this would access the sixth element of an array:

```
print $array[5];
```

Note that square brackets are still used to refer to the individual elements. With a hash you use braces:

```
print $hash{elem};
```

- When splicing elements from an array in Perl, you can either use the **splice** function or use commas and list operators in the square brackets to define the elements to splice (similar to, and identically named as, the subscript operator in Python). The **splice** function is the preferred option on named arrays; the subscript option should be used on the return values from lists.

- You must specify lists in Perl in surrounding brackets. The Python statement

```
a, b = 1, 2
```

will not work in Perl, even if you add the semicolon and **$** prefix to make

```
$a, $b = 1, 2;
```

What actually happens is that Perl sees three separate expressions in one large statement; only **$b** will actually be assigned a value. It should be rewritten as

```
($a, $b) = (1, 2);
```

- Variables within Perl are the actual storage containers of the data. Within Python all data storage is through a reference to an object. If you want to pass a variable reference to a function, you need to prefix the variable with a backslash to indicate to Perl that it is a reference. When de-referencing a variable, you need to specify the type of variable you are attempting to de-reference.

- Perl supports a number of internal functions that provide a lot of the functionality that Python requires external modules for. These functions include those for reading and writing files, using network sockets, handling arrays and hashes, and many other things.

- Perl includes most of the operating system information within the main interpreter. You can access the environment through the **%ENV** hash and the command-line arguments via the **@ARGV** array without having to import them from an external module.

- External modules are imported via the **use** function in Perl, which is effectively equivalent to the **import** keyword in Python. Note that when you **use** a module, the function is imported into the calling package:

```
use Cwd;
print getcwd();
```

The **from** construct in Python used to import specific functions is supported by appending a list of functions, variables, and other objects after the module name. For example,

```
use Cwd qw/getcwd/;
```

is synonymous with the Python construct:

```
from Cwd import getcwd
```

- If you are using objects in Perl, then to call a method you use the **->** operator:

```
FILEHANDLE->autoflush(1);
```

- Strings are concatenated in Perl using a single period; the Python statement

```
"Hello" "World" "\n";
```

in Perl would become

```
"Hello" . "World" . "\n";
```

Also, Perl interpolates variables and escape sequences (such as the new line above) only in certain quotes, excluding, unfortunately, single quotes; in Perl the value of

```
'\n'
```

is a string composed of a backslash and the lowercase character "n." However, this aspect does make **print** statements easier. You can place the variables straight into the double quotes, without having to specify a print format. If you want a formatted version of a string, use the **printf** function.

- Perl does not automatically append a new line to a **print** statement; you must add the string **\n** within double-quotes somewhere within your **print** statement.

- Code blocks in Perl must be enclosed in braces. An **if** statement looks like this:

```
if ($test)
{
}
```

The block starts after the opening brace and ends before the last brace.

Platform Migration Traps

When programming Perl on a number of different platforms you tend to take some things for granted. Although Perl is pretty platform independent, there are some differences that will trip you up if you're not concentrating. Most of the problems are relatively obvious, but some are obscure and difficult to treat.

As a general rule, don't assume that Perl supports all functions on all platforms, and don't use data without considering where it might have come from.

Function Support

The most obvious difference between platforms is the support for different functions and operators. The Perl porters are responsible for keeping things as flexible as possible across different platforms. However, Perl's Unix roots show through all too often, and you should keep the following points in mind if you find you have problems on a different platform:

- Functions that involve looking up details in one of the Unix files contained in **/etc**—generally these functions start with **set** or **get**. They include everything from the network information routines and also those routines related to group and/or password information. There are usually equivalents in a platform-specific module.

- Functions that adjust elements of a file system—although all the basic file interfacing options will work, others, such as **–X**, **stat**, and more Unix-centric functions such as **chmod** and **chgrp**, are unsupported. You should also remember that although MacOS and Windows support the notion of links via aliases and shortcuts, respectively, the **link** and **lstat** functions often do not work.

- Access to the internals of the operating system tables are also unsupported on many other platforms, particularly those that return unique process and group IDs, or those that return parent group and parent owner information for a process ID. Most of the time, however, the **$$** variable should provide you with a reasonable amount of information.

- Unix-specific utility functions are also generally unimplemented, such as the IPC systems **shm***, **msg***, and **sem***.

- Functions and operators that rely on the ability to run an application by name through a command-line–like interface may not work on all platforms. In particular, the MacOS, which doesn't have a command-line interface, does not natively support functions like **system** and the backticks, or **qx** operator. However, you can use the shell provided with the MPW (Macintosh Programmers Workbench) environment to run some commands in this manner.

You can get a more up-to-date list in the **perlport** manual page supplied with the Perl distribution.

Constant Compatibility

If you have problems with the operation of a function that normally uses a constant, make sure that you use the generic name rather than a fixed number. Although in theory the constants used for setting options with functions like **fcntl** and **ioctl** should be the same, some platforms use different values. Make sure you import the **POSIX** module and use the constant names defined there, rather than your own values.

Also, make sure you use the **POSIX** module when using the **seek** function; although the function itself is supported on nearly all platforms, the numbers used to search forward and backward, and move to the start and end of the file can differ among platforms.

Execution Environment

The environment in which Perl is executed can have a significant effect on your script. Many problems can arise because you rely on information or capabilities outside of Perl, but that may be directly available internally. Some examples are listed below:

- Try not to rely on the Unix environment variables or Perl's built-in variables to get certain pieces of information. In particular, avoid using things like **$>** and **$<** and other user/group ID variables, which are not set on all platforms. This advice is especially pertinent if you decide to use one of these variables in a unique ID or other identification string.

- Related to the above, don't rely on hostnames—or user names, either—especially if you intend to use them to store unique or identification information.

- Don't rely on commands that you want to execute being available within the **PATH** environment variable—set it yourself or, better still, use a full path to the application.

- Don't rely on signals unless you have to. Some platforms support signals and signal handlers, others don't, and those that do may only support a reduced set.

- Use shared files, network sockets, or a platform-specific module such as **Win32::Pipe** to exchange information. The **shm***, **msg***, and **sem*** functions are not supported on all platforms.

Errors

Perl reports most errors using the **$!** variable, but platform-specific errors on platforms other than Unix may not be included. Remember to report the information from **$^E** on platforms other than Unix, or use a platform-specific error function such as **Win32::GetLastError**.

Line Termination

One of the most fundamental problems of using Perl on multiple platforms is the line termination when reading and writing files. Different operating systems use different characters for line termination. In particular, Unix uses a newline (the **\n** or **\012** character) to terminate, whereas MacOS uses a carriage return (the **\r** or **\015** character). To complicate matters, DOS/Windows uses the carriage return, newline sequence (**\r\n** or **\015\012**).

Perl will automatically account for this difference under most conditions, but if you are transferring data as well as scripts between platforms, beware. Perl will automatically interpret

\n as the correct character or character sequence for the current platform. Under MacOS, Perl simply interprets **\n** as **\015**, but under DOS/Windows it is interpreted as **\015\012** when a file is accessed in text mode.

Under platforms other than Unix, you will need to use the **binmode** function on an open filehandle to read and write raw data and prevent Perl from doing the conversion automatically. Also, be careful when using **seek**, **tell**, and similar functions—the line termination is not taken into account automatically when calculating **seek** values.

When used with network sockets, more direct specification is required. In all communication between sockets, you should use numerical values instead of their character versions to ensure that **\012** can be identified correctly. Otherwise the interpretation of **\n** on the two platforms may differ. See the discussion on character sets later in this section. To make the process easier, the **Socket** module, which is part of the standard Perl distribution, can supply the values for you.

```
use Socket qw(:DEFAULT :crlf);
print "Message$CRLF";
```

These provide three constant variables, **$CR**, **$LF**, and **$CRLF**, which map to **\015**, **\012**, and **\015\012**, respectively, and are identical irrespective of the platform on which you are running.

Character Sets

Another popular misconception is that all platforms use the same character set. Although it's true that most use the ASCII character set, you can rely only on the first 128 characters (values zero to 127, or **\00** to **\0177**) as being identical. Even with this consideration, you shouldn't necessarily rely on the values returned by **chr** or **ord** across different platforms. The actual values of the character set may include all manner of characters, including those that may have accents, and may be in any order.

Since Perl 5.6, Perl is completely Unicode compliant, so you should be able to guarantee that the first 128 characters match the ASCII table, with each character being represented by a single byte. Further characters are represented by one or more bytes and include many of the accented and special characters. See the **perlunicode** documentation supplied with Perl.

Data Differences

Different physical and operating system combinations use different sequences for storing numbers. This characteristic affects the storage and transfer of numbers in binary format between systems, either within files or across network connections. The solution to the problem is either to use strings, which will of course be displayed in standard form, or to use the **n** and **N** network orders with the **pack** and **unpack** functions (see Chapter 7).

All times are represented in Perl by the number of seconds since the epoch. On nearly all systems the epoch is 0:00:00, 1 January, 1970. However, other platforms define other values (MacOS, for example). If you want to store a date, use a format that is not reliant on the epoch value, such as a single string like **YYYYMMDDHHMMSS**.

Files and Pathnames

The main three platforms show the range of characters used to separate the directories and files that make up a file's path. Under Unix it is /, but under DOS/Windows it is \, and on the Mac it is :. The Windows and DOS implementations also allow you to use the Unix / to separate the elements. To further complicate matters, only Unix and a small number of other operating systems use the concept of a single root directory.

On Windows and DOS, the individual drives, or partitions thereof, are identified by a single letter preceded by a colon. Under MacOS, each volume has a name that can precede a pathname, using the standard colon separator. The **File::Spec** module can create paths that use the appropriate character set and separator for you. Also be aware that different platforms support different file names and lengths. The following is a rough guide:

- DOS supports only names of no more than eight characters and extensions of three characters, and ignores case.

- Under Windows 95/NT the definition is slightly more complex: The full pathname has a maximum length of 256 characters and is case conscious.

- Under MacOS any element of a path can have up to 31 characters, and names within a directory are case insensitive—you cannot have two files called File and file.

- Older versions of Unix support only 31 characters, but newer versions, including Solaris, HP-UX 10.x and above, as well as Linux support a full 256 characters per path element.

You should also try to restrict file names to use only standard alphanumeric characters.

Modules

Be careful when using modules that contain platform-specific elements or that require the use of a C compiler when the module is built. You cannot guarantee that the module will be supported on all platforms or even that a C compiler will be available if you need it.

Performance and Resources

Not all platforms have the seemingly unlimited resources of the Unix operating system available to them. Although Windows provides a similar memory interface, the available memory on a Windows machine may be significantly less in real terms (physical/virtual) than that available under a typical Unix implementation, although this condition is changing as RAM becomes cheaper. MacPerl must be allocated its own block of memory and, once exhausted, it cannot automatically gain new memory, even if there is some available. You should therefore take care with statements that arbitrarily create large internal structures; for example,

```
foreach (1..1000000)
```

creates a list with one million elements, which will take up a significant amount of memory. This has been fixed in Perl 5.005, but earlier versions, including MacPerl, which is currently based on 5.004, will generate the huge list.

Also remember that other operating systems do not provide the same protected memory spaces or the multitasking features of Unix.

Platform Migration Tricks

There are a few things we can do within a script to identify where, and on what, the script is being executed. Most of the information is available as standard to the Perl interpreter; other pieces of information are available through the use of a supplied Perl module.

Knowing the following will help you to identify and trap some problems before they occur:

- Platform and operating systems
- Perl version
- Supported function lists

You can also use the information that is generated by Perl during the build process to help identify supported functions and abilities. Alternatively, we can use the **eval** function to trap and test for functions before you try to use them properly.

As a final trick, we'll look at the function overloading system that allows us to implement locally a built-in function that is not supported by the current Perl version.

Determining Your Platform

The **$^O** variable contains the name of the current platform. The information provided may not be very descriptive without knowing the significance of the name returned, but it should at the very least enable you to identify the main platform. Alternatively, you can use the value of the **$Config{'archname'}** variable (available via the **Config** module), which contains the name of the architecture on which the current Perl interpreter was compiled. The architecture string returned includes the platform name and the hardware architecture on which the binary was built.

Note the difference here: The build and the current platform are not essentially identical, although it may be safe to assume they are compatible. For example, a Perl binary built on Solaris 2.4 will also run on Solaris 2.6, or even Solaris 7. However, a Perl binary for the Intel version of Solaris will not run on the SPARC version. The value of **$Config{'osname'}** will tell you the name of the operating system on which the binary was built.

Some sample operating system names and **$^O** and **$Config{'archname'}** values are shown in Table 6-2.

On many platforms (particularly those derived from Unix), the value is extracted from that returned by **uname**. In all cases the value of **$^O** is probably of more use than the architecture name for writing cross-platform scripts.

OS	$^O/$Config{'osname'}	$Config{'archname'}
MS-DOS	dos	
Windows 95	MSWin32	MSWin32-x86
Windows NT	MSWin32	MSWin32-x86
MacOS	MacOS	
Linux	linux	i686-linux
SunOS 4	sunos	sun4-sunos
Solaris	solaris	sun4-solaris

Table 6.2   Operating Systems and Their Internal Equivalents

Determining the Perl Version

The Perl version relates very little to the level of support on different platforms. However, it can sometimes be a useful indicator of whether an official release exists for a platform as well as a useful reference point for a specific feature, irrespective of the platform on which you are working.

If all you want to do is find out what version of Perl you are using, the obvious solution is to check the version of Perl using the $] variable. This is the version number of the Perl interpreter added to the patch level and divided by one thousand. For example, v5.004 is Perl version 5, patch level 4. Sub-version numbers to the patch level are included for the maintenance and development releases of Perl and are indicated as the release number divided by 100,000; a value of 5.00553 is made up of Perl version 5, patch level 5, and development release 53. The maintenance release number increases from 1 to 49 and developmental releases from 50 to 99.

Since Perl 5.6, the information returned is much easier to determine. There are actually three components: the major version number, the minor version number, and the patch level. For example, the first version of Perl 5.6 was actually 5.6.0.

You can use the contents of the **perldelta** main page to determine what functions and abilities are available within each version of the Perl interpreter. The next section presents specific ways of determining the supported functions without requiring prior knowledge.

If you want to restrict a script so it runs only on certain platforms, you should use the **require** keyword with a numerical, rather than alpha, value. The number specified is taken as the Perl version required to execute the script. For example, the statement

```
require 5.00553;
```

places the simple restriction of requiring Perl 5.6 to continue. The value is taken literally, such that the comparison is made between the value passed to the **require** statement and the value of **$]**. If **$]** is numerically higher than the value passed to Perl, the script is allowed to continue. Thus, to ensure that the script runs only on the very latest version of Perl, you might want to try

```
require 5.6;
```

although this will probably be out of date by the time you read this. If the value specified does not match the current Perl interpreter, a runtime error will be produced:

```
perl -e 'require 6;'
Perl 6 required - this is only version 5.00553, stopped at -e line 1.
```

Checking for Supported Functions

The **Config** module we used earlier to determine the architecture and operating system name used to build the current Perl interpreter actually contains all the information discovered during the configuration process. You can use this information to determine the functions and the extensions supported within the current Perl interpreter. The data is stored in the form of a hash, **%Config**; so, to determine all of the values, you might use

```
use Config;
foreach (sort keys %Config)
{
    print "$_  : $Config{$_}\n";
}
```

The values output are not cryptic, but are also not obvious. The keys for underlying operating system functions start with **d_**, such that the existence of **chown** can be determined by

```
print "Have chown\n" if ($Config{'d_chown'} eq 'define');
```

Other features, such as extension modules to Perl (**NDBM, Socket,** for example), are in other keys within the same hash:

```
print "Extensions: $Config{extensions}\n";
```

To check for a specific function, use an **eval** block to execute the function within its own interpreter. If the call fails, the **eval** block will drop out, setting **$@** in the process. For example, to check once again for the **chown** function, you might use

```
eval { chown() };
warn "chown() $@" if $@;
```

Because **eval** blocks are executed within their own space at runtime, this will report a suitable error if **chown** doesn't exist.

Function Overloading

When you want to support a particular operation within a script that is not supported under multiple platforms, you may want to consider developing a special module that provides a personal interface to the built-in Perl functions. Another alternative is to provide your own set of "built-in" functions and then overload the real built-in functions with your own versions. You can do this through the use of a **BEGIN** block in your script and the **use subs** pragma.

The code fragment below shows the method required to determine which functions are supported:

```
BEGIN
{
    eval { chown() };
    push @functions,'chown' if $@;
}
```

```
use subs @functions;
use MyBuiltin @functions;

chown();
```

Note that the actual test must be done within the **BEGIN** block so that it is executed at compile rather than runtime; then, by the time compilation reaches the **use subs** pragma, the contents of **@functions** have already been populated with the required information.

The definition for **chown** is then placed into the **MyBuiltin** package, which is defined just like any other:

```
package MyBuiltin;

require Exporter;
@ISA = qw/Exporter/;
@EXPORT = ();
@EXPORT_OK = qw/chown/;

sub chown
{
    print "Changed mode!";
    return 1;
}
```

The contents of **@EXPORT** should be empty, since you don't want to import anything as standard. The value of **@EXPORT_OK** contains the list of built-in functions that you want to support and overload, if necessary. Thus, when you call **use MyBuiltin** with a list of unsupported built-in functions, you import your own list of replacements. In this example a simple **print** statement is used to show that the overloading is working. In an actual case, you'll probably want to put some real functionality into the functions you want to overload.

If you are testing a lot of functions, you will need to use loops and references to test the functions you want to overload:

```
BEGIN
{
    @subtest = qw/chown exec/;
    foreach $function (@subtest)
    {
        eval { &$function };
        push @functions,$function if $@;
    }
}
```

It's not possible in this to optimize the loop by placing the **foreach** loop within the **eval** block, since you're using each **eval** invocation to test the existence of each function. This is a performance hit, but the overall process improves compatibility, and it's one of the trade-offs examined at the beginning of the chapter.

Error Trapping

## CHAPTER 7

Basic Error Trapping

Even the simplest programs should have some basic form of error checking—taking the simplest possible application,

```
print "Hello World\n";
```

what problems could we experience? Well, for one, we don't know for certain that the **STDOUT** filehandle is open and ready to be written to. We don't test to make sure that the filehandle is open or that the **print** statement was successful. If we wanted to be really picky, we don't check that the **print** function is implemented within Perl on the current platform either.

All this might seem like we're going too far—do we really need to check so many things just to print a simple message to the screen? The simple answer is no; in this instance, we're probably going too far. In fact, if we even checked half of the things I'd mentioned earlier, we'd probably increase the size of the code by a factor of ten.

There is what I like to call the *error trap point*. This is the point at which your script moves from being a script that doesn't require error trapping to the point where it does. Some scripts are just so short or simple that they don't require trapping, or they would be made overly complex if error trapping were included. In the preceding example, even checking the return status of **print** would increase the script to four lines:

```
unless(print "Hello World\n")
{
    die "Can't print!";
}
```

Beyond the error trap point, you need error trapping to ensure that your script works correctly and accounts for 90 percent, if not 100 percent of all the possible errors and problems that could occur. Of course, there's also an upper limit to what you can, and indeed should, check. For example, in the above script, we report an error if the **print** function is unable to display our message—but what happens if **STDERR** is also closed?

In this instance, checking that as well would almost certainly be going too far, but where exactly do you draw the line? And more importantly, where do you start? What should you be checking, and what, in some circumstances, can you safely ignore?

This chapter aims to answer those questions. To that end, we'll be looking at the basics and mechanics of error checking and verification in Perl and at the different tricks and tools that can be used to help in that process.

Why Check for Errors?

If you don't already know the answer to that question, perhaps you ought to reconsider your role as a programmer!

There are actually two basic reasons for checking, and more importantly trapping, errors within your scripts:

- Trapping an error ensures that you identify a problem before it actually becomes apparent to the user that there is one. For example, with error trapping you would avoid the pointless exercise of trying to read from a file that you couldn't open in the first place.

- By trapping an error you can let your users know what has happened and why the program didn't do what they expected.

At the end of the day it's all related to protecting the user—either from doing something they didn't mean to do or from preventing your program from doing something it shouldn't.

Adding Error Checking to Your Scripts

You should already be adding error-checking processes to your scripts as you write them. It doesn't take long to get into the habit of always adding even basic error-checking sequences as you type, but you need to know which functions deserve checking and how to check and verify their operation.

Most of the basic functions and keywords within Perl and many of the standard CPAN extension modules follow the same basic format—a true value is returned if the function completed successfully or false if there was an error. You can then trap the error in a number of different ways.

Using **if**

The **if** statement is the obvious choice when you need to check the return value from a statement; for example,

```
if (open(DATA,$file))
{
    ...
}
else
{
    die "Woah: Couldn't open the file $!";
}
```

This procedure is most useful when you want to be able to account for two possible outcomes—if the statement works, continue and execute *these* statements; if it doesn't succeed, do *these* statements instead.

Alternatively, you can reduce the statement to one line in the those situations where it makes sense to do so; for example,

```
die "Woah: Something went wrong\n" if (error());
```

See the section on "Error Checking Guidelines" later in this chapter for more information on when, and indeed whether, to use this format.

Using **unless**

The **unless** function is the logical opposite of **if**: Statements can completely bypass the success status and only be executed if the expression returns false. For example,

```
unless(chdir("/etc"))
{
    die "Can't change directory!: $!";
}
```

The **unless** statement is best used when you want to raise an error or alternative only if the expression fails. The statement also makes sense when used in a single-line statement:

```
die "Can't change directory!: $!" unless(chdir("/etc"));
```

Here we die only if the **chdir** operation fails, although it's not pretty.

Using the Conditional Operator

For very short tests you can use the conditional operator:

```
print(exists($hash{value}) ? 'There' : 'Missing',"\n");
```

It's not quite so clear here what we're trying to achieve, but the effect is the same as using an **if** or **unless** statement. The conditional operator is best used when you want to quickly return one of two values within an expression or statement.

It's not really an error trapping statement since there's not enough scope to do anything, but it can be used to help communicate status information back to the user. Consider the following example:

```
chdir("/tmp") ? print "Using /tmp\n" : warn "Can't use /tmp: $!";
```

Here it's a useful way of highlighting a potential problem without actually doing anything about it. The same basic principles can be used from within functions when returning values:

```
return (@results) ? @results : undef;
```

Using Short-Circuit Logic

For many situations, especially where you want to immediately exit the script without actually handling the error, the short-circuit capabilities of the **or** operator work best:

```
mkdir("./tmp",0755) or die "Can't make directory!: $!";
```

See Chapter 2, "Symbolic Logical Or" for more details on why this works and the related dangers.

The ‖ symbolic logical **or** can also be used as a way to provide alternatives when the first-choice option doesn't work. For example, the line

```
$host = param('host') || $user->{prihost} || 'azus';
```

will use the browser-supplied value, then the user-configured value, and finally a default value if the other options fail.

Error Checking Guidelines

There are some general guidelines for testing for errors in this way. The first guideline is to make it obvious what you are testing and what you are trying to do. For example, the statement

```
if (!open(DATA,$file))
```

will work fine, except that it would make more sense to use the **unless** statement, as in

```
unless(open(DATA,$file))
```

The difference is that the **if** statement reads "If I didn't open," and the **unless** statement reads "Unless I can open." It's a minor difference that will make the code easier to read and, therefore, easier to debug. Here's another example that's difficult to read:

```
die "Couldn't change directory: $!" unless(chdir("/etc"));
```

This should be changed to

```
chdir("/etc") or die "Couldn't change directory: $!";
```

The second guideline is that you should make it obvious what the actual problem was; simply reporting that there was an error isn't enough, either for you to debug the program, or for your user to rectify it. Where relevant, also include information on the system error message, as provided by **$!**. Also remember the **$^E** variable, which contains the extended OS error on non-Unix platforms. For example, the line

```
open(DATA,$file) or die "Can't open";
```

is useless compared to

```
open(DATA,$file) or die "Can't open $file: $!, stopped";
```

Coupled to this, you should always report an error to **STDERR** by using either **warn** or **die**. The exception to this rule is when you're working with a GUI or Web-based application for which there is no logical **STDERR** file handle. See the end of this chapter for information on reporting errors when no terminal interface is available.

Error Checking Walkthrough

For an introduction, let's look at a simple script that copies lines one by one from one file to another. The script as it stands below does not use any type of error checking:

```
($filea, $fileb) = @ARGV;
open(FILEA, $filea);
open(FILEB, ">$fileb");
while(<FILEA>)
{
    print FILEB $_;
}
close(FILEA);
close(FILEB);
```

Even before we get to the first line, we've already got a few problems. First of all, we're not set up for Perl to issue warnings, and there's no **strict** pragma in force to ensure that we're not breaking any of the more lax laws provided by Perl. We'll ignore those issues for the moment—we'll actually be looking at the use and effects of these options in the next chapter.

Checking Command-Line Arguments

The first line makes a few assumptions. First, it assumes that information has been provided on the command line, and second it assumes that you've got two bits of information and that they will be the filenames.

We should really change that to

```
if (@ARGV == 2)
{
    ($filea, $fileb) = @ARGV;
}
else
{
    print "Usage: $0 filea fileb\n";
    exit 1;
}
```

We've done two things here: checked that we've got the right number of arguments and reported a useful message back to the user if that isn't the case. Note the terminology and content of the script—we've checked for exactly two arguments on the command line. If we'd checked for more than two arguments then the user could supply three and the script would still execute. There's nothing wrong with that process, but the user might expect something to happen to the rest of the arguments, so we need to highlight that we only *want* two arguments, not that we only *need* two.

Opening Files

Opening files, or indeed any process that involves connecting to an external data source, is something that you should always check. How you check and report the error depends on the situation—in this instance, we should probably call **die** if opening the file fails:

```
open(FILEA, $filea) or die "Can't open $filea: $!";
```

For the second file we're going to need something more complex. Although

```
open(FILEB, ">$fileb") or die "Can't open $fileb: $!";
```

will work, it will also overwrite any file with the name contained in **$fileb** without question; to do so might be a little unfriendly if the user types the wrong name. Instead, let's just check that the file doesn't exist first, and then warn the user—it will be up to the user to delete the file or change the name they are copying to:

```
die "$fileb already exists! Stopping.\n" if (-e $fileb);
open(FILEB, ">$fileb") or die "Can't open $fileb: $!";
```

Note the newline character at the end of **die**—it will make sure that Perl doesn't automatically add the location of the error; instead, it just prints the message and exits.

Reading from Files

The **while** loop is the most efficient method of reading from files on a record-by-record basis. It handles the end-of-file condition and will successfully leave the loop when the end of the file is reached. There's not really a lot we could improve on here.

Writing to Files

The line that prints the input line to the output,

```
print FILEB $_;
```

doesn't have any particular pitfalls, but it would probably be a good idea just to modify that slightly and check that the information has been written correctly. We can do that with an **unless** statement:

```
unless(print FILEB $_)
{
    die "Can't write to $fileb ($!)\n";
}
```

Closing Files

Perl uses buffered IO on most platforms, so some information is not written out to the file until the point at which the file is formally closed. You therefore need to make sure that the file is closed and that the process completed successfully, so you need to check the return value from the **close** function:

```
close(FILEA) or die "Couldn't close $filea properly: $!";
close(FILEB) or die "Couldn't close $fileb properly: $!";
```

There is a school of thought that thinks files opened only for reading shouldn't be checked—after all, if we haven't modified the file, why check to make sure that it closed properly?

The reason is that we need to ensure we have correctly read from and, in this case, reached the end of the file. Although it sounds implausible, it is possible for Perl to try to read from a file that has been deleted—Perl would pick this up as an end-of-file condition. The **close** function ensures that we have actually managed to close the file that we originally opened.

End Result

We've more than doubled the size of the script, although admittedly we could probably modify the formatting to reduce the number of source lines. We've also managed to produce a script that now checks most of the execution process to ensure that we don't do anything nasty, and the information is communicated back so the user knows what's going on.

```
if (@ARGV == 2)
{
    ($filea, $fileb) = @ARGV;
}
else
{
    print "Usage: $0 filea fileb\n";
    exit 1;
}
open(FILEA, $filea) or die "Can't open $filea: $!";
die "$fileb already exists! Stopping.\n" if (-e $fileb);
open(FILEB, ">$fileb") or die "Can't open $fileb: $!";

while(<FILEA>)
{
```

```
        unless(print FILEB $_)
    {
        die "Can't write to $fileb ($!)\n";
    }
}
close(FILEA) or die "Couldn't close $filea properly: $!";
close(FILEB) or die "Couldn't close $fileb properly: $!";
```

What to Check

The paranoid would say "everything," and the more relaxed and laid back would say "nothing." There are statements and operations that you should always check, whether you are interested in the return value or not, if only to prevent your script from doing something it shouldn't:

- The **open**, **close**, and related statements that provide a conduit to the outside world (including **socket** and **tie**) and external database connectivity

- Reading from or writing to a file or socket handle other than **STDIN**, **STDOUT**, or **STDERR**

- Reading from or writing to **STDIN**, **STDOUT**, or **STDERR** if they have been reassigned or redirected within the script

- Anything that makes changes to the operating system or file system, including calls like **unlink**

- Anything that changes the environment in which you are operating (for example, **chdir** and **chroot**) or modifying the **%ENV** hash

- Any system call not already covered above—system calls *always* return their status, so use it!

- Anything that relies on input or information supplied the user—don't automatically assume that users know what they are doing!

- Any calls to an external program, either through **open**, the **qx** operator, or **system**

- The object type when a reference that points to an internal object is dynamically generated—particularly vital for code references

Beyond this list, it comes down to a case of how the operation will affect the execution of your script. If the operation will affect the following statements, it needs to be traced and probably trapped to prevent it from it from a knock on effect. As a good example, using zero as a division value will raise an error, so it's a good idea to check the value beforehand.

What Not to Check

This list is obviously the inverse of our previous list. Beyond avoiding things that we don't need to worry about, there are some less obvious elements of our scripts that we can safely ignore. Most of the time, the things to avoid checking are those that will not immediately have an effect on what we are trying to achieve.

Don't Check Things that Don't Matter

There are some things in your script that just don't merit checking, either because the return values don't mean anything or because they have little or no relevance on the execution of your script. This is kind of an obvious statement, but it's worth taking the time to think about the process.

Here's a good example taken from a student's project. The script was supposed to ask the student's name and date of birth and calculate the user's age in days, without using any of the Perl modules that help you solve the problem. Right at the top of the script he had

```perl
unless (-d $ENV{HOME})
{
    die "You have no home!\n";
}
```

The script did not need to know the value of the user's home directory, nor did it to need to create any files, so why bother checking anything about the file system at all?

User Input

Following on from the last example, there are occasions when you need to verify that the input from the user matches a specific pattern (a number, for example) but you don't always need to check the user input to high levels of precision:

```perl
print "Enter your name: ";
$name = <STDIN>;
chomp $name;
if ($name =~ /[a-zA-Z0-9 ]+/)
{
    print "Hello $name\n";
}
else
{
    print "I dont know who you are\n";
}
```

Here we've probably gone too far. All we need to do is check that the user supplied some input; if he or she typed their name incorrectly or entered a string of punctuation characters, it won't affect the script—it just won't achieve what the user expects.

Substitution/Transliteration

When modifying a variable through the substitution or transliteration operators, don't bother checking that the operation completed successfully, unless you specifically want to match or identify regular expression elements. For example, the script

```perl
$string = 'hello';
if ($string =~ tr/a-z/A-Z/)
{
    print "Changed text\n";
```

```
}
else
{
    print "Raw\n";
}
```

might give you some useful information, but it doesn't actually check for anything useful—if the characters in the transliteration aren't found, it doesn't indicate an error, it just means nothing was changed.

When to Stop Checking

There are times when you can go too far. In the script we modified, for example, we checked the result when **close** is called, but nowhere did we actually check that the number of bytes that we read from the file matched the number of bytes in the file when we started. Checking that information is pointless—either we'll read everything from the file, or an error will be raised at some point (in this instance, probably when we try to close the file). On the other hand, there are situations in which checking to that level of granularity would be vital—transferring data over a network connection, for example.

Don't Check Things Twice

There's no point in checking the same thing twice in two different ways. Usually there is a simpler, one-shot solution that will identify the error for us. Here's a common mistake made by some programmers:

```
die "$file doesn't exist!" unless (-e $file);
open(FILE,$file) or die "Can't open $file: $!";
```

Aside from the fact that the second line would never be reached, the chances of the status of the file changing between the two lines is pretty remote. Furthermore, the first test might pass if the file exists, even though it might not necessarily be readable. By checking the return value of **open**, we actually verify that the file can be opened and read by Perl, not just the file's status.

Here's another example where the checking is basically verifying the same information, albeit it at different levels each time:

```
if ($name)
{
    if (length($name) > 0)
    {
        if ($name =~ /[a-zA-Z0-9 ]+/)
        {
            print "Hello $name\n";
        }
    }
}
```

The regular expression will tell us whether the information that was supplied was valid or not. Should the expression match fail, we'll already know that either it didn't match or that the supplied value wasn't long enough.

Functions, Return Values, and Nesting

If you've followed the guidelines in Chapter 5, you already know that you can improve and reduce the number and effects of bugs in your scripts by dividing and debugging the individual components. You know as well that the functions should ideally handle errors by returning the error to the caller and not by using its own error-handling statements to report problems (there are some exceptions; see "Reporting Errors Within Modules" later in this chapter). Therefore, in checking for errors when calling one of your own functions, you should avoid situations like this:

```
sub formatmessage
{
    my ($msg) = @_;
    if ($msg)
    {
        return "Hello $msg\n";
    }
    else
    {
        warn "No message!";
        return undef;
    }
}

$message = formatmessage(undef);
if ($message)
{
    print $message;
}
else
{
    warn "Invalid message!";
}
```

If you run this script, you get this:

```
No message! at t.pl line 10.
Invalid message! at t.pl line 22.
```

We've checked the same thing twice, once within the function and again with the returned value in the main script. This procedure could be avoided completely by just allowing the caller to handle the error condition and report the problem.

There are exceptions to this rule. There are occasions when it makes more sense to trap and, if necessary, report a problem within the function itself, yet still report an error condition back to the caller that could, if necessary, be trapped. For example, in the code here we have a function that reads information from a file and returns it to the caller:

```perl
sub template
{
    my $data = '';
    if (open(DATA,"template"))
    {
        $data .= $_ while (<DATA>);
        close(DATA);
        return $data;
    }
    else
    {
        return '';
    }
}

print template();
```

If the template file can't be opened, an empty string is returned—the error is still reported and indeed logged against the function in which the error occurs, but we ignore the error in the caller. We could have trapped the information and provided an alternative, but in this case it's safe to ignore the error.

Error Messages and Numbers

When reporting an error it's useful to supply the error that was returned by the operating system so that the problem can be identified. For example, when opening a file, the error could be caused by a lack of the file's existence or the user's privileges not allowing access to the file. Perl uses the special **$!** variable to hold the error number or error string for the last system error that occurred.

For example, we could update our **open** error message to

```perl
open FILE, 'myfile.txt' or warn "Didn't open the file: $!\n";
```

Whether the variable returns a numerical value or a string depends on the context in which it is used. If Perl is expecting a numerical value, the variable returns the numerical error code. For example, the modified statement

```perl
open FILE, 'myfile.txt' or warn "Didn't open the file: ", 0+$!, "\n";
```

will return an error code of 2 if the file didn't exist.

When called in a string context, the variable returns the corresponding error code string. The information for the error codes comes from the operating system's own headers, and the message contents and corresponding numbers will vary across different systems.

If required, you can set the value of **$!** in order to determine the error messages for a platform. The same trick can also be used if you want to set the error message and exit value for **die**; for example,

```
unless(open(DATA,$file))
{
    $! = 1;
    die "Couldn't open the file!";
}
```

will give an exit value of 1 from the script when it terminates.

For platform-specific error messages or extended error messages from outside Perl's normal execution space, you can use the **$^E** variable. This variable holds errors raised external to Perl or the functions that Perl uses to communicate with the operating system. Under Windows, for example, the **$^E** variable will usually hold the information that would otherwise be returned by the statement

```
Win32::FormatMessage(Win32::GetLastError());
```

However, don't rely on the value of **$^E** always being populated—it's quite possible that the value will always be undefined, regardless of the result of the previous system call.

Reporting Errors Within Scripts

The most obvious solution when you want to report an error is to use the **print** function and either send the output directly to **STDOUT**, or redirect it to **STDERR**. One advantage of **print** over the normal **warn** and **die** functions is that the output can also be redirected to another, previously opened file that you are using to log errors (see Chapter 9 for more details on log-based debugging).

The more usual method, however, is to report the error directly to **STDERR** using the **warn** and **die** functions. The basic format for both functions is

```
warn LIST
die LIST
```

In essence, the two functions are identical, and they both follow the same basic rules:

- The supplied **LIST** is concatenated and then printed to **STDERR**.
- If the final value to **LIST** does not end with a **\n** character, the current script name, line number, and input source line number (from an opened file) are appended.
- If **LIST** is empty and **$@** already contains a value (from an earlier **eval** call), then the string "\t...propagated" (for **die**) or "\t...caught" (for **warn**) is appended to **$@** and then printed with the current script name and line number.

We'll be returning to this last item later, as it applies specifically to the use of **warn** and **die** with an **eval** statement.

The major difference between the two functions is that **warn** only raises an error, whilst **die** raises an error and calls **exit**. Also see Chapter 9 for details on the signals raised by the **warn** and **die** functions.

The **Warn** Function

The **warn** function just raises a warning—a message is printed to **STDERR**, but no further action is taken. Aside from the rules already given, the **warn** function adds

- If **LIST** is empty and $@ does not contain a value, then the string "Warning: something's wrong" and the source file and line number are printed.

Otherwise, the function is fairly straightforward:

```
chdir('/etc') or warn "Can't change directory";
```

The **Die** Function

The **die** function works just like **warn**, except that it also calls **exit**. Within a normal script, this function has the effect of immediately terminating execution. The return code given by the script when **die** is called depends on the context. If the $! error variable contains a value, it is used as the error code. If $! is zero, the value of $! shifted to the right eight times ($! >> 8) is used. This correctly prints the error number retrieved from an external program execution via backticks. If the value is still zero, a value of 255 is passed to the **exit** function.

Beyond the rules given, the **die** function also adds:

- If **LIST** is empty and $@ is undefined, then the string "Died" is printed.

The function can be used in an identical fashion to **warn**:

```
chdir('/etc') or die "Can't change directory";
```

It's generally a good idea to add "stopped" or something similar to a **die** message just to make sure that it's obvious the script has abnormally terminated.

Propagation and **eval**

The **eval** function places some additional rules into the equation, especially when using **die**. The most critical difference is that any call to **die** from within an **eval** block will cause the $@ variable to be populated with the error message—as per the earlier rules—and the eval block to terminate instantly. The **warn** function has no effect on the $@ variable. You can actually verify this quite easily:

```
eval
{
    die "Exiting eval";
}
print $@;
```

The preceding script outputs

```
Exiting eval at t.pl line 2.
```

If we change that **print** statement to a **warn** statement without any arguments, the value of $@ is printed with "\t...caught" appended to the end, in addition to the input script and line number. For example,

```
Exiting eval at t.pl line 2.
        ...caught at t.pl line 4.
```

Also note that the "\t...caught" message is actually appended to $@ before printing—this means that the value of $@ has been updated. If we use **die** instead of **warn**, the value of $@ is printed with "\t...propagated" appended to the end, in addition to the input script and line number:

```
Exiting eval at t.pl line 2.
        ...propagated at t.pl line 4.
```

Now, if you call **warn** and then **die**, for example, like this,

```
eval
{
    die "Exiting eval";
};
warn;
die;
```

you get the original $@ value printed when **warn** is called, in addition to the updated $@ variable and the **die** information:

```
Exiting eval at t.pl line 2.
        ...caught at t.pl line 4.
Exiting eval at t.pl line 2.
        ...caught      ...propagated at t.pl line 5.
```

The propagation works across nested **eval** blocks, so,

```
eval
{
    eval
    {
        die "Exiting eval";
    };
    die;
};
die;
```

generates the expected:

```
Exiting eval at t.pl line 3.
        ...propagated at t.pl line 5.
        ...propagated at t.pl line 7.
```

Directives and Tokens

The special tokens **__FILE__** and **__LINE__** contain the currently executing line number and the file in which the line appears. These tokens are automatically populated by Perl and are the same tokens actually used by the **die** and **warn** functions when you supply a string not terminated by a new line character. For example,

```
chdir('/etc')
    or die "Can't change dir in ",__FILE__," line ", __LINE__, "\n";
```

If you failed to change the directory, this would print

```
Can't change dir in adduser.pl line 35
```

You can change the values that these tokens are populated with by using a special type of comment that includes a "line directive"; for example,

```
# line 200 "Parsing engine"
die "Fatal error";
```

produces the following:

```
Fatal error at Parsing engine line 200
```

It is important to note that the line number given here just resets the number for the following line of code—three lines down and an error would be reported as occurring on line 202. The line and file information is unique to the current input/source file, so when using **die** or a similar function, the information will be reported accordingly.

Also, because the line directive updates the **__FILE__** and **__LINE__** tokens, which are themselves used by **die** and similar functions, the modifications will work across all of the functions and tools used to report errors.

See Chapter 2 for more information on line directives and how they are identified.

Reporting Errors Within Modules

Although I've already stated that you should be using return values from functions to relate errors back to the caller, there are times when you need to raise an error within the confines of the module in which it appears. By highlighting a module-specific error you can more easily track down the problem, and also raise errors within a module that are too significant to be safely trapped through the use of an **if** statement.

There are two different situations we need to be able to handle:

- Reporting an error in a module that quotes the module's filename and line number—this is useful when debugging a module, or when you specifically want to raise a module-related, rather than script-related error.

- Reporting an error within a module that quotes the caller's information so you can debug the line within the script that caused the error. Errors raised in this fashion are useful to the end user, because they highlight the error in relation to the calling script's origination line.

The **warn** and **die** functions work slightly different from what you would expect when called from within a module – the **__LINE__** and **__FILE__** tokens are populated with the information about the module file, not the calling script. This causes a problem when you want to identify the line within the original script that triggered the problem. For example, the simple module

```
package T;

require Exporter;
@ISA = qw/Exporter/;
@EXPORT = qw/function/;
use Carp;

sub function
{
    warn "Error in module!";
}

1;
```

when called from a script

```
use T;

function();
```

produces the following error message:

```
Error in module! at T.pm line 11.
```

This is more or less what you might expect, but not necessarily what you want. From a module programmer's perspective the information is useful, because it helps to point to a bug within the module itself. For an end-user, the information provided is fairly useless, and for all but the hardened programmer, completely pointless.

Assuming that we know the module has only been imported from a calling script, we could use the **caller** function to identify the parent and then report the error (see Chapter 9, for more information). This is messy, and it also requires that you know the level to which the module has been called.

The solution is the **Carp** module, which provides a simplified method for reporting errors within modules that return information about the calling script—not the module. The **Carp** module provides four functions: **carp**, **cluck**, **croak**, and **confess**. With each function the location of the error is specified relative to the script or package that called the function. For errors more than one level deep it doesn't return the information on the calling script unless you use the **cluck** or **confess** functions to report a stack trace.

The **Carp** Function

The **carp** function is the basic equivalent of **warn** and prints the message to **STDERR** without actually exiting the script. The module actually uses **warn** so the same basic rules are followed. Thus, this example

```
carp "Error in module!";
```

would report the following:

```
Error in module! at test.pl line 3
```

Note that the function will always return the call that originated the error. If the script **test.pl** calls the module **S** which in turns calls the module **T**, and this is where **carp** is called, **carp** will return the call in **S** that triggered the error.

The **Cluck** Function

The **cluck** function is a sort of supercharged **carp**; it follows the same basic principle, but also prints a stack trace of all the modules that led to the function being called, including information on the original script. The **cluck** function is not exported by default by the module, so you'll need to import it explicitly. Following on from our **test.pl->S->T** example, we'd get this:

```
Error in module! at T.pm line 11
        T::function() called at S.pm line 13
        S::raise() called at test.pl line 3
```

The **Croak** Function

The **croak** function is the equivalent of **die**, except that it reports the caller one level up:

```
croak "Definitely didn't work";
```

Like **die**, this function also exits the script after reporting the error to **STDERR**:

```
Error in module! at S.pm line 13
```

As with **carp**, the same basic rules apply regarding the including of line and file information according to the **warn** and **die** functions.

The **Confess** Function

The **confess** function is like **cluck**: It prints a stack trace all the way up to the origination script.

```
confess "Failed around about there";
```

For example,

```
Error in module! at T.pm line 11
        T::function() called at S.pm line 13
        S::raise() called at t2.pl line 3
```

Reporting Errors Within GUIs and Web Applications

When writing an application that does not use the traditional command-line/terminal interface, the use of functions like **die** and **carp** should be deprecated in favor of a more user-friendly solution. For a start, the **STDERR** filehandle is unlikely to print anything useful to the user. For a Tk application there may be no **STDERR**, and for a web application, the output from **STDERR** is written to the server's error log.

For any interactive application, calling **die** on a script will also have the effect of immediately terminating the application. Within a Tk-based application this may cause the user to lose information, in addition to the stress caused by suddenly having their application apparently crash!

With a web application the same rules apply, albeit for different reasons. Immediately terminating a script that may not yet have communicated any information to the user, or that might be in the middle of returning information will leave the returned page largely unusable. Errors such as 'Document contained no data' or tables failing to be displayed are good examples of where the typical error systems just don't work.

The solution is therefore to provide a more suitable way of supplying an error condition, whether fatal or otherwise, without interrupting or otherwise affecting the rest of the flow of the application. This is where good functional design for your script comes into play—you can return from a function once an error has been raised without it affecting the remainder of the execution.

Within Tk this will mean trapping the error, supplying a dialogue box to warn the user of the error, and then returning to a state where the user can try again or give up. For a web application, it's more about supplying an error message while still supplying any of the other page elements still required.

Tk Dialogues

The **Tk** module and libraries provide a **Dialog** widget that presents a modal dialog to the user, waiting for them to press one of the buttons in order to continue. The return value from the module is the text of the button that was pressed.

```
$response = $main->Dialog(-text          => 'Overwrite File?',
                   -bitmap         => 'warning',
                   -title          => 'Warning',
                   -default_button => 'Cancel',
                   -buttons        => [qw/OK Cancel/);
```

This **bitmap** specification actually selects one of the predefined bitmaps that comes with the **Tk** library. The **warning** bitmap is an exclamation mark; other possibilities include **error**, **gray75**, **gray50**, **gray25**, **gray12**, **hourglass**, **info**, **questhead** and **question**.

Alternatively, you can create your own dialog box. The following script provides a simple **dialog** function that mirrors the basic functionality of the **Tk Dialog** widget:

```
#! /usr/local/bin/perl -w

use Tk;

sub dialog
{
```

```perl
my ($master, $title, $text, $bitmap, $default, @butdefs) = @_;

$w = MainWindow->new();
$w->title($title);
$w->iconname('Dialog');

$top = $w->Frame(relief => 'raised', borderwidth => 1);
$top->pack(side => 'top', fill => 'both');
$bot = $w->Frame(relief => 'raised', borderwidth => 1);
$bot->pack(side => 'bottom', fill => 'both');

$msg = $top->Message(width => '3i',
                     text => $text,
                     font=>'-Adobe-Times-Medium-R-Normal-*-180-*');

$msg->pack(side   => 'right',
           expand => 1,
           fill   => 'both',
           padx   => '3m',
           pady   => '3m');

if (defined($bitmap))
{
    $bm = $top->Label(bitmap => $bitmap);
    $bm->pack(side => 'left',
              padx => '3m',
              pady => '3m');
}

my $i = 0;
my $retval = 0;
my %buttons;
my %revbutton;
foreach $but (@butdefs)
{
    my $b = undef;
    if ($i == $default)
    {
        $bd = $bot->Frame(relief      => 'sunken',
                          borderwidth => 1);
        $bd->pack(side   => 'left',
                  expand => 1,
                  padx   => '3m',
                  pady   => '2m');

        $b = $bd->Button(text => $but);
        $b->configure(command => sub {$retval = $revbutton{$b} });

        $b->pack(in   => $bd,
                 side => 'left',
                 padx => '2m',
                 pady => '2m',
```

```
                              ipadx => '2m',
                              ipady => '1m');
        }
        else
        {
            $b = $bot->Button(text => $but);
            $b->configure(command => sub { $retval = $revbutton{$b} });
            $b->pack(side   => 'left',
                     expand => 1,
                     padx   => '3m',
                     pady   => '3m',
                     ipadx  => '2m',
                     ipady  => '1m');
        }
        $buttons{$i} = $b;
        $revbutton{$b} = $but;
        $i++;
    }

    if ($default >= 0)
    {
        $w->bind('<Return>',
                 sub { $buttons{$default}->flash(),
                       ($retval = $default) });
    }

    $w->waitVariable(\$retval);
    $w->destroy();
    return $retval;
}

$ret = dialog(undef,"Warning","Overwrite file?",
              'warning',1,"OK","Cancel");
print "Button $ret was pressed\n";

MainLoop();
```

You can see a sample of how to use the new dialogue function at the bottom of the script. Like the standard **Dialog** widget, you can display a suitable bitmap and have a default option that will be automatically chosen if the user presses **Return**.

How you handle the return value from either function is obviously entirely up to you and your script. In the preceding examples we check whether the user wants to overwrite a file, and this would probably be raised as the result of a file save dialog or save command. Remember that at all times you are trying to prevent the script from unceremoniously exiting without giving the user any sort of warning.

Web Error Reporting

Web error reporting is more complex, because there are two possible points at which an error could cause problems: before any information has been communicated back, and during the response.

The problem with the former is that you need to define a function that not only reports the error message but also sends the necessary HTTP header back to the user in order to display the message.

The general format is to define a function like this:

```
sub weberror
{
    my ($message) = @_;
    print "Content-type: text/html\n\n";
    print $message;
}
```

That's simplistic, but it does the job. An alternative to the problem of embedding the HTTP header into the error reporting function is to send back the HTTP header as early as possible, so that any errors are automatically reported back to the user. It's not uncommon, for example, to see the following:

```
BEGIN
{
    print "Content-type: text/html\n\n";
    close(STDERR);
    open(STDERR,'>-');
}
```

This not only returns the HTTP header information right at the start of the script, it also redirects the **STDERR** filehandle so that we could use **warn** to report error information to the user. It will only work if you are planning on return HTML in all cases—if you want to return non-standard HTTP headers or return an alternative file type you'll have to determine the type of error to report at runtime.

In terms of reporting errors during execution, the basic rule is to ensure that the error can be reported without affecting any of the other elements. For example, imagine we have a dynamically generated HTML table, using information that we've extracted previously from a database:

```
print "<table>\n";
%data = get_db_data();
foreach $key (sort keys %data)
{
    print "<tr><Td>$key</td>";
...
```

Raising an error at this point would cause a problem; we'd introduce text within a table row, but outside of a cell—this would cause the information to be displayed outside of the table. Instead, either build an error message that can be printed after the table has been completed, or check the information before starting the loop that outputs the table.

Error Watch *Although it's an HTML error, the sudden early termination of a web page that uses tables generally points to a failure to include the necessary </table> closing tag. You could fix this in Perl by using an END block to output any necessary tailing code.*

When working with complex HTML sites that employ tables for layout purposes, the trick is to use functions and abstraction to separate the different components that are displayed from the elements that are dynamically generated. For example, the following fragment is from a script that displays user information for the user's account:

```
print "Content-type: text/html\n\n";
print parse_template('topbar',
                     'login' => $session->{user},
                     'sessionid' => $session->{sessionid},);
print parse_template('sidebar',
                     'sessionid' => $session->{sessionid},);

display_account($user,$group,$session);

print parse_template('closepage',
                     'sessionid' => $session->{sessionid},);
```

The templates are static files read in dynamically during execution, and the **display_account** function is the one that does all the work. The templates themselves define a complex table that provides the basics for the layout, and when put together, the entire set of preceding tables would provide what could only be classed as a blank page.

The **display_account** function is then free to do whatever it likes in terms of displaying information or reporting errors. Any errors are displayed using **print**, and just become part of the overall page without affecting the layout. Any fatal error causes a **return**, rather than a **die** or **warn** call so that the remainder of the page can be displayed.

## CHAPTER 8

Using Pragmas and Warnings

At the risk of repeating myself, Perl is a very ambiguous language. The philosophy of DWIM (Do What I Mean), which is actually used by some areas of the Perl parsing engine, just helps this along. The problem with these ambiguities is that they are often the source of bugs and problems without you even realizing their effect.

There are ways to get around this—following the guides in the first section of this book will help. You can also trace and solve the problems using the debugging tips in the rest of this section. A better solution is get Perl to look at the decisions it makes and highlight the ambiguities in your code as it goes through the parsing and compilation process.

There are two basic methods: The first is to switch on warnings, and the second is to use the various Perl pragmas to control the parsing and execution of a script. Warnings are a good way of highlighting those ambiguities and the points in your code where Perl thinks you might have actually meant something different. Pragmas just change the way Perl looks at code. The **strict** pragma, for example, enforces stricter checking of certain elements—variable definitions and ambiguous references that can raise a fatal error during compilation.

Warnings

Warnings are one of the most basic ways in which you can get Perl to check the quality of the code that you have produced. As the name suggests, they just raise a simple warning about a particular construct that Perl thinks is either potentially dangerous or ambiguous enough that Perl might have made the wrong decision about what it thought you were trying to do.

There are actually two types of warning, the mandatory and optional warning:

- *Mandatory warnings* highlight problems in the lexical analysis stage.
- *Optional warnings* highlight occasions where Perl has spotted a possible anomaly.

As a rough guide, the Perl warnings system will raise a warning under the following conditions:

- Filehandles opened as read-only that you attempt to write to
- Files handles that haven't been opened yet
- Filehandles that you try to use after they've been closed
- References to undefined filehandles
- Redefined subroutines
- Scalar variables whose values have been accessed before their values have been populated
- Subroutines that nest with recursion to more than 100 levels
- Invalid use of variables—for instance, scalars as arrays or hashes
- Strings used as numerical values when they don't truly resolve to a number
- Variables mentioned only once
- Deprecated functions, operators, and variables

24x7

Warnings should be enabled by default on all your scripts—you'll discover more faults and possible areas where a fault may occur in the future than any amount of debugging. Get used to adding the **-w** command line argument when you execute a script and you'll save yourself hours in the long run.

These errors in your code are not serious enough to halt execution completely, but you can make Perl worried enough about them that it will raise a warning during compilation. For example, the code

```
$string = "Hello";
```

will pass the compiler checks if warnings are switched off, but if you turn warnings on, you get an error about a term that has only been used once:

```
Name "main::string" used only once: possible typo at -e line 1.
```

The traditional way of enabling warnings was to use the **-w** argument on the command line:

```
perl -w myscript.pl
```

You can also supply the option within the 'shebang' line:

```
#/usr/local/bin/perl -w
```

But be careful about using command-line options on operating systems that restrict the length of the shebang line you can use or that restrict the number of arguments that can be supplied.

You can also enable warnings using the **$^W** special variable. Older versions of Perl include the **warnings** pragma, which enables warnings within the script without needing the command line option. The pragma has been updated in Perl 5.6 to be more flexible—it even allows you to determine which type of warnings are displayed.

The $^W Variable

The **$^W** variable allows you to change—or discover—the current warnings setting within the script. If set to zero, the variable disables warnings; if set to one, they are enabled. In general, though, the use of the variable is not recommended—although it could be used to enable warnings on a lexical basis, it is open to far too many potential problems. It's possible, for example, to accidentally reset the warnings setting without realizing what you're doing. It is also difficult to differentiate between compiler-time and run-time warnings.

Ideally you should use either the command-line options, or use the **warnings** pragmas outlined here.

Option	Description
all	All warnings are produced; this is the default if none are specified.
deprecated	Only deprecated feature warnings are produced.
unsafe	Lists only unsafe warnings.

Table 8.1 Options for for the **warnings** pragma

The Old **warnings** Pragma

Older versions of Perl also supported a simple pragma that allowed you to switch warnings on and off within your script without the use of the command line. The options were fairly limited, in fact you could only choose three options": **all**, **deprecated** and **unsafe**, as detailed in Table 8-1.

You can switch on options with

```
use warnings 'all';
```

or you can switch off warnings with **no**:

```
no warnings 'deprecated';
```

Lexical Warnings in Perl 5.6

Perl 5.6, released at the beginning of April 2000, has changed slightly the way warnings are handled with the **warnings** pragma. This new method is actually now the preferred way of enabling warnings and has a few advantages over the traditional command-line switch or the **$^W** variable:

- Mandatory warnings become default warnings, and can be disabled.
- Warnings can now be limited to the same scope as the **strict** pragma—that is, they are limited to the enclosing block and propagate to modules imported using **do**, **use**, and **require**.
- You can now specify the level of warnings produced.
- Warnings can be switched off, using the **no** keyword, within individual code blocks.
- Both mandatory and optional warnings can be controlled.

24x7

If you've got Perl 5.6, use the **warnings** pragma instead of the **-w** command line switch for your warnings. However, as with the **-w** command line option, you should be using it all the time, not just when you think there might be a problem. In fact, get used to putting both the **warnings** and **strict** pragmas at the top of your scripts.

For example, the code

```
use warnings;
$a;
{
    no warnings;
    $b;
}
$c;
```

produces the following output:

```
Useless use of a variable in void context at t2.pl line 2.
Useless use of a variable in void context at t2.pl line 7.
Name "main::a" used only once: possible typo at t2.pl line 2.
Name "main::c" used only once: possible typo at t2.pl line 7.
```

The use of **$b** in line 5 does not raise an error.
To enable warnings within a block, use, one of

```
use warnings;
use warnings 'all';
```

and to switch them off within a block:

```
no warnings;
no warnings 'all';
```

More specific control of warnings is described in the remainder of this section.

Command-Line Warnings

The traditional **-w** command-line option has now been replaced with

Option	Description
-w	Works just like the old version—warnings are enabled everywhere. However, if you make use of the **warnings** pragma, then the **–w** option is ignored for the scope of the **warnings** pragma.
-W	Enables warnings for all scripts and modules within the program, ignoring the effects of the **$^W** or **warnings** pragma.
-X	The exact opposite of **-W**, it switches off all warnings, ignoring the effects of the **$^W** variable or the **warnings** pragma.

The switches interact with the **$^W** variable and the new lexical warnings according to the following rules:

- If no command-line switches are supplied and neither the **$^W** variable nor **warnings** pragma is in force, default warnings will be enabled and optional warnings disabled.

- The **-w** sets the **$^W** variable as normal.
- If a block makes use of the **warnings** pragma, both the **$^W** and **-w** flag are ignored.
- Lexical warnings enabled/disabled with the **warnings** pragma can be overridden only by the **-W/-X** command-line switches.

Warning Options

Beyond the normal control of warnings, you can now also define which warnings will be raised by supplying warning names as arguments to the pragma. For example, you can switch on specific warnings:

```
use warnings qw/void syntax/;
```

or turn off specific warnings:

```
no warnings qw/void syntax/;
```

The effects are cumulative, rather than explicit, so you could rewrite the preceding as

```
no warnings 'void';      # disables 'void' warnings
no warnings 'syntax';    # disables 'syntax' warnings in addition to 'void'
```

The **warnings** pragma actually supports a hierarchical list of options to be enabled or disabled, you can see the hierarchy in Table 8-2. For example, the **severe** warning includes the **debugging**, **inplace**, **internal** and **malloc** warnings options.

Making Warnings Fatal

Normally warnings are reported only to **STDERR** without actually halting execution of the script. You can change this behavior marking the options as "FATAL" when importing the pragma module:

```
use warnings FATAL => qw/syntax/;
```

Getting Warning Parameters Within the Script

When programming modules, you can configure warnings to be registered against the module in which the warning occurs. This effectively creates a new category within the warnings hierarchy. To register the module within the warnings system you import the **warnings::register** module:

```
package MyModule;

use warnings::register;
```

This creates a new warnings category called "MyModule." When you import the module into a script, you can specify whether you want warnings within the module category to be enabled:

```
use MyModule;
use warnings 'MyModule';
```

all	chmod	
	closure	
	exiting	
	glob	
	io	closed exec newline pipe unopened
	misc	
	numeric	
	once	
	overflow	
	pack	
	portable	
	recursion	
	redefine	
	regexp	
	severe	debugging inplace internal malloc
	signal	
	substr	
	syntax	ambiguous bareword deprecated digit parenthesis printf prototype qw reserved semicolon
	taint	
	umask	
	uninitialized	
	unpack	
	untie	
	utf8	
	void	
	y2k	

Table 8.2 The **warnings** Pragma Hierarchy

To actually identify if warnings have been enabled within the module, you need to use the **warnings::enabled** function. If called without arguments, it returns true if warnings have been enabled. For example,

```
package MyModule;

sub test
{
    if (warnings::enabled())
    {
        warnings::warn('deprecated',
                    'test is deprecated, use the object io');
    }
}
```

The **warnings::warn** function actually raises a warning—note that it raises an error even if warnings are disabled, so make sure you test that warnings have been enabled. Also note that the **warnings::warn** function accepts two arguments—the first is the word used to describe the warning, and the second is the additional text message printed with the warning. So, the line

```
warnings::warn('deprecated','test is deprecated, use the object io');
```

actually produces

```
test is deprecated use the object io at t2.pl line 5
```

The function name is inserted first—or the package or file name if it's within the global scope—just like the core **warn** function.

You can also be more specific about the warnings that you want to test for; if you supply arguments to the **warnings::enabled** function, it returns true only if the warning type specified has been enabled:

```
if (warnings::enabled('deprecated'))
...
```

The strict Pragma

The **strict** pragma restricts those constructs and statements that would normally be considered unsafe or ambiguous. Unlike warnings, which raise errors without causing the script to fail, the **strict** pragma will halt the execution of the script if any of the restrictions enforced by the pragma are broken. Although the pragma imposes limits that cause scripts to fail, the pragma generally encourages (and even enforces) good programming practice. For some casual scripts it does, of course, cause more problems than you might be trying to solve.

The basic form of the pragma is

```
use strict;
```

24x7

As with warnings, you should have the **strict** pragma enforced at all times. It will help you to pick more of those ambiguous instances where your script might fail without warning. It is no replacement for a full debugger, but it will highlight problems that a normal debugging process might overlook.

The pragma is lexically scoped, so it is in effect only within the current block. This means you must specify **use strict** separately within all the packages, modules, and individual scripts you create. If a script that uses the **strict** pragma imports a module that does not, only the script portion will be checked—the pragma's effects are not propagated down to other modules.

By using the pragma you should be able to identify the effects of assumptions Perl makes about what you are trying to achieve. It does this by imposing limits on the definition and use of variables, references, and barewords that would otherwise be interpreted as functions (subroutines). These can be individually turned on or off using the **vars**, **refs**, and **subs** options to the pragma. You supply the option as an argument to the pragma when the corresponding module is imported. For example, to enable only the **refs** and **subs** options, use the following:

```
use strict qw/refs subs/;
```

The effects are cumulative, so this could be rewritten as

```
use strict 'refs';
use strict 'subs';
```

The pragma also supports the capability to turn it off through the **no** keyword, so you can temporarily turn off strict checking:

```
use strict;

no strict 'vars';

$var = 1;

use strict 'vars';
```

Unless you have any very special reason not to, I recommend using the basic **strict** to enable all three levels of checking.

The **vars** Option

The **vars** option requires that all variables be predeclared before they are used, either with the **my** keyword, the **use vars** pragma, or through a fully qualified name that includes the name of the enclosing package in which you want the variable to be defined.

When using the pragma, the **local** keyword is not sufficient, because its purpose is only to localize a variable, not to declare it. Therefore the following examples work:

```
use strict 'vars';
$Module::vara = 1;
my $vara = 1;
use vars qw/$varb/;
```

but these will fail:

```
use strict 'vars';
$vars = 1;
local $vars = 1;
```

One of the most frustrating elements of the **vars** option is that you'll get a list of errors relating to the use of variables. For example, the script

```
use strict;

%hash = ('Martin' => 'Brown',
         'Sharon' => 'Penfold',
         'Wendy'  => 'Rinaldi',);

foreach $key (sort keys %hash)
{
    print "$key -> $hash{$key}\n";
}
```

raises these errors when executed:

```
$ perl -w t2.pl
Global symbol "%hash" requires explicit package name at t2.pl line 3.
Global symbol "$key" requires explicit package name at t2.pl line 7.
Global symbol "%hash" requires explicit package name at t2.pl line 7.
Global symbol "$key" requires explicit package name at t2.pl line 9.
Global symbol "%hash" requires explicit package name at t2.pl line 9.
Global symbol "$key" requires explicit package name at t2.pl line 9.
Execution of t2.pl aborted due to compilation errors.
```

The obvious solution to the problem is to declare the variables using **my**:

```
use strict;

my %hash = ('Martin' => 'Brown',
            'Sharon' => 'Penfold',
            'Wendy'  => 'Rinaldi',);

foreach my $key (sort keys %hash)
{
    print "$key -> $hash{$key}\n";
}
```

When developing modules, the use of **my** on variables that you want to export will not work, because the declared variables will be lexically scoped within the package. The solution is to use the **vars** pragma:

```
package MyModule;

use vars qw/@ISA @EXPORT/;

require Exporter;
@ISA = qw/Exporter/;
@EXPORT = qw/
    open_db
/;
```

As a general rule, you should always use the **vars** option, even if you neglect to use the other **strict** pragma options.

The **refs** Option

The **refs** pragma generates an error if you use symbolic (soft) references—that is, use a string to refer to a variable or function. Thus, the following will work:

```
use strict 'refs';
$foo = "Hello World";
$ref = \$foo;
print $$ref;
```

but these do not:

```
use strict 'refs';
$foo = "Hello World";
$ref = "foo";
print $$ref;
```

Care should be taken if you're using a dispatch table, because the traditional solutions don't work when the **strict** pragma is in force. The following will fail, because you're trying to use a soft reference to the function that you want to call:

```
use strict refs;
my %commandlist = (
                    'DISK'  => 'disk_space_report',
                    'SWAP'  => 'swap_space_report',
                    'STORE' => 'store_status_report',
                    'GET'   => 'get_status_report',
                    'QUIT'  => 'quit_connection',
                    );
...
my ($function) = $commandlist{$command};
die "No $function()" unless defined(&$function);
&$function(*CHILDSOCKET, $host, $type);
```

To get around this, find a reference to the subroutine from the symbol table, and then access it as a typeglob and call it as a function. This means you can change the last three lines in the preceding script to

```
if (defined($main::{$commandlist{$command}}))
{
    *code = \$main::{$commandlist{$command}};
    &code($user,$group,$session);
}
```

> **Note** *You can also use the **exists** function to determine if a function has been created, but it will return true even if the function has only been forward-defined by the **subs** pragma or when setting up a function prototype, not just when the function has actually been defined.*

The **subs** Option

The final option controls how barewords are treated by Perl (see Chapter 2 for a description of barewords). Without this pragma in effect, you can use a bareword to refer to a subroutine or function. When the pragma is in effect, then you must quote or provide an absolute reference to the subroutine in question.

Normally, Perl allows you to use a bareword for a subroutine. This pragma disables that ability, best seen with signal handlers. The examples

```
use strict 'subs';
$SIG{QUIT} = "myexit";
$SIG{QUIT} = \&myexit;
```

will work since we are not using a bareword, but

```
use strict 'subs';
$SIG{QUIT} = myexit;
```

will generate an error during compilation because **myexit** is a bareword.

Other Perl Pragmas

Beyond the **warnings** and **strict** pragmas, there are others that can help to control and change the way Perl treats different aspects of your script. Although not always useful when debugging, the effects of pragmas can cause unexpected problems in scripts if you fail to notice that the pragma is in effect. Others help you get by the effects of the **strict** pragma, such as the **vars** and **subs** pragmas.

To recap on how pragmas work: All pragmas are just modules. You enable them with the **use** keyword, supplying any optional parameters as a string or array after the pragma name. For example,

```
use vars qw/$var $string/;
```

To turn off a specified pragma, you need the **no** keyword, which is the logical opposite of the **use** keyword. If you specify **no** at the same level as a previous **use** statement, it acts as a toggle, switching off the earlier pragma until a new **use** statement is seen, or until the end of the block. If you use **no** within an enclosed block (a function or loop) inside a block with the corresponding **use** statement, the pragma is disabled only for the duration of the enclosed block. For example,

```
use integer;
function intdivide
{
    print "67/3","\n"; #Uses integer math
}

function divide
{
    no integer;
    print "67/3","\n"; #Uses floating point math
}

print "67/3","\n"; #Integer math
no integer;
print "67/3","\n"; #Floating point math
```

Other pragmas work in similar ways, although some of the effects are dependent on other pragmas or on the specific implementation.

autouse

The **autouse** pragma postpones the loading of the module until one of **funca** or **funcb** is actually used:

```
use autouse 'Module' => qw(funca funcb);
```

This is similar in principle, but not identical, to the **Autoload** module. Note that you must specify the functions that will trigger the **autouse** process; otherwise, there is no way for the Perl interpreter to identify the functions that should be imported. The preceding line is therefore equivalent to the standard method for importing selected functions:

```
use Module qw(funca funcb);
```

You can also supply function prototypes to the **autouse** pragma to trap errors during the compilation, rather than execution, stage:

```
use Module qw(funca($$) funcb($@));
```

The effect of the **autouse** pragma is to reduce the loading and compilation time for a script and also to reduce the number of modules that are loaded at startup in scripts where specific external functions are used only in certain execution trees. Unfortunately, the pragma also has the effect of delaying the loading of the module until execution time, thus bypassing the usual checks that are made when importing a module and shifting the responsibility of reporting any errors to the execution, rather than compilation stages.

Problems can occur when there are bugs or typographical errors in the modules being **autoused**, because your program will not fall over when the module is imported, but when a function is actually used. Additionally, any module that relies on early initialization (say, within a **BEGIN {}** block) might fail because it expects the initialization to occur during the initial compilation of the whole script.

You can get around the bugs in **autouse** modules during the development phase by placing a genuine **use** statement for the **autouse** modules. For example,

```
use File::Basename
use autouse 'File::Basename' => qw(basename dirname);
```

The first line masks the second; when you come to release your script and/or module to the public, just comment out the first line and let the **autouse** pragma do its work.

base

The **base** pragma establishes a relationship with a base class at compile (rather than execution) time. In effect, this operation is equal to adding the specified classes to the **@ISA** array during the module initialization, such that

```
package Object;
use base qw(Foo Bar);
```

is effectively equal to

```
BEGIN
{
    require Foo;
    require Bar;
    push @ISA, qw(Foo Bar);
}
```

The primary problem that can be experienced here is that you fail to import the base class on which you want to inherit. See Chapter 3 for other problems relating to using objects.

blib

The **blib** pragma forces Perl to look for modules in the blib directory structure, as created by the **MakeMaker** module. This feature is especially useful for testing modules before you intend to publish them and make them available to the general Perl community. Ideally, it should be used only on the command line with the **-M** option:

```
perl -Mblib script
perl -Mblib=dir script
```

If **dir** is specified, it looks in that directory (and subdirectories) for the **blib** structure. If you do not specify **dir**, it assumes you want to include the current directory.

You can also use

```
use blib;
use blib 'dir';
```

but this is not the preferred solution because it requires modification of the script to disable the behavior.

constant

Although there are other techniques for introducing constant variables, the most practical solution is the **constant** pragma. The advantages of a constant are obvious: If you use the same constant value throughout all your calculations and programs, you can be guaranteed that the values calculated will also remain constant.

The rule applies even when the constant is used over many different platforms. For example, the value of π can be endlessly calculated, and there are varying methods and degrees of precision used for the value. You can create a constant value to be used in all calculations like this:

```
use constant PI => 3.141592654;
```

The value can be any normal Perl expression, including calculations and functions such that the following also work:

```
use constant PI   => 22/7;
use constant USER => scalar getpwuid($<);
```

Once it's defined, you can use a constant directly; there is no need for a preceding character to denote the variable type:

```
$zero = (cos(PI/2));
```

The values supplied are evaluated in a list context, allowing you to define constant lists as well as scalars. Note that constants are lists, so you must subscript, not array, notation. Therefore, the statement

```
$quota = USERDATA[5];
```

will not work; you must use

```
$quota = (USERDATA)[5];
```

Also note that constants can be directly interpolated, although you must use indirect notation:

```
print "I want to eat some @{[PI]}\n";
```

It's also worth noting that, because constants are actually just subroutines, you cannot use them in contexts where a bareword is automatically quoted, such as hashes. Instead, use an empty parenthesis or the + operator in front of the constant to force Perl to identify it as a function:

```
$hash{PI()};
$hash{+PI};
```

Although it is not essential, constants should have names composed only of uppercase characters to help distinguish them from normal variables. All constants must begin with a letter.

Constant definitions are package-scoped rather than block-scoped, so you can have different constant values within the confines of different packages, and you can also refer to constants using fully qualified names.

Error Watch *Be careful when using constants; the uppercase convention can interfere with filehandles.*

diagnostics

The **diagnostics** pragma inserts additional diagnostic capabilities into the Perl script. Although Perl normally outputs a fair number of errors and warnings when it discovers a problem—at both compile and runtime—the messages are often terse single-line descriptions. Even if you know what the error message signifies, the exact cause of the problem might be difficult to determine.

The **diagnostics** pragma prints out not only the terse one-line warnings but also the additional descriptive text that you find in the *perldiag* main page. Although you still don't have the further benefit of a more in-depth description of the problem, the description can often highlight things you have overlooked.

To use, insert the **diagnostics** pragma at the top of the script you want to examine for problems, and then run the script (preferably with warnings switched on) and examine the extended output. The program below will produce a few errors:

```
use diagnostics;
print DUMMY 'Wont work';
```

When it's run, you get the following:

```
$ perl -w nodiag.pl
Name "main::DUMMY" used only once: possible typo at t.pl line 2 (#1)

    (W) Typographical errors often show up as unique variable names.
    If you had a good reason for having a unique name, then just mention
    it again somehow to suppress the message.  The use vars pragma is
    provided for just this purpose.

Filehandle main::DUMMY never opened at t.pl line 2 (#2)
```

```
(W) An I/O operation was attempted on a filehandle that was never
initialized. You need to do an open() or a socket() call, or call
a constructor from the FileHandle package.
```

Alternatively, leave your script as it is and pipe the error output to a file. The **splain** program (installed with Perl) can then be used to analyze the errors and produce the full descriptions for the error messages and warnings:

```
perl -w nodiag.pl 2> nodiag.err
./splain <nodiag.err
```

 *Under MacPerl there is no separate **splain** application, but the pragma still works if specified within the script.*

If you specify the **-verbose** option when specifying the pragma, the introduction from the *perldiag* main page will be printed out before the diagnostic warnings and extended information:

```
use diagnostics -verbose;
```

Once they are imported, you can control the behavior of individual elements of the script by switching the diagnostics messages on and off using the **enable** and **disable** functions:

```
enable  diagnostics;
disable diagnostics;
```

These changes affect only any runtime errors. It's not possible to switch off the diagnostics process during the parsing/compilation stage.

If your program is making use of the **$SIG{__WARN__}** and **$SIG{__DIE__}** handlers to trap errors in your program, you can still use them in conjunction with the **diagnostics** module. However, the **diagnostics::splainthis** function will be executed first, so you'll get the extended warning information before your own extensions are executed. See Chapter 9 for information on using signals for error trapping.

If you want to examine exactly what the **diagnostics** module is doing, you can switch on "debugging" for the **diagnostics** module by defining

```
BEGIN { $diagnostics::DEBUG =1 }
```

before the script starts the rest of the execution process.

See Chapter 9 for more information on debugging noninteractive scripts, including information on how to make use of the **diagnostics** pragma in theses situations.

fields

The **fields** pragma affects the compile-time error checking of objects. Using the **fields** pragma enables you to predefine class fields, such that a call to a specific class method will fail at compile time if the field has not been specified. This is achieved by populating a hash called **%FIELDS**. When you access a hash with a typed variable holding an object reference, the type is looked up in the **%FIELDS** hash, and if the variable type exists, the entire operation is turned into an array access during the compilation stage. For example,

```
{
    package Foo;
    use fields qw(foo bar _private);
}
...
my Foo $var = new Foo;
$var->{foo} = 42;
```

If the specified field (in this case "foo") does not exist, a compile-time error is produced.

For this to work, the **%FIELDS** hash is consulted at compile time, and it's the **fields** and **base** pragmas that facilitate this. The **base** pragma copies fields from the base class definitions, and the **fields** pragma adds new fields to the existing definitions. Field names that start with an underscore character are private to a class; they are not even accessible to subclasses.

The result is that objects can be created with named fields that are as convenient and quick to access as a corresponding hash. You must access the objects through correctly typed variables, or you can use untyped variables; providing a reference to the **%FIELDS** hash is assigned to the 0th element of the array object. You can achieve this initialization with the following:

```
sub new
{
    my $class = shift;
    no strict 'refs';
    my $self = bless [\%{"$class\::FIELDS"], $class;
    $self;
}
```

integer

Perl does all its calculations in floating point by default. Although you can normally force integer results from specific calculations using the **int** function, it can be more useful to specify that all calculations are performed with integers only. For example,

```
use integer;
print 67/3,"\n";
```

The **use integer** pragma lasts only as long as the current block, so it can safely be used within individual functions without affecting the rest of the script. In addition, you can switch off the **integer** pragma with the **no** keyword:

```
use integer;
print 67/3,"\n";
no integer;
print 67/3,"\n";
```

You can also use **no** within an enclosed block to temporarily turn off integer math, as seen in the introductory example under "Other Perl Pragmas."

less

The **less** pragma is currently unimplemented:

```
use less;
```

The intention is to allow you to specify reductions for certain resources such as memory or processor space. This capability might be useful in situations where you want to ensure that the effects of the script do not upset the rest of your system.

Meanwhile, see Chapter 14 for more information on stress testing your system when executing a script.

lib

When importing modules with **use**, the interpreter examines the **@INC** array for a list of directories to search for the modules to be imported. Since **use** statements are evaluated during the compilation process, you cannot insert additional directories in the main part of the script. You can, of course, use a **BEGIN {}** block:

```
BEGIN { unshift @INC, LIST }
```

Or you can use the **lib** pragma. The equivalent of the above block would be

```
use lib LIST;
```

Note that the directories are added (using **unshift**) before the standard directories to ensure that you use the local modules in preference to the standard ones. For all directories added in this way, the **lib** module also checks that a **$dir/$archname/**auto exists, where **$archname** is the name of the architecture of the current platform. If it does exist, it is assumed to be an architecture-specific directory and is actually added to **@INC** before the original directory specification.

Once added, it is not normally necessary to remove directories. Furthermore, you shouldn't ever remove standard directories from the array. It's also worth remembering that you might affect the future operation of a later module if you remove a directory that contains a module on which it relies. Although you could argue that it is the module's responsibility to make sure it has access to the modules it needs, it's also sensible to assume that in the interests of good relations you shouldn't be removing directories anyway. There is no advantage to removing them; it doesn't take a considerable amount of extra memory or processing power for the interpreter to search for what it's looking for.

With all this in mind, you remove directories with a **no lib** pragma, which removes the first instance of the named directory from **@INC**. If you want to remove multiple instances, you will need to call **no lib** multiple times. You can also remove all the specified names from **@INC** by specifying ":ALL" as the first parameter of **no lib**. For example,

```
no lib qw(:ALL .);
```

For each directory, the opposite of the earlier process is executed. The architecture-specific directories are also searched for in the **@INC** array before they too are removed.

Although in practice you shouldn't need to, if you want to reinstate the original (standard) list of directories in **@INC**, you need to use

```
@INC = @lib::ORIG_INC;
```

ops

The **ops** pragma switches off specific opcodes during the compilation process. The synopsis is as follows:

```
perl -Mops=:default
```

which enables only reasonably safe operations. Or you can specify that opcodes be removed from those available, using

```
perl -M-ops=system
```

Note that the best way to use this option is via the command-line incorporation; otherwise you open yourself up to abuse before the compilation process starts through the use of **BEGIN {}** statements. Alternatively, you can use the **Safe** and **Opcode** modules, which provide a more comprehensive method for executing Perl code using a restricted set of opcodes.

re

The **re** pragma alters regular expression behavior. The pragma has three options: **taint, debug**, and **eval**. One additional pragma is really just a modification of an earlier one, called **debugcolor.** The only difference is in the color of the output. In all cases the **re** pragma applies to the entire file (it is not lexically scoped), and the effect is felt at both compile and execution time.

The **taint** option ensures that variables modified with a regular expression are tainted in situations where they would otherwise be considered cleaned during the regular expression exercise:

```
use re 'taint';
```

That is, in situations where matches or substitutions on tainted variables would ordinarily produce an untainted result, the results are in fact marked as tainted. Information that is already untainted remains unchanged—the use of the taint option does not taint all regular expression data.

The **debug** and **debugcolor** options force Perl to produce debugging messages during the execution of a regular expression:

```
use re 'debug';
use re 'debugcolor';
```

This is equivalent to using the **-Dx** switch during execution if the **-DDEBUGGING** option was specified during the build process. The information provided can be very large, even on a relatively small regular expression. The **debugcolor** option prints out a color version if your terminal supports it. See Chapter 10 for more information on the effects of the **-D** switch.

The **eval** option enables regular expressions to contain the (**?{...}**) assertions, even if the regular expression contains variable interpolation:

```
use re 'eval';
```

Ordinarily this is disabled because it's seen as a security risk, and the pragma is ignored if the **use re 'taint'** pragma is in effect.

Individual pragmas can be switched off with **no re**.

sigtrap

The **sigtrap** pragma enables simple signal handling without the complexity of the normal signal handling routines:

```
use sigtrap;
```

The pragma supports three handlers: Two are supplied by the module itself (one provides a stack trace and the other just calls **die**), and the third is one that you supply yourself. Each option supplied to the module is processed in order, so the moment a signal name is identified, the signal handler is installed.

Without any options specified, the module defaults to the **stack-trace** and **old-interface-signals** options. The individual options are listed here:

```
use sigtrap qw/stack-trace HUP INT KILL/;
```

This generates a Perl stack trace to **STDERR** when the specified signals are received by the script. After the trace has been generated, the module calls **dump** to dump the core.

```
use sigtrap qw/die HUP INT KILL/;
```

This calls **croak** (see Appendix D), reporting the name of the message that was caught.

```
use sigtrap 'handler' => \&my_handler, HUP, INT, KILL;
```

This installs the handler **my_handler** for the specified signals.

The pragma defines some standard signal lists. If your system does not support one of the specified signals, the signal is ignored rather than producing an error.

```
normal-signals
```

These are signals that might ordinarily be trapped by any program: **HUP, INT, PIPE, TERM**.

```
error-signals
```

These are the signals that indicate a serious error: **ABRT, BUS, EMT, FPE, ILL, QUIT, SEGV, SYS, TRAP**.

```
old-interface-signals
```

The list of signals were trapped by default by the old **sigtrap** pragma. This is the list of signals that is used if you do not specify others: **ABRT, BUS, EMT, FPE, ILL, PIPE, QUIT, SEGV, SYS, TERM, TRAP.**

```
untrapped
```

This special option selects from the list of signals that follow or specifies all the signals that are not otherwise trapped or ignored.

```
any
```

applies handlers to all subsequently listed signals; this is the default.

See Chapter 9 for information on using signals as a way of debugging scripts.

subs

The **subs** pragma predeclares a function so that the function can be called without parentheses even before Perl has seen the full definition.

```
use subs qw(func);
```

This option can also be used to override internal functions by predefining the subroutines you want to override:

```
use subs qw(chdir);
chdir $message;
sub chdir
{
...
}
```

The overriding versions can be defined in the local file (as in the preceding example), or they can be imported from an external module, although it's possible to override functions from external modules by defining the function specifically to the import process, as in

```
use MyBuiltin 'chdir';
```

Obviously, you will need to define the **chdir** function in the **@EXPORT_OK** array as part of the module initialization. See Chapter 4 for more information on problems when defining and using subroutines.

The **subs** pragma is not block scoped, so the function definitions are global to the entire execution—as you'd expect.

vars

The **vars** pragma predeclares the variables defined in the list, which has the effect of preventing typographical warnings for variables not yet created. It is also the best way to declare variables that are to be shared with other modules if you do not want to use the **local** keyword. The use of **my** variables won't work since the variables will be localized strictly to the module. Because the variables are declared globally, it's also the easiest way to declare global variables that would otherwise trip up the **use strict** pragma.

```
use vars qw($scalar @array %hash);
```

Note that **vars** is not block-scoped. The variables are truly global within the current file.

## CHAPTER 9

Manual Debugging Techniques

Up to now, we've concentrated on how to identify and resolve bugs in your scripts, but without paying much attention to the actual process of debugging. The reason for this approach is not that debuggers aren't useful, but rather that I believe by understanding the language better, and with a greater appreciation about how the interpreter does its work, you can eliminate most bugs before they happen.

It's also true that Perl, for all of its freeform nature, does have tools that help to reduce the likelihood of those errors ever making it into your scripts in the first place. The previous chapter, which looked at the Perl warnings, and pragmas like **strict**, should have demonstrated that quite nicely. There's more to be said for stricter programming, planning, and documentation than you might think.

Although many people treat debuggers as the ultimate solution to the bugs, the truth is that they simply aren't. Debuggers don't find the bugs for you or explain to you why they happened or how to fix them. What they do provide is a useful tool for monitoring the execution of your script.

Debuggers also rely on the person running the debugged code to understand what is happening—not always practical if you are trying to help an end user identify a bug or problem in your code. In these situations you need something that is "inline"—that is, modifications to the source code that will enable you to trace the execution and any possible problems at any time without the use of a separate debugger.

In this chapter we're going to look at some of the "manual" techniques for debugging. All of these methods require you to modify your code and, therefore, require manual intervention. They also all produce output that will need to be separately studied before you can identify and trace a problem to a specific part of the application.

In addition to using the humble **print** statement, we'll also look at the **caller** function, which provides useful background information on the function calls that led up to the current statement, and at signals, which can provide a useful alternative to the direct debugging solutions. We'll also look at using **eval**, which allows us to execute statements within a separate Perl compartment. This feature can be used as an effective debugging tool. Finally, we look at how to create a separate debug log, which can be later examined without the effects of the failure affecting the user's experience.

Using **print**

To me, **print** statements have always seemed easy, and, providing you're careful, they can usually provide enough information for you to trace the bug without having to resort to a full-blown debugger. In fact the easiest way to use the humble **print** statement is during the development of a script—just inserting a quick "this variable has this value" is great way for you to check that your script is doing what you think.

We can also use the **print** statement as a way of reporting debugging information in the final release version of the script. You usually use this method in combination with a global variable, perhaps set via the script's command line, to enable or disable some simple debugging information. The benefits of a script that outputs debugging information in this way is that it allows both the user and programmer to perform a post-mortem debug on the script. The only place where **print** is often useless is within a loop, because it produces a voluminous amount of information that needs to be processed manually after the execution is complete. On occasion the loop mechanism can prove useful if you want to continually monitor a single variable as it is processed, or when you want to monitor the input or output to a filehandle.

Usage is pathetically simple. Using a statement such as

```
print "Got here!\n";
```

you can trace the execution path of a program. You can use the same basic layout for any valid piece of data that you want to output. Because you can print whatever you like, you can be quite explicit about the information:

```
print "Data before processing: $data\n";
#process some data
print "Fieldname: $field, data: $data, leftovers: $leftover\n";
```

More usually, though, you'll want to be a bit more explicit about the location in which the debug report occurred. Here you can use the **__LINE__** and **__FILE__** directives, which insert the line number and current file in which the message was printed, respectively. For example,

```
print __FILE__,'(',__LINE__,"): Data before processing $data\n";
```

might produce

```
process.pl(19): Data before processing Name: Martin
```

Note that the **__FILE__** and **__LINE__** tokens must be outside of quotes in order for them to be included in the printed line.

Quoting Information

When using **print** to output data it's a good idea to delimit the information that you are outputting. This limit helps to make it clear *exactly* what the actual data was. For example, the report line

```
process.pl(19): Data before processing Name: Martin
```

doesn't tell us if there are any trailing tabs or spaces to the information, which may or may not be important. A simple set of braces on either side of the data highlights the full data string:

```
process.pl(19): Data before processing [Name: Martin          ]
```

Here it's obvious that we have some trailing spaces or tabs.

Design Tip   *Don't use angle brackets, <>, to delimit information, especially when displaying debugging data within a CGI or other HTML script. The HTML parser may either identify the entry as a proper HTML tag or simply ignore the data entirely!*

You can also go one stage further and quote the special characters. The script below defines two functions—the interface to the whole thing is the **mapascii** function. This takes a string and then converts the special characters into their equivalent sequence:

```
sub mapasciichar
{
    my ($char) = @_;
```

```
@map = qw/
    \0 [SOH] [STX] [ETX] [EOT] [ENQ] [ACK] \a \b \t \n \v \f \r
    [SO] [SI] [DCE] [DC1] [DC2] [DC3] [DC4] [SYN] [ETB] [CAN]
    [EM] [SUB] [ESC] [FS] [GS] [RS] [US]
        /;

    return $map[ord($char)] if (exists($map[ord($char)]));
    return $char;
}

sub mapascii
{
    my ($string) = @_;
    join('',map { $_ = mapasciichar($_) } split //,$string);
}

print mapascii("Hello\nThis is a raw test\t\r\n"),"\n";
```

When you run the script, you get

```
Hello\nThis is a raw test\t\r\n
```

Other control characters will also be printed out with their ASCII names or in the format that you would normally use when interpolating special characters into strings.

Tracing Execution

The line and file directives that we saw earlier provide a useful way of isolating the exact script position that raised a particular error. Of course, it makes more sense to include a more detailed report, such that the output produced is as detailed as necessary and describes exactly what the script was doing at the point of the error. Here's the output from a **print** debugged script that processes a file. The output includes the contents of the variables that we are using to process the data:

```
$ foo.pl
Opened file (input.dat)
Read data (hello)
Read data (world)
Closed file
```

Remember at all times that when producing a debug report in this way you should be producing an annotated sequence of events. Doing this will help you and your users to understand what is going on without having to look back at the script.

Design Tip   *It's a good idea to switch off the file buffering when outputting this information, so that it's updated in real time, rather than chunks. The easiest way to do this is:*

```
use IO::Handle;
autoflush FILEHANDLE 1;
```

Using a Debug Option

The best way to employ the **print** statement is through a simple debug variable that can be switched on and off at will within the script, either by a simple modification or through the use of a command line argument. Doing this enables both the developer and the end-user to obtain extended debugging information when a problem is discovered.

Debug options are often employed by third-party modules as well; you set the value of a variable in the package at the initialization. For example, here is some output from a script that uses the **Net::FTP** module by Graham Barr:

```
grfile.pl ftp://martinb:foo@twinspark.mcslp.com/pub/filelist.txt
Net::FTP: Net::FTP(2.33)
Net::FTP:   Exporter
Net::FTP:   Net::Cmd(2.11)
Net::FTP:   IO::Socket::INET
Net::FTP:     IO::Socket(1.1603)
Net::FTP:        IO::Handle(1.1504)

Net::FTP=GLOB(0xb68ec)<<< 220 twinspark FTP server (UNIX(r) System V
Release 4.0) ready.
Net::FTP=GLOB(0xb68ec)>>> user martinb
Net::FTP=GLOB(0xb68ec)<<< 331 Password required for martinb.
Net::FTP=GLOB(0xb68ec)>>> PASS ....
Net::FTP=GLOB(0xb68ec)<<< 230 User martinb logged in.
Net::FTP=GLOB(0xb68ec)>>> CWD /pub
Net::FTP=GLOB(0xb68ec)<<< 250 CWD command successful.
Net::FTP=GLOB(0xb68ec)>>> PORT 198,112,10,130,128,13
Net::FTP=GLOB(0xb68ec)<<< 200 PORT command successful.
Net::FTP=GLOB(0xb68ec)>>> RETR filelist.txt
Net::FTP=GLOB(0xb68ec)<<< 150 ASCII data connection for filelist.txt
(198.112.10.130,32781) (1328 bytes).
Net::FTP=GLOB(0xb68ec)<<< 226 ASCII Transfer complete.
Net::FTP=GLOB(0xb68ec)>>> QUIT
```

24x7

You can create your own debug setting variables within your own scripts and modules. All you have to do is create a global variable with **use**, **vars**, or **our** (for Perl 5.6) to hold the debug setting and then append each debug statement with a suitable **if** statement:

```
print "Got an error whilst parsing, probably ignorable\n" if ($debug);
```

You can also use the same principle to offer different levels of debugging information:

```
print "Read a line from $source\n" if ($debug);
print "Input: [$line]\n" if ($debug > 1);
```

You can also use the same method within a module to set the debug option. For example,

```
package MyModule;
require Exporter;
@ISA = qw/Exporter/;
@EXPORT = qw/setdebug readfile/;

use vars qw/$debug/;
$debug = 0;

sub setdebug
{
    my ($deblevel) = @_;
    $debug = $deblevel;
}
```

From the calling script you then have two choices: either set the value directly:

```
$MyModule::debug = 1;
```

or use the **setdebug** function to set the debug level. Similar tricks can be employed on a function-by-function basis:

```
sub readfile
{
    my ($infile, %options) = @_;
    my $debug = $options{debug} if (exists($options{debug}));
...
}
```

Now, just supply the debug level to the function when you call it; for example,

```
$source = readfile($infile, debug => 1);
```

Design Tip   *Try to avoid exporting the debug variable so that you can selectively turn on debugging for individual modules and/or function calls without affecting other modules. Further, don't combine the use of a global debug variable and a function-specific debug variable, just in case in you inadvertently switch on debugging for the entire script.*

Using caller

Printing your own debug information requires a lot of manual entry if you are trying to trace the execution path through a program. For each **print** statement you include in your source, you will need to include a reference about the location of the statement in order for your debug output to make sense.

To ease the process, you can use the **caller** function, which returns the current context information for a subroutine. The information includes details about the subroutine (or **eval** or **require**) statement:

```
caller EXPR
caller
```

In a scalar context, the function simply returns the package name. In a list context (without arguments), the function returns the package name, file name, and line of the caller of the current subroutine or **eval** or **require** statement:

```
($package, $filename, $line) = caller;
```

If **EXPR** is specified, **caller** returns extended information. The value of **EXPR** should be the number of subroutine calls on the stack to go back to before the current one. That is, if you specify a value of *one*, the parent subroutine information will be printed, a value of *two* will print the grandparent subroutine, and so forth. The information returned is

```
($package, $filename, $line, $subroutine,
 $hasargs, $wantarray, $evaltext, $is_require) = caller($i);
```

The **$evaltext** and **$is_require** values are only returned when the subroutine being examined is actually the result of an **eval()** statement. As an example, examine this script:

```
sub bar
{
    Top::top();
}

bar();

package Top;

sub top
{
    my $level = 0;
    print "Top of the world, Ma!\n";
    while ((($package, $file, $line,
            $subname, $hasargs, $wantarray) = caller($level++)))
    {
        $hasargs    = $hasargs    ? 'Yes' : 'No';
        if (defined($wantarray))
        {
            $wantarray = 'Yes';
        }
        else
        {
            $wantarray = 'No';
        }
        print <<EOF;
Stack:
        Package: $package
           File: $file
           Line: $line
```

```
        Subroutine: $subname
    Has Arguments?: $hasargs
      Wants Array?: $wantarray
EOF
    }
}
```

When the code is executed, the resultant information shows the stack trace for the **top** function, including its original call from **main** and from the **bar** function:

```
Top of the world, Ma!
Stack:
            Package: main
               File: ././t.pl
               Line: 5
         Subroutine: Top::top
     Has Arguments?: Yes
       Wants Array?: No
Stack:
            Package: main
               File: ././t.pl
               Line: 8
         Subroutine: main::bar
     Has Arguments?: Yes
       Wants Array?: No
```

The information provided should enable you to pinpoint the location within a script. If you want to report the information to a log, you may want to introduce a wrapper function like this one:

```
sub callerlog
{
    my $reference = shift;
    open(DATA,">>caller.log") || return;
    print DATA join(' ',@_),":$reference\n";
    close(DATA);
}
```

Then to call the function, you would use a line such as

```
callerlog("Writing data",caller());
```

to report the information for the current stack trace. Note that you can't directly use the information from **callerlog**, since doing so would introduce its own frame of information at location zero within the stack. You could, however, use a modified form of the **callerlog** function that returns the stack trace from frame one onward:

```
sub callerlog
{
    my $reference = shift;
    my $level = 1;
```

```
    while ((((@data) = caller($level++)))
    {
        print join(' ',@data),":$reference\n";
    }
}
```

The information provided by **caller** is actually used by the Perl debugger to provide the tracing information used in the debugging environment.

Using **eval**

The **eval** function provides a very simple way of checking certain events without affecting the overall execution of your script. In essence, the **eval** function just initiates a new instance of the Perl interpreter in order to evaluate a particular string or block. It's used in all sorts of places within Perl—including in the debugger where it allows you to execute those arbitrary statements—but it can also be employed as a debugging tool.

Because **eval** evaluates a Perl statement or block within its own interpreter, we can use it in situations that might otherwise cause the Perl interpreter to fail. This process works because an embedded **eval** block reports any errors raised by a call to **die** through the **$@** variable. In fact, any unexpected exit is reported through **eval** to the **$@** special variable.

We can demonstrate this with a simple **eval** block used to test the existence of a particular module:

```
eval
{
    require Net::FTP;
}
print "Error: Module failed to load ($@)" if $@;
```

outputs

```
$ perl eval.pl
Failed to load Net::FTP: Can't locate Net/FTP.pm in @INC (@INC contains:
/usr/local/lib/perl5/5.6.0/i686-linux /usr/local/lib/perl5/5.6.0
/usr/local/lib/perl5/site_perl/5.6.0/i686-linux
/usr/local/lib/perl5/site_perl/5.6.0 /usr/local/lib/perl5/site_perl .) at
eval.pl line 1.
```

Armed with this information, we can now check anything (except statements executed at compile time, such as **use**) that might raise an error and trap and report the problem.

The same operation can be followed for more simple statements, such as for checking a possible divide by zero error. You could do this:

```
if ($b == 0)
{
    print "Can't divide by zero\n";
}
else
```

```
{
    print "Result is ", $a/$b,"\n";
}
```

But it's slightly more convenient to do this:

```
eval { $a/$b };
print $@ if $@;
```

Here's another example, this time of a function that uses an **eval** to execute its statements so that it can return a single error back to the caller instead of simply calling **die** and executing the script completely:

```
if ($error = writedata("debug", "some error text\n"))
{
    print("Raised an error writing to the log: \n",$error,
        "Continuing...\n");
}


sub writedata
{
    my ($file, $data) = @_;

    eval
    {
        open (FILE, ">$file") or die "Can't open file ($file): $!";
        print FILE $data or die "Can't write to file ($file): $!";
        close(FILE) or die "Can't close file ($file): $!";
    };
    return $@ if ($@);
}
```

Here we've got essentially three places where we could potentially drop out of the script. By embedding all three statements into an **eval** block and then checking the return value from the whole function, we've managed to trap what might otherwise be a critical failure into something that we can safely recover from. This capability becomes incredibly useful in situations where you need to continue working even if a particular option fails, but you want to avoid producing your own exception and error handling system.

In this example, just running the script produces

```
Raised an error writing to the log:
Can't open file (debug): Permission denied at eval.pl line 15.
Continuing...
```

In this case we've just ignored the error, but you could redirect the sequence and error-report to a Tk widget or another HTML page if this was a CGI script.

Design Tip *The same trick also provides an ideal way of converting an existing script from a command-line basis to a CGI or Tk basis without having to make major changes to the code. Instead of changing the individual cells to 'die', you can place program segments into an eval, and then use a CGI or Tk-based error function to report the problem. For example, with a standard (non-eval) **writedata** function, we can place the eval outside function call and then use the dialog function to report an error through Tk.*

```
eval
{
    writedata("debug", "some error text\n")
}
dialog("Raised an error writing to the log: \n",$error,
"Continuing...\n") if $@;
```

Signals

Most people are aware of the tricks available when using the **alarm** function, which raises the **SIGALRM** signal when the specified period expires. For example, we can use the **alarm** function to provide a timeout when entering information:

```
use IO::Handle;

$name = 'unknown';

eval
{
    local $SIG{ALRM} = sub { die "alarm\n" };
    autoflush STDOUT 1;
    print "What is your name [unknown] ? ";
    alarm 10;
    $name = <STDIN>;
    alarm 0;
};
if ($@ && $@ eq "alarm\n")
{
    print "(using default...)\n";
}
print "Hello $name\n";
```

We can also use signals as a way of indicating a particular problem without resorting to one of the built-in functions or a custom error function. There are also two special signals supported in Perl that can be used to trap **die** and **warn** calls.

Signals as Exceptions

It's actually possible to use signals as a form of exception—instead of calling **warn** or **die** or some other function to indicate an error, you instead raise one of the available user signals to trap and indicate an error. This procedure can be useful in situations when you want to jump to a user-configurable error handler rather than rely on a fixed function. To do this, all you need to do is create a suitable signal handler, install it, and then use **kill**. For example,

```
sub error_handler
{
    print STDERR "Trapped an error!\n";
}

$SIG{USR1} = \&error_handler;

open(FILE, "hhhdhd") or kill USR1, $$;
```

The only problem with this method is that you cannot easily exchange information. The only data available with the signal handler is the name of the signal raised that triggered the handler in the first place. You could use a global variable, but then operation becomes tricky if you decide to use the system within a multimodule script. A much better solution is to employ the __WARN__ and __DIE__ signals and then continue to use the **warn** and **die** functions.

The __WARN__ and __DIE__ Signals

The special signals __WARN__ and __DIE__ can be used to execute statements when **warn** and **die** are called. This method allows you greater control over exactly what happens when these two functions are called. Normally, **warn** reports the supplied error to **STDERR** and then continues, while a call to **die** reports the error and then calls **exit()**. This automatic operation causes a problem if you want to close files safely or even to report the problem to the user directly and still use the "standard" error trapping tools.

You can of course use any of the tricks we've seen above—both the **eval** and exception signals will work in most cases, but they still require micro-management of your scripts in order for the processes to work effectively. By using these two signals instead, you can trap errors dynamically and even make decisions about how to report the error without making major modifications to your code.

Using $SIG{__WARN__}

The **warn** handler is called whenever the **warn** function is called. The handler is passed any arguments that are passed to the **warn** function, but the **warn** function does not actually operate—the handler acts as a complete replacement for the normal operation of the function. For example,

```
sub warn_handler
{
    print STDERR "Woah - trapped a warning!\n\t",@_;
}

$SIG{__WARN__} = \&warn_handler;

warn "Something went awry\n";
warn "Something went awry again\n";
```

Running this produces the following output:

```
Woah - trapped a warning!
    Something went awry
Woah - trapped a warning!
    Something went awry again
```

You can see that the message is printed out only once—in this case by the embedded call to **print** in the signal handler.

The **__WARN__** handler is best employed when you want to provide an alternative way of reporting or recording an error. You'll find examples elsewhere in this chapter for reporting information directly to logs; all you need to do is install a handler at the top of your script that traps and handles the warning in an alternative fashion. For example, here's a handler that uses the **writelog** function (see "Using a Logging Function," below) to report the error to a log, instead of to the screen:

```
sub warn_handler
{
    writelog("warning: (%s)",join(', ',@_));
}

$SIG{__WARN__} = \&warn_handler;
```

We don't need to make any further modifications to the code (aside from adding the **writelog** function definition). From now on, all calls to **warn** will trigger this handler and force the output to be written to a file instead of **STDERR**. Similar tricks allow us to report warnings through Tk:

```
sub warn_handler
{
    dialog(undef,"Warning", join(', ',@_),
           'warning',1,"OK");
}
```

See Chapter 7 for an example of the **dialog** function.

Using $SIG{__DIE__}

Unlike **__WARN__**, the **__DIE__** handler merely acts as an interloper into the process—the handler is called, but the **die** function continues as normal, both printing out the error and calling **exit()**. Consider the following script:

```
sub die_handler
{
    print "Woah - trapped a call die\nTrying to exit gracefully...\n";
}


$SIG{__DIE__} = \&die_handler;
die "Something went completely wrong\n";
```

Note that the handler will be passed the text as formatted by **die**—this means we can adapt the text and then call **die** again to actually output the updated version of the text. For example, the line

```
die "Just couldn't it anymore!";
```

generates

```
Just couldn't it anymore! at sigdiemod.pl line 7.
```

but add a handler:

```
sub die_handler
{
    my ($error)  = @_;
    die "Trapped an error: $error";
}

$SIG{__DIE__} = \&die_handler;
```

and the error becomes

```
Trapped an error: Just couldn't it anymore! at sigdiemod.pl line 9.
```

The **die_handler** function will be called only once, as the signal handler is reset after the first call.

The **__DIE__** handler is best used when you want to gracefully exit from a script—perhaps providing a simple prompt to the user and safely closing files or network connections before finally allowing the script to die. It's true that you could use an **END** block for this process, but doing so means that the closing statements are executed *after* **die** has actually been called. It also relies on the functions, filehandles, and other artifacts being accessible to the **END** block at the time of termination.

Design Tip — *Currently the __DIE__ (and __WARN__) handler is called even within an* **eval** *block. This can cause problems as the $@ variable may not yet be populated, so consider using the $^S variable to check the status of the interpreter at the point the handler is called. The $^S variable will be true if the statements are being called from within an* **eval** *string or block.*

Writing a Log

There are times when you'll need to write debugging style information to something other than the standard output and error filehandles. In these situations you can redirect the information directly to another file—we've already seen examples of this with the **caller** function earlier in this chapter.

There are a number of different ways in which we can do this. At the simplest level you can just use **print** to send the output somewhere else. For a more comprehensive solution you should think about redirection. This approach will ensure that **warn** and **die** also output their information to the log, rather to than to the real **STDERR**. The final solution is to report information to the **syslog** daemon on a Unix machine, or to the Event Log on a Windows machine. This procedure is useful for scripts that play a vital role in an administration environment where you need the information to be reported to a central, rather than an application-specific, log.

Redirecting **STDOUT/STDERR**

The simplest way of creating a log without seriously affecting the output of your script is to simply redirect the default **STDOUT** and **STDERR** to somewhere else, which you can do like this:

```
open(SECOUT,">&STDOUT");
open(SECERR,">&STDERR");
open(STDOUT,">stdlog.txt");
open(STDERR,">stderr.txt");
```

Now to print to the real standard output, you need to send output to **SECOUT**.

 *If you're going to redirect the complete output of a script, consider placing the redirection statement into a **BEGIN** block, so that everything is redirected to the log files, even if an error is raised by an imported module.*

In fact, it's probably best to follow those statements with

```
select SECOUT;
```

to ensure that standard **print** and other calls send their output to the real standard output and not the redirected one.

 It's a good idea to switch off the file buffering when sending information to a log; doing this prevents overruns and ensures that data is written even if the script crashes.

Since you will have control over the filehandle on which you provide the user interface, but not the filehandle used to print the debugging information from the contributed module, redirecting only **STDERR** is often a more practical solution.

It's also possible, using this method, to create a log file of the debug output you create. This file is especially useful when using an indirectly accessed script, such as that used on a web server. Here, printing the debug information to the standard output will cause the information to be included as part of the document that is sent back to the user's web browser. Instead you can redirect to a file.

Using a Logging Function

If you don't want to redirect the **STDOUT** and **STDERR** filehandles, the other solution is to create a function that opens and then writes the information you supply directly to a log file.

```
sub writelog
{
    my ($format,@rgs) = @_;
    open(LOGFILE,">>debug.log")
        or die "Can't open debug log!: $!\n";
    printf LOGFILE ($format,@args);
    close LOGFILE;
}
```

Now you can just make calls to the **writelog** function:

```
writelog("Had an error in the line %s from %s", $line, $file);
```

A more efficient solution is to use a global variable as the filehandle and then change the function so that it only opens the file if it isn't already open:

```
my $logfile = undef;

sub writelog
{
    my ($format,@rgs) = @_;
    unless(defined($logfile))
    {
        open($logfile,">>debug.log")
            or die "Can't open debug log!: $!\n";
    }
    printf $logfile ($format,@args);
}
```

24x7

Using a debug log is the best way of capturing debugging information in non-interactive scripts. To get the best use out of the function, make sure you also record the time that the error was reported, the process ID, and, if relevant, the machine and/or user name. That way when you examine the log it should be clearer both when and why the error occurred.

Now the file will be opened once—when the first call to **writelog** is made—and then just appended to for each subsequent call. Note that we've removed the call to **close**; I suggest that you instead put it into an end block:

```
END
{
    close($logfile) if (defined($logfile));
}
```

Doing this will ensure that the file is properly closed when the script terminates.

> **Design Tip** *If you like, you can also put a call to the **warn** function within your own **writelog** function, thereby ensuring that the error is logged to a file and reported to the user during runtime.*

Reporting to syslog

Perl comes with the **Sys::Syslog** module, which provides a very simple interface for reporting information to the syslog system, which in turn is written to the system logs, often held at /var/log/syslog (or similar). The best way to use the system if you intend to log information in this way is to call the **openlog** function at the start of your script:

```
openlog($myprog, 'cons,pid', 'user')
```

The first argument is the identity of the program. This string is prepended to each message within the log. The second argument defines the options used when writing to the log, defined as a comma-separated list of words. The available options are shown in Table 9-1. The last argument defines the facility that the error affects. For example, you might log an error with a user's script with the **user** option, or a problem with authorization to the authorization/security facility. Again, keeping in mind that these are system-dependent, Table 9-2 lists some likely candidates.

Option	Description
pid	Include the process ID with the message.
ndelay	Open the connection to the syslog system immediately, rather than waiting until the first message is reported.
cons	Send the error directly to the console if the log cannot be written.
nowait	Do not wait for children forked to log messages on the console. This option should be used by processes that enable notification of child termination via **$SIG{CLD}**, because **syslog** might otherwise block, waiting for a child whose exit status has already been collected.

Table 9.1   Syslog Logging Options

Facility	Description
authpriv	Security/authorization messages
cron	Scheduling (cron and at)
daemon	Other system daemons
kern	Kernel messages
lpr	Line printer subsystem
mail	mail subsystem
news	USENET news subsystem
syslog	Messages generated internally by **syslog**
user	Generic user-level messages
uucp	UUCP subsystem level

Table 9.2   Syslog Facilities

To actually report an error you make a call to the **syslog** function. This uses the options you've supplied when the log was opened in addition to the arguments you supply. For example, consider the line

```
syslog('debug',"Got the error %m from %s", $function);
```

The first argument is the priority of the message. It's actually a combination of the facility and priority settings that determine how and where the information is reporting. The **syslog** system is configured through the syslog.conf file that determines what the **syslog** daemon does when a message is sent to the system. Priorities supported by Perl are listed in Table 9-3.

The second argument is a format, as defined by **printf**, which formats the message; any remaining arguments are applied to the corresponding elements in the **printf** format. The only difference is that the format string **%m** is replaced with the string value of **$!**.

Priority	Description
emerg	system is unusable
alert	action must be taken immediately
crit	critical conditions
err	error conditions
warning	warning conditions
notice	normal, but significant, condition
info	informational message
debug	debug-level message

Table 9.3   Syslog Message Priorities

Once you've finished writing to the log, use **closelog** to close the connection. As a complete example, the snippet

```
use Sys::Syslog;

openlog('perl', 'cons,pid', 'user');
syslog('warning' ,'Something happened');
closelog();
```

produces the following entry on a Solaris system:

```
Jul 19 11:13:57 twinspark perl[2686]: Something happened
```

Reporting to the Windows NT/2000 Event Log

The Windows NT Event Log is a central logging system similar in principle to the **syslog** system, but slightly more advanced. Primarily, the **Event Log** is used to record errors and warnings, but it can also be used just to store simple informational messages and also audit events—that is, those events configured by the administrator to be specifically tracked and recorded.

The Event Log also stores a lot more information than **syslog** does in its standard format. For example, the **syslog** system can be configured and set to report the computer and user information, but it's not enforced. With the Event Log this information is automatically recorded. In addition, you can include any data that was being processed at the time; extended message strings, categories, and event types.

The number of event logs on your machine is dependent on the configuration; the standard logs for both Windows NT and Windows 2000 are shown in Table 9-4. Other logs can be set up by the system to log specific OS services and applications. The most likely log you will want to use is the Application log, although for some specific instances the System or Security logs might be more appropriate.

Log	Platform	Description
Application	NT, 2000	Used to store information, warnings, and errors raised by individual applications.
Security	NT, 2000	Records successful and unsuccessful network login attempts, security breaches (when recognized), and attempts by users to access a secured resource.
System	NT, 2000	OS-specific errors and warnings such as the failure to start a service or communicate with a device.

Table 9.4   Event Logs Supported by Windows NT/2000

Log	Platform	Description
Directory Service	2000	Errors/warnings/information raised by the Windows 2000 Active Directory system.
DNS Server	2000	Errors/warnings/information raised by the DNS server, including inability to resolve and address, contact a named server, or communicate with one of the root servers.
File Replication Service	2000	Errors/warnings/information raised by the file replication service used to distribute files over a Windows 2000 network.

Table 9.4   Event Logs Supported by Windows NT/2000 *(continued)*

To report an error to the event log system, you need to create a new **Win32::EventLog** object and then use the supplied methods to actually introduce a new report to the system. The general format for creating the **Event Log** is

```
use Win32::EventLog;
$object = new Win32::EventLog(EVENTLOG [, SERVER])
```

The **new** class method returns an **Event Log** object, opening the **EVENTLOG** on **SERVER**. The **EVENTLOG** argument should be supplied as a string using one of the standard identifiers listed in Table 9-4. If **SERVER** is not specified or is blank, then the log is opened on the local machine. For example, to open the application log on the local machine:

```
$eventlog = new Win32::EventLog('Application');
```

To actually introduce a log entry, you need to call the **Report** method. This accepts a reference to a hash that contains the information that you want to report. The keys of the hash are shown in Table 9-5, and Table 9-6 shows the constants exported by the module that can be used with the **EventType** key.

Key	Description
Category	An application-specific category number.
Computer	The name of the computer from which the event was reported.
Data	The event data reported—this is displayed in the data portion of the event log viewer entry.

Table 9.5   Hash Keys for an Event Log Entry

Key	Description
EventID	An application-specific ID number. The ID is normally looked up in the corresponding DLL for the event message, but doesn't apply to a Perl script.
EventType	An integer relating to one of the constants shown in Table 9-6.
Source	The name of the application or service that reported the entry.
Strings	Application-specific text strings. This is the error string reported within the description for the event log entry.

Table 9.5 Hash Keys for an Event Log Entry *(continued)*

For example, the snippet

```
use Win32::EventLog;

my $eventlog = new Win32::EventLog('Application');

%event = (Data => 'Some data',
          Source => 'Perl',
          EventID => 1,
          EventType => EVENTLOG_WARNING_TYPE,
          Strings => 'I failed to pick up some info I was expecting',
          Category => 0);

$eventlog->Report(\%event);
```

will log an Application error into the **Event Log**. Note here that I've used a hash and then called the **Report** method instead of embedding the information directly—it's quicker and easier to use the same hash and update only the relevant information when you need to report a new error.

You can view event log entries using the **Event Viewer** application. Figure 9-1 shows the entry as reported under Windows 2000.

Event Type	Description
EVENTLOG_ERROR_TYPE	The event was an error.
EVENTLOG_WARNING_TYPE	The event was a warning.
EVENTLOG_INFORMATION_TYPE	The event indicates a particular piece of information, but is not a warning or an error.

Table 9.6 Event Log Entry Types

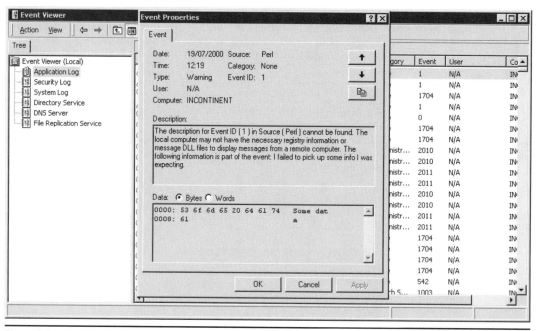

Figure 9.1 A Perl-sourced event error.

## CHAPTER 10

The Perl Debuggers

A t the start of the previous chapter we looked at the different possible ways of debugging an application. Real debuggers of course work on different principles than those given in the last chapter and, to a greater or lesser extent, work on different principles than those of the Perl debugger.

For a start, most modern language debuggers work in two basic ways: by postmortem debugging or by live debugging of the application. A *postmortem debugger* studies a core dump or other executable image created during the execution process. Using the information within that file in combination with the original application, it can determine the problems within the application itself.

Generally postmortem debugging is of use only when an application crashes, although there are systems that will monitor execution and post-process the details. There are also tools such as **truss** under Solaris that will monitor system calls. Postmortem techniques can also be used for other application improvements—see the Perl profiler in Chapter 12, for example.

Live debugging makes use of a separate application that monitors the execution of your application as it proceeds. Unlike postmortem debugging , with live debugging we can monitor the execution of the application in real time, monitoring individual lines and even monitoring and evaluating expressions based on the functions and variables available within the current scope of the program.

Perl doesn't lend itself well to postmortem debugging. Aside from the profiler and other similar tools as well as the techniques shown in the previous chapter, there's not a lot we can do with a Perl script after the event. For a start, postmortem really makes more sense when you are armed with a core file after a crash, something that doesn't, as a rule, happen in Perl unless there's a problem with the interpreter itself.

Perl does, however, come with a mechanism for debugging a running script. In fact, the debugger itself is just another Perl script that allows you to interactively monitor the execution of your own script. Most usefully of all, because it is a Perl script and because Perl is an interpreted, and not compiled, language, we can execute any Perl statement we like as part of the debugging process.

In this chapter we'll look at the two main debuggers available for Perl—the built-in debugger and the ActiveState Debugger, which is available as part of the Perl Development Kit. Before we look at those two debuggers, we'll look at the principles of using any debugger.

Using a Debugger

There are three basic tools available to you when you are using a debugger: watches, stepping, and breakpoints. We'll have a look at each of these tools and describe how they can best be used to help you when debugging your scripts.

Watches

Watches are the variables that you want to monitor as you execute a script. You set a watch on a variable, and then, for each statement that is executed, you are shown the corresponding value of the variable. By using watches you can monitor how a variable is updated and isolate those instances where a variable is modified without you realizing it.

Stepping

Stepping is the action of executing Perl statements, either individually or as a group (as when you execute an entire function call in one go). By stepping you can monitor the execution and variables used and affected by a statement on a line-by-line basis. There are three basic step commands, although some debuggers will offer some additional options:

- **Step Into** executes the current statement, following the execution of any functions or methods found within the statement. Execution goes as far as calling the function or method, bypassing any variable initialization, and stops at the first executable statement within the called function.

- **Step Over** executes the current statement. Any functions or methods that are called are executed without being processed by the debugger, so execution stops on the next executable statement within the current file.

- **Step Out** continues execution until the current function or method ends. Execution stops at the next executable statement, either within the next function call of the current line from the calling script or on the next statement from the caller.

The advantage of stepping over breakpoints is that it allows you to monitor each line individually. This capability is particularly useful when you want to study a sequence or each iteration of a loop in detail.

Breakpoints

Breakpoints offer a different approach. Instead of laboriously stepping through each line of a script, you can set a breakpoint at a future point in the script and then start execution. The Debugger will execute all of the lines up until the given breakpoint. In addition, you can also set a breakpoint to be triggered only when a variable matches a certain condition.

For example, imagine you are having trouble within a loop, but only when the loop counter reaches 1,000; you can set a breakpoint to be triggered when the counter value is greater than or equal to 1,000. The loop will parse and execute 1,000 times, and then the debugger will halt to allow you to process each individual line until you trace the problem.

The Perl Debugger

The Perl Debugger is a bit of a misnomer. The debugger is in fact just a suite of modules and a script that ends up sitting almost simultaneously between and behind the script you are attempting to run and the Perl interpreter that will execute it. By sitting in this position, the debugger script can extract the individual lines of your source file and incrementally execute each one—the stepping process.

In addition, the debugger allows us to set watches and breakpoints and provides us with a way of directly executing Perl statements that can interface to the underlying script. For example, when reaching a breakpoint you might want to perform a simple calculation on a value generated by the script.

The main difference between Perl and many other languages is that we can run the debugger directly—in fact straight from the command line. There isn't a separate application for doing the debugger, and there's no reason to make any changes to your code.

The User Interface

To start the debugger, you need to specify the **–d** option on the command line to the Perl interpreter:

```
perl -d t.pl
```

Alternatively, it can be used with a dummy **–e** statement to drop you straight into a dummy debugger environment:

```
perl -de 1
```

Once the debugger is invoked, you are placed into it at the first executable statement within the defined script:

```
Loading DB routines from perl5db.pl version 1.0401
Emacs support available.

Enter h or `h h' for help.

main::(-e:1):    1
  DB<1>
```

The value in the angle brackets—1, in this example—is the number of the debugger command. This can be recalled with the **!** debugger command. The number of angle brackets shows the current depth of the debugger. Calling a new subroutine via an **s**, **n**, or **t** command will introduce a new set of brackets as a new execution path is created within the script. You can specify multiline commands by using the \ character, which has the effect of escaping the newline that would ordinarily end the command.

Rather confusingly, the line that is displayed before the prompt is the line that is *about* to be executed, rather than the line that has been executed. Therefore, on first entry into the debugger, no lines (other than compiler directives and package imports) have actually been executed.

The normal operation is to set a breakpoint on a line or statement that you want to monitor and then use the **T** command to produce a stack trace. For example,

```
  DB<4> b 16
  DB<5> r
Top of the world, Ma!
main::callerlog(t.pl:16):               print join(' ',@data),":$reference\n";
  DB<6> T
. = main::callerlog('Printed Message') called from file 't.pl' line 23
. = main::top() called from file 't.pl' line 5
. = main::bar() called from file 't.pl' line 8
```

The actual execution process for each line in the script is as follows:

1. Check for a breakpoint.
2. Print the line, using tracing if the **AutoTrace** option has been set.
3. Execute any actions defined.
4. Prompt the user if there is a breakpoint or single step.
5. Evaluate the line.
6. Print any modified watchpoints.

Once the execution has halted, you can step through the script, either by every line, using the **s** command, or by each line, stepping over subroutine calls using the **n** command.

Note that compile-time statements are not trapped by the debugger, which means that those enclosed in a **BEGIN** block, or statements such as **use**, are not stopped by the debugger. The best method for trapping them is to specify the value of the **$DB::single** variable that is part of the Perl debugger. Although it requires modification of the code, it does not affect anything if the debugger is not running. A value of 1 for the **$DB::single** variable is equivalent to having just typed **s** to the debugger. A value of 2 indicates that **n** should be used. Alternatively, you can monitor the status of the commands using the **AutoTrace** option.

You can set watchpoints, which display the value of a variable if it has been modified in the just executed statement. For example, in the script

```
while (<DATA>)
{
    chomp;
...
}
```

you could set a watchpoint for $_, which would print the value of $_ for each iteration of the loop.

Debugger Commands

The debugger supports a wide range of commands that are outlined below. As a general rule, anything that is not immediately identified as a command, or alternatively any input line beginning with a space, is interpreted as a Perl statement that is executed via an **eval** function.

> **Tip** *Any debugger command can be piped through an external program by using the pipe symbol, just as at a Unix shell prompt. This feature is primarily useful for parsing output through a pager, but could be used for anything.*

h

```
h COMMAND
h
```

Prints out help information for **COMMAND** or general help if **COMMAND** is not specified. If you use the special **h h** command, a condensed version of the general help is printed—it should fit onto a standard screen without scrolling. See the **O** command later for details on how to change the default paging program.

p

```
p expr
```

Prints the evaluated value of **expr** using the standard print built-in function. The value of **expr** can include variables and functions defined within the current script being debugged.

The usual rules for the print function apply—nested structures and objects will not be printed correctly. (See the **x** command for a more useful version of this.)

x

```
x expr
```

Evaluates its expression in list context and dumps out the result in a pretty-printed fashion. Nested data structures are printed out recursively, unlike with the print function. See the options in Table 10-1.

V

```
V PACKAGE VARS
V PACKAGE
V
```

Displays the list of variables specified in **VARS** within the package **PACKAGE** if both are specified. If **VARS** is omitted, all variables for **PACKAGE** are printed. If no arguments are specified, it prints out all the variables for the **main** package. Information is intelligently printed, with the values of arrays and hashes and nested structures being formatted before output. Control characters are also converted into a printable format.

If you specify the variables, you should omit the variable type characters (**$**, **@**, or **%**). You can also specify a pattern to match, or a pattern not to match, using **~PATTERN** and **!PATTERN** arguments.

X

```
X VARS
X
```

Same as **V VARS** for the current package.

T

```
T
```

Prints a stack backtrace, as determined by the **caller** function and the value of the current stack frame array. See the section "Debugger Interface" later in this chapter for some examples.

s

```
s EXPR
s
```

Executes only the next statement (single step), following subroutine calls if necessary. If **EXPR** is supplied, it then executes **EXPR** once, descending into subroutine calls as necessary. This process can be used to drop directly into a subroutine outside of the normal execution process.

n

```
n EXPR
n
```

Single-steps the next statement, but steps over the subroutines instead of stepping into them. If **EXPR** is specified, any subroutines are stepped into.

Carriage Return

Repeats the last **n** or **s** command.

c

```
c LINE
c SUB
c
```

Continues execution (all statements) until the next configured breakpoint of the end of the script. If **LINE** or **SUB** is specified, then a breakpoint, active for one break only, is inserted before **LINE** or the subroutine **SUB**.

l

```
l
```

Lists the next page of lines for the current script from the current line.

```
l MIN+INCR
```

Lists **INCR+1** lines from the line specified by **MIN**.

```
l MIN-MAX
```

Lists the lines from line **MIN** to **MAX**.

`l LINE`

Lists the line **LINE**.

`l SUB`

Lists the first page of lines for the subroutine **SUB**.

`-`

Lists the previous page of lines.

w

```
w LINE
w
```

Lists a page of lines surrounding the current line, or **LINE** if specified.

`.`

Returns the line pointer to the last line executed and prints it out.

f

`f FILENAME`

Changes the file currently being viewed to **FILENAME**. The value of **FILENAME** should match either the main script or the name of a file identifiable within the **%INC** variable. If still not found, it is interpreted as a regular expression that should resolve to a file name.

/PATTERN/

Searches forward within the current file for the regular expression **PATTERN**.

?PATTERN?

Searches backward within the current file for the regular expression **PATTERN**.

L

Lists all the currently set breakpoints and actions.

S

```
S PATTERN
S !PATTERN
S
```

Lists all subroutines matching the regular expression **PATTERN**. If **PATTERN** is preceded by an exclamation mark, then lists those not matching the regular expression **PATTERN**.

t

```
t EXPR
t
```

Toggles trace mode. Trace mode enables the printing of each statement as it is executed. If **EXPR** is specified, traces the execution of **EXPR**. See also the **AutoTrace** option in Table 10-1.

For example, the script

```
sub one { 1 };
sub two { 2 };
print one()*two();
```

prints out only the final value of *two*. With trace mode switched on, it also prints the statements

```
DB<1> r
main::one(t2.pl:1):    sub one { 1 };
main::two(t2.pl:2):       sub two { 2 };
2
```

b

```
b LINE CONDITION
b LINE
b CONDITION
b
```

Sets a breakpoint on the current line when no arguments are specified. If **LINE** is specified, then the breakpoint is set on the specified line. If **CONDITION** is specified, then each time the breakpoint is reached, it breaks execution only if the condition resolves to true. The **CONDITION** does not use an **if** statement; it is purely the test. If you use **/PATTERN/**, the breakpoint breaks only if the statement matches the regular expression **PATTERN**.

```
b SUB CONDITION
b SUB
```

Sets a breakpoint on subroutine **SUB**, using **CONDITION** if specified.

```
b postpone SUB CONDITION
b postpone SUB
```

Sets a breakpoint on subroutine **SUB** only after it has been compiled.

```
b compile SUB
```

Sets a breakpoint on the first executable statement of the subroutine **SUB** after it has been compiled.

```
b load FILENAME
```

Sets a breakpoint at the first executed line of **FILENAME**.

d

```
d LINE
d
```

Deletes the breakpoint specified on **LINE**, or the breakpoint on the line that is about to be executed if **LINE** is omitted.

D

Deletes all the currently set breakpoints.

a

```
a LINE COMMAND
a COMMAND
```

Sets the action specified by **COMMAND** to be executed before the current line, or the line specified by **LINE**, is executed. For example, this can be used to print the value of a variable before it is used in a calculation.

A

Deletes all currently installed actions.

W

```
W EXPR
W
```

Sets a watch on the variable specified by **EXPR**. A change to the specified variable will be printed before the next line to be executed is printed. If **EXPR** is not specified, then all watchpoints are deleted.

O

```
O OPT?
O OPT=VALUE
O
```

The first form, **O OPT?**, prints the value of the option named **OPT**. The second format specifies the value for **OPT**; if no value is specified, it defaults to one. If no arguments are given, the values of all the current options are printed. The option name can be abbreviated to the minimum identifiable name; for example, the **pager** option can be reduced to **p**.

A list of the most commonly used options is shown in Table 10-1. For others, refer to the **perldebug** man page.

Option	Description
RecallCommand	The character(s) used to recall a command.
ShellBang	The character(s) used to spawn a shell.
Pager	The program to use for paging the output using the | command within the debugger. The value of the **PAGER** environment variable will be used by default.
TkRunning	Run **Tk** when prompting. (See "Alternative Interfaces" later in this chapter for a discussion of the Tk interface to the Perl debugger.)
SignalLevel	The level of verbosity applied to signals. Default operation is to print a message when an uncaught signal is received. Set to zero to switch this off.
WarnLevel	The level of verbosity applied to warnings. Default operation is to print a backtrace when a warning is printed out. Set to zero to switch this off.
DieLevel	The level of verbosity applied to warnings. Default operation is to print a backtrace when a warning is printed out. Set this option to a value of two to enable messages to be printed by surrounding **eval** statements. Set to zero to switch this off.
AutoTrace	Trace mode, identical to the **t** option on the command line. Set to zero to disable tracing.
LineInfo	The file or pipe to print line number information to. This is used by debugger interfaces with a pipe to enable them to obtain the information.
inhibit_exit	When set to zero, allows you to step to a point beyond the normal end of the script.
PrintRet	When set to zero, does not print the return value resolved when the **r** command is used. When set to one (the default), the return value is printed.
Frame	Controls how messages are printed during the entry and exit process from subroutines. The value is numeric, based against a bitset. If the value is zero, then messages are printed only on entry to a new subroutine. If bit 1 (value of 2) is set, then both entry and exit to the subroutine is printed. If bit 2 (4) is set, then the arguments to the subroutine are printed, and bit 4 (8) prints the values parsed to **tied** functions and methods. Bit 5 (16) also causes the return value from the subroutine to be printed. Thus, a value of 18 prints the entry and exit to a subroutine with the returned value.
MaxTraceLen	The maximum number of arguments printed when bit 4 of the **frame** option is set.
ArrayDepth	The maximum number of elements printed from an array. An empty string prints all elements.
HashDepth	The maximum number of keys and values printed from a hash. An empty string prints all keys.
CompactDump	Sets the style of the array or hash dump. Short arrays may be printed on a single line.
VeryCompact	Sets the style of the array or hash dump to be very compact.
GlobPrint	Sets whether the resolved file name globs are printed.
TTY	The TTY device to use for debugging I/O.
NoTTY	If set, goes into a nonstop debugging mode, as if there is no controlling terminal. See the examples under the **O** command for more information.
ReadLine	When set to zero, disables **readline** support within the debugger, so that scripts that use **ReadLine** can be debugged.
NonStop	Automatically set by **noTTY**, sets the debugger into non-interactive mode.

Table 10.1   Internal Options for the Debugger

The default values for the options can be obtained by typing **O** into a new debugger process:

```
perl -de 1

Loading DB routines from perl5db.pl version 1.0401
Emacs support available.

Enter h or 'h h' for help.

main::(-e:1):    1
  DB<1> O
            hashDepth = 'N/A'
           arrayDepth = 'N/A'
          DumpDBFiles = 'N/A'
         DumpPackages = 'N/A'
           DumpReused = 'N/A'
          compactDump = 'N/A'
          veryCompact = 'N/A'
                quote = 'N/A'
              HighBit = 'N/A'
            undefPrint = 'N/A'
            globPrint = 'N/A'
             PrintRet = '1'
            UsageOnly = 'N/A'
                frame = '0'
            AutoTrace = '0'
                  TTY = '/dev/tty'
                noTTY = ''
             ReadLine = '1'
              NonStop = '0'
             LineInfo = '/dev/tty'
          maxTraceLen = '400'
        recallCommand = '!'
            ShellBang = '!'
                pager = '|more'
            tkRunning = ''
            ornaments = 'us,ue,md,me'
          signalLevel = '1'
            warnLevel = '1'
             dieLevel = '1'
         inhibit_exit = '1'
        ImmediateStop = 'N/A'
         bareStringify = 'N/A'


<

< EXPR
<
```

Sets a Perl command, specified in **EXPR**, to be executed before each debugger prompt. If **EXPR** is omitted, the list of statements is reset.

<<

```
<< EXPR
```

Sets a Perl command, specified in **EXPR**, to be executed before each debugger prompt.

>

```
> EXPR
>
```

Sets the Perl command **EXPR** to be executed after each debugger prompt and after any command on the prompt has been executed. If **EXPR** is not specified, the list of commands is reset.

>>

```
>> EXPR
```

Sets the Perl command **EXPR** to be executed after each debugger prompt and after any command on the prompt has been executed.

{

```
{ EXPR
{
```

Sets a debugger command, specified in **EXPR**, to be executed before each debugger prompt. If **EXPR** is omitted, the list of statements is reset.

{{

```
{{ EXPR
```

Sets a debugger command, specified in **EXPR**, to be executed before each debugger prompt.

!

```
! EXPR
!
```

Redoes the previous command specified by the number **EXPR** (as shown in the debugger prompt), or the previous command if **EXPR** is not specified.

```
! -EXPR
```

Redoes the **EXPR** to the last command.

```
! PATTERN
```

Redoes the last command starting with **PATTERN**.

!!

```
!! EXPR
```

Runs **EXPR** in a subprocess.

H

```
H -EXPR
```

Displays the last **EXPR** commands—if **EXPR** is omitted, then it lists all of the commands in the history.

q or ^D
Quits from the debugger.

r
Returns immediately from the current subroutine. The remainder of the statements are ignored.

R
Restarts the debugger. Some options and history may be lost during the process, although the current specification allows for histories, breakpoints, actions, and debugger options to be retained. Also, the command-line options specified by **-w**, **-I**, and **-e** are retained.

|

```
|EXPR
```

Runs the command **EXPR** through the default pager.

||

```
||EXPR
```

Runs the command **EXPR** through the default pager, ensuring that the filehandle **DB::OUT** is temporarily selected.

=

```
= ALIAS EXPR
ALIAS
```

Assigns the value of **EXPR** to **ALIAS**, effectively defining a new command called **ALIAS**. If no arguments are specified, the current aliases are listed. Note that the aliases do not accept arguments, but you can simulate the effects of arguments by defining **EXPR** as a regular expression:

```
$DB::alias{'strlen'} = 's/strlen(.*)/p length($1)/';
```

This effectively re-executes the original **strlen** command as **print length($1)**, where **$1** is the value of the first matching parentheses.

m

```
m EXPR
```

Evaluates expression and lists the currently valid methods that could be applied to it.

```
m PACKAGE
```

Lists the available methods defined in **PACKAGE**.

Using Non-Interactive Mode

The interactive interface is great if you're trying to locate a very specific bug or problem, but it may be overkill if all you want is a quick guide or overview of the execution path of a particular script. There are other, perhaps better, tools (see the "Perl Compiler" in Chapter 12).

You can get round this by using a "non-interactive" mode, which is basically just a trick using the **PERLDB_OPTS** environment variable to get Perl to execute a series of debugger commands when the debugger is started. It's not officially a way of executing the debugger, but it is a solution when you want to print a stack trace or watch variables during execution without having to manually introduce **print** statements or having to drop into the interactive debugger interface.

To do this you need to set the value of the **PERLDB_OPTS** environment variable before running the debugger. The following example, which assumes you have the **bash** shell, switches on full frame information for called subroutines and runs the debugger without human intervention, outputting the full trace to the standard output:

```
$ export set PERLDB_OPTS="N f=31 AutoTrace"
$ perl -d t.pl
Package t.pl.
8:        bar();
in  .=main::bar() from t.pl:8
 5:           top();
 in  .=main::top() from t.pl:5
  22:          print "Top of the world, Ma!\n";
Top of the world, Ma!
  23:          callerlog("Printed Message");
  in  .=main::callerlog('Printed Message') from t.pl:23
```

```
   12:        my $reference = shift;
   13:        my $level = 1;
   14:        while (((@data) = caller($level++)))
   15:        {
   16:            print join(' ',@data),":$reference\n";
main t.pl 5 main::top 1 :Printed Message
   14:        while (((@data) = caller($level++)))
   15:        {
   16:            print join(' ',@data),":$reference\n";
main t.pl 8 main::bar 1 :Printed Message
   14:        while (((@data) = caller($level++)))
   15:        {
  out .=main::callerlog('Printed Message') from t.pl:23
 out .=main::top() from t.pl:5
out .=main::bar() from t.pl:8
```

The **PERLDB_OPTS** environment variable is actually part of the customization system for the debugger, which we'll have a look at separately.

Customization

There are two ways of customizing the Perl debugger. The first is to specify the internal debugger options within the value of the **PERLDB_OPTS** environment variable, as you have already seen. The other option is to specify options and aliases and commands to be executed when the debugger starts by placing commands into the .perldb file, which is parsed at the time of execution by the debugger module.

The normal use for this file is to specify new aliases to the debugger, which you do by specifying the keys and values of the **%DB::alias** hash. The key is the name of the alias, and the value is the command that should be executed. See the = command in the earlier "Debugging Commands" section for details.

You can change options to the debugger by calling the **parse_options** function, which takes a single argument—a string such as would be specified in the **PERLDB_OPTS** variable. Note, however, that the definitions in .perldb are parsed before the string defined in the environment **PERLDB_OPTS** variable.

Alternative Interfaces

The **emacs** editor provides an interface to the Perl debugger that enables you to use the **emacs** editor as a complete development and debugging environment. There is also a mode available that allows **emacs** to understand at least some of the debugger commands that can be used during the debugging process.

There are also a number of modules available on CPAN that provide Windows-based interfaces to the Perl debugger. The most friendly of the interfaces I have come across is the **ptkdb** interface.

The **ptkdb** debugger interface uses the **Tk** interface system to provide a windowed interface to the Perl debugger. All of the normal interface elements are available, with buttons and entry points for the most regularly used items. You invoke the **ptkdb** interface (once it has been installed) using the debug extension command-line option:

```
$ perl -d:ptkdb t.pl
```

You can see a sample window for the chapter's example debug script in Figure 10-1. The left side of the window shows the listing of the original Perl script. The right panel displays variables, expressions, subroutines, and breakpoints for the current debugger invocation. The information printed is the same as that produced within the normal text-based debugger interface, albeit within a nice preformatted and windowed environment.

ActivePerl Debugger

While there is actually nothing wrong with the text-based debugger, for many Windows-based programmers it will feel a little restrictive and complicated to use. The ActiveState Perl Debugger (APD), which comes with the Perl Development Kit, provides a GUI interface to a debugger that will be familiar to users of Visual Studio and other integrated development environments.

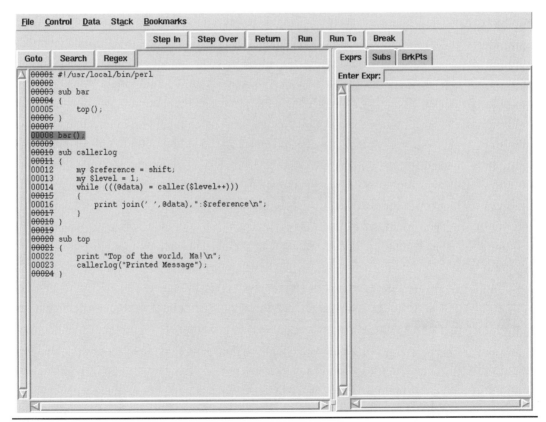

Figure 10.1   The ptkdb debugger interface

The Debugger Interface

Once you have installed the Perl Development Kit, the APD replaces the default debugger installed as part of the core Perl distribution. Therefore, to actually start the APD you use the same command-line option:

```
C:\> perl -d script.pl
```

There is unfortunately no way of using the standard Perl debugger once the ActiveState version has been installed. The default ActivePerl debugger window can be seen in Figure 10-2.

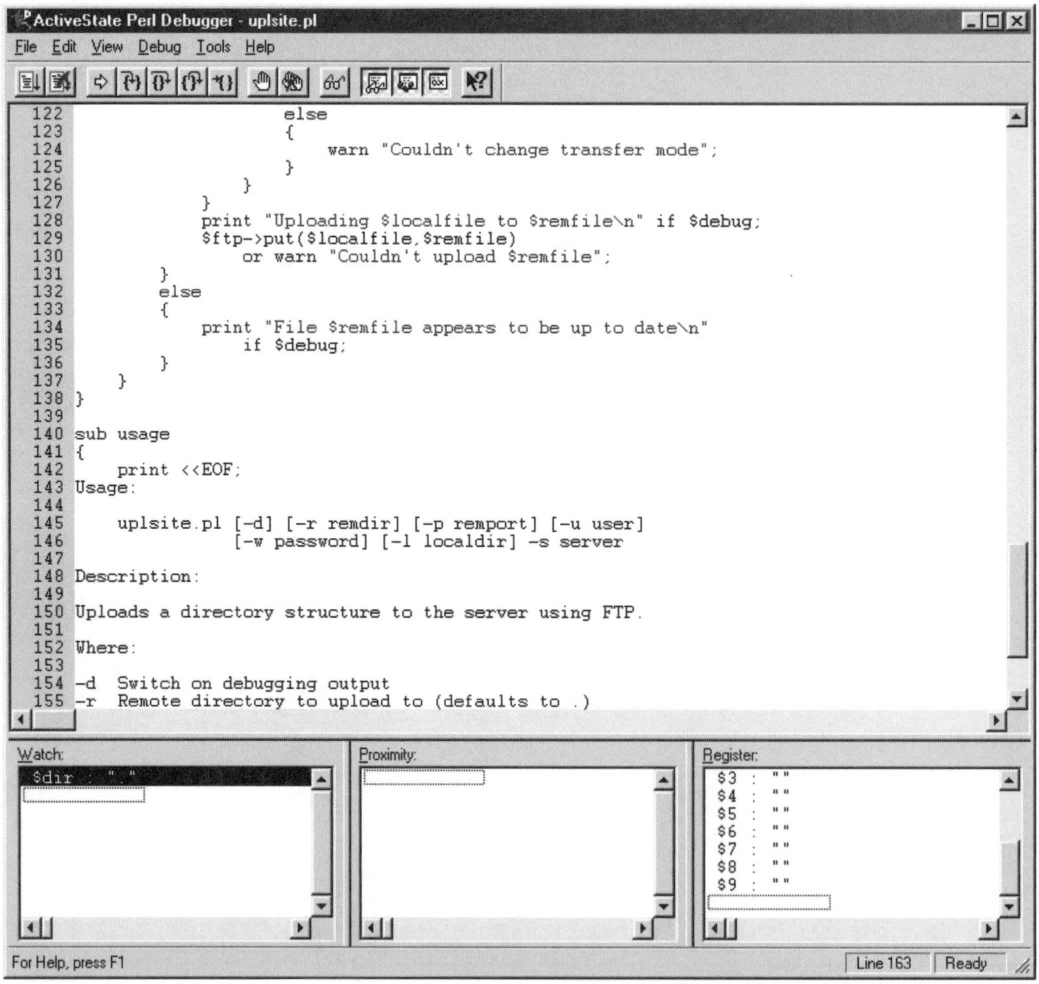

Figure 10.2   The ActiveState Perl Debugger

Once started, the debugger automatically opens your script and executes any **use** statements and any **BEGIN** blocks. The starting location for the script is therefore the first statement that would ordinarily be executed by the compiler *after* the compilation process.

By default, the window is split into four areas, the main **Source** window, which shows the source script currently being debugged, and the **Watch**, **Proximity** and **Register** panels, which show information about the current state of execution.

Note that any changes that you make to the configuration of the Perl debugger are permanent. The next time you use the debugger the same watches, window, and tools will be available to you.

The Source Panel

The **Source** panel shows the source for the currently executing statement. Initially this will show the script you are debugging, but if your script also imports any external modules, then the debugger will trace through to those modules, also showing their source. You can always tell what file you are currently debugging by looking at the window title—this will always show the path of the file.

Within the source panel, the left-hand side shows the line numbers for the file being debugged. Although the line numbers seem trivial, they are handy when you want to set breakpoints—we'll look at these in more detail later.

The yellow arrow shows the statement/line that will be executed next—not the statement that has just been executed. The blue arrow shows the location of the current "cursor" used when creating new breakpoints and bookmarks.

We'll cover the actual execution process of the script later.

Syntax Colorization

For ease of identification while looking at the source code, it is colored according to the individual components that make up each statement. You can configure the coloring by using the **Colors** panel of the **Options** window, available from the **Tools** menu. You can see an example in Figure 10-3.

To enable syntax coloring you need to check the **Enable Syntax Coloring** checkbox. If the box is left unchecked, all the text is shown using a black foreground and white background.

For ease of use, each component of a script can be colorized individually, and for each component you can set the foreground and background color. You can see a list of the components recognized by the debugger in Table 10-2.

Component	Description
Source	The default color for the source not otherwise colored according to the other configuration settings from this table.
Margin	The color of the margin along the left side of the window used to list the line numbers.
Watch	The colors used to display the contents of the Watch, Proximity, and Registers panels.
Comments	The colors used for comments in the code. Comments are identified using the normal comment rules—all text after a # that does not immediately follow a $ sign up to the end of line. Any embedded POD document is also colored using the same settings.

Table 10.2   Syntax Colorization

Component	Description
Keyword	Sets the color for any keywords in the source code. The debugger comes with a predefined number of keywords that match the list of keywords supported by Perl. You can edit the list of the keywords by editing the **keywords.txt** file installed in the debugger directory.
'String'	Sets the color used for single-quoted strings, whether they are identified by the ' single quote character or matching the **q//** operator.
"String"	Sets the color used for double-quoted strings, whether they are identified by the " double quote character or matching the **qq//** operator.
`String`	Sets the color used for backquoted strings, whether they are identified by the ` backquote character or matching the **qx//** operator.
Match	Sets the color used to identify regular expression matches. A match expression is identified by the **//** operator or the **m//** operator.
Substitution	Sets the color used to identify substitution expressions. A substitution expression is identified by the **s///** operator.
Translation	Sets the color used to identify translation expressions. A translation expression is identified either by the **tr///** or by the **y///** operators.

Table 10.2 Syntax Colorization *(continued)*

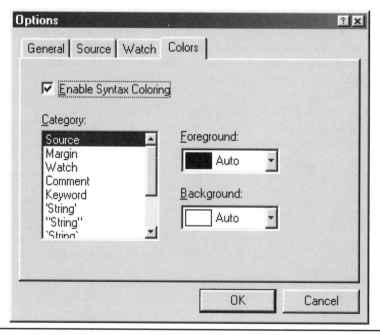

Figure 10.3 Setting Syntax Colors

To actually change the color, select the component from the list in the left-hand list and then select the foreground and background colors from the pop-up menus on the right. Clicking the OK button at any time will accept all the changes that you've made, while clicking Cancel will reject the changes.

Colorizing code changes only the color of what is displayed—no other modification is made. Although this may seem obvious, there are times when it would be convenient for it to be otherwise. For example, I often use the debugger with the comment component set to white on both the foreground and background. This effectively hides the comments from the program, useful if I'm debugging my own code when the comments don't add to my understanding. Unfortunately, it also has the effect of introducing blank areas within the debugger source window.

Source Options

The **Source** panel from the **Options** item in the **Tools** menu allows you to configure the look and feel of the main source panel. There are five options: you can control the fonts, tab size, watch and break tip display, and the use of line numbers.

The **Set Font** option allows you to set the font style and size used to display the source code. The **Tab Size** is the number of spaces used to replace each tab used as indent within the code. The default is a value of 4 (as used in this book).

WatchTips and **BreakTips** define whether the information about a watch or breakpoint is shown in a tooltip when the cursor points to a watched variable or breakpoint.

The **Display Line Numbers** option defines whether line numbers are shown in the left-hand margin. Note that this option does not affect the display of the current statement arrow or breakpoints, only the line numbers.

The Registers

The register simulates the operation of the register panel in a normal debugging tool. Perl doesn't actually use internal registers, even within the Perl virtual machine, but there are some global variables that can have an effect on the overall execution of your script. For example, the $_ variable, which is used as the scratchpad throughout your script, is often the default variable used by many functions and operators if you fail to supply any arguments.

The register panel therefore lists the core global variables used by the Perl interpreter. The list of variables displayed is shown in Table 10-3.

Register	Description
$_	The scratchpad variable.
$.	The current line within the file currently being used.
$&	The string matched by the last successful pattern match.
$`	The string preceding the information matched by the last pattern match.
$'	The string following the information matched by the last pattern match.
$1..$9	The variables used to store the result of the corresponding parentheses from the last regular expression match.

Table 10.3   Registers Displayed by the Debugger

The entries listed in Table 10-3 are the defaults; you can add your own list of registers to be watched by right-clicking within the register window. The menu provides three options: you can add, modify, or update the watches within the list. The changes you make are permanent—the next time you open and use the debugger the list of watches will be as you last used them. You can reset the list of register watches to the default by clicking the **Reset** button in the **Watch** panel under **Tools** and **Options** when configuring debugging options. (Watches are a common feature of the debugger; see the section on the **Watches** panel later in this chapter for details on adding watches to the registers panel.)

You can hide the registers window by selecting **Hide** from the pop-up menu displayed when you right-click within the **Registers** panel or by selecting the **Registers** option from the **View** menu.

Proximity Panel

The proximity panel displays the values of the variables surrounding the current line. You cannot configure the variables that are displayed, nor can you control how the listed variables are displayed. You can, however, control how many lines above and below the current line are examined to determine which variables to monitor.

To adjust the **Proximity** properties, select the **Options** item from the **Tools** menu. Doing this will present the options window. If you switch to the **Watch** tab, seen here in Figure 10-4, you can see the configurable options. The lines above and below the next line in the execution control how many lines are monitored by the **Proximity** panel.

The other options allow you to reset the list of watches displayed in the Registers panel and to set the font used in all three **Watch** panels. The setting of this font does not affect the display of the main window, only the panels.

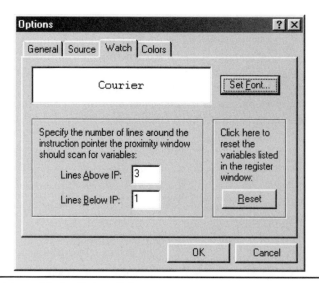

Figure 10.4   The Watch panel in the Options dialog

Watches

The **Watch** panel allows you to set specific variables to be watched at all times. Doing this bypasses the normal **Register** display and the **Proximity** display. The information listed within the **Watches** panel remains, no matter where you are within the execution of the script being debugged.

To add a new watch, you can either right-click on a variable in the **Proximity** panel and select **Copy to Watch**, or right-click within the **Watch** panel.

Watches (either in the **Watch** or **Register** panel) are not simply static variables—the statement used when creating a new watch is evaluated just like any other Perl statement. Watches can therefore be used in complex expressions, or you can embed expressions and functions into the watch to format the variable that you want to in a more human-readable format.

For example, when watching an array you might want to use this:

```
join(', ', @array)
```

as the watch statement. If you want to get even more creative, you can also enter multiline or block-based statements. Here's one that monitors a hash:

```
foreach $key (sort keys %hash) { $string .= "$key -> $hash{$key}\n" } $string
```

The only problem with all watches is that, because the source for the watch is displayed within the panel, long watch statements like the one above may not be displayed properly. This problem is not significant, but it can be a constant frustration!

Watches are always evaluated using the current context. This means that if you switch to a block or function that uses a variable with the same name, the local variable will be displayed. Special care should be taken if you use a scalar to hold a reference to another data type, since the watch may not evaluate properly.

Executing Statements

Once you have opened the script you want to debug, you will need to decide how to execute it. There are two basic methods offered by all debuggers: stepping and breakpoints.

Stepping

The ActiveState debugger supports four main step commands. The **Step Into**, **Step Over**, **Step Out** and **Run to Cursor** commands work exactly as described earlier in this chapter, allowing you to execute and follow, execute and ignore, step out of a function, and run to the current cursor position, respectively. The key combinations for each operation are shown in Table 10-4.

Key	Description
F11	Step Into
F10	Step Over
Shift+F11	Step Out
Ctrl+F10	Run until Cursor

Table 10.4 Script Execution

Breakpoints

To create a breakpoint within the ActivePerl debugger, move the cursor to the line on which you want to set the breakpoint and then press F9, right-click and select **Toggle Breakpoint** or select it from the **Edit** menu. The option is a toggle, so you can use the same process to remove an existing breakpoint.

Alternatively, you can insert a breakpoint at a specific line using the **Insert Breakpoint** option. Doing this allows you to select the line on which the breakpoint should occur (it defaults to the current cursor line) and to enter a condition to use in order to trigger the breakpoint. The condition should be in the same format as conditions used in **if, while**, and other control statements, if the result of the condition is a positive integer then it's treated as a success and triggers the breakpoint and halts execution.

To edit all of the breakpoints that you've configured, choose the **Edit Breakpoints** option. This will provide you with a list of all the breakpoints, as seen here in Figure 10-5.

Pressing F5 will start execution, which will stop only when it reaches a breakpoint; otherwise the entire script will execute. For most scripts it's a good idea to insert a couple of breakpoints just to allow you to interrupt processing of the script so that you can monitor what is going on.

Debug Tools

Instead of using watches, proximity lists, and registers, you can get immediate information about the script being debugged by using the **Quick Eval**, **Dump Variable** and **Call Stack** options from the **debug** menu. These provide information about variables and the stack trace for the current statement, according to the context of the current line.

Quick Eval

The **Quick Eval** option allows you to execute any Perl statement within the context of the script being debugged. You have access to all of the variables defined within the current debugger location within the script. For a more permanent view on the statement that you enter you can click on the **Add Watch** button.

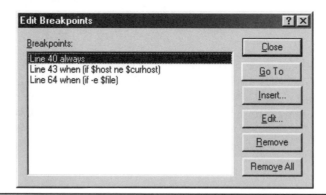

Figure 10.5 Editing all breakpoints

Dump Variable

The **Dump Variable** option dumps the contents of a variable into a scrollable box. For very large variables this function is vital since it enables you to view the entire contents without the restrictions enforced by the individual panels.

Unlike with the other watches, you cannot supply a statement to be evaluated, only a variable or variable component (such as an array or hash element). The debugger displays the variable formatted according to the variable's type and content. The actual dump is handled by the **Data::Dumper** module.

Call Stack

The **Call Stack** option displays a trace of the function calls used to reach the current statement and information about how those functions were called. The actual output is handled by the **caller** function, a function built into the Perl compiler. The **Call Stack** option uses the extended version of the **caller** function described below.

If you want to use the **caller** function on your own programs, the information on using the function is included here. The data returned by the **caller** function includes details about the subroutine (or **eval** or **require**) statement:

```
caller EXPR
caller
```

In a scalar context, it simply returns the package name. In a simple list context, the function returns the package name, file name, and line of the caller of the current subroutine, **eval**, or **require** statement:

```
($package, $filename, $line) = caller;
```

If **EXPR** is specified, **caller** returns extended information. The value of **EXPR** should be the number of frames on the stack to go back to before the current one. That is, if you specify a value of one, the parent subroutine information will be printed, a value of two will print the grandparent subroutine, and so forth. The information returned is

```
($package, $filename, $line, $subroutine,
 $hasargs, $wantarray, $evaltext, $is_require) = caller($i);
```

The **$evaltext** and **$is_require** values are returned only when the subroutine being examined is actually the result of an **eval()** statement. As an example, examine the following script:

```
sub bar
{
    Top::top();
}

bar();

package Top;

sub top
{
```

```perl
        my $level = 0;
        print "Top of the world, Ma!\n";
        while ((($package, $file, $line,
                $subname, $hasargs, $wantarray) = caller($level++))))
        {
            $hasargs   = $hasargs   ? 'Yes' : 'No';
            if (defined($wantarray))
            {
                $wantarray = 'Yes';
            }
            else
            {
                $wantarray = 'No';
            }
            print <<EOF;
Stack:
            Package: $package
               File: $file
               Line: $line
         Subroutine: $subname
     Has Arguments?: $hasargs
       Wants Array?: $wantarray
EOF
        }
    }
```

After execution, the resultant information shows the stack trace for the **top** function, including its original call from **main** and from the **bar** function:

```
Top of the world, Ma!
Stack:
            Package: main
               File: ././t.pl
               Line: 5
         Subroutine: Top::top
     Has Arguments?: Yes
       Wants Array?: No
Stack:
            Package: main
               File: ././t.pl
               Line: 8
         Subroutine: main::bar
     Has Arguments?: Yes
       Wants Array?: No
```

The information provided should enable you to pinpoint the location within a script. If you want to report the information to a log, you may want to introduce a wrapper function like this one:

```perl
sub callerlog
{
    my $reference = shift;
```

```
    open(DATA,">>caller.log") || return;
    print DATA join(' ',@_),":$reference\n";
    close(DATA);
}
```

Then to call the function, you would use a line such as

```
callerlog("Writing data",caller());
```

to report the information for the current stack trace. Note that you can't directly use the information from **callerlog**, since doing that would introduce its own frame of information at location zero within the stack. You could, however, use a modified form of the **callerlog** function that returns the stack trace from frame one onwards:

```
sub callerlog
{
    my $reference = shift;
    my $level = 1;
    while (((@data) = caller($level++)))
    {
        print join(' ',@data),":$reference\n";
    }
}
```

Bookmarks

You can introduce a bookmark into any piece of code. A bookmark operates in a similar function to Internet bookmarks—it allows you to go straight to a location within a script file at any time. This feature can be useful when you want to jump to a particular function that is called regularly and monitor its status.

To set a new bookmark, use the mouse to select the line (as marked by the blue arrow) and then select **Toggle Bookmark** (CTRL-F2). This is a toggle, so you can also use it to remove the bookmark from an individual line. To view a bookmark, use the **Next** (F2) and **Previous Bookmark** (SHIFT-F2) items from the **Edit** menu.

 Bookmarks are also retained after the debugger completes execution. To clear all bookmarks, select Remove All Bookmarks (CTRL-SHIFT-F2) from the Edit menu.

Using Tools

You can configure a number of tools that you can access directly from the debugger. These can be used to open the script you are debugging in an editor or to execute the script directly or through another tool—perhaps a web browser, if you are developing a web-based interface.

To configure the tools available within the debugger, choose the **Customize** option from the **Tools** menu. You'll get a window like the one in Figure 10-6.

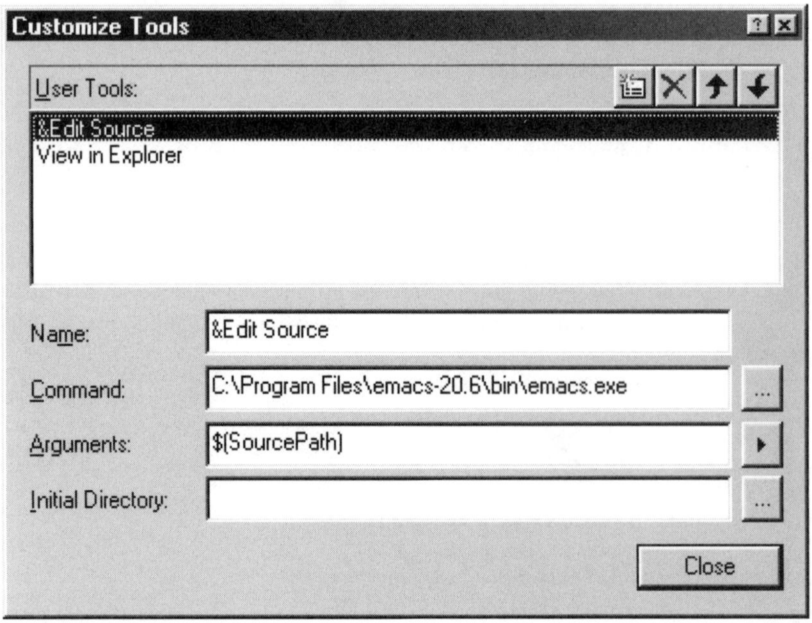

Figure 10.6 Customizing tools

To set up a new tool, click the left-most button at the top of the window, and then enter the tools name as it will appear in the menu. If you prefix the name with an ampersand, then the command will be given a menu shortcut using the normal letter prefix. The first nine tools are always available as ALT-#, where # is the number from 1–9. You can configure which tool appears at the top of the list—and therefore has a shortcut of ALT-1—by selecting the tool item and then using the up and down arrow buttons to adjust its position.

The Command box configures the program that will be executed when the tool is selected. You can use the browse button to select the program using a normal file dialog box. The Command box must only contain the path to a program; if you want to add arguments you must use the Arguments box.

The Arguments box allows you to introduce additional arguments to be appended to the line during execution. You can place any text into this box, but the tool is most useful when you use one of the predefined arguments supplied by the debugger tool. You can see a list of the arguments and their descriptions in Table 10-5.

Argument	Description
Source Path	The full path to the source file currently being debugged. Note that this is the active debug script, not necessarily the script that you were debugging.
Source Directory	The directory component of the current file's path.
Source Name	The name (without extension) of the current file.

Table 10.5 Custom Tool Variables

Argument	Description
Source Extension	The extension (with leading period) of the current file.
Current Directory	The current directory. This is the directory in which the script was and where the debugger was started, not the current directory within the execution of the script.
Current Line	The line number of the statement being debugged.
Current Text	The text of the current line being debugged.

Table 10.5   Custom Tool Variables *(continued)*

Note that the Source Extension argument includes the period used to separate the base name and its extension. For example, when debugging a CGI script, you might create a Tool with the following properties:

```
Name: View in Explorer
Command: C:\Program Files\Internet Explorer\Iexplore.exe
Arguments: incontinent/www/$(SourceName)$(SourceExtension)
```

The final entry allows you to configure the directory in which execution starts. Although not useful (or necessary) for editing files, it can be useful if you want to create a tool that executes the script outside the confines of the debugger.

Command-Line Debugging

When you compile Perl you can configure the interpreter to include additional debugging capabilities. These debugging hooks provide an interface to the internals of the Perl interpreter and so debug the script at a level slightly lower than that of the Perl debugger. To enable this, you'll need to rebuild Perl from the sources and enable the debugging option by running **Configure** again:

```
$ sh Configure -Doptimize='-g'
```

Doing this forces the C compiler to rebuild the executable, first with debugging for the application itself, so you could run it through **gdb**. It also switches on the **-DDEBUGGING** flag, which enables the interpreter's debugging features. These features are more technical than those of the Perl debugger, in that they report internal information rather than script information.

The information available is extensive and really relates more to the internal workings of Perl than to your script. In fact, in some cases the information is useless when used as a script debugging tool because the information is directly related to the interpretation or parsing process of the interpreter. That said, using these tools can help you to better understand how Perl works and why different operations work or fail.

More useful of the options are those that can be used to identify specific problems relating to memory usage, hashes, or regular expressions. There are also tools for outputting the execution tree and information on the opcodes employed by the script, which can help if you are developing a script for a secure environment and need to use the **Safe** or **Opcode** modules or the **ops** pragma.

Note	*These tools are not for the faint-hearted! Unless you are trying to trace a specific bug that you cannot resolve elsewhere, stay away. These options are no substitute for the Perl debugger, or some of the simpler techniques we've seen in Chapter 10.*

The list of available options is shown in Table 10-6, and we'll have a look in detail at each option shortly. To actually obtain the debugging output, selected options either by their letter combination or by specifying the decimal value of the combined options. For example, to switch on taint checks and memory allocation, you would use **–Dmu** or **–D2176**.

Remember that in each case, the amount of information actually output by these options can be huge—even a simple script can output thousands of lines of "debugging" information. I recommend redirecting the output to a file, or at the very least piping the output through a pager. Because the output is to **STDERR**, use

```
$ perl -Dmu t.pl 2>debug.out
```

for redirection, or

```
$ perl -Dmu t.pl 2>&1 | more
```

when paging.

Number	Letter	Description
1	p	Tokenizing and parsing.
2	s	Stack snapshots.
4	l	Context (loop) stack processing.
8	t	Trace execution.
16	o	Method and overloading resolution.
32	c	String/numeric conversions.
64	P	Print preprocessor command for **-P**.
128	m	Memory allocation.
256	f	Format processing.
512	r	Regular expression parsing and execution.
1024	x	Syntax tree dump.
2048	u	Tainting checks.
4096	L	Memory leaks.
8192	H	Hash dump.
16384	X	Scratchpad allocation.
32768	D	Cleaning up.
65536	S	Thread synchronization.

Table 10.6   Debugging Flags

24x7

These debug options produce copious amounts of information and can act as a useful cross-references for your application once you've finished programming. If you decide you want to use them in this way, consider saving the output from the **tcmrx** options. If you're working with tainted data use the **u** option, and for threads the **S** option. Save the information along with the documentation for your script.

> **Tip**   *If you really want to see what Perl is doing when it outputs the debug information, search the Perl source tree for the string **DEBUG_#** where # is the debug letter shown in Table 10-6.*

Tokenizing and Parsing

The first of the options outputs the parsing process handled by the **yacc** parser built into Perl. To really understand the output from this option, you'll need to know how the **yacc** parser works, which is unfortunately beyond the scope of this book. In essence though, the parser works by *tokenizing* each element of an input line and identifying or resolving each token. The resolving process follows a series of states that identify each component. Once each component has been identified, it can then be resolved, executed, or otherwise discarded according to the identified type.

The actual process is extensive, and the parsing will work through a number of different states and reductions before the final statement can be executed. As an example, consider the following lines:

```
$ perl -Dp -e 'print $hello;'
yydebug: after reduction, shifting from state 0 to state 2
yydebug: state 2, reducing by rule 7 (lineseq :)
yydebug: after reduction, shifting from state 2 to state 3
### Tokener expecting STATE at
yydebug: state 3, reading 286 (LSTOP)
yydebug: state 3, reducing by rule 44 (label :)
yydebug: after reduction, shifting from state 3 to state 15
yydebug: state 15, shifting to state 46
### Tokener expecting REF at  $hello;

yydebug: state 46, reading 36 ('$')
yydebug: state 46, shifting to state 65
yydebug: state 65, reading 257 (WORD)
yydebug: state 65, shifting to state 92
yydebug: state 92, reducing by rule 190 (indirob : WORD)
yydebug: after reduction, shifting from state 65 to state 147
yydebug: state 147, reducing by rule 185 (scalar : '$' indirob)
yydebug: after reduction, shifting from state 46 to state 116
### Tokener expecting OPERATOR at ;
...
```

```
yydebug: after reduction, shifting from state 2 to state 3
### Tokener expecting STATE at
yydebug: state 3, reading 0 (end-of-file)
yydebug: state 3, reducing by rule 2 (prog : $$1 lineseq)
yydebug: after reduction, shifting from state 0 to state 1

EXECUTING...
```

I've actually trimmed the output; the full output is 59 lines for a relatively simple statement. You can imagine the output from a larger script.

Stack Snapshots

The stack snapshot option produces a simplified list of the argument stack used to exchange information during subroutine calls. For example, this simple script

```
sub add
{
    $_[0]+$_[1];
}

print add(1,2);
```

produces the following output:

```
perl -D2 t.pl

EXECUTING...

    =>
    =>
    =>
    =>   *
    =>   **
    =>   **   IV(1)
    =>   **   IV(1)   IV(2)
    =>   **   IV(1)   IV(2)   GV()
    =>   *    IV(1)   IV(2)
    =>   *
    =>   *    IV(1)
    =>   *    IV(1)   IV(2)
    =>   *    NV(3)
    =>   *    NV(3)
    =>   SV_YES
```

This shows quite clearly the status of the stack—the value 1 is placed on the stack first (as an integer value), and then 2. The glob value (GV) is the call to the **add** function where the two values are then taken off and replaced with the numerical value 3. The **SV_YES** is the indicator that describes the return context from the **print** statement—a scalar value.

Context (Loop) Stack Processing

The context stack processing output actually displays the progress of each statement as it enters the different scopes and blocks that make up your script. This feature can be useful if you want to trace any jumps in and out of a specific block or loop. In addition, it also displays the corresponding source file responsible for executing that statement or fragment, useful if you want to identify the location of specific opcode operation for debugging your interpreter.

For example, in the same script as that preceding:

```
$ perl -D4 t.pl
(t.pl:4)        ENTER scope 2 at op.c:6393
(t.pl:3)        LEAVE scope 2 at op.c:6722
(t.pl:6)        ENTER scope 2 at op.c:6393
(t.pl:6)        LEAVE scope 2 at op.c:6722
(t.pl:0)        LEAVE scope 1 at perl.c:1278
(t.pl:0)        ENTER scope 1 at perl.c:1286
(t.pl:0)        Setting up jumplevel 0xbffff9c8, was 0x81364c0

EXECUTING...

(t.pl:0)        ENTER scope 2 at pp_hot.c:1465
Entering block 0, type BLOCK
(t.pl:6)        ENTER scope 3 at pp_hot.c:2303
Entering block 1, type SUB
Leaving block 1, type SUB
(t.pl:6)        LEAVE scope 3 at pp_hot.c:2047
Leaving block 0, type BLOCK
(t.pl:0)        LEAVE scope 2 at pp_hot.c:1587
(t.pl:0)        LEAVE scope 1 at perl.c:388
```

you can see that the call to **add**, which is scope 3, is actually entered from line 6. Scope 2 is the **main** package and execution path. Scope 1 is the initial interpretation/parsing stage, where things like the command line arguments are extracted and then passed on to the script.

This option really comes into its own when debugging loops, as it gives the clearest indication of when a particular iteration of a loop jumps out to a different scope (subroutine or other block). For example, the slightly modified script:

```
sub add
{
    $_[0]+$_[1];
}

foreach (1..100)
{
    print add($_,$_);
}
```

produces a jump in/jump out report for each of the 100 iterations. A cropped version looks like this:

```
(t2.pl:4)     ENTER scope 2 at op.c:6393
(t2.pl:3)     LEAVE scope 2 at op.c:6722
(t2.pl:9)     ENTER scope 2 at op.c:6393
(t2.pl:6)     ENTER scope 3 at op.c:6393
(t2.pl:6)     LEAVE scope 3 at op.c:6722
(t2.pl:6)     LEAVE scope 2 at op.c:6722
(t2.pl:0)     LEAVE scope 1 at perl.c:1278
(t2.pl:0)     ENTER scope 1 at perl.c:1286
(t2.pl:0)     Setting up jumplevel 0xbffff9c8, was 0x81364c0


EXECUTING...

(t2.pl:0)     ENTER scope 2 at pp_hot.c:1465
Entering block 0, type BLOCK
(t2.pl:6)     ENTER scope 3 at pp_ctl.c:1658
(t2.pl:6)     ENTER scope 4 at pp_ctl.c:1688
Entering block 1, type LOOP
(t2.pl:8)     ENTER scope 5 at pp_hot.c:2303
Entering block 2, type SUB
Leaving block 2, type SUB
(t2.pl:8)     LEAVE scope 5 at pp_hot.c:2047
(t2.pl:8)     ENTER scope 5 at pp_hot.c:2303
Entering block 2, type SUB
Leaving block 2, type SUB
...
(t2.pl:8)     LEAVE scope 5 at pp_hot.c:2047
Leaving block 1, type LOOP
(t2.pl:6)     LEAVE scope 4 at pp_ctl.c:1775
(t2.pl:6)     LEAVE scope 3 at pp_ctl.c:1776
Leaving block 0, type BLOCK
(t2.pl:0)     LEAVE scope 2 at pp_hot.c:1587
(t2.pl:0)     LEAVE scope 1 at perl.c:388
```

Here it should be obvious that block 1 (scope 4) is the main loop, and block 2 (scope 5) is the **add** function.

By the way, you might think that scope 1 is also where the **BEGIN** and **END** blocks are handled. You'd be wrong. Running a simple script with one of each statement reveals that they are treated with their own scopes just like the main script. Furthermore, it also shows that these are executed using a call to **eval**. This in itself is probably not that surprising, but it does help us to understand how these blocks and the **eval** function work.

Trace Execution

You can very simply trace the internal execution of a script or statement by using the trace execution option. Doing this actually outputs an unformatted version of the opcode tree as each code fragment is executed. Using our sample script again, you can see how the values are pushed onto the stack, the **add** sub is called, and then the **print** sub is called to output the result:

```
$ perl -D8 t2.pl

EXECUTING...

(t2.pl:0)        enter
(t2.pl:0)        nextstate
(t2.pl:6)        pushmark
(t2.pl:6)        pushmark
(t2.pl:6)        const(IV(1))
(t2.pl:6)        const(IV(2))
(t2.pl:6)        gv(main::add)
(t2.pl:6)        entersub
(t2.pl:6)        nextstate
(t2.pl:3)        aelemfast
(t2.pl:3)        aelemfast
(t2.pl:3)        add
(t2.pl:3)        leavesub
(t2.pl:6)        print
(t2.pl:6)        leave
```

You can use this information in combination with the **Safe** module for creating a safe compartment in which to execute your script.

For information on opcodes see Chapter 2 or refer to Chapter 12—the Perl compiler has its own way of outputting a parsed opcode tree that may make more sense.

Method and Overloading Resolution

When using objects and methods that need to be resolved through the inheritance system used by Perl it's sometimes useful to monitor where a particular method is being inherited from. You can do this using the **-Do** debug option—this prints the trace followed by Perl when looking for a given method. For example, consider the simple call:

```
perl -D16 -e 'use Cwd;'
(/usr/local/lib/perl5/5.6.0/Cwd.pm:71)  Looking for method import in package Carp
(/usr/local/lib/perl5/5.6.0/Cwd.pm:71)  Looking for method import in package Exporter
(/usr/local/lib/perl5/5.6.0/warnings.pm:67)    Looking for method import in package Carp
(/usr/local/lib/perl5/5.6.0/warnings.pm:67)    Looking for method import in package Exporter
(-e:1)  Looking for method import in package Cwd
(-e:1)  Looking for method import in package Exporter

EXECUTING...
```

We can see that when importing **Cwd** the **import** method is required. This is the method called by the **use** statement to import the functions exported by **Cwd** into the current namespace. First we look in **Carp**, which has been imported by **Cwd**, and then **Exporter**, which is the class used to export/import functions.

The same basic rules and processes will be followed when you call an overloaded function of method.

String/Numeric Conversions

This option produces a list showing where Perl has made assumptions about the desired format of a string or numerical value and converted it. For example, the following:

```
$string = "The result is: ";
$string .= '45' + 99;
print $string;
```

produces

```
0x813e190 num(99)
0x813e190 1nv(99)
0x813e1c0 1nv(45)
0x813e1cc 2iv(144)

EXECUTING...

0x813e1cc 2pv(144)
```

when run through the debug option in Perl. You can see that it identifies 99 as a raw number and assigns it to a numerical value, converts the 45 to a numerical value, the result of the calculation to an integer, and finally sets the result to a string (PV) value.

You can use this option to track the situation where a number seems to be interpreted incorrectly. For example, the modified version of the above script

```
$string = "The result is: ";
$string .= '99/33' + 1;
print $string;
```

will obviously return 100—Perl's string to numeric conversion converts only raw numbers, so the division symbol acts as a terminator. The result is clearer when run through the debug option:

```
0x813e190 num(1)
0x813e190 1nv(1)
0x813e1c0 1nv(99)
0x813e1cc 2iv(100)

EXECUTING...

0x813e1cc 2pv(100)
```

The same option can also be used to identify the precedence rules applied to a calculation; for example,

```
$ perl -D32 -e '34 + 55 * 99'
0x813e0ac num(99)
0x813e0ac 1nv(99)
0x813e0a0 num(55)
0x813e0a0 1nv(55)
```

```
0x8136c50 2iv(5445)
0x8136c50 num(5445)
0x8136c50 lnv(5445)
0x813e094 num(34)
0x813e094 lnv(34)
0x813e0ac 2iv(5479)
```

From this it's obvious that the * operator has a higher precedence than the + operator. A more usable example can be obtained using the **Deparse** engine supplied with the Perl compiler (see Chapter 12 for more information).

Print Preprocessor (for CPP)

The print processor outputs the information and execution call when using the C preprocessor on a Perl script, as initiated by the **–P** option on the command line. In addition, it will print out a list of the number of opcodes called for a given script. Here is an example:

```
$ perl -DP -P myext.pl

EXECUTING...

Not enough args at ch10/cron2nt.pl line 8.
     7 pushmark
    17 const
     2 gvsv
     5 gv
...
    19 nextstate
     3 unstack
     2 enter
     1 enteriter
     4 iter
     1 leaveloop
     1 require
     1 leaveeval
     1 method_named
```

Memory Allocation

You can get an extensive list of the memory allocated during the execution of a Perl script using this option. The information is really not very useful—it probably won't tell you what you expect. The information can also be misleading, since a lot of the allocations are actually made solely for the purpose of holding the built-in special variables and other meta-data used by Perl during the execution of any script.

The information given is listed by its virtual address within the address space the interpreter allocates for scripts, and each call to the malloc/free memory allocation system is given a simple sequential number. Unless you know the size of a particular object it'll be hard to track using this tool—a better overview can be obtained using the **-DL** option.

Format Processing

When using Perl's internal format system, it's impossible to trace and identify a problem without manually producing and studying each line before output. You can get around that by using the **-Df** debug option.

This option outputs the progress of the formatting process as it works through a given format. For example, this simple script

```
format STDOUT_TOP =
Variable            Value
================================================================
.
format STDOUT =
@<<<<<<<<<<<<<<<<  ^<<<<<<<<<<<<<<<<<<<<<<<<<<<<<<<<<<<<<<<<<<<<
$key,                 $data{$key}
.

%data = ('MC' => 'Martin C Brown',
         'Dan' => 'Dan the Man');

foreach $key (%data)
{
    write;
}
```

outputs the following when run through the debugger:

```
$ perl -Df fmtdebug.pl

EXECUTING...

LINEMARK
FETCH            19
CHECKNL
ITEM
SPACE
LITERAL          1
FETCH            47
CHECKCHOP
ITEM
CHOP
NEWLINE
END
left=0, todo=1
LINEMARK
LITERAL          25
NEWLINE
LINEMARK
LITERAL          67
NEWLINE
END
```

```
left=60, todo=2
Variable              Value
=====================================================================
left=58, todo=1
MC                    Martin C Brown
LINEMARK
FETCH             19
CHECKNL
ITEM
SPACE
LITERAL           1
FETCH             47
CHECKCHOP
ITEM
CHOP
NEWLINE
END
left=57, todo=1

LINEMARK
FETCH             19
CHECKNL
ITEM
SPACE
LITERAL           1
FETCH             47
CHECKCHOP
ITEM
CHOP
NEWLINE
END
left=56, todo=1
Dan                   Dan the Man
LINEMARK
FETCH             19
CHECKNL
ITEM
SPACE
LITERAL           1
FETCH             47
CHECKCHOP
ITEM
CHOP
NEWLINE
END
left=55, todo=1
```

The **left** figure is the number of lines left within the current page, while **todo** is the number of lines currently held in the $A accumulator variable. The rest of the output is devoted to determining the exact format of the lines and fields being output. The **FETCH** lines indicate the number of characters for the current field. **LINEMARK** indicates the start of a newline (including continuation), **CHECKNL** indicates whether the source data includes a newline, and **CHECKCHOP** indicates whether the text needs to be chopped or split to make up a multiline entry.

Regular Expressions

The **–Dr** command-line option allows you to debug regular expressions. You can achieve the same basic output results by using the **use re 'debug'** pragma. The result is an extensive list of the compile-time output for the regular expression engine. For example,

```
$ perl -Dr -e '"top o the world" =~ m/top [of]\s+the (world)/;'
Compiling REx 'top [of]\s+the (world)'
size 23 first at 1
rarest char w at 4
rarest char p at 2
   1: EXACT <top >(3)
   3: ANYOF[fo](12)
  12: PLUS(14)
  13:    SPACE(0)
  14: EXACT <the >(16)
  16: OPEN1(18)
  18:    EXACT <world>(21)
  21: CLOSE1(23)
  23: END(0)
anchored 'top ' at 0 floating 'the world' at 6..2147483647 (checking floating) minlen 15

Omitting $' $& $' support.

EXECUTING...
```

We'll have a look at each section individually, starting with the preamble:

```
Compiling REx 'top [of]\s+the (world)'
size 23 first at 1
rarest char w at 4
rarest char p at 2
```

The preamble before the numbered list shows the size of the compiled expression and the rarest characters found in the expression. This information is used by the internal regular expression tables during the actual execution. This information can be invaluable if you want to see the advantage of using the **study** function. In this case, both the source text (**$_**, which will be empty) and the regular expression are not complex enough to warrant a call to **study** first. The actual decision made by Perl of which are the rarest is based on known tables of letter frequency within the English language.

```
   1: EXACT <top >(3)
   3: ANYOF[fo](12)
  12: PLUS(14)
  13:    SPACE(0)
  14: EXACT <the >(16)
  16: OPEN1(18)
  18:    EXACT <world>(21)
  21: CLOSE1(23)
  23: END(0)
```

The numbered list then indicates the individual nodes for a given rule. Each node indicates a particular construct within the regular expression language. We'll return to the specific node types later, but this example can be easily understood; match the exact string "top," any of the specified characters (in the square brackets), followed by any number of spaces, the exact string "the," and then the first group (1) matching the exact string "world." You can see that for the grouping and minimal/maximal matches the meaning is nested.

```
anchored 'top' at 0 floating 'the world' at 6..2147483647 (checking floating) minlen 15
```

The summary statement is where the initial search will be anchored—in this case at the first exact string match, while the string "the world" can be at any position within the string. The absolute minimum number of characters required to match the regular expression is 15, a requirement that is part of the optimization and in fact really reflects common sense. Any match string supplied that is less than 15 characters in length can be skipped (no match). The individual elements of the summary statement can be made up of a number of different fields beyond those seen here. The full list is given in Table 10-7.

```
Omitting $' $& $' support.
```

Field	Description
anchored **STRING** at **POS**	Shows that **STRING** has been identified as appearing only at the precise location specified by **POS**.
floating **STRING** at **POS1..POS2**	Shows that the **STRING** could be found within the character range **POS1** and **POS2**.
matching floating/anchored	Shows which substring should be checked first.
minlen	Shows the minimum length of the match.
stclass **TYPE**	The type of the first matching node.
noscan	Advises not to scan for the found substrings.
isall	Specifies that the optimizer info is in fact all that the regular expression contains. That is, the regular expression does not actually need to be executed in order for a match to be made. For example, the expression /s/ doesn't require the expression engine to find a match; it's not a regular expression.
GPOS	Displayed if the pattern contains \G.
plus	Shown if the pattern starts with a repeated character, as in /s+/.
implicit	Shown if the pattern starts with .*.
with eval	Shown if the pattern contains evaluated group expressions.
anchored(TYPE)	Shown if the pattern will match only at a number of places. **TYPE** is one of **BOL** (beginning of line), **MBOL** (beginning of multiline), **GPOS** (matches where the last **m//g** left off).

Table 10.7   Summary Fields for Debugged Regular Expressions

The last line just indicates whether the special variables that can be populated by the regular expression system have been enabled and populated.

Node Types

The regular expression engine works by resolving components down into nodes (see the introduction to this section). Individual nodes indicate the type of match to perform, and some can be nested to produce complex expressions, such as **[a-z]+**. The full list of nodes is shown in Table 10-8.

Node Type	Description
END	End of the expression.
SUCCEED	Indicates a successful return from a subroutine call.
BOL	Match at the beginning of a line.
MBOL	Match at the beginning of a multiline string.
SBOL	Match at the beginning of a single line.
EOS	Match at end of string.
EOL	Match at end of line.
MEOL	Match at the end of a multiline string.
SEOL	Match at the end of a single line.
BOUND	Match at a word boundary.
BOUNDL	Match at a word boundary in current locale.
NBOUND	Match at a non-word boundary.
NBOUNDL	Match at a non-word boundary in current locale.
GPOS	Matches where the last **m//g** left off.
ANY	Match any single character, except newline.
SANY	Match any single character.
ANYOF **expr**	Match any of the characters within (or not within) **expr**.
ALNUM	Match any alphanumeric character.
ALNUML	Match any alphanumeric character in the current locale.
NALNUM	Match any non-alphanumeric character.
NALNUML	Match any non-alphanumeric character in the current locale.
SPACE	Match any whitespace character.
SPACEL	Match any whitespace character in the current locale.
NSPACE	Match any non-whitespace character.
NSPACEL	Match any non-whitespace character in the current locale.
DIGIT	Match any numeric character.
NDIGIT	Match any non-numeric character.

Table 10.8 Nodes Used to Describe a Regular Expression

Node Type	Description
BRANCH **node**	Match the current node or switch execution to the supplied **node**. Even a simple **m/a|b/** expression contains two branch statements, one to match against **a** or progress to the node for **b**. The second branch statement will match against **b** or progress to the end of the expression.
BACK	Points back to a previous branch.
EXACT **expr**	Match the string **expr**.
EXACTF **expr**	Match the string **expr** (folded).
EXACTFL **expr**	Match the string **expr** (folded in locale).
NOTHING	Match an empty string.
TAIL	Match an empty string when inside a group and go back to previous branch.
STAR **node**	Match this node 0 or more times.
PLUS **node**	Match this node 1 or more times.
CURLY **start**, **end**	Match this simple node between **start** and **end** times.
CURLYN **start**, **end**	Match the next node between **start** and **end** times.
CURLYM **start**, **end**	Match this medium complex node between **start** and **end** times.
CURLYX **start**, **end**	Match this complex node between **start** and **end** times.
WHILEM	Perform a nested curly brace match, repeating until the entire node expression matches.
OPEN **expr**	Open the group identified by **expr**.
CLOSE **expr**	Close the group identified by **expr**.
REF **expr**	Match an already matched string within the confines of the group **expr**.
REFF **expr**	Match an already matched and folded string within the confines of the group **expr**.
REFFL **expr**	Match an already matched and folded string within the current locale string within the confines of the group **expr**.
IFMATCH **offset**	If the following node match succeeds, branch to the character at **offset** within the regex.
UNLESSM **offset**	If the following node match does not succeed, branch to the character at **offset** within the regex.
SUSPEND **offset**	Match the independent regex within the current node.
IFTHEN **offset**	Switch execution to a given offset if matched.
GROUPP **expr**	Indicates whether the entire group matched.
LONGJMP **offset**	Jump to the given **offset** within a large regular expression. This is more efficient for matching large regular expressions than jumping to a specific node when the match (or failure) can be easily determined.
BRANCHJ **offset**	Branch using an offset, rather than node argument.
EVAL **eval**	Evaluate the Perl code **eval** using a call to the **eval** function.

Table 10.8   Nodes Used to Describe a Regular Expression (*continued*)

Node Type	Description
MINMOD	Set minimal, rather than maximal, match.
LOGICAL	Next node should set the flag for logical matches, without conducting/branching against a logical expression.
RENUM **offset**	Renumber the group (normally group references increment as they are used) starting at **offset**. This is not yet used, but will allow you to return a group match even if the group is spread across more than one group of logical nodes.
OPTIMIZED	Indicates an optimized node sequence.

Table 10.8 Nodes Used to Describe a Regular Expression *(continued)*

The Matching Process

If you actually supply a string to match against, then following the standard **EXECUTING** statement you'll see the actual matching process in action. In our case, this produces the following:

```
EXECUTING...

Guessing start of match, REx 'top [of]\s+the (world)' against 'top o the world'...
Found floating substr 'the world' at offset 6...
Found anchored substr 'top ' at offset 0...
Guessed: match at offset 0
Matching REx 'top [of]\s+the (world)' against 'top o the world'
  Setting an EVAL scope, savestack=3
   0 <> <top o the wo>      |  1:   EXACT <top >
   4 <top > <o the wo>      |  3:   ANYOF[fo]
   5 <top o> < the wo>      | 12:   PLUS
                                    SPACE can match 1 times out of 32767...
  Setting an EVAL scope, savestack=3
   6 <op o > <the wor>      | 14:   EXACT <the >
  10 < o the > <world>      | 16:   OPEN1
  10 < o the > <world>      | 18:   EXACT <world>
  15 < o the world> <>      | 21:   CLOSE1
  15 < o the world> <>      | 23:   END
Match successful!
Freeing REx: 'top [of]\s+the (world)'
```

The engine starts by verifying the initial information first highlighted in the compiled regular expression summary—it has found the floating string and the anchor string at the start of the expression. The rest of the process is given over to matching the individual node descriptions against the supplied string.

Using the Regex Debugger

The best way to use this debugger is not as a postmortem debugger to verify a particular regular expression (regex) has worked on a string. Instead, supply the regex only and make sure that the node listing and description that has been given matches what you think the regular expression means.

There's far too much information provided in the matching process to make it useful unless you are dealing with a very complex string and regular expression combination. Even so, most of the techniques we saw back in Chapter 4 will probably be more useful to you.

Again, the utility of this particular debug option is of more use to the writers and maintainers of the Perl language or to those wishing to gain a greater understanding of how Perl works on the inside.

Syntax Tree

The syntax tree dump, **-Dx**, is a bit like the opcode engine supported by the Perl compiler. It produces a tree-like structure containing the opcodes used to execute a particular statement. For example,

```
$ perl -Dx -e 'print 1+2;'
{
6    TYPE = leave  ===> DONE
     FLAGS = (VOID,KIDS,PARENS)
     REFCNT = 0
     {
1        TYPE = enter  ===> 2
     }
     {
2        TYPE = nextstate  ===> 3
         FLAGS = (VOID)
         LINE = 1
         PACKAGE = "main"
     }
     {
5        TYPE = print  ===> 6
         FLAGS = (VOID,KIDS)
         {
3            TYPE = pushmark  ===> 4
             FLAGS = (SCALAR)
         }
         {
4            TYPE = const  ===> 5
             FLAGS = (SCALAR)
             SV = IV(3)
         }
     }
}
```

You can follow the actual execution by following the opcode branches. Each branch is numbered and given in the first column of the output. Like the compiler backend, the opcode tree produced is based on the optimized version of the code—so you can see in this example that the calculation "1+2" has been optimized away to a simple constant value of 3 in node 4 of the execution.

This debug option can be useful if you want to find where, or why, a particular statement is being forwarded to a given opcode branch. At first glance the sequence is difficult to identify, but with practice you can turn even a large tree like this into something your brain can understand, manipulate, and ultimately identify.

Tainting Checks

When working with tainted data, identifying why the data is tainted is not normally a problem—the taint engine will be specific about where, and what, raised the error. But it is sometimes useful to understand why a taint verification failed. Generally, the reason for a security failure on scripts that have been modified to take account of tainted data is a problem with the setuid system. Either a user has tried to execute the code as someone else or the setuid system has failed.

Although we could manually print out the current taint setting, user ID (uid) and effective user ID (euid), a better way is to use the **-Du** debug option. When called, it produces a list of the information, taint value, uid and euid. For example,

```
$ perl -Du -T -e '$path = $ENV{PATH}; system "echo";'

EXECUTING...

$ENV{PATH} 1 1000 1000
Insecure $ENV{PATH} while running with -T switch at -e line 1.
```

In this example we have of course forced the taint failure. When debugging your own scripts, make sure that the uid and euid are identical; if doing that doesn't resolve the problem, then you will need to modify your script to check and verify any data from tainted sources. See the **perlsec** man page for more information on taint checking.

Memory Leaks

We've already seen one example of how Perl allocates memory. This example wasn't particularly useful because it didn't give us a feel for how much memory Perl was using in full. The **–DL** debug option outputs a list of the memory allocated, including the different bucket sizes, for a given Perl operation. I've taken the sample here from the Perl documentation:

```
!!! "after" at test.pl line 3.
   Id  subtot    4    8   12   16   20   24   28   32   36   40   48   56   64   72   80  80+
  0 02  13752    .    .    .    .  294    .    .    .    .    .    .    .    .    .    .    4
  0 54   5545    .    .    8  124   16    .    .    .    1    1    .    .    .    .    .    3   .
  6 02   7152    .    .    .    .    .    .    .    .    .  149    .    .    .    .    .    .
  7 02   3600    .    .    .    .  150    .    .    .    .    .    .    .    .    .    .    .
  7 03     64    .   -1    .    1    .    .    2    .    .    .    .    .    .    .    .    .
  7 04   7056    .    .    .    .    .    .    .    .    .    .    .    .    .    .    .    7
  7 17  38404    .    .    .    .    .    .    .    1    .  442  149    .    .  147    .
  9 03   2078   17  249   32    .    .    .    .    2    .    .    .    .    .    .    .
```

The **Id** is a unique id given to different operations within the interpreter. You can identify a particular operation by using **grep** on the Perl source code. For example, the code 903 indicates the creation of a glob.

The information represented here is not very useful unless you are trying to identify a specific operation's memory leaks—the most useful time is when you are either embedding or extending Perl. If you just want a simple indication of the memory usage by Perl, see the "Debugging Memory Usage" section later in this chapter.

Hash Dump

The **-DH** debug option forces an override of the **values** statement so that instead of printing out the value of a given hash key, it prints out the information about the computed hash value and the array used to store that information. Taking a simple script that populates a hash with four entries—**a => b**, **c => d**, and so on—and then prints each value, you get the following output:

```
104%8=0
106%8=2
100%8=4
102%8=6
```

The format of the output for each value within a hash is as follows:

```
computed_hash%array_max+1 = array_index
```

To understand how this works and its significance, you need to understand how hashes work. The Perl hash system works on a simple premise called *collision chaining*. Here, strings are converted into an integer (the *computed_hash* above). This computed value is used as an array index to the dynamic array **xhv_array**, a component of the hash object used internally by Perl. However, because different strings may result in the same computed value, the index within **xhv_array** is actually used to point to a linked list, and it's this linked list that actually contains the real hash keys.

With this procedure, a number of different hash keys may be stored within the same linked list if the key results in the same integer hash value and, therefore, the same element within **xhv_array**. When you access the hash, the key string you supply is converted to its integer hash value, which gives Perl the starting point within **xhv_array** for the linked list that contains the true key value. This process explains why hash lookups are so fast, even on large complex hashes. When you look up a specific key, instead of traversing over the entire array of hash keys, Perl examines only the linked list that relates to your key's hash value.

In order for the whole thing to be efficient, Perl also needs to ensure that the distribution of linked lists is fairly even—if we had a hash of 1,000 elements, and 900 of them existed within the same linked list, lookups would take an excessive amount of time. Perl gets round this by doubling the size of the **xhv_array** and then re-indexing the hash entries to improve the distribution.

Of course, we still need to actually store the hash value in an array. To convert the hash value into a real array index, Perl folds the computed hash value into the maximum size of the array used to store a given linked list (*array_max* above) using the calculation

```
array_index = computed_hash & array_max;
```

So, taking all of this information in hand, we can use the debug option **-DH** to get an overview of the hash values and the corresponding array of linked lists. Going back to our sample, the value **104%8=0** indicates that the hash value is 104, that it's stored within the **xhv_array** with a maximum of 8 linked lists, with the linked list actually stored at index 0 within **xhv_array**.

For more complex hashes, the output will be a more informative overview of the distribution of hash keys and linked lists. This information can help you to adjust the key-base that you use in order to improve the distribution and, therefore, performance.

Incidentally, if you print a hash in scalar context it outputs the ratio of the number of elements within **xhv_array** that actually store linked lists to the total number of elements in **xhv_array**. This figure gives you a quick indication, without having to resort to debugging, of the efficiency of an array. The lower the ratio between those two numbers, the faster the performance, since a lower ratio indicates that the linked lists are short. For example, the script

```
foreach ('aa' .. 'zz') { $hash{$_} = 1; }

print scalar %hash, "\n";
```

produces a hash of 676 elements and outputs

```
676/1024
```

indicating that there are 676 array elements with linked lists out of a possible 1024. That will give us the highest performance, since the computed hash will take us straight to the value. On the other hand, the script

```
foreach (1 .. 1000) { $hash{"key-$_"} = 1; }

print scalar %hash, "\n";
```

creates 1,000 entries and produces

```
509/1024
```

indicating that there are almost two entries in each linked list for a given hash value, which will slow performance just slightly since each hash key will need to be checked against two entries before we find the value we are looking for.

You can adjust the maximum size of the **xhv_array**, and therefore improve efficiency, by assigning an integer to the **keys** statement for the hash, as in the following:

```
keys %hash = 1000;
```

Perl will round up the figure to the next nearest power of 2, 1024 in this case. Doing this is really useful only if you know you are going to be introducing a lot of entries to a hash, because it stops Perl from performing the re-indexing process as the hash increases in size. The difference is difficult to calculate precisely, since it depends entirely on the hash keys you are using, and in most instances is unlikely to have much significance.

Scratchpad Allocation

Perl creates a number of scratchpad variables that are used to store scalar values before they are finally allotted, either to a scalar variable or optimized or executed away during the execution of an opcode. For example, the statement **4 + 5** actually allocates three scratchpads, one each for the values and one for the result of the **add** opcode. The **–DX** option shows the allocation of these scratchpads during the initial compilation of a script:

```
perl -DX -e '4 + 5;'
Pad 0x813d3c0 alloc 1 for add
Pad 0x813d3c0 sv 1
Pad 0x813d3c0 sv 1
Pad 0x813d3c0 swipe 1
Pad 0x813d3c0 free 1

EXECUTING...
```

Note that the allocation of a scratchpad variable is actually the result of an element allocation within the scratchpad array. Scratchpad arrays are created for individual opcodes and initially have a size of just one element. When using a recursive subroutine call, the size of the scratchpad array will increase by one for each level of recursion. Obviously, if you have a subroutine that contains many levels of recursion, you can end up with a huge scratchpad array for a given opcode.

The same rules and problems can also apply to threads, which also have the potential for creating a number of execution pointers to the same subroutine. In both case, the **-DX** command-line option helps you keep a tag on this.

Cleaning Up

The **-DD** debugger shows where Perl has opted to clean up an object reference, a named glob object, or when cleaning loops within object references. The information produced by this process is large, as the object being cleaned is dumped using the internal object dumper. For example, here's the dump information for a single object reference:

```
Cleaning object ref:
 SV = RV(0x8140c40) at 0x8141534
  REFCNT = 1
  FLAGS = (ROK)
  RV = 0x8136ba8
```

This shows the memory location of the reference, and the reference count. For a named glob object, the information is more explicit:

```
Cleaning named glob object:
 SV = PVGV(0x813e260) at 0x813de18
  REFCNT = 1
  FLAGS = (GMG,SMG,MULTI)
  IV = 0
  NV = 0
  MAGIC = 0x813e2d0
    MG_VIRTUAL = &PL_vtbl_glob
    MG_TYPE = '*'
    MG_OBJ = 0x813de18
    MG_LEN = 5
    MG_PTR = 0x813e2f0 "STDIN"
  NAME = "STDIN"
  NAMELEN = 5
  GvSTASH = 0x8136ad0    "main"
  GP = 0x813e298
    SV = 0x813de24
    REFCNT = 1
```

```
        IO = 0x813de30
        FORM = 0x0
        AV = 0x0
        HV = 0x0
        CV = 0x0
        CVGEN = 0x0
        GPFLAGS = 0x0
        LINE = 0
        FILE = "t12.pl"
        FLAGS = 0x2
        EGV = 0x813de18       "STDIN"
```

This check can be useful in obscure situations when you want to identify where a particular object or glob is being destroyed. You can usually determine this information much easier by using the debugger or even **print** statements to monitor the status of a given object or reference.

Thread Synchronization

The last of the command line debugging options lists all the thread-based operations, including the creation, detaching, joining, and expiration of threads. It will also force Perl to list the current status when the parent thread exits while child threads are still executing. Although it has been updated in Perl 5.6, the thread support is still largely experimental, and this option provides a very simple way for you to monitor how threads are being executed and handled within your script.

Even running the test scripts can raise errors. The following example is the result of executing the **create.t** thread test:

```
$ perl -DS create.t
find_threadsv: new SV 0x8111f78 for $"
entersub: 0x810a850 grabbing 0x811576c:CV(BEGIN) in stash main
entersub: 0x810a850 grabbing 0x8115928:CV(BEGIN) in stash Thread
0x810a850 unsetting CvOWNER of 0x8115928:CV(BEGIN)
restore svref: 0x810a998 0x810aca8:PV("\n"\0) -> 0x811579c:PV("\n"\0)
find_threadsv: new SV 0x8121b28 for $_
entersub: 0x810a850 grabbing 0x8115b2c:CV(load) in stash XSLoader
0x810a850 unsetting CvOWNER of 0x8115b2c:CV(load)
entersub: 0x810a850 grabbing 0x81218a0:CV(import) in stash Exporter
restore svref: 0x8116804 0x8117db0:\CV(__ANON__) -> 0x8117dc8:PVMG()
0x810a850 unsetting CvOWNER of 0x81218a0:CV(import)
0x810a850 unsetting CvOWNER of 0x811576c:CV(BEGIN)
restore svref: 0x810a998 0x810aca8:PV("\n"\0) -> 0x81122f0:PV("\n"\0)
entersub: 0x810a850 grabbing 0x81158b0:CV(BEGIN) in stash main
entersub: 0x810a850 grabbing 0x812b53c:CV(BEGIN) in stash Config
0x810a850 unsetting CvOWNER of 0x812b53c:CV(BEGIN)
restore svref: 0x810a998 0x812b56c:PV("\n"\0) -> 0x81289b4:PV("\n"\0)
find_threadsv: new SV 0x812dd5c for $1
entersub: 0x810a850 grabbing 0x8139dd8:CV(TIEHASH) in stash Config
0x810a850 unsetting CvOWNER of 0x8139dd8:CV(TIEHASH)
entersub: 0x810a850 grabbing 0x812b668:CV(import) in stash Config
restore svref: 0x81207d0 0x812b494:IV(1) -> 0x8117fa8:IV(0)
0x810a850 unsetting CvOWNER of 0x812b668:CV(import)
0x810a850 unsetting CvOWNER of 0x81158b0:CV(BEGIN)
restore svref: 0x810a998 0x810aca8:PV("\n"\0) -> 0x81122f0:PV("\n"\0)
```

```
entersub: 0x810a850 grabbing 0x8139f7c:CV(BEGIN) in stash main
entersub: 0x810a850 grabbing 0x81331c4:CV(BEGIN) in stash Tie::Hash
entersub: 0x810a850 grabbing 0x81218a0:CV(import) in stash Exporter
restore svref: 0x8116804 0x8133494:\CV(__ANON__) -> 0x8117dc8:PVMG(""\0)
0x810a850 unsetting CvOWNER of 0x81218a0:CV(import)
0x810a850 unsetting CvOWNER of 0x81331c4:CV(BEGIN)
restore svref: 0x810a998 0x810aca8:PV("\n"\0) -> 0x812dc78:PV("\n"\0)
entersub: 0x810a850 grabbing 0x81332fc:CV(BEGIN) in stash Tie::Hash
entersub: 0x810a850 grabbing 0x8143e24:CV(BEGIN) in stash warnings
entersub: 0x810a850 grabbing 0x81218a0:CV(import) in stash Exporter
restore svref: 0x8116804 0x8143ef0:\CV(__ANON__) -> 0x8117dc8:PVMG(""\0)
0x810a850 unsetting CvOWNER of 0x81218a0:CV(import)
0x810a850 unsetting CvOWNER of 0x8143e24:CV(BEGIN)
restore svref: 0x810a998 0x8143e54:PV("\n"\0) -> 0x8141d10:PV("\n"\0)
entersub: 0x810a850 grabbing 0x8141a34:CV(import) in stash warnings::register
entersub: 0x810a850 grabbing 0x8141a04:CV(mkMask) in stash warnings::register
0x810a850 unsetting CvOWNER of 0x8141a04:CV(mkMask)
entersub: 0x810a850 grabbing 0x8141a04:CV(mkMask) in stash warnings::register
0x810a850 unsetting CvOWNER of 0x8141a04:CV(mkMask)
0x810a850 unsetting CvOWNER of 0x8141a34:CV(import)
0x810a850 unsetting CvOWNER of 0x81332fc:CV(BEGIN)
restore svref: 0x810a998 0x810aca8:PV("\n"\0) -> 0x812dc78:PV("\n"\0)
0x810a850 unsetting CvOWNER of 0x8139f7c:CV(BEGIN)
restore svref: 0x810a998 0x810aca8:PV("\n"\0) -> 0x81122f0:PV("\n"\0)

EXECUTING...

main thread is 0x810a850
entersub: 0x810a850 grabbing 0x8117e04:CV(async) in stash Thread
new_struct_thread: copied threadsv 0 0x810a850->0x8115008
new_struct_thread: copied threadsv 1 0x810a850->0x8115008
new_struct_thread: copied threadsv 14 0x810a850->0x8115008
new_struct_thread: copied threadsv 18 0x810a850->0x8115008
new_struct_thread: copied threadsv 30 0x810a850->0x8115008
0x810a850: newthread (0x8115008), tid is 1, preparing stack
new thread 0x8115008 waiting to start
0x810a850 unsetting CvOWNER of 0x8117e04:CV(async)
new thread 0x8115008 starting at \CV(__ANON__)
entersub: 0x8115008 grabbing 0x812b44c:CV(__ANON__) in stash main
Starting new thread now
Segmentation fault
```

The initialization shows how Perl identifies the different threads and starts to set up the objects (actually code values) that will make up the threads we want to create. You can even see in the execution how the threads are duplicated and a new thread is created—however, we get a segmentation fault when Perl actually tries to start the thread!

Debugging Memory Usage

Perl has a separate mechanism for debugging memory usage. This check, which works only if Perl was built using Perl's own **malloc** memory allocation function, provides some useful insights into how Perl uses and allocates memory.

To use it, you need to set the value of the **PERL_DEBUG_MSTATS** environment variable. If unset, or set to a value of zero no stats are printed. If set to one, Perl prints out the statistics only after execution; if set to a value greater than one, then it outputs the memory stats after compilation and execution. For example,

```
PERL_DEBUG_MSTATS=2 perl -e 'use Cwd'
Memory allocation statistics after compilation: (buckets 4(4)..16376(16384)
   93388 free:    255   106    447     59     16    3    0     3    2 0 0 3
                  279    168    124    118     11
  214376 used:    255   402   1191    406     16   13    8    65    0 1 2 0
                  232    172    811    470     14
Total sbrk(): 322872/39:187. Odd ends: pad+heads+chain+tail: 1336+3532+2048+8192.
Memory allocation statistics after execution:   (buckets 4(4)..16376(16384)
   93388 free:    255   106    447     59     16    3    0     3    2 0 0 3
                  279    168    124    118     11
  214376 used:    255   402   1191    406     16   13    8    65    0 1 2 0
                  232    172    811    470     14
Total sbrk(): 322872/39:187. Odd ends: pad+heads+chain+tail: 1336+3532+2048+8192.
```

We'll look at each component separately, using the execution stats as a guide.

```
Memory allocation statistics after execution:   (buckets 4(4)..16376(16384)
```

Perl allocates memory for variables, code, and other objects in the form of buckets. Information is placed into these buckets, with the figure above being given in terms of the smallest bucket size, in this case 4 bytes, through to the largest, 16,384 bytes. The numbers in brackets give the overall size of the bucket—the numbers outside of the brackets indicate the maximum size of user data that could fit into the bucket. In this case, we have an overhead of 8 bytes at the largest bucket size, since we can only actually store 16,376 bytes in the largest bucket.

```
93388 free:    255   106    447     59     16    3    0    3    2 0 0 3
               279    168    124    118     11
```

The **free** rows show the number of buckets of different sizes that remain unused. The numbers in the first row relate, in order, to the buckets between the smallest bucket size (or one size larger) and the largest. The second row shows the number of buckets that are unused of a size in between the two numbers above. The whole thing is made clear if it's rewritten as:

```
#Bckt size       8     16     32     64    128 256 512   1024 ...
93388 free:    255   106    447     59     16    3    0      3    2 0 0 3
#Bckt size 4    12     24     48     96
               279    168    124    118     11
```

This shows, for example, that we have 255 buckets of 8 bytes in size that have been allocated but remain unused. While we have 11 buckets of 96 bytes that remain unused.

The **used** rows show the same information, but for the buckets that have been allocated and used. In both cases, the number preceding **free** or **used** shows the total number of bytes allocated.

```
Total sbrk(): 322872/39:187. Odd ends: pad+heads+chain+tail: 1336+3532+2048+8192.
```

The summary **sbrk** row shows the total number of bytes allocated for the script. The **sbrk()** function increases the memory allocation for a running process and is used in conjunction with **malloc()** to help allocate memory within the Perl interpreter. For Perl, this allocation of memory is for the execution of your script. The primary figure, in this case 322,872, gives the total amount of memory that Perl allocated, and 39 is the number of calls that Perl made to the **sbrk()** function. The final figure, 187, shows the number of chunks that Perl thinks are continuous.

The "odd ends" figure gives extended information about how the memory has been allocated. The **pad** figure shows the amount of memory required to keep the individual buckets aligned.

The **heads** shows the overhead required for storing smaller buckets. Remember that the smallest bucket size in our example was 4 bytes, but the bucket size and usable area were the same size: 4 bytes. The overhead is stored in a separate block, which is what the **heads** figure shows.

The **chain** figure gives the amount of memory left over after larger buckets have been split into two or more smaller buckets. The individual fragments are recorded separately and stored as a linked list.

The final **tail** figure gives the amount of memory requested by **sbrk()** but not allocated by **malloc()**.

What It Actually Means

Ignoring all the of the detail given in this report, the really important figure is the total number of bytes allocated through the **sbrk()** call. In our sample, the script used a total of 322,872 bytes of memory. It's worth remembering however that the figure given includes all of the memory allocated by Perl, including that given to internal variables, symbol tables, and scratchpads. Even the simplest of scripts uses a fair amount of memory:

```
$ PERL_DEBUG_MSTATS=1 perl -e '1;'
Memory allocation statistics after execution:    (buckets 4(4)..8184(8192)
   19020 free:    199     80     53     23     11     3     0      2    1 0 0
                  455    126     71      1     22
   39720 used:     56     47     10     39      5     5     0     16    0 1 1
                   56     44     99     41      3
Total sbrk(): 60728/7:155. Odd ends: pad+heads+chain+tail: 1336+652+0+0.
```

The detail is relatively trivial, unless you want to examine the storage mechanisms and trade-offs afforded by storing data in different types of internal structures. Hashes obviously imply a bigger overhead than arrays, and arrays more than simple scalars. Also remember that Perl creates a number of internal structures just to hold information in different formats—accessing the string "1" as an integer and string will almost double the required storage allocation.

The granularity of the information given at this level is probably far too specific for most casual programmers. If you want some quick tips on how to identify possible memory and resource problems, see Chapter 11.

Optimizing Your Code

CHAPTER 11

Manual Optimization

In Chapter 1 we looked at the different processes behind debugging code. There are of course just general problems with code, the bugs and little traps that cause programs to fall over, and we've spent a large portion of the book looking at those problems and how to track, trace, and, hopefully, resolve them. There is, though, another type of bug that, while not as serious, can still cause problems and unnecessary delays in your code.

The type of problems I'm referring to are those that can be optimized away—areas of your code that in essence work fine, but slow the execution down or make inefficient use of Perl's abilities.

Tracing these bugs can be difficult. Some of them are easy to spot, and an expert will be able to cast an eye over a script and spot where you can make better use of Perl to speed up your program. For less experienced users it takes more time, and making their task easier is the aim of this chapter—some guidelines and ideas will be presented for improving the speed of applications without affecting their operation. As with all other areas of debugging, over time these practices will become automatic, but even an experienced programmer will sometimes use the quick, rather than the efficient, method just to make sure the algorithm works.

There are in fact two sides to the optimization process: improving the speed and improving the memory usage. The speed angle is the easiest to spot since it relates directly to the execution flow of your program—using a **for** loop to iterate over each item in an array instead of just using a hash, for example. Memory is more difficult. Although tools are available for tracking memory usage (see Chapter 10), these really give an idea only of the entire memory usage, not of the areas within a script that might be making bad use of memory.

What we won't be doing in this chapter is sorting out problems with inefficient algorithms used in your programs. These problems are difficult to provide guidance on, although Donald Knuth's *The Art of Computer Programming* (three volumes on basic algorithms, searching and sorting, and semi-numerical algorithms) will help. For tools that will help you spot problem areas, see Chapter 12, "Automatic Optimization."

Tracing Execution

Manual optimization, by its very definition, is a *manual* process. The tools we look at in Chapter 12 will help you only to identify those areas within your script that are causing problems; they won't do the optimization for you. Even though Perl does do its own sort of optimization, it's highly focused on the elements that it can find and optimize away—it can't spot, or indeed fix, a bad algorithm or approach.

This situation is something that may change in the future—compilers and interpreters are getting smarter, and building in the capability to spot possible bad approaches to a problem is probably not many years away.

Until that time, the only solution is to manually trawl through your scripts and find and fix the problems. One simple way is to use some of the manual debugging techniques we looked at back in Chapter 9—using a **print** statement just to highlight a possible problem area is useful. For example, if you're debugging a program that uses a number of loops and other nested statements, just putting a single **print** statement that gives the name of the loop or function should give you a good idea of the number of times each is being called.

If you're worried about the actual timing, think about using **time** to get the start and end times for specific functions, or better still, use the Perl profiler in Chapter 12.

When actually looking through your code there are three main areas you should probably concentrate on

- *Variables* Efficient use of variables means creating only those that you need, using locally scoped variables (using **my**) where possible, and avoiding the creation of scalars, lists, or hashes that are more than a few hundred bytes or elements in size.

- *Function* Passing large lists to functions should be avoided; using small, compact, self-contained functions should be favored when a specific function will be called a number of times in a loop. See Chapter 5 for information on creating and optimizing your programs using functions.

- *Program Control* Structures that imply loops, nested function calls, and repetitive iterations should be avoided. Always think about what the options are during a test expression—think of using a predefined default value and testing only for non-default entries.

We'll have a look at some of the specifics in the next few pages.

Spotting Resource Sinks

The two areas we will be looking at are ways to increase the speed of execution and ways to reduce memory usage. As in all things, there is usually a trade-off for both sides of the equation. It *is* possible to increase speed—but often at the risk of increasing memory usage. Reading a large file into memory, for example, will reduce the number of calls to the system for more data—on the other hand it will also mean allocating a large chunk of memory to hold the file content.

There is no hard-and-fast rule for which to choose. In the modern world, speed is more important than memory, especially when disk and RAM storage is so cheap. However, keep in mind that large memory usage will slow down the execution of web-based solutions, where the possibility of multiple instances of a script executing simultaneously are a reality.

There's also a certain amount of crossover—some of the techniques that are listed as purely speed improvements will actually also help to reduce memory usage. I've tried to note both the crossover and complementary techniques where possible.

Increasing Speed

Increasing the speed of execution relies on your ability first to produce a good algorithm and second to make the best use of Perl's capabilities to help the algorithm along. Simple things like keyword lists are much better handled by a hash than an array because the internal hashing algorithms have already been optimized. We can go straight to a hash value, and even using hashes as a way of de-duping material is still more efficient than using arrays and iteration.

Program Structure

The program structure is the general layout of the script, and some of the generic statements that you'll use in all parts of the application.

- Avoid using **goto** when a function or loop control statement will achieve the same result. Any call to **goto** causes the parser to search for the specified label; Perl doesn't keep an internal table.

- Don't use **eval** when you can use braces to expand information (such as variable names) inline. You can use something like this:

```
${$prefix . $var} = "String";
```

- Also, avoid using **eval** inside a loop, since doing so will cause Perl to run the parser over the **eval** statement for each iteration. Instead, put the iteration inside the **eval** so the block will only have to be parsed once.

- Within the context of a loop, always place control statements as early as possible to prevent Perl from executing statements it then never uses. For example, the following code is wasteful:

```
while (<DATA>)
{
    chomp;
    next if /^#/;
...
}
```

You don't have to take the newline off the end of the string in order for the regular expression test to match.

- Replace **if..else** statements used to select from a range of single values with a logical **or**. You can always use

```
$login = getlogin || (getpwuid($<))[0] || "Anonymous";
```

- Avoid calling complex subroutines in large loops, especially those with few other steps. The overhead in copying arguments to the stack and back again will slow the process down. If you can, use references rather than static lists; or, if that becomes a real problem, rewrite the function in C.

- Use lists to functions that accept them in place of concatenating a string. Using concatenation with **print**, for example, involves copying each value into a new string before returning the concatenated version and moving on to the next element. Using a list speeds up the process considerably. Alternatively, try using **join** with a null separator value, since **join** will add each string to a new string, instead of performing multiple copies on each element.

Variables and Constants

Good variable design should help to reduce most of the overhead—for example using arrays instead of lists of individual variables. Other tips are shown here:

- Avoid using default values for variables. Perl always initializes variables to 0 or empty anyway.

- Pre-extending an array or string can save time, as it pre-allocates memory that Perl would otherwise attempt to allocate on the fly.

- Use hashes instead of arrays to hold information like keywords (for which you would otherwise use an array and a search mechanism to find). Also, remember that you can use hashes to remove duplicates from a list.

Don't waste time doing the manual math on static expressions:

```
$day_seconds = 24*60*60;
```

Perl will optimize this away into a single value during compilation for you. Even better, use the expression where it's needed and don't waste time introducing yet another variable.

- Use **my** instead of **local**.

- Don't **undef** variables you may want to use again later for a different purpose. More specifically, don't create multiple variables when a single temporary variable will do. Better still, use $_ if you can get away with it.

Printing, Interpolation, and Manipulation

The display and interpolation of text can be quite a time consuming process, especially within script that makes heavy use of text output—for example parsers or CGI scripts.

- Avoid using quotes that interpolate on text that doesn't require interpolation. Although doing this won't save you much time, it will mean that Perl has to investigate fewer strings when interpolating data.

- Use **print** in place of **printf** unless you absolutely have to print a specific format. Remember that variables can be interpolated directly into certain quoted strings.

- Avoid using **substr** many times on a long string when a regular expression could perform the conversion or extraction quicker. For example, to extract the elements from a date in the form "19980326," using **substr**

```
$date = '19980326';
$year = substr($date,0,4);
$month = substr($date,4,2);
$day   = substr($date,6,2);
```

is almost certainly quicker using a regular expression:

```
$date = '19980326';
($year, $month, $day) = $date =~ '/(d{4})(\d{2})(\d{2})/'
```

Better still, use **pack** and **unpack** for strings. You could rewrite the above example as:

```
($year, $month, $day) = unpack("c4c2c2",$date);
```

- Use **substr** to modify a string, rather than extracting the elements and concatenating the new version. Better still, use a regular expression substitution.

- Use **tr///** instead of **s///g** to delete characters from a string.

- When working with multiple filehandles, especially if they are network sockets, use **select** rather than a round-robin approach. Better still, consider using **fork** or the new **Thread** module so that you can service requests asynchronously. Remember, though, that **fork** implies an overhead as the process is copied, and threads imply a memory overhead.

Regular Expressions

Regular expressions can be huge resource sinks. The backtracking process used to match groups and repeating elements implies a large overhead as it requires a number of iterations over the same section of text. Other traps and solutions are outlined below:

- Optimize regular expressions by reducing the number of quantifiers and assertions in a single expression. Doing this is especially useful when using expression groups, since this causes the regular expression engine to backtrack and populate the **$#** variables each time.

- Avoid using the **$&**, **$`**, and **$'** variables. At the first point of use, Perl starts to track the information for every regular expression used afterwards.

- Using a logical **or**, **||**, outside of a regular expression can sometimes be quicker than using the alternative within a regular expression. So use

```
$found = if /one/ || /two/;
```

instead of

```
$found = if /one|two/;
```

- When testing a string for a number of times with many regular expressions, group all the a's, all the b's, and so on. Perl works faster this way because the internal tables will have already been built.

- If the string is large and the regular expressions are complex, use the **study** function to improve performance.

Files and Filesystems

Because they are external, many people neglect to consider the effects of a file or filesystem call into overall equation. Although such a call won't affect the Perl script execution, it does take time for the OS to process the request. Reducing the number of calls, or the size of such calls will help both performance and memory usage.

- Use **sysread** to get information in blocks, not **getc**.

- Use **grep** and **opendir** for reading directory listings to avoid large lists being returned from the **glob** function.

- Use the OS **mkdir** command (if supported) when creating multiple directories instead of using multiple calls to the built-in **mkdir**.

- Don't use **eof** when operators and functions detect **eof** automatically.

Calling External Applications

You don't have any control over the execution time and sequence of an external program, but you can reduce the effects by using internal functions or by forcing direct, rather than shell-based execution.

- Avoid making calls to operating system functions when the predefined variables built into every Perl script at execution time are likely to contain the information you want.

- Use the **Cwd** module instead of making an external call to **pwd**. Using **system** creates a subprocess and possibly a shell, involving a lot of extra instructions and processor time.

- Use lists with **system** and **exec** instead of using one big string that you have to quote and format in order to get the right information.

Reducing Memory

When we're talking about reducing the memory footprint for Perl, we're really talking about reducing the RAM footprint, rather than disk space. Internally, Perl will allow you to do all sorts of things that potentially increase the memory footprint without your being aware that this is happening. The obvious instances are loading entire files into memory for processing, but less obvious problems can be caused by creating temporary arrays and lists.

The places where we can reduce the memory footprint are few and far between. Perl's practicality comes from its automatic handling of things like memory and variable allocation, and garbage collection when variables go out of context. There is no way to control Perl's memory usage beyond the tips given here, although such control is planned for a future version.

Variables and Data

It's very easy to let Perl use a lot of memory without considering the consequences. The tips below should help you to reduce the memory footprint of your variables:

- Use the **vec** function to store very small numbers in a single variable, rather than individual variables for each.

- Use **pack** and **unpack** to store information efficiently in external files.

- Use **substr** to store small fixed-length strings in one larger string.

You can also follow this through to arrays and hashes, which can be stored in a file if memory space is really tight. If necessary, use temporary files to store very large arrays. In addition, consider using a DBM file to store hash and list information out of memory. If you want to store small pairs of information in hashes, consider using the **Tie::SubstrHash** module, which will compact hash data much more tightly than the normal 1K (or larger) key/value pair size.

Iteration and Program Control

Certain Perl statements automatically imply large memory overheads; the more significant ones are listed here:

- Use **each** in place of **keys** for iterating through hashes when order is not important. It reduces the size of the temporary list passed to the loop control statement.

- Try to avoid creating large temporary lists, for example,

```
foreach (0..$#array)
{
    #Do something with $array[$_];
}
```

Although this has been optimized in recent versions of Perl, it's still best avoided if possible. Use a **while** or **for** loop with a simple variable and test.

- In general, try to avoid any list operations that could be avoided; creating an array and then using it frequently uses a lot of temporary storage space, even on relatively small arrays.

- Use **undef** and **delete** to remove variables or hash elements that you no longer need.

- Pass around references to variables, especially lists and hashes, rather than supplying lists to the function each time.

- Avoid creating temporary lists that are used solely to support a sequence for a hash, for example,

```
@sort = keys %hash;
foreach (sort @sorted)
...
```

Sort the list inline, that is,

```
foreach (sort keys %hash)
```

If the list is complex and you need to process each element in order to sort, remember that you can supply your own sorting function to **sort**. This process can even be used on complex data—for example, to sort dates you could use this:

```
foreach (sort sortdate keys %errors)
{
    print "$_\n";
```

```
}


sub sortdate
{
    my ($c,$d) = ($a,$b);

    $c =~ s{(\d+)/(\d+)/(\d+)}{sprintf("%04d%02d%02d",$3,$1,$2)}e;
    $d =~ s{(\d+)/(\d+)/(\d+)}{sprintf("%04d%02d%02d",$3,$1,$2)}e;

    $c <=> $d;
}
```

Here we've copied the values of **$a** and **$b** supplied to the function and then compared the modified values—doing this prevents us from modifying the originals, since **$a** and **$b** are really references to the list contents.

In this instance the space optimization means a decrease in speed!

## CHAPTER 12

Automatic Optimization

The title of this chapter is probably a little misleading, since it implies that we can get Perl to do its own optimization. Of course this is partly true—back in Chapter 2 we had a look at the execution process of a Perl script, and one of the stages that Perl goes through is a sort of optimization process. A drawback of this process is that it's fairly simplistic, and all it really does is try to fold multiple statements into a single opcode to improve the final performance.

So, the problem with this process is that it doesn't really optimize your program. It doesn't pick out and fix the traps that we saw in the last chapter, like pointless loops, using arrays when hashes would be better (or vice versa), or inefficient uses of **eval**.

To pick up most of these efficiency errors you need to manually trawl through your code, as we did in Chapter 11, or you need to use a tool that will help you to identify and optimize parts of your program so that you can make modifications yourself.

There are two tools supplied with Perl that will help you spot possible areas that can be optimized, the Perl profiler and the Perl compiler. The Perl profiler is a special extension to the debugging backend that also supports the debugger we saw back in Chapter 10. The profiler works by monitoring how long it takes to execute individual subroutines and then produces a report based on this information. The profiler doesn't optimize the subroutines for you, but it will identify which ones require a closer look to see if they can be hand-optimized.

The Perl compiler is a relatively new feature to Perl. Its primary purpose is to allow you to convert your Perl script into a standalone executable, embedding the script and the interpreter into a single application. However, the backends supplied with the compiler can also be used to help you identify statements that Perl has optimized. Alternatively, you can produce a precompiled version of a script that you can then execute directly, thereby eliminating the normal parser/optimization stage used for executing text scripts.

The Perl Profiler

The Perl Profiler takes a typical script and, using the debugging backend, monitors the execution of individual subroutines within the script. The profiler monitors both the functions or methods defined within the confines of the script itself and any subroutines/methods imported from outside— including the **import** method employed during a **use** statement.

The actual process is in two stages:

- Run the script using the **DProf** debugging extension. Doing this produces a separate file called **tmon.out**.

- Run the **dprofpp** script, which analyzes the information within **tmon.out** and produces a variety of reports based on that information.

The first stage is easy, just supply the **DProf** extension as the name of the debugger to use when you execute the script. For example,

```
$ perl -d:DProf slow.pl
```

The **tmon.out** file contains information for each individual subroutine call, including how long it took to execute and the name of the subroutine that called it. From this information you can gain a fairly clear understanding of precisely what was executed, and when, and how long it took. Although you can analyze and process this information yourself, Perl comes prepared with its **dprofpp** script.

The **dprofpp** script is installed when you install Perl and should exist within your execution path ready to use to post-process the profiling. It takes the **tmon.out** file, collates all of the information, and then outputs a summary of the timing information as a straight list, a nested tree, or in a variety of other formats.

The options for the **dprofpp** script are shown in Table 12-1. If you regularly use a specific set of options, you can use the **DPROFPP_OPTS** environment variable to store the list of default options. The default value would be **–z –O 15 –E**.

Option	Description
-a	Sorts the list of subroutines alphabetically.
-A	Reports the time for functions loaded via the AutoLoad module as ***::AUTOLOAD**, showing the total time for all autoloaded modules. The default is for individual functions (autoloaded or otherwise) to have their own time calculated.
-E	This is the default option, displaying all subroutine times exclusive of child subroutine times.
-F	Generates fake exit time values. This gets around the problem introduced by subroutines calling **exit** or **exec**, which causes the normal execution process of the script to end prematurely.
-g subroutine	Shows the results only for **subroutine** and the subroutines it calls.
-I	Displays child as well as parent execution times.
-l	Sorts the list of subroutines by the number of times each subroutine has been called.
-O count	Displays only the first **count** subroutines.
-p script	Executes **script** and then outputs report.
-Q	Quits after profiling the script with **–p** without producing a report.
-q	Displays report without headers.
-R	Counts anonymous subroutines within the same package scope individually. The normal operation is to count each invocation separately.
-r	Displays only elapsed real times. Individual user and system times are not displayed.
-s	Displays only system times. User times are not displayed.
-S	Displays merged subroutine call tree, with statistical information for each branch, to **STDOUT**. Making multiple calls to the same function within the same branch creates a new branch at the next level. Repeat counts are displayed for each function within each branch. Sort order is by total time per branch.
-T	Displays subroutine call tree to **STDOUT**. Statistics are not printed.
-t	Displays subroutine call tree to **STDOUT**, and subroutines called multiple consecutive times are simply displayed with a repeat count. Statistics are not printed.
-U	Do not sort subroutine list.
-u	Displays only user times. System times are not displayed.

Table 12.1 Options for the dprofpp Profiling System

Option	Description
-V	Prints the version number of the **dprofpp** script and prints the **Devel::Dprof** version number stored in the statistics file if found or specified.
-v	Sorts by the average time elapsed for child calls within each call.
-z	Sorts the subroutine list by the amount of user and system time used.

Table 12.1   Options for the dprofpp Profiling System *(continued)*

The default output of the **dprofpp** script is shown here:

```
Total Elapsed Time = 40.28038 Seconds
  User+System Time = 40.18038 Seconds
Exclusive Times
%Time ExclSec CumulS #Calls sec/call Csec/c  Name
 100.   40.21 40.215    1001   0.0402 0.0402  First::foo
 0.31   0.125 40.291       1   0.1254 40.290  Second::foo
 0.00   0.000 40.340       1   0.0000 40.340  main::bar
```

By default, the information output shows the total amount of time elapsed to produce the script. Note that this might give a slightly extended figure, since it will depend on the other processes running on your machine. The user and system time is the total time spent actually executing your script. User time is that spent by Perl actually processing, and the system time is that spent by the system servicing requests—for example, reading data from a file or outputting information to the screen.

The remainder of the figures relate to the individual functions in a columnar format, and the descriptions for each column are summarized below.

- **%Time**   The amount of time relative to the other functions spent in this single function.
- **ExclSec**   The amount of time spent executing this function—this figure does not include the time taken by other functions called by this one.
- **CumulS**   The amount of time spent executing this function and any functions called by this function.
- **#Calls**   The number of calls to this function.
- **Sec/call**   The average number of seconds spent executing each invocation of this function—this figure does not include the time taken by other functions called by this one.
- **Csec/c**   The average number of seconds spent executing each invocation of this function and any other functions called by this one.

You can see from this example that the function called most often, and the one that soaks up the most amount of time, is the **foo** function in the **First** package.

You can also produce a report that shows the nesting and relative execution times of the individual functions and how they were called

```
main::bar x 1    40.34s = (0.00 + 40.34)s
  Second::foo x 1        40.29s = (0.13 + 40.17)s
    First::foo x 1000     40.17s
  First::foo x 1          0.05s
```

The remainder of the command-line options essentially just modify these two basic reports, either changing the order, the calculation parameters, or the tree display.

Sample Script Profile

For our sample script we're going to use a simplified version of an HTTP log processor. It extracts a single field (the date/time string) and then produces a list of the unique entries. The log file used is about 8Mb in size—consisting of 90,300 lines. It's actually a 180Kb file duplicated many times—this is deliberate, both to stress-test the script and provide us with enough samples to get a good idea of the relative execution times. The first version of the script looks like this:

```perl
#!/usr/local/bin/perl -w

use strict;
my @datetime;
process();

sub process
{
    open(DATA,"../access.log") or die "can't open log: $!";
    while(<DATA>)
    {
        chomp;
        my @fields = split;
        process_fields(@fields);
    }
}

sub process_fields
{
    my (@fields) = @_;
    add_to_datetime($fields[3]);
}

sub add_to_datetime
{
    my ($datetime) = @_;
    foreach (@datetime)
    {
        return if ($datetime eq $_);
    }
    push @datetime,$datetime;
}
```

The profiler doesn't pick up on the **main** section of script, aside from lumping it all into the overall execution time; we've therefore split out the main processing loop into its own function to get a precise timing value. Those who've followed the tips in the last chapter should already be able to spot the two obvious resource sinks in the preceding example.

Running the profiler on this script and then calling **dprofpp** without any arguments gives the following output:

```
Total Elapsed Time = 91.55104 Seconds
  User+System Time = 91.79165 Seconds
Exclusive Times
%Time ExclSec CumulS #Calls sec/call Csec/c  Name
 72.4   66.47 65.511  90300   0.0007 0.0007  main::add_to_datetime
 23.7   21.84 95.886      1   21.841 95.885  main::process
 11.5   10.58 74.044  90300   0.0001 0.0008  main::process_fields
 0.01   0.010  0.010      1   0.0100 0.0099  main::BEGIN
 0.00   0.000 -0.000      1   0.0000      -  strict::import
 0.00   0.000 -0.000      1   0.0000      -  strict::bits
```

The biggest sink is the **add_to_datetime** function, which is responsible for adding a unique entry to the **datetime** array. This is a lengthy process, because it means stepping through the array each time (in fact, 90,300 times). Although there's only about 405 unique items, there's still a lot of iterations to go over before we either pick up the one we need or determine that we need to add the current entry to the list. This particular resource sink is a good example of where using an array is a really bad idea—we could replace it with a hash and eliminate the loop.

The main **process** function we can ignore for the moment—there's not a lot we can do to speed up the parsing of the individual lines that we read from the file. Actually, there is the fact that we call an external function to process. This final execution sink, the **process_fields** function, accepts a relatively large array from the **process** function and in turn calls the **add_to_datetime** function.

Again, according to the last chapter, calling a function repetitively, especially when there are a number of different arguments, is a resource sink. This is because Perl has to copy the arguments onto the stack before calling the function. We could try using references or a global variable, but, in conjunction with the other sink, there's probably a better solution.

If we fix both of these problems, we can produce a new script that uses a hash rather than two functions and an array. The new version of the script looks like this:

```perl
#!/usr/local/bin/perl -w

use strict;
my %datetime;

process();

sub process
{
    open(DATA,"../access.log") or die "can't open log: $!";
    while(<DATA>)
    {
        chomp;
        my @fields = split;
```

```
        $datetime{$fields[3]} = 1;
    }
}
```

Running the script with the profiler enabled and then reporting on it using **dprofpp** we get this:

```
Total Elapsed Time = 19.75992 Seconds
  User+System Time = 19.68992 Seconds
Exclusive Times
%Time ExclSec CumulS #Calls sec/call Csec/c  Name
 99.6  19.62  19.620      1   19.620 19.620  main::process
 0.00  0.000  -0.000      1   0.0000      -  main::BEGIN
 0.00  0.000  -0.000      1   0.0000      -  strict::import
 0.00  0.000  -0.000      1   0.0000      -  strict::bits
```

A big difference—we've managed to reduce the execution time from 91 seconds down to less than 20, just by using a hash. We've also eliminated two function calls—because we don't need them anymore—and ended up with just one function that does all of the work.

This is a great demonstration of why hashes are faster for these sorts of summary calculations. The hashing algorithm has done all of the nasty work for us. For a description of the hashing algorithm and why it is so much faster than a normal progressive array lookup, see Chapter 10, under "Command-Line Debugging: Hash Dump."

One-Hit Profiling

If all you want to do is produce a profile for a single hit of a script, you can use the **dprofpp** script directly:

```
$ dprofpp -S -p t.pl
```

However, if what you want is to continually probe the original results for different combinations and different reports, perhaps targeting a different selection of functions each time, then you should run the script through the profiler to create the **tmon.out** file. You can then compile reports based on the raw data without having to run the script again. Comparing the results of multiple executions of the script is often a waste of time, since the minor differences between each execution may introduce wildly different figures for certain functions.

Also be aware of the size of the raw data file created. For this small script, a 16K data file is generated. Larger scripts with more functions and, more importantly, more function calls will generate significantly more data. Our slow script example above produces a 1.6Mb data file for processing.

Profiling Alternatives

At the simplest level, just record the timings given by **time** before and after calling a function:

```
$before = time();
myfunction();
$after = time();
$duration = $before-$after;
```

The only problem with this solution is that we get to know the duration only in seconds—useful when you are calling a function that will take a long time, but not fine enough if want you want to profile the individual calls to functions.

A better solution is the **Benchmark** module, which is part of the standard Perl distribution. This works in the same basic fashion as the **time** example above, except that we get a granularity of milliseconds (through the use of the **times** function). For example, the code

```
$t = timeit(1000000,'cos(3.141)');
print "Calculation time: ", timestr($t), "\n";
```

will place the timing information for a million iterations of the calculation into **$t**, which will be a reference to a **Benchmark** object. The **timestr** function then prints out a suitably formatted message:

```
Calculation time:  1 wallclock secs ( 1.70 usr + -0.07 sys =  1.63 CPU) @
6134969.33/s (n=10000000)
```

Alternatively, you can calculate the timings for an arbitrary set of statements:

```
$ta = new Benchmark;
&render_object();
$tb = new Benchmark;
print "Calculation time: ", timestr(timediff($ta,$tb)), "\n";
```

The problem with both these solutions is that they require you to modify your scripts before you get any useful data. While this is not a huge problem, it adds to the development time. The profiler doesn't have this problem—you can just get the information instantly.

The tricks are, on the other hand, useful either if you want to provide information directly to your users or if you want to monitor a sequence of statements as a whole. The profiler will deal only with functions, so without splitting your code into a number of subroutines (which will of course slow it down) there's no way to identify the timing information for small sections of code.

Using the Compiler

The obvious solution with the Perl compiler is just to turn your scripts into standalone applications. Doing that will, theoretically, make them run faster, although this won't always be the case. There are other solutions related to the compiler that we can use—in fact, there are tools provided with the compiler that will merely improve the speed at which we can develop without necessarily optimizing the execution of the script itself.

The Perl compiler is a relatively new inclusion in the Perl distribution and is still considered largely experimental. It's been updated and improved upon heavily in Perl 5.6 to the point where most of the features of the compiler now work more or less as expected.

The Perl compiler works by taking the internal opcode tree produced by the Perl parser/compiler and then reproducing it in the desired format. At this point, the opcode tree can be converted into a number of different formats, including, if we want, an optimized version of the Perl source script.

When producing a standalone executable, the opcode tree is embedded along with some C-based wrapper code into a C source file. This, in turn, can be compiled using a standard C compiler such as **gcc** to produce the final executable. Because the source file includes the Perl source code and is linked to the Perl interpreter, we get a fully standalone application. Further, because the Perl source is taken after the normal Perl parsing and optimization procedures have taken place, we end up with an already optimized version of the original script.

The entire system works using a series of backend modules, such as **B::C** for the C source code creator, or **B::Xref** for the cross reference backend. When producing a standalone executable, you can also use the **perlcc** front end, which does the conversion and compilation stages for you. We'll have a look at the backends first.

The Backends

There are two parts to the compiler backends. The **B** modules actually contain the backend code itself—these modules turn the raw opcode tree into a number of different formats. The **O** module just provides a nice friendly frontend to enable us to use the backends available.

We will examine nine backends with respect to both optimization and debugging: **C**, **CC**, **Bytecode**, **Terse**, **Debug**, **Xref**, **Lint**, **Deparse**, and **ShowLex**. All backends work in the same basic way. You call the **O** module as part of the command line to a normal Perl interpreter and then specify the backend and any options you want to define:

```
$ perl -MO=Backend[,OPTIONS] foo.pl
```

Most backends support three options. The **-v** option forces the backend to report extensive information about the compilation process. The **-D** option enables a debugging—different backends support a number of different debugging options, so check the individual backends for more information on how to uses these. The **-o** option (followed by a file name) redirects the output of the backend to another file. Multiple options to the frontend can be separated by commas.

C Backend

The **C** backend is the fundamental part of the conversion of a Perl script into its **C** opcode equivalent. The backend produces code based on the state of the Perl script just before execution begins; that is, the compilation, parsing, and optimization processes normally conducted by the interpreter have already been completed. The compiled program can, therefore, execute more or less identically to the original interpreted version. Unfortunately, this process also means that the speed of execution is identical.

The basic options, shared with the **CC** backend, are shown in Table 12-2. There are also a number of options specific to the **C** backend, shown in Table 12-3.

Option	Description
-	End of options.
-uPackname	Include functions defined in **Packname** to be compiled if they have not otherwise been selected. Normally, only functions that are identified as being used are included in the opcode tree. Unused functions are ignored. Using this option allows functions that are used via an **eval** to be compiled with the rest of the Perl script. Obviously, this also increases the size of the source code created as well as the eventual size of the executable.

Table 12.2   Basic **C** Backend Options

For example, the following creates the C source code of the **foo.pl** Perl script to the file **foo.c**, with optimization:

```
$ perl -MO=C,-O1,-ofoo.c foo.pl
```

You can then compile the **foo.c** program using any C compiler, remembering to link to the Perl library in order to produce a final executable. It's quicker and easier to use the **perlcc** frontend to the whole process, which will not only produce the source, but also compile the file for you.

CC Backend

The **CC** backend produces C code equivalent to the tree that would be executed at runtime. This is in effect like writing the script as it would be executed. The optimization and reduction stages have taken place already, allowing for much better performance. See Chapter 2 for an example of the sort of optimizations that take place during the compilation and optimization of a Perl script.

Option	Description
-Do	Debug opcodes; prints each opcode as it is processed.
-Dc	Debug construct opcodes (COPs); prints COPs as they are processed, including file and line number.
-DA	Debug; prints array value information.
-DC	Debug; prints code value information.
-DM	Debug; prints magic variable information.
-fcog	Copy-on-grow; string values are declared and initialized statically. Can have an effect on speed, since each time the string grows in size a new string variable is created and the information is copied over. The opposite action, **-fno-cog** incurs less of a penalty but may also cause memory-related failures during execution of the final application.
-fno-cog	No copy-on-grow; string values are initialized dynamically.
-On	Set optimization to the value of **n**. Values of one and higher set **–fcog**.

Table 12.3   Options Specifically for the **C** Backend

At the moment, the compiler still deals with the raw bytecode of the script directly. This is still not as efficient as it could be—for example, when using an integer within a Perl script, we still actually deal with a Perl scalar variable object, instead of just using a genuine C integer, which obviously impacts performance.

The **CC** backend supports the same basic options as the **C** backends that are shown in Table 12-3. The **CC**-specific options are shown in Table 12-4.

For example, to create the C source code of the **foo.pl** Perl script to the file **foo.c**:

```
$ perl -MO=CC,-ofoo.c foo.pl
```

Again, it's probably better to use the **perlcc** frontend, which we'll look at shortly, to produce and compile your script into its executable format.

Option	Description
-mModulename	Generates source code for an XSUB, creating a hook function named **boot_Modulename** suitable for identification by the DynaLoader module.
-Dr	Debug; outputs debugging information to **STDERR**. If not specified, the debugging information is included as comments in the C source code produced.
-DO	Debug; prints with opcode as it's processed.
-Ds	Debug; prints the shadow stack of the opcode as it's processed.
-Dp	Debug; prints the contents of the shadow pad of lexical variables as loaded for each block (including the main program).
-Do	Debug; prints the name of each fake PP function just before it is processed.
-D	Debug; prints the source file name and line number of each line of Perl code as it is processed.
-Dt	Debug; prints the timing information for each compilation stage.
-ffreetmps-each-bblock	Forces the optimization of freeing temporaries to the end of each block until the end of each statement.
-ffreetmps-each-loop	Forces the optimization of freeing temporaries to the end of each enclosing loop, instead of the end of each statement. You can set only one of the **freetmps** optimizations at any one time.
-fomit-taint	Disables the generation of the tainting mechanism.
-On	Sets the optimization to level **n**. A level of **–O1** implies **–ffreetmps-each-bblock**, and **-O2** implies **-ffreetmps-each-loop**.

Table 12.4   Options Specifically for CC Backend

Bytecode Backend

We can produce a permanently optimized version of a Perl script by storing the bytecode produced during the normal parsing and optimization stage. That way, when we execute the produced bytecode, we've already gone through the parsing/optimization process, thus saving us some time. This is the solution offered by web accelerators like **mod_perl** and **PerlEx**; they store the compiled version and execute it using an already loaded interpreter.

The easiest interface for producing a bytecode version of a script is to use **perlcc** with the **-b** option:

```
$ perlcc -b foo.pl
```

This will produce a file, **foo.plc**, that is actually ready to run Perl script. It includes the bytecode and the **ByteLoader** module, which reads and executes the bytecode for you. The produced file is platform independent—it's still essentially a Perl source file, just in its compiled, rather than raw, state. To execute it, just run the script as normal:

```
$ perl foo.plc
```

Alternatively, you can produce a bytecode file, without the **ByteLoader** preamble, by using the backend directly:

```
$ perl -MO=Bytecode,-ofoo.bc foo.pl
```

Note that by default the bytecode file is sent to **STDOUT**, which will most likely upset your terminal. You should always use the **–ofilename** option to specify an alternative file in order to store the compiled program. Other options are listed in Table 12-5.

Option	Description
-Do	Debug; prints out each opcode as it is processed.
-Dt	Debug; prints out the compilation progress.
-Da	Debug; includes source assembler lines in the bytecode as comments.
-DC	Debug; prints each code value as taken from the final symbol tree.
-S	Produces bytecode assembler source instead of the final bytecode binary.
-m	Compiles the script as a module.
-fcompress-nullops	Completes only the required fields of opcodes that have been optimized by the compiler. Other fields are ignored (saves space). Can be switched off with **-fno-compress-nullops**.
-omit-sequence-numbers	Ignores the code normally produced that populates the **op_seq** field of each opcode (saves space). This is normally used only by Perl's internal compiler. Can be switched off with **-fno-omit-sequence-numbers**.
-fbypass-nullops	Ignores null opcodes; the code skips to the next non-null opcode in the execution tree (saves space and time). Can be switched off with **-fno-bypass-nullops**.

Table 12.5   Options Specifically for Bytecode Backend

Option	Description
-f-strip-syntax-tree	Does not produce the internal pointers that compose the syntax tree. This does not affect execution, but the produced bytecode cannot be disassembled. This has the effect of rendering **goto LABEL** statements useless. It also works as a suitable security measure to stop bytecode-compiled scripts from being reverse-engineered. Can be switched off with **-fno-strip-syntax-tree**.
-On	Sets optimization to level n. Currently, **-O1** implies **-fcompress-nullops** and **-fomit-sequence** numbers. **-O6** implies **-fstrip-syntax-tree**.

Table 12.5   Options Specifically for Bytecode Backend (*continued*)

Terse Backend

The **Terse** backend is useful when you want to examine the exact execution path of a script in its opcode-compiled format. The information output is, as the name suggests, very terse, but it should provide you with a basic idea of the process that is taking place when a script executes. By default the information is formatted and printed in syntax order; for example,

```
$ perl -MO=Terse -e '$a = $b + 2;
-e syntax OK
LISTOP (0x13c530) pp_leave
    OP (0x1349a0) pp_enter
    COP (0x13c5f0) pp_nextstate
    BINOP (0x1435a0) pp_sassign
        BINOP (0x12eb40) pp_add [1]
            UNOP (0x12eb00) pp_null [15]
                GVOP (0x12eae0) pp_gvsv  GV (0xc9864) *b
            SVOP (0x1435c0) pp_const  IV (0xbc9d8) 2
        UNOP (0xbf6c0) pp_null [15]
            GVOP (0xbf660) pp_gvsv  GV (0xc6ba0) *a
```

The backend supports only one option, **exec**, which outputs the opcodes in execution order. Unfortunately, it removes much of the formatting available in the default mode:

```
$ perl -MO=Terse,exec -e '$a = $b + 2;'
-e syntax OK
OP (0x1349a0) pp_enter
COP (0x13c5f0) pp_nextstate
GVOP (0x12eae0) pp_gvsv  GV (0xc9864) *b
SVOP (0x1435c0) pp_const  IV (0xbc9d8) 2
BINOP (0x12eb40) pp_add [1]
GVOP (0xbf660) pp_gvsv  GV (0xc6ba0) *a
BINOP (0x1435a0) pp_sassign
LISTOP (0x13c530) pp_leave
```

Debug Backend

For a more detailed view of the execution of opcodes than that provided by the **Terse** backend, you can use the **Debug** backend instead, which works in a similar way but provides more detailed information. By default, the information is output in syntax order:

```
$ perl -MO=Debug -e '$a = $b + 2;'
-e syntax OK
LISTOP (0x133530)
            op_next             0x0
            op_sibling          0x0
            op_ppaddr           pp_leave
            op_targ             0
            op_type             177
            op_seq              7065
            op_flags            13
            op_private          0
            op_first            0x151bf8
            op_last             0x141dc0
            op_children         3
OP (0x151bf8)
            op_next             0xcf1d0
            op_sibling          0xcf1d0
            op_ppaddr           pp_enter
            op_targ             0
            op_type             176
            op_seq              7058
            op_flags            0
            op_private          0
COP (0xcf1d0)
            op_next             0x12eae0
            op_sibling          0x141dc0
            op_ppaddr           pp_nextstate
            op_targ             0
            op_type             173
            op_seq              7059
            op_flags            1
            op_private          0
            cop_label
            cop_stash           0xbc87c
            cop_filegv          0xbca50
            cop_seq             7059
            cop_arybase         0
            cop_line            1
...
```

The output above has been trimmed for brevity. The full list from this simple statement is 173 lines long!

Like the **Terse** backend, **Debug** also supports the output in execution order, but once again the formatting is lost:

```
$ perl -MO=Debug,exec -e '$a = $b + 2;'|more
-e syntax OK
OP (0x151bf8)
        op_next         0xcf1d0
        op_sibling      0xcf1d0
        op_ppaddr       pp_enter
        op_targ         0
        op_type         176
        op_seq          7058
        op_flags        0
        op_private      0
COP (0xcf1d0)
        op_next         0x12eae0
        op_sibling      0x141dc0
        op_ppaddr       pp_nextstate
        op_targ         0
        op_type         173
        op_seq          7059
        op_flags        1
        op_private      0
        cop_label
        cop_stash       0xbc87c
        cop_filegv      0xbca50
        cop_seq         7059
        cop_arybase     0
        cop_line        1
```

The information provided here is probably only of real use to someone who is investigating the internal opcodes of a script.

Xref Backend

During the development of a project with Perl, it's sometimes difficult to see the wood for the trees. Looking for that elusive function definition or trying to find where a particular function is used can be a time-consuming process. Sure, we could use the debugger, or perhaps even **grep**, but there is an easier way that also gives us a useful document that we can keep with the Perl source code and use for future reference.

The **Xref** backend produces a report that details the use of all the variables, subroutines, and formats in a program. The report includes cross-references (including line numbers) indicating where the variables are used and which subroutine uses which variable, along with other valuable cross-referencing details.

The level of detail includes not only the subroutines and variables from the original file but also all of the modules and files the original script relies upon. This means that even a relatively short script can produce a huge amount of information. The format of the report is as follows:

```
    File filename1
      Subroutine subname1
        Package package1
            object1         C<line numbers>
            object2         C<line numbers>
```

```
        . . .
    Package package2
        . . .
```

Here's an example from a five-line script that prints the contents of a DBM file:

```
File dbmdump.pl
  Subroutine (definitions)
    Package UNIVERSAL
        &VERSION          s0
        &can              s0
        &isa              s0
  Subroutine (main)
    Package main
        $!                11
        $0                3, 11
        $datafile         7
        $df               i5, 11, 11
        $key              15, 15
        %db               11, 13, 15, 17
        &O_RDONLY         &11
        *key              13
        @ARGV             3
```

The output has been trimmed for brevity; the full report runs to 246 lines.

The information can prove invaluable if you are trying to optimize the original source or find out which functions rely on certain variables. Normally this information should be obtainable through the use of the internal debugger or by using one of the debugging methods outlined in Chapter 10. There are instances, however, when a cross-reference report is quicker, and it provides ancillary information that can help trace other bugs.

The function supports only two options, **-r** and **-D**. The **–r** option produces raw output. Rather than the formatted version shown above, a single line is printed for each definition or use of a function, package, or variable. Here's a fragment from the same script used to produce the above report:

```
dbmdump.pl (main)        3 main      @ ARGV       used
dbmdump.pl (main)        3 main      $ 0          used
dbmdump.pl (main)        5 main      $ df         intro
dbmdump.pl (main)        7 main      $ datafile   used
dbmdump.pl (main)       11 main      % db         used
dbmdump.pl (main)       11 main      $ df         used
dbmdump.pl (main)       11 main      & O_RDONLY   subused
dbmdump.pl (main)       11 main      $ 0          used
dbmdump.pl (main)       11 main      $ df         used
dbmdump.pl (main)       11 main      $ !          used
dbmdump.pl (main)       13 main      % db         used
dbmdump.pl (main)       13 main      * key        used
dbmdump.pl (main)       15 main      $ key        used
dbmdump.pl (main)       15 main      % db         used
dbmdump.pl (main)       15 main      $ key        used
dbmdump.pl (main)       17 main      % db         used
```

I've stripped the full pathname from the preceding example and, once again, trimmed it for size. Otherwise, this is identical to the output produced. The columns are, in order, file, full package name (includes references to functions included via **AutoLoad**), line number, short package name, object type, object name, and how it was used in the specified line. Once the information is produced, it is quite voluminous. Using a suitable Perl script, it should be possible to summarize the information in a more readable form, perhaps by selectively excluding those modules you are not interested in. I'll leave that particular exercise to the reader.

The **-D** option supports two sub-debugging flags, both of which are best used in combination with the **-r** option. Using **-Dt**, the object on top of the object stack is printed as it is tracked, allowing you to trace the object as it is being resolved in each of the packages. The **-DO** function prints each operator as it is processed during the cross-referencing process.

Remember that much of the information that can be gleaned from the data supplied is also available via more traditional debugging methods. By the same token, a similar portion of the information is also only available via this backend.

Lint Backend

Under many C environments there is a program called **lint**, which checks C source code for any parsing errors, including those that may not normally have been picked up by the C compiler. The Lint backend is a similar module for Perl. It can pick up many errors that may not be identified by the Perl interpreter even with warnings switched on.

You can see from the options shown in Table 12-6 the errors that Lint attempts to identify.

Option	Description
context	Warns when an array is used in an implied scalar context, such as **$foo = @bar**. Ordinarily, the Perl interpreter ignores this and just sets the value of **$foo** to the scalar value of **@bar** (the number of elements in the array). You can prevent the error from being reported by explicitly using the **scalar** function.
implicit-read	Warns whenever a statement implicitly reads from one of Perl's special variables, such as $_.
implicit-write	Warns whenever a statement implicitly writes to a special variable.
dollar-underscore	Warns when the $_ variable is used, either explicitly or implicitly, as part of a **print** statement.
private-names	Warns when a variable, subroutine, or method is used when the name is not within the current package, or when the name begins with an underscore.
undefined-subs	Warns when an undefined subroutine is called.
regexp-variables	Warns when one of the special regular expression variables, $', $&, or $`, is used.
All	Turns on all warnings.
None	Turns off all warnings.

Table 12.6　Options for the **Lint** Backend

| Note | *The use of this module is not intended as a replacement for either the **-w** command line option or the **use strict** pragma (see Chapter 8 for more information). It augments the options available for finding possible performance and/or parser problems.* |

Deparse Backend

We've already seen some examples of the **Deparse** engine. It takes in a script and regurgitates it in its optimized form, but unlike the **Bytecode** backend, the regurgitated script is in its source format. This means that we can use the **Deparse** engine to get an idea, in source format, of what the Perl interpreter thinks it is executing, rather than what you wrote. When debugging and optimizing code it picks out the following:

- Statements and expressions that can be folded or optimized away
- Ambiguous statements, and how Perl interpreted them
- Badly formed expressions that didn't take into account the precedence rules

The specific options for the **Deparse** backend are shown in Table 12-7.

Option	Description
-p	Prints additional parentheses that would otherwise have been optimized away. Many parentheses can be ignored (or are implied) in the source code. For example, parentheses are not necessarily required around function arguments. This option ensures that all locations where parentheses are implied are actually printed. This can be useful when you want to discover how Perl has interpreted your implied parentheses in a statement. (See the examples below for more information.) Perl will reduce away any constant values, which will appear as ??? in the resulting output.
-uPACKAGE	Includes subroutines from PACKAGE that are not called directly (that is, those loaded by AutoLoad or those that are not resolved to subroutines during runtime). Normally these are ignored in the parsed output.
-l	Adds **#line** declarations to the output, based on the source code line and file locations.

-sC	"Cuddle" **elsif, else,** and continue blocks, for example,
	
	`if ()`
	`{`
	`}`
	`else`
	`{`
	`}`
	
	will be printed as
	
	`if () {`
	`} else {`
	`}`

Table 12.7   Options for the Deparse Backend

The parentheses option is useful for demystifying the operator precedence that Perl uses. For example, here's a Deparsed calculation:

```
$ perl -MO=Deparse,-p -e '$a + $b * $c / $d % $e;'
-e syntax OK
($a + ((($b * $c) / $d) % $e));
```

See Chapter 2 for the list of operators and their precedence.

Showlex Backend

The **Showlex** backend shows the lexical variables (those defined by **my** rather than **local**) used by a subroutine or file. Any options to the backend are assumed to be the names of the subroutines whose list of lexical variables you want to summarize.

For example, to summarize the lexical variables in the **uplsite.pl** script:

```
$ perl -MO=Showlex uplsite.pl

Pad of lexical names for comppadlist has 30 entries

0: PV (0x810af00) "@_"

1: PVNV (0x8315e48) "$debug"
2: PVNV (0x8339de8) "$remserver"
3: PVNV (0x8339dc4) "$remport"
4: PVNV (0x8339db8) "$user"
5: PVNV (0x8339ecc) "$password"
6: PVNV (0x8339ef0) "$dir"
7: PVNV (0x8339f14) "$localdir"
8: PVNV (0x8339f38) "$curxfermode"
9: SPECIAL #1 &PL_sv_undef
10: SPECIAL #1 &PL_sv_undef
11: SPECIAL #1 &PL_sv_undef
12: PVNV (0x8339ff8) "$ftp"
13: SPECIAL #1 &PL_sv_undef
14: SPECIAL #1 &PL_sv_undef
15: SPECIAL #1 &PL_sv_undef
16: SPECIAL #1 &PL_sv_undef
17: SPECIAL #1 &PL_sv_undef
18: SPECIAL #1 &PL_sv_undef
19: SPECIAL #1 &PL_sv_undef
20: SPECIAL #1 &PL_sv_undef
21: SPECIAL #1 &PL_sv_undef
22: SPECIAL #1 &PL_sv_undef
23: SPECIAL #1 &PL_sv_undef
24: SPECIAL #1 &PL_sv_undef
25: SPECIAL #1 &PL_sv_undef
26: SPECIAL #1 &PL_sv_undef
```

```
27: SPECIAL #1 &PL_sv_undef
28: SPECIAL #1 &PL_sv_undef
29: PVNV (0x833a154) "$currentdir"
etc/mcslp/books/paa/ch07/uplsite.pl syntax OK
```

The **perlcc** Frontend

The main method for compiling a Perl script into a final executable is the **perlcc** script. This takes a number of command line options that control the generation process. It also automates the entire process from the generation of the C source code right through to the compilation and linking stages. Using it at its simplest level, the command

```
$ perlcc foo.pl
```

will compile the foo.pl script into the executable **foo**.

When converting a script into a standalone executable, the process assumes you have installed Perl and have a C compiler on your system. The **perlcc** script (which is written in Perl) should account for the specific file locations of your Perl installation and the required tools for building.

> **Note**   *The Perl compiler is not currently supported under Windows or MacOS. Under Windows you can use the PerlApp extension supplied with the Perl Development Kit from ActiveState to convert an application into a standalone executable.*

The **perlcc** frontend supports a number of command line arguments. These control the compilation, code generation, and linking process for translating a Perl source script into an executable program. Most of the options are actually passed on to the underlying backend modules. The command line options also control the calls to the compiler and linker used to build the final executable. Certain options simplify both the process of compiling large programs consisting of many Perl scripts and modules and the compilation of multiple scripts into multiple executables.

Using **perlcc**

The basic way of using **perlcc** is just to supply the name of the script on the command line:

```
$ perlcc foo.pl
```

Doing this will convert and compile **foo.pl** into the ready-to-run executable **foo**. Note that, because it converts and compiles the full version of the script (including any imported modules), we don't need any other options. It will determine any required modules, extensions, or libraries and either incorporate the extensions into the executable or provide the necessary hooks so that dynamic libraries can be loaded.

If you supply a Perl module, then it gets converted into a shared library that you can use directly within Perl using **use Module**:

```
$ perlcc Bar.pm
```

This produces the library **Bar.so**.

Finally, you can produce a standalone bytecode script using the **-b** option:

```
$ perlcc -b foo.pl
```

which produces **foo.plc**, ready for running directly through Perl.

Command-Line Arguments

The frontend also supports a number of additional arguments that control different aspects of the compilation process. They are outlined below for reference.

```
-L DIRS
```

Adds the directories specified in **DIRS** to the C/C++ compiler. Each directory should be separated by a colon.

```
-I DIRS
```

Adds the directories specified in **DIRS** to the C/C++ compiler. Each directory should be separated by a colon.

```
-C FILENAME
```

Gives the generated C code the file name specified by **FILENAME**. Only applicable when compiling a single source script.

```
-o FILENAME
```

Gives the generated executable the file name specified by **FILENAME**. Only applicable when compiling a single source script.

```
-e LINE
```

Identical to the Perl **–e** option. Compiles **LINE** as a single-line Perl script. The default operation is to compile and then execute the one-line script. If you want to save the executable generated, use the **–o** flag.

```
-regex NAME
```

NAME should specify a regular expression to be used when compiling multiple source files into multiple executables. For example, the command

```
$ perlcc -regex 's/\.pl/\.bin/' foo.pl bar.pl
```

would create two executables, foo.bin and bar.bin.

```
-verbose LEVEL
```

Sets the verbosity of the compilation process to the level specified by **LEVEL**. This should be in the form of either a number or a string of letters. Except where specified via the **–log** option, the information is sent to **STDERR**. The available levels are given in Table 12-8.

Numeric	Letter	Description
1	g	Code generation errors to **STDERR**.
2	a	Compilation errors to **STDERR**.
4	t	Descriptive text to **STDERR**.
8	f	Code generation errors to file (**-log** flag needed).
16	c	Compilation errors to file (**-log** flag needed).
32	d	Descriptive text to file (**-log** flag needed).

Table 12.8   Verbosity Levels for the **perlcc** Command

For example, to set the maximum verbosity level, you might use

```
$ perlcc -v 63 -log foo.out foo.pl
```

Note that some options require that the name of a suitable file be given via the **–log** option (see the following for more details). If the **–log** tag has been given and no specific verbosity level has been specified, the script assumes a verbosity level of 63. If no verbosity or log file is specified, a level of 7 is implied.

```
-log NAME
```

Logs the progress of the compilation to the file **NAME**. Note that the information is appended to the file; the contents are not truncated before more information is added. The effect of this option is to make the entire process of compilation silent—all output is redirected to the specified file.

```
-argv ARGS
```

Must be used with the **–run** or **–e** options. Causes the value of **@ARGV** to be populated with the contents of **ARGS**. If you want to specify more than one argument, use single quotes and separate each argument with a space.

```
-sav
```

The intermediate C source code that is generated during the compilation is saved in a file with the same name as the source with ".c" appended.

```
-gen
```

tells **perlcc** to generate only the C source code—the file will not be compiled into an executable.

```
-run
```

Immediately runs the executable that was generated. Any remaining arguments to **perlcc** will be supplied to the executable as command-line arguments.

```
-prog
```

This specifies that all files supplied are programs. The option causes Perl to ignore the normal interpretation that .pm files are actually modules, not scripts.

```
-mod
```

This specifies that the files should be compiled as modules, not scripts. The option overrides the normal interpretation that files ending in .p, .pl, and .bat are Perl scripts.

Environment Variables

You can change some of the implied logic of the **perlcc** process using environment variables. These modifications will affect all compilation, unless you use the command line arguments to override the new defaults.

The **PERL_SCRIPT_EXT** variable contains a list of colon-separated regular expressions. These define the extensions that **perlcc** automatically recognizes as scripts. For example, the default value is

```
PERL_SCRIPT_EXT = '.p$:.pl$:.bat$';
```

Note the use of **$** to define that the extension should be at the end of the file name.

The **PERL_MODULE_EXT** operates in the same way, only for those files that should be recognized as modules. The default value is **.pm$**.

During the compilation process, the **perlcc** module creates a number of temporary files. All of these files' names are based on the value of the **$$** Perl variable, which refers to the current process ID. Thus the temporary file for the **–e** option is perlc$$.p, the file for temporary C code is perlc$$.p.c, and a temporary executable is stored in perlc$$.

Differences Between Interpreted and Compiled Code

Because of the methods used to produce an executable version of a Perl script, there are minor differences between interpreted and compiled code. For the most part, the bugs are related to the behavior of the compilation process, and in time they should be able to be modified such that the compiled and interpreted versions of the same script work identically. Unfortunately, other bugs are directly related to the way the compiler operates, and it's unlikely that these will be able to be changed.

The currently known list of differences are as follows:

- Compiled Perl scripts calculate the target of **next**, **last**, and **redo** loop control statements at compile time. Normally these values are determined at runtime by the interpreter.

- The decision of Perl to interpret the **..** operator as a range or flip-flop operator is normally decided at runtime, based on the current context. In a compiled program the decision is made at compile time, which may produce unexpected results.

- Compiled Perl scripts use native C arithmetic instead of the normal opcode-based arithmetic used in interpreted scripts. This shouldn't cause too many problems (in fact, it makes things quicker), but it may affect calculations on large numbers, especially those at the boundaries of the number ranges.

- Many of the deprecated features of Perl are not implemented in the compiler.

Comparing Script and Executable Speeds

Many factors affect the speed of execution of a typical program. The platform on which you are running obviously has an effect, including the memory, hard disk, and other application requirements at the time the program is run. When considering a Perl script, there are additional overheads to the execution process.

With a C program, the time to execute a program can be split into three elements:

- The time to load the program, including any dynamic loading of libraries.

- The execution of any user-defined components.

- The execution of any system functions. These include any access to the operating system proper, such as files and network sockets, and any access to the memory system. Depending on the implementation, you can also add the library loading time to this figure.

With a Perl script that is interpreted, the list is longer, and, as such, the equivalent process should take longer, even for a very simple statement:

- The time to load the Perl interpreter.

- The time for Perl to load the Perl script.

- The time taken for the Perl interpreter to parse the script and translate it into the opcode tree.

- The execution of the Perl opcode tree.

- The execution of any system functions.

It should be obvious that Perl should, in theory, be a lot slower than a compiled version of the same program written in C. When a Perl script is compiled into a binary executable, two of the above elements can be removed. The script is already in the format of a binary executable; all you need to do is load the binary and execute it. This is where the speed advantage becomes apparent.

When comparing times, you need to compare the following operations:

- Time taken to compile the C program.

- Time taken to execute the C program.

- Time taken to execute the interpreted Perl script.

- Time taken to compile the Perl script into a binary.

- Time taken to execute the Perl binary.

It's also worth considering the overall time taken to

- Compile the C program and then execute it 100 times.

- Execute the Perl script 100 times with the interpreter.

- Compile the Perl script into a binary and then execute it 100 times.

These figures will show the difference in total execution time between the C program, interpreted Perl, and compiled Perl. Remember that when a Perl script is interpreted, it must be compiled before it is executed, which takes a finite amount of time.

Usually the reason for using a compiled binary is to increase the speed of execution. By checking the combined times for running the script 100 times, you should get a rough idea of how much of a speed increase you can expect. Obviously, it's likely that the script will be run significantly more than 100 times, but the same calculation can be applied to any number of executions.

Tests

We'll be comparing three basic programs. The first performs a repetitive calculation on an ascending number for a specific number of iterations. This tests the relative speed of calculations and loops, something we already know is slower in Perl than in a compiled C program. Following is the C version used in the tests:

```
#include <math.h>

int main()
{
  int i;

  for(i=0;i<10000;i++)
    {
      sqrt(abs(sin(i)+cos(i)));
    }
}
```

The code below shows the Perl version. Note that it's much slower; it shows the brevity with which programs can be written in Perl. You don't have to worry about any of the initialization that the C equivalent requires. Also notice that, otherwise, the two versions are very similar.

```
for(my $i=0;$i<10000;$i++)
{
    sqrt(abs(sin($i)+cos($i)));
}
```

The next test is a simple text-processing test. We'll count the number of lines in a document. The document in question is actually a list of all the words in a public domain dictionary that begin with "a" (for reasons that will become apparent in the next script). This tests basic I/O in the two languages. Essentially, the performance of the two should be largely identical, since Perl will optimize the process down to an almost identical structure.

```
#include <stdio.h>

int main()
{
  char *line;
  FILE *data;
```

```
   long count=0;

   data = fopen("wordlist","rw");

   while(!feof(data))
      {
         fgets(line,255,data);
         count++;
      }
   printf("%d lines\n",count);
}
```

The Perl version of Test 2 can be seen below. Once again, note that the overall structure is largely identical, although Perl's **<FH>** operator makes reading in the information much easier.

```
open(DATA, "<wordlist")

while(<DATA>)
{
     $lines++;
}
close(DATA);

print "$lines lines\n";
```

The final test is an advanced version of Test 2. We'll read in the words from the file and then calculate the number of unique lines. Within C we'll use a simple keyword table stored in the **words** array. This will hold the list of words we have already recorded. To identify whether the word has already been seen, we just compare the new word against every entry in the array. This process is slow and inefficient, but it is the shortest (in lines) of the methods available. We could have used a binary tree or even a hashing system, but doing so would have added significantly more lines to an already long C program.

```
#include <stdio.h>

char words[32000][260];
long wordidx=0;

void addtolist(char word[255])
{
  int i=0;
  for(i=0;i<wordidx;i++)
     {
        if (strcmp(word,words[i]) == 0)
            return;
     }
  strcpy(words[++wordidx],word);
}

int main()
```

```
{
  char line[255];
  FILE *data;
  long count=0;

  data = fopen("wordlist","rw");

  while(!feof(data))
    {
      fgets(line,255,data);
      addtolist(line);
    }
  printf("%ld unique lines\n",wordidx);
}
```

The Perl script for Test 3 is significantly shorter, but only because we can directly use hashes, instead of having to use a separate function and loop to search an array.

```
open(DATA,"<wordlist") || die "Can't open file";

my %words;

while(<DATA>)
{
    $words{$_} = 1;
}
close(DATA);

print scalar keys %words," unique lines\n";
```

Summary Results

Each test was run three times, and the **times** command that is standard with the **bash** shell was used to test the execution of each item. This calculates the elapsed time and the user and system time for each command. The times shown are the elapsed amount of time for the program to load, execute, and quit.

The tests show a significant difference in execution times both between the C and Perl programs and also between the interpreted and compiled versions of the Perl scripts. The times are shown in Table 12-9.

Operation	Test 1	Test 2	Test 3
Compile C to binary	8.41	6.74	6.75
Execute C program	0.81	0.62	10.97
Compile C program once, execute 100 times	89.41	68.74	1103.75
Execute interpreted Perl script	2.48	1.04	1.97

Table 12.9 Summary Times for Comparison Tests

Operation	Test 1	Test 2	Test 3
Compile Perl script to binary	51.96	51.09	51.27
Execute Perl script to binary	1.95	1.09	1.32
Execute interpreted Perl script 100 times	248.33	104.00	197.00
Compile Perl program once, execute 100 times	246.63	160.09	182.94

Table 12.9   Summary Times for Comparison Tests *(continued)*

The figures show two things: first, the difference in execution time between a C program and a Perl script and, second, the performance gain between executing a Perl script in its interpreted form and then its compiled form. For additional comparison, the table also shows the time taken to perform 100 C, interpreted Perl, and compiled Perl executions.

Irrespective of the values, it should be noted that these are fairly immature benchmark tests, although they do show many of the advantages of compiling a Perl script into an executable. It's also worth remembering why the time taken to compile the Perl script into a binary is very high. Creating a Perl binary involves not only the compilation of the script into its native Perl format, but also a significant amount of translation to make that into a C source that can be compiled. It also needs to be linked to the Perl library that supplies all of the core Perl functions and the Perl interpreter.

The most obvious difference is the drop in speed from a raw C program to a Perl version. In the case of the interpreted version of the script, some of this difference can be attributed to the time taken to compile the script into opcodes, optimize it, and then execute the opcode tree. However, the difference in times is so great on the first test that it's obvious the problems are with the mathematical calculations in Perl, combined with the large loops.

The compiled version of the Perl script does at least narrow the gap. It is likely that a good deal of the overhead here is related to loading a binary that is about 686K, compared to the 23K for the C version. The Perl binary is large because we used a static, rather than a dynamic, Perl library. With a dynamic Perl library, the size is much smaller—about 11K—but many of the functions from the dynamic library will also need to be loaded.

For the second test, both the Perl and C versions are incredibly quick; the program is very simple, and probable differences between the cores of both programs are likely to be very small. The biggest difference is of course in the last test, where the Perl version is significantly quicker than the C equivalent. The main reason is that we've cheated and used a hash to do the deduping operation. Within the C source we had to use a different method to achieve the same result. The C version is also much longer, by source lines, and the algorithm used here is not ideal. Had I coded a binary tree or even a hash system in the C program, there might have been a smaller difference in the speed tests between the two. However, to add a C-based hashing system or binary tree system would have increased the length of the C program considerably.

The figures comparing the execution of the interpreted Perl script 100 times and the compiled and then interpreted version are much more telling. You can see very clearly that executing the compiled Perl script is much faster than executing the interpreted version. This difference is significant if you are expecting to install a script in a live environment where it may be called a large number of times, as, for example, on a website.

The other benefit of a compiled executable is that you can continue to develop and test with the interpreted version while using a final compiled production version in the live environment. You can be guaranteed that the interpreted and compiled versions will work identically, and they will both retain the same compatibility. They can even use the same configuration and data files without requiring any modifications.

This is a much more efficient development environment than using C or some other language that requires separate compilation each time you want to test a feature or bug fix. As you saw in the last chapter, when debugging a Perl program, you only need to change the source and run the interpreter again. A C program needs to be recompiled and relinked between each test of a bug fix.

As a further comparison, let's imagine the program in Test 2 is riddled with 100 bugs, and we recompile the program between each fix. Ignoring the time to edit the source, the C version would take 736 seconds for each compilation and execution. The Perl version would take 155.09 seconds, including a final compilation to an executable binary. That's an efficiency gain of 475 percent!

## PART V

Testing Your Code

## CHAPTER 13

Testing Methods

If the experts are to be believed, you should be spending only 20 percent of the total development time for a project actually coding the application. The other 80 percent should be given over to testing your code once it's been completed to make sure that it works okay. But what should you actually be testing? And how far do you go when testing?

There are actually two levels of testing that you should conduct on all code: normal usage and stressed usage. *Normal usage* applies to the execution of the application under normal conditions, that is, when supplied with the sort and amount of data the application could normally expect to receive. *Stressed usage* applies to those situations when an unexpected event takes place, such as supplying more data than the application expected or data beyond the limits of a particular function.

Testing the application at the normal level is fairly straightforward and should help you to find all sorts of problems that you can either trap (using the techniques in Chapter 7) or adjust so that the condition doesn't cause a problem. Stressing your application (or the system on which the application runs) is more difficult, but it should make your application more stable in situations that you might not be willing or able to handle. It can also help to highlight possible security problems with your script.

Take a CGI script for example. One of the most common security breach attempts is to supply either invalid information or so much information that the CGI script is unable to handle it. If you were to deliberately send too much data to the script you'd be able to spot where and how to trap that fault and then deal with it accordingly. Just testing the script with normal parameters wouldn't have picked up this error.

Most of this book has dealt with the processes for trapping and debugging your code, but if you are producing a commercial product, or code that you expect to distribute to either your clients or the general public, then you need to approach the testing in a more thorough and methodical fashion.

In this chapter, we'll concentrate on what and how to test the different elements of your script. We'll also look at the Perl "standard" for test scripts and at the **Test** and **Test::Harness** modules that help the process.

The Test Harness Role

Although we've tucked this right at the back, testing with some sort of formal testing process should be an ongoing part of any project. In fact, that's really what debugging is all about, tracing the problems that you find when you test your code and find a problem. Most of the techniques here are as applicable during development as they are once development has been completed, but there are also reasons for producing a standalone test suite that is separate from your main debugging process.

Although it may not be the best way of doing things, the typical sequence that most programmers go through when developing an application is as follows:

1. Write code feature.

2. Test parts of feature.

3. Debug parts of feature (return to step 1 until application complete).

4. Write test harness.

The reality is that most programmers don't follow a rigid development structure, and the test harness is there as the final failsafe for the application. It's also the case during Perl development that, for modules and extensions, the testing is the final phase of the development process.

The role of the test harness therefore is one of validation that your script/function/module works as you expect and advertise, rather than being a part of the ongoing development effort. This is actually quite practical—you can use the test suite as a way to validate your project when it's moved to a different platform or environment or on a new version of Perl. Any discrepancies can thus be fixed in the next revision of your software.

Testing Strategies

When I was in college I remember being told by our tutor that big commercial systems are tested by providing every possible combination of arguments when calling a specific function. This meant that all the possibilities had not only been tested, but eventually accounted for. This approach can be impractical, even for a simple function. Consider something as innocent as

```
sub add
{
    return($_[0]+$_[1]);
}
```

If we wanted to test that function properly we'd have to supply every number between the ranges of both an integer and floating point value, and at every value in between, in order to ensure that there won't be a problem. And we'd have to have to do that for both arguments to the function—even if the limits were only 10,000, we'd have to perform 100,000,000 calculations just to make sure it worked okay.

In practice, of course, we don't need to worry about anything quite so trivial. Computers are not infallible, but it's a pretty good bet that adding two numbers together will work correctly without us having to test every combination.

For more complex functions, however, there are operations and combinations that we need to test, and there are ways of determining the limits

24x7 Testing Modules

If you use the **h2xs** utility to build your module templates, then it will automatically create a very simple test script that you can modify to include specific tests for your module to check that it's working OK. On a simple Perl module you might think this is overkill, but remember that if you release the code to the public the module may well end up executing on a platform other than your development platform. For a module that actually makes use of the XS extension system, it will also provide a way to test that your module loads the necessary library properly and that the Perl to C/C++ code interface is working correctly.

The test script also provides the best way for you to get other people to test the module on a variety of platforms. You should be able to utilize the output of that test script to help you migrate the script to the new platform.

Test Samples

If we go back and look at our **add** function we should be able to spot some possible problems that could arise when the function is used. On something as simple as this it seems silly to test it—but consider the following calls:

```
add(1,2);
add(1000000000,300000000);
add(-99,100);
add('Hello',4);
add('Some','Numbers');
add('4','5');
add(3,4,5,6,8);
add(1);
add();
```

There could be problems with every one of these function calls, so let's take each one in turn and check the result. I've switched warnings on to highlight some possible problems during the execution:

```
add(1,2);
3
```

This one works fine, and we could easily test the return value of this function call to make sure that it operated correctly.

```
add(1000000000,300000000);
1300000000
```

And so does this one:

```
add(-99,100);
1
```

And this one appears to work too:

```
add('Hello',4);
Argument "Hello" isn't numeric in addition (+) at t13.pl line 3.
4
```

This one clearly doesn't, and for an obvious reason: We've supplied a string when the **+** operator is expecting a number. The warning tells us why it failed, but the return value hides the fact that the function really failed—because we've seen a positive value returned, a simple true/false test would resolve to true, as would checking a value of 4.

```
add('Some','Numbers');
Argument "Numbers" isn't numeric in addition (+) at t13.pl line 3.
Argument "Some" isn't numeric in addition (+) at t13.pl line 3.
0
```

Now this one is bound to fail—we've supplied two string arguments that Perl can't convert to a numerical value, and, in turn, the function has returned a false (zero) value. Although this one will return a failure, it's actually clear from the return value why there is a failure.

```
add('4','5');
9
```

This one works, but only because we've supplied two numerical strings, which Perl automatically converts for us.

```
add(3,4,5,6,8);
7
```

This one has worked too, insofar as the first two arguments have been correctly added together. The function, though, has completely ignored the remainder of the arguments.

```
add(1);
Use of uninitialized value in addition (+) at t13.pl line 3.
1
```

Here the lack of a second argument has raised an error, but we've still got a return value that might not help us.

```
add();
Use of uninitialized value in addition (+) at t13.pl line 3.
Use of uninitialized value in addition (+) at t13.pl line 3.
0
```

In this last one, we've failed to supply any arguments to the function, which has, in turn, raised two errors and a false result, which could inadvertently point to a problem that does not in fact exist.

When testing we therefore need to take into account not only the expected operation of the function, but also the values it returns.

Writing a Suitable Test

Our first problem is to write a suitable testing strategy that will help to highlight these problems. There is really only one rule to apply when testing any function:

- Check the return value

It's that straightforward: You need a "control," some piece of expected or manually calculated piece of information that you can use as a comparison against the function you are going to test.

The simple tests we've conducted above have actually highlighted a few problems with the function itself that we need to be aware of and be equipped to handle:

- What happens when text arguments are supplied?
- What happens when more than two arguments are supplied?
- What happens when fewer than two arguments are supplied?

For the first situation, we'll just add a filter so that we don't add text arguments. We can solve problems in the second and third arguments by using a default value of zero and using an accumulator to add arguments to the final return value. If we're not supplied anything, then a zero gets returned; if we're supplied 50 arguments, then the function returns the sum of all 50, providing of course they are numbers. The final function looks like this:

```perl
sub add
{
    my $return = 0;
    foreach my $value (@_)
    {
        next unless ($value =~ m/^[-_.\d]+$/);
        $return += $value;
    }
    return $return;
}
```

It's important to realize here that it was the testing that gave rise to the change in the function—if we hadn't supplied so many different combinations of arguments, then we would never have found the errors that gave rise to the function design change in the first place.

To actually write a suitable set of tests, we need to add some code to our test function calls. Perl uses the "ok/not ok" text to indicate a functional success or failure, so we can update the test sequence to:

```perl
print ((add(1,2) == 3 ? '' : 'not '),"ok\n");
print ((add(1000000000,300000000)
            == 1300000000 ? '' : 'not '),"ok\n");
print ((add(-99,100) == 1 ? '' : 'not '),"ok\n");
print ((add('Hello',4) == 4 ? '' : 'not '),"ok\n");
print ((add('Some','Numbers') == 0 ? '' : 'not '),"ok\n");
print ((add('4','5') == 9 ? '' : 'not '),"ok\n");
print ((add(3,4,5,6,8) == 26 ? '' : 'not '),"ok\n");
print ((add(1) == 1 ? '' : 'not '),"ok\n");
print ((add() == 0 ? '' : 'not '),"ok\n");
```

If we run this in combination with the change to the **add** subroutine, we should get this:

```
ok
ok
ok
ok
ok
ok
ok
ok
ok
```

It works!

Although this has been a very simplistic example, it does demonstrate the basic principles of any testing system that you plan to introduce. What this should have highlighted is that there are essentially two elements to any test harness: the items and functions that you test and the limits and scope of the data that you supply to the functions when testing.

What to Test

In our earlier sample, three different function calling cases were tested for:

- **Correct Arguments**   The function was expected to handle numerical values, so we supplied values both large and small, and in varying numbers from 1–5 arguments.
- **Bad Arguments**   Because the function expected numerical values, we also supplied some bad arguments to make sure that the function was able to handle them, either by providing a warning or bad value or (as in the sample) by simply ignoring the invalid arguments.
- **Argument Numbers**   You can't always guarantee that the function will be supplied with the correct number of arguments, and your script should know how to handle too few or too many.

Your testing script should follow the same rules; you need to supply good and bad arguments to your functions and script (see "Limits and Scope" later in this chapter) and a varying number of arguments.

Good Arguments

The best way to test any script or function is to supply it with data that it is expecting and able to handle and to check the result against the value you are expecting. For example, in our **add** function we know that adding 1 and 1 together should give 2. Well, in this universe anyway.

Bad Arguments

You should use bad arguments—that is, ones that the function or script isn't expecting—so that you can check that it's able to recover from such situations gracefully. For example, when writing a script that parses a file, supply the name of a file that you know doesn't exist. If you are writing to a file, then supply the name of a file that cannot be overwritten.

Argument Numbers

You should also be testing the number of arguments that you supply, either to the script as a whole or to an individual function. This will let you know if the script or function involved is equipped to handle the situation properly. You can also use this test as a way to check known combinations. Good examples here are command line arguments that switch different options—make sure that all of the arguments are parsed whether you supply only 1 or 20.

Limits and Scope

Although earlier I implied that checking every possible combination was considered the best way to test, in practice that just isn't possible. For our sample subroutine we'd have to run the function 1.84E19 times—that's over 100,000 trillion iterations. Even on a fast machine that would take months to run its course.

It gets even more complicated when you start to think about strings or, worse, lists and hashes. In these cases, it would be plain impractical to consider even generating every possible combination, nevermind actually testing a function that makes use of that information to ensure that there isn't a problem.

Instead, the approach you should use is to think about testing the limits and different combinations of arguments that you supply to your function. For example, for our test function we checked some small values, large values, and some non-numeric values. We also supplied too many and too few arguments than we might have originally catered for. In each case the idea was to test the limits, rather than all possible permutations. The same general rules should be applied to all functions.

Integer and Floating Point Data

Testing integer and floating point information is really just a case of supplying some trivial values. For numerical values you should check:

- **Lower limits**   For most cases this will be zero, but also think about checking negative values, especially to a function that handles only positive values (think about instances like the third argument to the built-in **split** function). Check something near, and potentially beyond the limits that you think your function can handle.

- **Upper limits**   Check something near and beyond the upper limit that your function should be capable of handling. Try not to think in terms of the physical limits of Perl or the platform that you are working on, but the potential limits of the function. For example, if you're testing a function that handles entries from **/etc/passwd**, there's little point in going beyond 70,000—most systems handle only 65536 values.

- **Mid values**   Just because a function can handle the upper and lower limits doesn't mean that there won't be a problem in the middle, so check some innocent-seeming numbers in the midrange.

- **Zero**   It's very easy to forget that zero is a number too, and your script may not be set up to handle such an innocent value.

String and Textual Data

For strings you have a more difficult decision. You can't test limits because, in theory at least, there are no limits on strings in Perl. However, you can test strings from the point of view of what the script expects. If you've written a script that parses some information, then supply it with that information during the test.

Again, it's worth supplying one that you know will work and one that you know will fail—your script or function should be capable of handling both instances with relative grace.

We can therefore summarize the list into:

- Data that should parse correctly

- Data that shouldn't parse correctly

- Empty strings or text

- The undefined value

Arrays and Hashes

The rules here are the same as for strings—the information contained within the array or hash that you supply will by its very nature be application-specific, so there are no hard and fast rules. But we can summarize the categories you should test into:

- Data that should parse correctly
- Data that shouldn't parse correctly
- Empty arrays/lists/hashes

Remember that you are testing not only that your script works as advertised, but also that it can handle problems—and lists and hashes can be the root of many different problems.

References

If you are using references to exchange information, then you should be checking first that those references are populated correctly and second that they are of the correct type. Using a simple **ref** call will tell you if the type of information returned was correct.

Generating Raw Information

For some scripts and instances you will need to generate some raw data that you can use as a source for the script to work on. There are no hard and fast rules here, but make sure that the data you produce is both suitably diverse and in reasonable quantities. Using a data file that is a repeat of 10 identical items is not a good test. Similarly, a file with only 10 entries in it is also unlikely to be a good test.

You should base the size of your file on the number of fields or elements in the source. I tend to produce 100 times the number of records as there are fields. For example, if you are testing a web log analyzer there should be about 700 entries, and I'd recommend that there be at least 10 variations for each field.

Building a Test Harness

By now you should already know the sort of things you should be testing, and the limits and scope that you should be testing. Now you need to build a script or system that will enable you to test the different elements of your application. The script or scripts will go to make up the "test harness" for your program. The harness should test and then report on the status of those tests. The harness acts as an external net that traps the errors that your test harness is designed to highlight.

After a number of years of development, the Perl development team has perfected a testing system that is used not only to test the Perl interpreter itself during compilation, but also for testing Perl scripts and modules. Perl's testing system works by checking the result of a specific operation and then reporting whether the operation worked "ok" or "not ok."

The "ok" is important here—if you run one of the test scripts that come with Perl (I've used **base/cond.t** here) then you get:

```
1..4
ok 1
ok 2
ok 3
ok 4
```

The **1..4** indicates the test number range, and each "ok" indicates the number of the test that completed successfully. If an error occurred, then "not ok" is printed.

The same basic principles are applied to the test script produced by **h2xs** when developing a new Perl module, which builds a template test script that contains the following executable code:

```
BEGIN { $| = 1; print "1..1\n"; }
END {print "not ok 1\n" unless $loaded;}
use MyModule;
$loaded = 1;
print "ok 1\n";
```

This tests that the module loads successfully—a failure will trigger the **END** block to be executed, which in turn prints the "not ok" message.

This procedure might not sound like a ground breaking solution, but its simplicity is also its power. Because we output a combination of the number of tests, and a list of which tests are completed successfully, it becomes very easy to detect which test failed. It's also very easy to post-process the output (using Perl) in order to produce a summary of the number of tests that completed or failed.

This is the purpose behind the **Test** module, which performs basic tests and outputs the "ok"/ "not ok" message, and the **Test::Harness** module, which monitors the output from **Test** (or any compatible test script).

There are other ways to build a test harness, but you should probably be using the Perl standard system, as it will help you to understand how Perl itself is tested and how the tests in modules and extensions that you download work. By understanding the testing system employed by these modules you should be able to track problems in places other than your own scripts.

 A test harness can also be a useful way of testing your script/module when a new version of Perl has been released.

We'll also have a look at how to produce a test harness for CGI scripts that will work independently of a web server and also allow you to supply arbitrary requests to the script without using a browser.

Using the **Test** Module

The **Test** module supports a single function, **ok**, that prints the "ok" or "not ok" test depending on the result of the test that you perform. The primary way to use the module is to call **ok** with zero, which indicates a failure, or 1, which indicates a success. For example,

```
@unsorted = qw/wilma barney fred bambam/;
ok(1) if (join('',sort split //,$unsorted) eq 'abcdef');
```

If you want to run multiple tests, then use a **BEGIN** block to specify the parameters for the tests you are about to conduct. For example,

```
use Test;
BEGIN { plan tests => 2}

ok(1);
ok(0);
```

Each call to **ok** should indicate a successful test or failure. The resulting report and output matches the format used by Perl's own testing system available when Perl has been built from a raw distribution. For example, the above script would output

```
1..2
ok 1
not ok 2
# Failed test 2 in test.pl at line 5
```

Note that each call to **ok** iterates through the available test numbers, and failures are recorded and reported accordingly.

You can also use the **ok** function directly to check the return value from a script—for example, for a function or expression that returns true on success:

```
ok(mytest());
```

The return value or resolved expression must be expected to return true or false according to the success or otherwise of the test. You can also use a two-argument version that compares the values of the two arguments:

```
ok(mytest(),mytest());
```

If you want to trap additional information with the error, you can append additional arguments to the **ok** function:

```
BEGIN { plan tests => 1 }
ok(0,1,'Math Error');
```

The resulting error and mismatch information are reported when the script exits:

```
1..1
not ok 1
# Test 1 got: '0' (t13.pl at line 3)
#   Expected: '1' (Math Error)
```

You can mark tests as "to do" tests by specifying which test numbers are to be fixed directly within the test suite. These tests are expected to fail. You specify the information to the **plan** function during the **BEGIN** block. The **todo** argument should be supplied with a reference to an array that lists the tests that are expected to fail:

```
use Test;
BEGIN { plan tests => 4, todo => [2,4] }

ok(1);
ok(0);
ok(1);
ok(0);
```

The resulting failure message notes the existence of an expected failure:

```
1..4 todo 2 4;
ok 1
not ok 2
# Failed test 2 in t13.pl at line 5 *TODO*
ok 3
not ok 4
# Failed test 4 in t13.pl at line 7 *TODO*
```

and also notifies you when it sees a success in a test it was expecting to fail:

```
1..2 todo 2;
ok 1
ok 2 # Wow! (test.pl at line 5)
```

You can skip tests based on the availability of platform-specific facilities, using the **skip** function:

```
skip(TEST, LIST)
```

TEST is a test that evaluates to true only if the required feature is *not* available. Subsequent values in **LIST** work identically to the **ok** function. For example, you could use this to test a multi-platform script where certain functions or external commands are available only on some platforms:

```
skip($platform eq 'hpux', [3,5,9]);
skip($platform eq 'solaris', [2,4,8]);
```

You can also supply a subroutine to handle additional diagnostics after the tests have completed. The function is passed an array reference of hash references that describe each test failure. The keys of each hash are **package**, **repetition**, and **result**. To configure the function, specify its reference in the call to **plan** in the **BEGIN** block:

```
BEGIN { plan tests => 2, onfail => \&errdiags }
```

The resulting function is executed within an **END** block and can be used to report either additional diagnostic information or details on how errors should be reported back to the author.

Using **Test::Harness**

The **Test::Harness** module acts as a wrapper around a number of test scripts. It monitors the output generated by each script and then produces a summary based on the success, or otherwise, of the tests within the system. Although you can use this module in conjunction with your own scripts that output suitable "ok" messages, it's best used in conjunction with the **Test** module we saw earlier.

The method for using the module is to call the **runtests** function with a list of test script file names:

```
use Test::Harness;
runtests(LIST)
```

LIST should be a list of valid test scripts to be executed. It parses the output produced by a typical Perl test script and analyzes the output. The output produced by the **Test** module is suitable for correct parsing.

For example, a nine-test script with three failures would output the following:

```
test.pl................
# Failed test 2 in test.pl at line 5
# Failed test 5 in test.pl at line 8
# Failed test 9 in test.pl at line 12
FAILED tests 2, 5, 9
        Failed 3/9 tests, 66.67% okay
Failed Test  Status Wstat Total Fail  Failed  List of failed
-----------------------------------------------------------------
test.pl                        9     3  33.33%  2, 5, 9
Failed 1/1 test scripts, 0.00% okay. 3/9 subtests failed, 66.67% okay.
```

You can see from this that it produces both statistical and specific information on the tests that failed.

A CGI Harness

When testing CGI scripts you have a separate set of problems owing to your need to be able to supply form data to the CGI script during its execution. If you are using the **CGI** module, the easiest way to do this is to either populate the environment with suitable information or supply the data as input to a script. I use the following script to test my CGI scripts. It acts as a wrapper around a CGI call, populating the environment accordingly. In the sample here, it's configured for testin`g a script that shows television information:

```
#!/usr/local/bin/perl -w

use strict;
use URI::Escape;
```

```
%ENV = (REQUEST_METHOD => 'GET',
        QUERY_STRING   => '',
        REQUEST_URI    => '',
        PATH           => '/bin:/sbin:/usr/bin',
        );

my %request = (t => 'c',
               c => 'BBC 1');
my $request;

foreach (sort keys %request)
{
    $request .= "$_=uri_escape($request{$_})";
}

$ENV{QUERY_STRING} = $request;
$ENV{QUERY_LENGTH} = length($ENV{QUERY_STRING});
$ENV{CONTENT_LENGTH} = length($ENV{QUERY_STRING});

system('./index.cgi >testharness.out 2>testharness.warn');
```

To use the wrapper, change the **%request** hash, populating it with the information that would normally be submitted by a form. Each element of the hash is parsed by the **URI::escape** module to ensure that it's in a suitable format for posting to a CGI script, and then the script is executed with the STDOUT and STDERR redirected to suitable files.

> **Design Tip**   *Notice in the script that the %ENV array has been overwritten with new data. This is deliberate and ensures that we get a web server type environment and not that of the enclosing shell. The environment specified here is fairly typical (although it's missing some web-specific entries) and will also trap errors in your script where you've used relative, rather than absolute, names for external commands. It'll pass the taint checks.*

The method above relies on the **GET** method. If you've written a custom handler (instead of using the **CGI** module) that supports only **PUT**, you'll need to modify the script so that it uses **echo** to supply the request string and then pipes that into the CGI script itself. For example,

```
system('echo $request|./index.cgi >test.out 2>test.warn');
```

Remember to change the **%ENV** at the top to reflect a **PUT** rather than **GET** request.

## CHAPTER 14

Breaking Your Code

Building a test harness is a great way to test your code, but it tests the code only in "ideal" conditions. Very few people ever test their code on a system that is heavily loaded or in situations where their script would fail not because of a problem within the script, but because of the effects of the environment within which the script is being executed.

We saw the internal testing process in the previous chapter. The next level of testing is to present your script or module with an environment that is deliberately designed to break your code from the outside, rather than simply testing the script's limits or abilities from the inside. In this chapter we're going to concentrate on these external influences that can interrupt the flow of your program and suggest some ways in which you can test these scripts and pick up these problems before your project reaches the final stages of development.

There are lots of different systems that can affect the environment in which your script is executed. The most obvious is the physical environment in which it is running: disk space and CPU time. The environment variables and their contents should be also be considered as a physical aspect. Finally, the security and permissions on the files and resources that you are using should be considered.

Another obvious way to break your code is to use the Perl tainting mechanism. Doing this will help you to trace possible areas of your script where you are using information that could be from a questionable source. It can also act as a method for tracing data as it progresses through a script.

Running a script within the confines of a web server raises its own issues. The environment is often severely restricted, and depending on the platform you are working on, and facilities such as external programs and the availability of different files and systems may also be restricted. The data supplied to your script while working under a web server is also subject to a certain amount of interpretation. Assuming that the information supplied to your CGI script will be the correct size and format is a bad idea, and deliberately supplying the wrong information is a good way to test your script.

The final effect we'll look at is that of running the same script a number of times simultaneously. It's surprising how many people forget the effects and problems associated with such a simple device, especially with applications such as CGI or system administration scripts—both have a high potential for being run simultaneously.

In this chapter we'll look at the effects of all of these and, where applicable, ways in which you can deliberately break your code by reducing or restricting the resource in question.

Disk Space

Restricting the amount of disk space on your machine should be a vital part of any testing strategy when developing a script that makes use of the filesystem for any kind of storage. Most of the time you should be able to pick up errors by checking calls to **open** and **print**, but also remember to check the operation of tied hashes and calls to **mkdir** and even **chmod**. You should probably be doing this anyway, but it's worth paying special attention to what happens when it's a lack of disk space, not a permission problem, that is causing the error.

24x7   Reducing Disk Space

Under Unix, the quickest way to deliberately reduce the amount of disk space is to use the **mkfile** command. This produces a file based on the supplied size and name; for example,

```
$ mkfile 16M bigfile
```

produces a file 16Mb in size. Under Windows and MacOS, and Unix if you don't want to use or have access to the **mkfile** command, use the following script, which does the same thing:

```perl
#!/usr/local/bin/perl -w

use strict;
use Fcntl;

unless (@ARGV == 2)
{
    print "$0 size name\n";
    exit 0;
}

my ($size,$modifier);

if ($ARGV[0] =~ m/([0-9]+)([A-Za-z]*)/)
{
    ($size,$modifier) = ($1,$2);
}
else
{
    die "Invalid size specification: $ARGV[1]";
}

$modifier = lc($modifier);
my $block;

if ($modifier eq 'k')
{
    $size *= 1024;
    $block = 'x' x 1024;
}
if ($modifier eq 'm')
{
    $size *= 1024*1024;
    $block = 'x' x 16384;
```

```
}
if ($modifier eq 'g')
{
    $size *= 1024*1024*1024;
    $block = 'x' x 16384;
}

my ($written,$blocksize) = (0,length($block));

sysopen(FILE,$ARGV[1],O_CREAT|O_WRONLY) or die "Can't create $ARGV[1]: $!";

while($written < $size)
{
    syswrite FILE, $block, $blocksize
        or die "Error writing to file: $!";
    $written += $blocksize;
}
close(FILE);
```

You use it in exactly the same way as the **mkfile** command; the command

```
$ mkfile.pl 1G bigfile
```

would create a 1Gb file.

CPU Time

Not all scripts work well under heavy CPU loads. In particular, scripts that themselves imply a heavy load or that use timeouts to wait for the completion of specific operations can be problematic. For example, imagine a script that employs an **ALRM** signal handler to pause and wait for an operation. Irrespective of the CPU load, the delay period supplied to the **alarm** function is specified in real seconds.

If the CPU load is particularly heavy, the handler could kick in before the operation has completed, even though the script would have eventually completed successfully if given a suitable amount of time considering the load. For scripts that are communicating with a filesystem or using sockets to communicate with a remote machine, this type of operation can become a problem, especially if it leaves sockets or files unnecessarily open.

In practice this particular scenario is unlikely to happen, since even under very heavy loads your system should be responding correctly. That doesn't mean that the CPU threat isn't real. For time-critical applications—including those on the web—it's an element that you should account and test for. Of course, if your system isn't responding quickly enough for your script, you've got bigger problems than just running Perl scripts effectively!

It's conceivable to use the output from **uptime** (on Unix) to determine the current system load and modify the timeout period accordingly, but in practice doing this involves probably far too complex a system to use in most scripts. Instead, you should test your script under different loads and then adjust the timing accordingly.

To imply a heavy load on your system the best solution is to run one or more scripts that will stress your system. Make sure, though, that your script does more than just a simple calculation. You'll need to write something that copies data around in order to help stress the system, and consider including a call to the system—something like **glob** should be enough. I use the following script:

```perl
#!/usr/local/bin/perl -w

sub funca
{
    my (@data) = @_;
    foreach (@data) { $_ =~ tr/[a-z]/[A-Z]/; }
    return @data
}

sub funcb
{
    my (@data) = @_;
    foreach (@data) { $_ =~ tr/[A-Z]/[a-z]/; }
    return @data;
}

while(1)
{
    @data = glob("/etc/*");
    funca(funcb(funca(@data)));
}
```

You can run this as many times as you like in order to stress up your system—I've used it to run up a loading of 20–30 processes requesting time to execute within the last minute.

I try to stick to a rough guide of 15 concurrent processes per processor, but the exact amount will depend on your system. Remember to use the **uptime** command to help gauge the load. On Windows machines you can use the built-in resource monitor to check the load on the system. Under MacOS it gets more difficult—to run multiple Perl scripts you'll need to duplicate the Perl application. It's probably easier just to run some other processor-intensive task—running a Gaussian Blur (at 3.5 pixels) on a large file in Adobe Photoshop is one way, but there are others.

Once the system has been suitably stressed, try the script and see the effects. Don't worry too much about obvious effects such as slow execution; instead, concentrate on failures and missing data where the application otherwise worked at normal load.

Design Tip *If you are using a Perl script that communicates with a database, either local or remote, write a script that stresses the database (use large or repetitive SELECT...ORDER BY queries), rather than the system in general. This should help to highlight problems in your script during the database connectivity phase as well as during a SELECT or similar query.*

Environment Variables

It's a really bad idea to rely on external variables for information, especially when the information can generally be found somewhere else. Some classic examples are usernames, user IDs, and the PATH, but there are plenty of others. Table 14-1 lists some Unix environment variables that you should either avoid using or that you should define yourself to ensure proper operation. Table 14-2 lists Windows variables and includes information on which platforms define those variables as standard.

Where relevant, the tables show a probable default value that you can use. The tables also list alternative locations where you can find the same information without relying on an environment variable. MacOS and other non-interactive platforms don't rely so heavily on environment variables for the execution of scripts anyway.

Variable	Description	Alternate
COLUMNS	The number columns for the current display. Can be useful for determining the current terminal size when developing a terminal/text interface. However, it's probably better to rely on a user setting or just use the **Term::*** modules and let them handle the effects. If you do need a base value, then use vt100, which most terminal emulators support.	None
EDITOR	The user's editor preference. If it can't be found then default to **vi** or **emacs** or, on Windows, to **C:/Windows/Notepad.exe**.	None
EUID	The effective user ID of the current process. Use **$>**, which will be populated correctly by Perl even when using **suidperl**.	**$>**
HOME	The user's home directory. Try getting the information from **getpwuid** instead.	**getpwuid**.
HOST	The current hostname. The **hostname.pl** script included with the standard Perl library provides a platform-neutral way of determining the hostname.	**hostname.pl**
HOSTNAME	The current hostname.	**hostname.pl**
LINES	The number of lines supported by the current terminal window or display. See **COLUMNS** earlier in the table.	None
LOGNAME	The user's login. Use the **getlogin** function or, better still, the **getpwuid** function with the **$<** variable.	**getlogin**, **getpwuid($<)**
MAIL	The path to the user's mail file. If it can't be found, try guessing the value; it's probably **/var/mail/LOGNAME** or **/var/spool/mail/LOGNAME**.	None
PATH	The colon-separated list of directories to search when looking for applications to execute. Aside from the security risk of using an external list, you should probably be using the full path to the applications that you want to execute, or populating **PATH** within your script.	None

Table 14.1   Environment Variables on Unix Machines

Variable	Description	Alternate
PPID	The parent process ID. There's no easy way to find this, but it's unlikely that you'll want it anyway.	None
PWD	The current working directory. You should use the **Cwd** module instead.	**Cwd**
SHELL	The path to the user's preferred shell. This value can be abused so that you end up running a suid program instead of a real shell. If it can't be determined, **/bin/sh** is a good default.	None
TERM	The name/type of the current terminal and therefore terminal emulation. See **COLUMNS** earlier in this table.	None
UID	The user's real ID.	$<
USER	The user's login name. See **LOGNAME** earlier in this table.	**getlogin**, **getpwuid($<)**
VISUAL	The user's visual editor preference. See **EDITOR** earlier in the table.	**EDITOR**
XSHELL	The shell to be used within the X Windows System. See **SHELL** earlier in the table.	**SHELL**

Table 14.1   Environment Variables on Unix Machines *(continued)*

You can use the script at the end of the Chapter 13 that we used for CGI testing to actually fake a reduced, or even nonexistent, environment—just remove the references for creating the CGI request variables and then populate the **%ENV** hash by hand.

Variable	Platform	Description	Alternate
ALLUSERSPROFILE	2000	The location of the generic profile currently in use. There's no way of determining this information.	None
CMDLINE	95/98	The command line, including the name of the application executed. The Perl **@ARGV** variable should have been populated with this information.	**@ARGV**
COMPUTERNAME	NT, 2000	The name of the computer.	**Win32::NodeName**
COMSPEC	All	The path to the command interpreter (usually **COMMAND.COM**) used when opening a command prompt.	None

Table 14.2   Environment Variables for Windows

Variable	Platform	Description	Alternate
HOMEDRIVE	NT, 2000	The drive letter (and colon) of the user's home drive.	None
HOMEPATH	NT, 2000	The path to the user's home directory.	None
HOMESHARE	NT, 2000	The UNC name of the user's home directory. Note that this value will be empty if the user's home directory is unset or set to local drive.	None
LOGONSERVER	NT, 2000	The domain name server the user was authenticated on.	None
NUMBER_OF_PROCESSORS	NT, 2000	The number of processors active in the current machine.	None
OS	NT, 2000	The name of the operating system. There's no direct way, but the **Win32::IsWin95** and **Win32::IsWinNT** return true if the host OS is Windows 95/98 or Windows NT/2000, respectively.	**Win32::IsWin95** **Win32::IsWinNT**
OS2LIBPATH	NT, 2000	The path to the OS/2 compatibility libraries.	None
PATH	All	The path searched for applications within the command prompt and for programs executed via a **system**, backtick, or **open** function.	None
PATHEXT	NT, 2000	The list of extensions that will be used to identify an executable program. You probably shouldn't be modifying this, but if you need to define it manually, **.bat**, **.com**, and **.exe** are the most important.	None
PROCESSOR_ARCHITECTURE	NT, 2000	The processor architecture of the current machine. Use the **Win32::GetChipName**, which returns 386, 486, 586 and so on for Pentium chips, or Alpha for Alpha processors.	**Win32::GetChip Name**

Table 14.2   Environment Variables for Windows (*continued*)

Variable	Platform	Description	Alternate
PROCESSOR_IDENTIFIER	NT, 2000	The identifier (the information tag returned by the CPU when queried).	None
PROCESSOR_LEVEL	NT, 2000	The processor level, 3 refers to a 386, 4 to a 486, and 5 to the Pentium. Values of 3000 and 4000 refer to MIPS processors, and 21064 refers to an Alpha processor. See the **PROCESSOR_ ARCHITECTURE** entry earlier in the table.	**Win32::GetChipName**
PROCESSOR_REVISION	NT, 2000	The processor revision.	None
SYSTEMDRIVE	NT, 2000	The drive holding the currently active operating system. The most likely location is **C:**.	None
SYSTEMROOT	NT, 2000	The root directory of the active operating system. This will probably be **Windows** or **Win**.	None
USERDOMAIN	NT, 2000	The domain the current user is connected to.	**Win32::Domain Name**
USERNAME	NT, 2000	The name of the current user.	None
USERPROFILE	NT, 2000	The location of the user's profile.	None
WINBOOTDIR	NT, 2000	The location of the Windows operating system that was used to boot the machine. See the **SYSTEMROOT** entry earlier in this table.	None
WINDIR	All	The location of the active Windows operating system, this is the directory used when searching for DLLs and other OS information. See the **SYSTEMROOT** entry earlier in this table.	None

Table 14.2   Environment Variables for Windows *(continued)*

Security and Permissions

For scripts that communicate with the outside world using files and other file based resources (named *pipes*, or *raw devices*), special attention needs to be given to the files to which the scripts require access. Different users will have access to different files on the basis of their user and group settings and, of course, the individual file permissions.

The easiest way to test the accessibility of different files for script is to run the script as a different user. If you can, try running the script as a user with identical capabilities to the final environment or, for a general-purpose script, create a special user that doesn't have any special privileges. Under Unix just create a user without a primary group, and under Windows create a new user with only Guest privileges.

From within the script ensure that you are testing all file operations, both the obvious **open** and **print** statements and the **stat** and other statistical operators.

Tainted Data

Supplying invalid data provides a good way of testing your script's capability to handle unexpected situations. The real threat is from supplying too much data or the wrong type of data without the script checking either its source or validity. The most obvious example is when a CGI script is used to return the contents of a file—allowing the user to supply a system file, such as **/etc/passwd**, is quite obviously a bad idea.

The simple rule here is *not* to trust any of the data that is supplied by the user, either from the standard input or from environment variables. Manually tracing and tracking the problem is what the Perl taint mechanism is all about.

Using Taint Mode

Perl provides a facility called *taint checking*. This option forces Perl to examine the origin of the data used within a script. Information gleaned from the outside world is tainted, effectively marking it as unsafe. Further, variables derived from tainted data are also tainted. Perl examines where these unsafe variables are used and whether they affect something else outside your script. If, for example, they are involved when running a command or modifying the filesystem, an error is raised. Data is marked as tainted if it comes from outside the script, including the following:

- Command-line arguments
- Environment variables
- Locale information
- readdir function
- readlink function
- shmread function (the data variable only)
- msgrcv function (messages only)
- getpw* function set (the password, gcos, and shell fields)
- Any file input

Tainted data cannot be used in the following:

- Commands that invoke a subshell (including **system**, **open**, **exec** and the **qx//** operator. The exception is the multi-argument forms of **system** and **exec**).

- Commands that modify file contents, permissions, or filesystem attributes—including creating new files.

- Commands that modify directory permissions or names.

- Commands that run new processes or manage existing ones.

Some of the checks are relatively simple, such as verifying that the directories within a given path are not writable by others. Some are more complex and rely on Perl's compiler and syntax checker to accept or reject the statement.

The following code fragments show the results of running some statements with taint checking switched on:

```
$cmd = shift;             # tainted - its origin is the command line
$run = "echo $cmd";       # Also tainted - derived from $cmd
$alsoran = `echo Hello`;  # Not tainted
system "echo $cmd";       # Insecure - external shell with $cmd
system "$alsoran";        # Insecure - until $PATH set
system "/bin/echo", $cmd; # Secure - doesn't use shell to execute
```

If you try to execute this as a script with taint checking switched on, you will receive errors such as "Insecure dependency" or "Insecure $ENV{PATH}" for lines 4 and 5.

Also note that anything that implies the use of an external command or function also makes the data insecure. Therefore, anything that accesses the environment (via **%ENV**), calls to file globbing routines (**glob** or **<*.c>**), and some **open** constructs also returns tainted information. Finally, any system functions, such as **umask**, **unlink**, **link** and others, when used with tainted variables, are also considered insecure. In each case, there are some exceptions.

If you modify the environment from Perl before accessing it, then the information is not tainted (Perl "remembers" that you made the modification); so the code

```
$ENV{'PATH'} = '/bin:/usr/bin';
$path = $ENV{'PATH'};
```

does not taint **$path**, since its source was originally internal.

With the **open** command, reads from tainted file names are allowed, because reading is nondestructive. However, writes to files referred to by tainted variables are not allowed; thus the code

```
$file = shift;
open(DATA,">$file");
```

will generate an error, since the **$file** variable has come from an external source.

Using pipes is also an insecure option if the command or data you are using with a command has come from an external source, such that

```
$file = shift;
open(FOO,"gunzip -c $file|");
```

is considered unsafe, since you must call a shell in order to interpret the entire command line. You can get around this by using the alternative pipe notation,

```
$file = shift;
open(FOO,"-|") or exec 'gunzip', '-c', $file;
```

which is considered safe, because you do not use a shell to execute the command.

To switch on taint checking, you must specify the **–T** option on the command line. Doing this works for Unix and Windows NT. Taint checking with MacPerl is available but not particularly useful. Even if you enable taint checks it wouldn't make a huge difference since the MacOS is not capable of executing external programs. In any case, it is not prone to the same security breaches as a Unix or NT system.

Taint checking is also automatically enabled by Perl if you attempt to run a script that is running with different real and effective user and group IDs. If the setuid or setgid bit has been set on a Unix system, this automatically implies taint checking. Once switched on, taint checking is enabled for the rest of your script; you cannot switch it off until the script ends.

Checking and Untainting Data

To detect whether a variable is tainted, you can use the function **is_tainted** from the **tainted.pl** script supplied in the standard library of the Perl distribution. The only way to untaint variables is to reference substring regular expression matches. For example, for an email address you might use the following code fragment to extract an untainted version of the address:

```
If ($addr =~ /^([-\@\w.]+)$/)
{
    $addr = $1;
}
else
{
    die "Bad email address";
}
```

Obviously, running an expression match on every tainted element defeats the object of taint checking in the first place. You can, therefore, switch this untainting behavior on and off within the script by using the **re** pragma,

```
use re 'taint';
```

which means that all regular expressions taint data if their source data is already tainted.

Because variables from CGI scripts are tainted (they come from either an external environment variable or the standard input), tainting Perl CGI scripts is a good idea.

Web Servers

Web servers provide a restricted environment for running CGI scripts. Many of the environment variables covered earlier in this chapter, for example, will simply not exist or contain a severely reduced set of information—especially for security conscious variables like the **PATH**. Other factors also need to be taken into consideration: communicating with the outside world, either through a socket or command, can be problematic. The user used to execute a script in this environment is also likely to have a reduced set of capabilities. Finally, the use of timeouts can incorrectly indicate a script failure.

The easiest way to test code under these conditions is to actually run it under the web server and see what happens. Use the techniques in Chapters 7 and 9 to record errors during the execution, rather than relying on the server's error log file, which you might not have access to.

Web Environment

The environment variables available to any script running under a web server are severely restricted. Most of the information would be unusable or available elsewhere (see "Environment Variables" earlier in this chapter). In fact it's probably best to assume that all the environment variables that you might normally have access to *will not*, rather than *might not*, exist. The variable you are most likely to experience a problem with is the **PATH** variable, but given the other problems I've highlighted above, you should be defining your own path anyway. I've listed the environment variables defined when executing a CGI script under the two most popular web browsers, Apache and IIS, in Table 14-3 for reference.

Environment Variable	Platform
CONTENT_LENGTH	Apache, IIS
DOCUMENT_ROOT	Apache
GATEWAY_INTERFACE	Apache
HTTPS	IIS
HTTP_ACCEPT	Apache, IIS
HTTP_ACCEPT_CHARSET	Apache, IIS
HTTP_ACCEPT_ENCODING	Apache, IIS
HTTP_ACCEPT_LANGUAGE	Apache, IIS
HTTP_CONNECTION	Apache, IIS
HTTP_COOKIE	IIS
HTTP_EXTENSION	Apache
HTTP_HOST	Apache, IIS
HTTP_IF_MODIFIED_SINCE	Apache
HTTP_UA_CPU	Apache, IIS
HTTP_UA_OS	Apache, IIS
HTTP_USER_AGENT	Apache, IIS
LOCAL_ADDR	IIS
PATH	Apache
PATH_INFO	IIS

Table 14.3   Environment Variables Defined when Executing a CGI Script

Environment Variable	Platform
PATH_TRANSLATED	IIS
QUERY_STRING	Apache, IIS
REMOTE_ADDR	Apache, IIS
REMOTE_HOST	Apache, IIS
REQUEST_METHOD	Apache, IIS
REQUEST_URI	Apache
SCRIPT_FILENAME	Apache
SCRIPT_NAME	Apache, IIS
SERVER_ADDR	Apache
SERVER_ADMIN	Apache
SERVER_NAME	Apache, IIS
SERVER_PORT	Apache, IIS
SERVER_PORT_SECURE	IIS
SERVER_PROTOCOL	Apache, IIS
SERVER_SIGNATURE	Apache
SERVER_SOFTWARE	Apache, IIS
TZ	Apache

Table 14.3   Environment Variables Defined when Executing a CGI Script *(continued)*

Network Communication

Talking to other machines from within Perl over a network can be problematic when the script is executing under a web server. The reason is normally something simple like timeouts (see below) but can also be related to a reduced set of permissions or a lack of the resources required. A good example here is a script that downloads a page from another site and filters and then displays the information back to the browser. Even the LWP and libnet toolkits can cause problems in these situations.

The only way to test and resolve this problem is to try running the script—if you are having problems, try the trick listed in the "Timeouts" section later in this chapter.

External Programs

Relying on external programs for information is a bad idea for any script, but more so for a web-based script because it relies on creating a new process from within a script that may not have either the permissions or resources to do so. Unless you have a real need to communicate directly with an external command, avoid doing so all costs. Most of the time a Perl module will have already been written to talk with most systems. For example, when reading and writing compressed files and other archives, check out the **Archive::*** series of modules available on CPAN. If the extension you are looking for does not exist, consider writing one!

When using the ISAPI toolkit (part of the ActivePerl distribution) to execute Perl scripts through the ASP interface, you get a different set of problems. The PerlIS.dll library creates different threads for each script that it executes.

Because Perl for ISAPI runs as a thread within the web server process and not as a separate process with its own threads, there can be potential problems spawning new applications directly from a Perl for ISAPI script. The cause is that you are attempting to load a program within the scope of the web server's memory space (because it will be a child of the Perl script, which is in turn a thread of the web server). Since you can do most things within the confines of Perl, this wont always be a problem, but if you are worried about the need to call an external program, then use the Perl interpreter directly rather than the PerlIS DLL for executing that script.

User Security

Most web servers will be run either by using the "nobody" account or by using a special named account, such as **www**; for Microsoft's IIS server, the **IUSER_<nodename>** user will be used instead. By default these users have very few permissions and can't really do much beyond access the files within the web server or execute the basic files defined within the reduced **PATH**. Care should be taken with scripts used on these web servers that files and commands are referenced using their fully-qualified names and that any files beyond the scope of the local web server are either suitably secured or given suitable permissions so the script can access them.

If you're connecting to a database, you should explicitly specify the login and password information to connect to the database engine and not rely on the user permissions inherited from the environment. Doing this will only affect databases that default to using the "current" user, such as MySQL and PostGreSql.

The simplest way to test, and possibly break, your code under these conditions is to log in as the restricted user and try running the script.

Timeouts

Most servers and browsers use a series of timeouts when waiting for information to ensure that they don't wait an infinite amount for data. Scripts that are overly complex or that rely on the output of external commands should take this into account. It's quite possible for a script to take so long to execute that the browser times out, even though the script may actually be working correctly.

You can get around this problem by supplying some blank data (a simple newline character will do) while you are waiting for the operation to succeed. To do this, make sure you switch off the normal output buffering,

```
$| = 1;
```

and then output the empty text. This will reset the timeout for the server and browser and stop your script from triggering a failure message.

Running the script under normal conditions may not be enough to trace a fault here. Instead, you'll need to run the script within its CGI environment.

Web Data

The number of attacks on Internet sites is increasing. Whether this is because the meteoric rise of the number of computer crackers or to the number of companies and hosts who do not take the threat seriously is unclear. The fact is that it's incredibly easy to ensure that your scripts are secure if you follow some simple guidelines. However, before we look at solutions, let's look at the types of scripts that are vulnerable to attack:

- Any script that passes form input to a mail address or mail message

- Any script that passes information that will be used within a subshell

- Any script that blindly accepts unlimited amounts of information during the form processing

The first two danger zones should be relatively obvious: anything that is potentially executed on the command line is open to abuse if the attacker supplies the right information. For example, imagine an email address passed directly to **sendmail** that looks like this:

```
mc@foo.bar;(mail mc@foo.bar </etc/passwd)
```

If this were executed on the command line as part of a **sendmail** line, the command after the semicolon would mail the password file to the same user—a severe security hazard if not checked. You can normally get around this problem by using taint checking to highlight the values that are considered unsafe. Since input to a script is either from standard input or an environment variable, the data will automatically be tainted.

There is a simple rule to follow when using CGI scripts: *Don't trust the size, content, or organization of the data supplied.* Here is a checklist of some of the things you should be looking out for when writing secure CGI scripts:

- Double-check the field names, values, and associations before you use them. For example, make sure an email address looks like an email address, and that it's part of the correct field you are expecting from the form.

- Don't automatically process the field values without checking them. As a rule, come up with a list of ASCII characters that you are willing to accept, and filter out everything else with a simple regular expression.

- Check the input size of the variables or, better still, of the form data. You can use the **$ENV{CONTENT_LENGTH}** field, which is calculated by the web server to check the length of the data being accepted on **POST** methods, and some web servers supply this information on **GET** requests, too.

- Don't assume that field data exists or is valid before use; a blank field can cause as many problems as a field filled with bad data.

- Don't ever return the contents of a file unless you can be sure of what its contents are. Arbitrarily returning a password file when you expected the user to request an HTML file is open to severe abuse.

- Don't accept that the path information sent to your script is automatically valid. Choose an alternative **$ENV{PATH}** value that you can trust, hardwiring it into the initialization of the script. While you're at it, use **delete** to remove any environment variables you know you won't use.

- If you are going to accept paths or file names, make sure they are relative, not absolute, and that they don't contain **..**, which leads to the parent directory. An attacker could easily specify a file of ../../../../../../../../etc/passwd, which would reference the password file from even a deep directory.

- Always validate information used with **open**, **system**, **fork**, or **exec**. If nothing else, ensure any variables passed to these functions don't contain the characters **;|()**. Better still, think about using the **fork** and piped **open** tricks to provide a safe interface between an external application and your script.

- Ensure your web server is not running as **root**, which opens up your machine to all sorts of attacks. Run your web server as **nobody**, or create a new user specifically for the web server, ensuring that scripts are readable and executable only by the web server owner, and not writable by anybody.

- Use Perl in place of **grep** where possible. Doing this will negate the need to make a system call to search file contents. The same is true of many other commands and functions, such as **pwd** and even **hostname**. There are tricks for gaining information about the machine you are on without resorting to calling external commands. Your web server provides a bunch of script-relevant information automatically for you in using environment variables, and much of this is available in untainted format from the **CGI** module. Use it.

- Don't assume that hidden fields are really hidden—users will still see them if they view the file source. And don't rely on your own encryption algorithms to encrypt the information supplied in these hidden fields. Use an existing system that has been checked and is bug free, such as the **DES** module available from your local CPAN archive.

- Use taint check or, in really secure situations, use the **Safe** or **Opcode** modules to provide a restricted set of functionality for executing your Perl script.

If you follow these guidelines, you will at least reduce your risk from attacks, but there is no way to completely guarantee your safety. A determined attacker will use a number of different tools and tricks to achieve his or her goal.

The basic rule should always be remembered: Don't trust the size, content, or organization of the data supplied.

Multiple Execution

It's surprising to note that many scripts that are used in situations where they might be executed a number of times concurrently are never actually tested under these conditions. Any script that relies on reading and writing from a resource has the potential to cause a problem. The situations to look out and test for include the following:

- **Network Servers**   You're probably using **select** or **fork** to actually support the individual clients, but beware when supporting commands that write to the same file. Remember to test both **open** and **close** operations and use **flock** or a lock file for other operations, such as tied database access.

- **Database Interfaces**   For interfaces to commercial and other RDBMS systems through modules like the DBI toolkit you shouldn't have a problem, as the databases will handle their own row, column, and table locking. Make sure that you test all operations to pick up any problems. For DBM and text-based databases use either **flock** or the GDBM or Berkeley toolkits, which come with their own locking mechanisms. If none of these work reliably, create a function that tests database operations and waits a short period before retrying, rather than simply failing. Even something as simple as this

```
while(!(tie %metadata, 'GDBM_File' ,"$dbfile", &GDBM_WRCREAT, 0666))
{
    sleep 5;
    last if ($retry++ >6);
}
```

will have the desired effect.

- **CGI Scripts**   Related to the preceding examples, any CGI script that attempts to talk to a resource that can be locked or unavailable should be capable of handling the situation. Again, check any operation that communicates with external data storage, including files, databases, and filesystems.

If you are going to use some form of locking mechanism, including a simple lock file, use **BEGIN** and/or **END** blocks to ensure that the lock file is created before the rest of the program executes and is deleted when the script quits by whatever method. In situations where you're using **die**, go one stage further and use the **__DIE__** signal with a suitable handler to close any lock files. Doing this will help prevent a permanent lock situation where new scripts always fail because the lock file is never removed.

When testing for multiple execution, the easiest method is to place

```
$input = <STDIN>;
```

or

```
sleep(60);
```

somewhere within the script while you execute one or more other instances of the same script in different windows (or the same window if your shell supports job control). Always perform the tests on non-critical data just in case there is an error and the data files you are using get overwritten.

Appendix

Error Message Cross Reference

This appendix contains a list all the errors generated by Perl v5.6.0. In addition to an error description, some indication is given of why the error may have occurred and, if relevant, a method for fixing it.

All error messages are divided into the categories shown in Table A-1. Check the references for each error message for details on why or how to trap or avoid the error.

Some warnings can be controlled using the **warnings** pragma. For those that can, the warning category is given in brackets (see Chapter 8 for more details on using and controlling warnings using the **warnings** pragma). Note that *Severe Warnings* are always displayed unless they have been explicitly disabled with the **warnings** pragma or the **-X** option. For trappable errors, try embedding the statement that is causing the problem within an **eval**.

Note that the error messages include their **printf** formats—for example, **%s** indicates that a string will be inserted into the error message. See the error descriptions for the information on what information will be inserted.

See Chapters 2 through 4 for more information on some of the regularly occurring traps that trip people up.

"%s" variable %s masks earlier declaration in same %s   Warning (misc)

You've tried to declare the same variable twice using the **my** or **our** keywords within the same scope; for example,

```
my $string = 'Hello';
my $string = 'World';
```

Usually this is a typographical error, or you've cut and pasted a section of code and neglected to remove the keywords. Note that the second definition overrides the first.

"my sub" not yet implemented   Fatal Error

You cannot declare subroutine with the **my** or **our** keywords—almost certainly a typographical error.

Warning Type	Trappable	When Reported
Warning	No	When warnings enabled
Deprecated Feature	No	When warnings enabled
Severe Warning	No	Always
Fatal Error	Yes	Always
Internal Error	Yes	Always
Very Fatal Error	No	Always
External Error (not generated by Perl)	No	Depends

Table A.1   Error Types report by Perl

"my" variable %s can't be in a package   Fatal Error

Variables declared with **my** are lexically scoped and therefore don't really exist within a package, so the code

```
my $MyModule::error = 'Not in here';
```

will raise the above error.

"no" not allowed in expression   Fatal Error

As with the **use** keyword, you can't use **no** within an expression. The following is guaranteed not to work:

```
if (no strict)
{
    print "Strict disabled\n";
}
```

"our" variable %s redeclared   Warning (misc)

You've tried to redeclare a variable with **our** within the same lexical scope; probably you've tried

```
our $string;
our $string;
```

"use" not allowed in expression   Fatal Error

You can't place the **use** keyword into any expression. The following will fail:

```
if (use strict)
{
    print "Strict disabled\n";
}
```

'!' allowed only after types %s   Fatal Error

You can use the ! character only with **pack** formats after the s, S, l, and L formats.

/ cannot take a count   Fatal Error

You've tried to use the / template character with **pack** or **unpack** which allows the packed string or list to supply the format length, but the template character does not itself accept a repeat value. For example, you might have typed

```
unpack 'a2/3a*', "03Martin";
```

when really should have typed

```
unpack 'a2/a*', "03Martin";
```

/ must be followed by a, A or Z   Fatal Error

You've probably tried to **unpack** a variable non-string element from a packed string, but you can use only the **a, A,** and **Z**. For example, the following won't work:

```
unpack 'a2/b8',$binary;
```

Alternatively, you might have just introduced a space into the **unpack** format string:

```
unpack 'a2/ a*',$binary;
```

/ must follow a numeric type   Fatal Error

You've tried to unpack a variable length element but didn't supply a suitable format for extracting the numerical value; for example,

```
unpack 'x2/a*',"01binary";
```

% may only be used in unpack   Fatal Error

You can't get checksum information using **pack**—only **unpack**. The following will fail:

```
pack 'a*%','Hello';
```

/%s/: Unrecognized escape \\%c passed through   Warning (regular expressions)

You used a backslash-character combination not recognized by Perl. For example,

```
s/\q//g;
```

This will also happen within an interpolated string.

/%s/: Unrecognized escape \\%c in character class passed through   Warning (regular expressions)

You used a backslash-character combination that is not recognized by Perl inside character classes. The character was understood literally.

/%s/ should probably be written as "%s"   Syntax Warning

You've used regular expression syntax at a point where Perl was expecting a quoted string. This is usually caused by inadvertently using a **split** format on a **join**.

%s (...) interpreted as function   Syntax Warning

Perl interprets any list operator followed by parentheses as a function, rather than an operator. This usually points to either use of the wrong function or placement of parentheses in the wrong place. Using soft references for function names is also another potential problem.

%s() called too early to check prototype   Prototype Warning

You've defined a function that has a prototype, but actually called the function before Perl had a chance to interpret and verify the prototype. For example,

```
message();

sub message($)
{
    print "Hello World\n";
}
```

Either introduce a forward declaration at the start of the script, which will work for all function calls:

```
sub message($);
```

or move the function definition to the start of your script.

%s argument is not a HASH or ARRAY element   Fatal Error

You've supplied something other than a hash or array element to the **exists** function. Passing an entire hash or array, or any other type of object, will raise this error. It may possibly be the result of passing an incorrect reference to the function—the following are all valid:

```
exists($hash{key});
exists($array[0]);
exists($ref->{'key'});
```

%s argument is not a HASH or ARRAY element or slice   Fatal Error

The **delete** function accepts only a hash or array element or a hash or array slice. Passing anything else will raise the above error. This might be the result of an incorrect or undefined reference or object.

%s argument is not a subroutine name   Fatal Error

When using **exists** to verify a function, only supply the function name, don't make it a function call. For example,

```
exists(&function)
```

is fine, but

```
exists(&function($text));
```

will fail.

%s did not return a true value   Fatal Error

You've probably created a file or module that is being imported, but the file doesn't return a true value at the end. Two possibilities exist: either you've neglected to include a simple

```
1;
```

line at the end of the file, or you're using a system to check that the export worked correctly, and it's just failed.

%s found where operator expected   Severe Warning

Perl found a term when it was expecting an operator—you've probably forgotten a delimiter or operator or it's an early indication that the line hasn't been terminated with a semicolon.

%s had compilation errors   Fatal Error

The final failure message when calling Perl with the **-c** command-line option.

%s has too many errors   Fatal Error

Perl lists only 10 errors before it gives up—if you've got more than this, it probably indicates some form of typographical error, such as a missing bracket, quotation mark, or semicolon.

Note that there is no limit to the number of potential errors reported by the **strict** pragma.

%s matches null string many times   Warning (regular expressions)

The pattern you've specified would be an infinite loop if the regular expression engine didn't specifically check for that.

%s never introduced   Severe Warning

This indicates a problem within the interpreter, rather than your script. Basically Perl went to use a previously defined object but it was out of scope by the time Perl wanted to use it. This can be generated by an **eval** call, a dynamically generated signal handler, or a thread-based script.

%s package attribute may clash with future reserved word: %s   Warning

You've used a lowercase name for an object attribute or method that might one day be used internally by Perl.

This almost always indicates that you've mistyped a function, method, or attribute name or accidentally omitted the data type character from a variable.

%s syntax OK   Fatal Error

The final summary message when calling Perl with the **-c** command-line option used to check a script without execution.

%s: Command not found   External Error

You've probably set the execution permission on a Perl script without modifying or adding a suitable shebang (#!) line. This results in the script being run through a shell, not Perl. Check that the shebang line is correct; it should probably read one of these these:

```
#!/usr/local/bin/perl
#!/usr/bin/perl
#!/bin/env perl
```

%s: Expression syntax   External Error

You've probably set the execution permission on a Perl script without modifying or adding a suitable shebang (#!) line. This results in the script being run through a shell, not Perl.

%s: Undefined variable   External Error

You've probably set the execution permission on a Perl script without modifying or adding a suitable shebang (#!) line. This results in the script being run through a shell, not Perl.

%s: not found   External Error

You've probably set the execution permission on a Perl script without modifying or adding a suitable shebang (#!) line. This results in the script being run through a shell, not Perl.

(in cleanup) %s   Warning (misc)

This indicates that an error has occurred when the interpreter called a **DESTROY** method on an object. Only one such error is listed for each object that causes the problem. It may also indicate a problem when communicating with a Perl interpreter from within C when the function callback has failed.

(Missing semicolon on previous line?)   Severe Warning

Perl has made an educated guess about the previous error and thinks it might have been caused by a missing semicolon. However, it could as well be caused by a missing quotation mark, term, list element, or parenthesis.

-P not allowed for setuid/setgid script   Fatal Error

You can't run the C preprocessor on a script that has **setuid** or **setgid** permissions.

-T and -B not implemented on filehandles   Fatal Error

You're operating system can't determine the type of file by examining the buffer of the filehandle. You'll need to supply the file name of the file that you were trying to open instead.

-p destination: %s   Fatal Error

When processing a script with the **-p** command-line option, Perl discovered an error when trying to output the resulting file.

?+* follows nothing in regexp   Fatal Error

You've probably tried to do something like this:

```
s/*//g;
```

which you intended to match either all the text in the expression or a literal. The *, +, and ? modifiers must follow a character or expression definition; for example,

```
s/.*//g;
```

To match a literal character, escape it with a backslash:

```
s/\*//g;
```

@ outside of string   Fatal Error

You've supplied a template to **unpack** that refers to a character location beyond the limits of the string.

<> should be quotes   Fatal Error

You've tried to use C formatting to include a file. The statement

```
require <file.pl>;
```

should be written

```
require 'file.pl';
```

accept() on closed socket %s   Warning

You've tried to call the **accept** function on a socket that is closed. Either the socket was never opened or it was closed before **accept** reached it.

Allocation too large: %lx   Fatal Error

MS-DOS has a limit of 64K for data and code, and you've tried to load a script that exceeds the 64K limit.

Applying %s to %s will act on scalar(%s)   Warning (misc)

You've supplied an array or hash to a match, substitution, or transliteration call. The effect is that the array or hash is interpreted as a scalar (as if supplied to the **scalar** function). If you were trying to perform an operation to every element of an array or hash, use a loop:

```
foreach (keys %hash)
{
    $hash{$_} = tr/a-z/A-Z/;
}
```

or use **map**:

```
map { s/text/string/g } @array;
```

Arg too short for msgsnd   Fatal Error

You've supplied a string to **msgsnd** that is too short. The string should be at least as long as the size of the **long** data type on the current platform. Most platforms use a 32-bit **long**, so you can pad the string to 4 characters using **sprintf**:

```
$message = sprintf("%-4s",$string);
```

Don't be tempted to use **pack** with a 4-byte format unless you know that the string is likely to be shorter than 4 bytes—**pack** will trim the string to exactly the number of characters that you specify; **sprintf** will not.

Ambiguous use of %s resolved as %s   Severe Warning

You've supplied a term that Perl assumed to be a function, method, or string. Usually points to a typo: a missing quote, operator, or parenthesis.

Ambiguous call resolved as CORE::%s(), qualify as such or use &   Warning

You've created a function that has the same name as a Perl keyword but haven't qualified the name when calling it. This causes the interpreter to make the assumption that you want the built-in version rather than your locally defined function. For example,

```
sub log
{
    print STDERR "Log: @_\n";
}
log "Result is " log 5;
```

To call the real **log** built-in, use **CORE::log**. To call your own function, either qualify it completely using **main::** or **package::** or prefix the function call with an ampersand to ensure that a function is called. Alternatively, use the **subs** pragma to forward-declare the function or import it from a module.

Args must match #! line   Fatal Error

When running in **setuid** mode with the **setuid** emulator, the arguments supplied on the command line must match the arguments set in the **#!** shebang line. It's possible that splitting individual switches on the command line on an OS that supports only a single switch is the cause of the problem. Try combining switches—for example, **-w -T** into **-wT**.

Argument "%s" isn't numeric %s   Warning

You've supplied a string to an operator that was expecting a numerical value. The second argument should include the name of the operator affected. For example,

```
$a = 3 * 'hello';
```

raises

```
Argument "hello" isn't numeric in addition (+) at - line 1.
```

Array @%s missing the @ in argument %d of %s()   Deprecated

You've supplied the name of an array without supplying the @ prefix. For example,

```
$ perl -e "push nonchalant,'hello';"
```

```
Unquoted string "nonchalant" may clash with future reserved word at - line 1.
```

Array @nonchalant missing the @ in argument 1 of push() at - line 1.

assertion botched: %s   Internal Error

The **malloc** package that comes with Perl had an internal failure.

Assertion failed: file "%s"   Internal Error

A general assertion within a Perl source file failed. Check the named file and then consider reporting the error to the Perl maintainers.

Assignment to both a list and a scalar   Fatal Error

If you assign to a conditional operator, the second and third arguments must either both be scalars or lists. Otherwise, Perl won't know which context to supply to the right side.

Attempt to free non-arena SV: 0x%lx   Internal Error

The interpreter has created a scalar value outside of the normal SV-defined area. Normally this area is cleared automatically by Perl when the interpreter exits, but this indicates that the interpreter was unable to do so.

Attempt to free nonexistent shared string   Internal Error

Perl maintains a reference-counted internal table of strings to optimize the storage and access of hash keys and other strings. This message indicates that someone tried to decrement the reference count of a string that can no longer be found in the table.

Attempt to free temp prematurely   Internal Error

Mortal variables (that is, those that should be deleted) are supposed to be freed by the **free_tmps()** routine. This message indicates that something else is freeing the SV before the **free_tmps()** routine gets a chance, which means that the **free_tmps()** routine will be freeing an unreferenced scalar when it does try to free it.

Attempt to free unreferenced glob pointers   Internal Error

The reference counters in the symbol table for the **glob** have become corrupted.

Attempt to free unreferenced scalar   Internal Error

The interpreter tried to free the memory used by a scalar variable that had already been freed.

Attempt to join self   Fatal Error

You've tried to join a thread to itself, which is impossible. Check the logic around your calls to **join** to make sure that the right thread is being specified.

Attempt to pack pointer to temporary value   Warning

You've tried to use a temporary variable (from a function or expression) as the template string to **pack**. You must use either a literal string or a real variable.

Attempt to use reference as lvalue in substr   Warning

You cannot use references as the first argument to **substr**, because it is effectively a lvalue. Make sure to de-reference the variable before using it.

Bad arg length for %s, is %d, should be %d   Fatal Error

You passed a buffer of the wrong size to **msgctl**, **semctl**, or **shmctl**. Check the size of the **msqid_ds**, **semid_ds**, or **shmid_ds** structures defined in the C include files.

Bad evalled substitution pattern   Fatal Error

The expression that you supplied in the replacement portion of a regular expression uses an elevated statement, but the expression is invalid due to a syntax error. Check brackets, braces, commas, quotes, and argument types and counts.

Bad filehandle: %s   Fatal Error

You've supplied a symbol to an operator or function that was expecting a filehandle, but the symbol is not a filehandle. Check the name you supplied and that the variable you are using has been populated correctly with **open**.

Bad free() ignored   Severe Warning

The Perl interpreter has tried to call the internal **free()** function on something that had never been allocated memory through **malloc()** in the first place. If you think the warning has been reported in error, you can set the **PERL_BADFREE** environment variable to 1.

Bad hash   Internal Error

One of the internal hash routines was passed a null HV pointer.

Bad index while coercing array into hash   Fatal Error

The index used to identify an entry in the internal pseudo-hash table is not legal.

Bad name after %s::   Fatal Error

You supplied the full name of a variable, including the type prefix, after a package name; for example,

```
print MyPackage::$variable;
```

Be especially careful when using soft references—remember that names interpolate only within quotes. For example,

```
package MyPackage;
$var = 99;

package main;

print "MyPackage::$var\n";
print "$MyPackage::var\n";
```

The first line simply prints "MyPackage::" with the interpolation of **$var** (which doesn't exist in this scope) being appended.

Bad realloc() ignored   Severe Warning (**malloc()**)
The internal **realloc()** function used to re-allocate memory for a variable has been called on something that had never been allocated with **malloc()** in the first place—can be disabled by setting environment variable **PERL_BADFREE** to 1.

Bad symbol for array   Internal Error
An internal request asked to add an array entry to something that wasn't a symbol table entry.

Bad symbol for filehandle   Internal Error
An internal request asked to add a filehandle entry to something that wasn't a symbol table entry.

Bad symbol for hash   Internal Error
An internal request asked to add a hash entry to something that wasn't a symbol table entry.

Badly placed ()'s   External Error
You've accidentally run your script through **csh** instead of Perl. Check the shebang (**#!**) line or manually feed the script to Perl.

Bareword "%s" not allowed while "strict subs" in use   Fatal Error
When using the **strict subs** pragma, you cannot use a bareword, except when calling a subroutine or specifying the key of a hash using the **=>** operator. This usually indicates a function name typo.

Bareword "%s" refers to nonexistent package   Warning (bareword)
You've used a bareword to refer to a package that hasn't been predeclared or imported yet.

Bareword found in conditional   Warning (bareword)
The compiler found a bareword when it expected a conditional operator. This usually points to a problem with the last argument to a function or operator when combined with the ‖ or **&&**; for example,

```
open FOO || die;
```

It may also indicate a misspelled constant that has been interpreted as a bareword:

```
use constant TYPO => 1;
if (TYOP) { print "foo" }
```

The **strict** pragma will normally identify these problems.

BEGIN failed—compilation aborted   Fatal Error
The compiler failed while executing a **BEGIN** block—since these are executed during the compilation rather than execution stage, failure causes the interpreter to exit.

BEGIN not safe after errors—compilation aborted   Fatal Error
The interpreter identified a **BEGIN** block, but a number of compilation errors had already been identified that may cause the block to fail.

Binary number > 0b1111111111111111111111111111111 non-portable   Warning (portability)

The binary number you specified is larger than 32 bits—that is, 2**32-1 (4294967295)—and therefore non-portable between systems.

bind() on closed socket %s   Warning

You tried to do a **bind** on a closed socket. Make sure that you check the return value of the **socket** function.

Bit vector size > 32 non-portable   Warning (portability)

You've specified a bit vector larger than 32 bits, which is non-portable.

Bizarre copy of %s in %s   Internal Error

Perl detected an attempt to copy an internal value that cannot be copied.

Buffer overflow in prime_env_iter: %s   Warning (internal), VMS only

While Perl was preparing to iterate over %**ENV**, it encountered a logical name or symbol definition that was too long, so it was truncated to the string shown.

Callback called exit   Fatal Error

A subroutine from an external packaged called **exit**().

Can't "goto" out of a pseudo block   Fatal Error

You cannot use **goto** to get out of a pseudo block (as used by **sort**, **grep**, and **map**).

Can't "goto" into the middle of a foreach loop   Fatal Error

You can't use **goto** to jump into the middle of a **foreach** loop.

Can't "last" outside a loop block   Fatal Error

The **last** statement can only be used to exit from a block generated for a loop, such as **while** or **for/foreach**, and cannot be used in conditional blocks, such as **if**, or pseudo blocks (**sort**, **map** and **grep**). If you need to use **last** in such a block, create a new unnamed block, which Perl will treat as a single-iteration loop. For example, change

```
if ($value)
{
    last;
}
```

to

```
if ($value)
{
    { last; }
}
```

Can't "next" outside a loop block   Fatal Error

The **next** statement can be used only to exit from a block generated for a loop, such as **while** or **for**, and cannot be used in conditional blocks, such as **if,** or pseudo blocks (**sort, map** and **grep**). Consider inserting an unnamed block (see previous entry).

Can't read CRTL environ   Severe Warning, VMS only

Perl tried to read an element of **%ENV** from the CRTL's internal environment array and discovered the array was missing. You need to figure out where your CRTL misplaced its environment or define **PERL_ENV_TABLES** so that the environment is not searched.

Can't "redo" outside a loop block   Fatal Error

The **redo** statement can be used only to exit from a block generated for a loop, such as **while** or **for/foreach**, and cannot be used in conditional blocks, such as **if**, or pseudo blocks (**sort, map**, and **grep**). Consider inserting an unnamed block (see the "Can't 'last' outside a loop block" entry).

Can't bless nonreference value   Fatal Error

You can only bless a hard reference into an object—soft references cannot be blessed.

Can't break at that line   Severe Warning (internal)

A warning that should be printed only when using the Perl debugger—indicates that the specified line number wasn't the location of a statement at which execution could be stopped.

Can't call method "%s" in empty package "%s"   Fatal Error

You called a method from a package that doesn't actually define any methods or, in fact, any classes. Check that you are calling the right method on the right object. You might also want to check the @**ISA** array to make sure you are not inheriting methods from a package that is otherwise empty.

Can't call method "%s" on unblessed reference   Fatal Error

You cannot call a method on anything except a suitably blessed object reference. Check that the variable you are supplying is actually an object and not a reference and that it has been suitably blessed. If you're calling a method from within another, ensure that you've captured the object correctly—it should have been supplied as the first argument to the function.

Can't call method "%s" without a package or object reference   Fatal Error

You tried to call a method but the entity you supplied is not an object reference of package name. For example,

```
$object = 1;
$object->parse();
```

Note that a different message is returned when calling a method on a string-based variable. Running

```
$object = 'hello';
$object->parse();
```

produces

```
# Can't locate object method "parse" via package "hello".
File 'Untitled'; Line 2
```

Can't call method "%s" on an undefined value   Fatal Error

You've called a method on a variable that contains the undefined value, rather than a true object. This is probably because you failed to check the value of an object when it was first created. Either perform a simple test on the newly generated object:

```
die "Couldnt create object" unless ($object);
```

or use **ref** to check that the returned value was a proper reference rather than a real variable.

Can't chdir to %s   Fatal Error

The directory you supplied to Perl on the command line via the **-x** option doesn't exist. Perl will not continue if it cannot execute within the specified directory.

Can't check filesystem of script "%s" for nosuid   Internal Error

The filesystem isn't allowing Perl to check the status of the **nosuid** setting used to determine whether a **setuid** script can be executed.

Can't coerce %s to integer in %s   Fatal Error

You cannot convert a **typeglobs** and some other types of scalar values into an integer; you've probably tried to do something like this:

```
*value += 1;
```

Check that you're operating on the correct value, or transfer the **typeglob** to a scalar and modify that

```
$value = *value;
$value += 1;
```

Remember that **$value** will no longer be a **typeglob**.

Can't coerce %s to number in %s   Fatal Error

You cannot convert a **typeglobs** and some other types of scalar values into a number.

Can't coerce %s to string in %s   Fatal Error

You cannot convert a **typeglobs** and some other types of scalar values into a string.

Can't coerce array into hash   Fatal Error

You've supplied an array when a hash was expected, but the array contains no information on how to map from keys to array indices. You can do that only with arrays that have a hash reference at index 0.

Can't create pipe mailbox   Internal Error, VMS only

The process is suffering from exhausted quotas or other plumbing problems.

Can't declare class for non-scalar %s in "%s"   Severe Warning

You can declare scalar variables with a specific class qualifier and optional attribute only in a **my** or **our** declaration.

Can't declare %s in "%s"   Fatal Error

You can specify scalar, array, and hash variables only using **my** or **our**. Other variable types are not supported.

Can't do inplace edit on %s: %s   Sever Warning (inplace edits)

While processing a file for an inplace edit (via the **-i** command-line option), the new destination file could not be created. Check permissions on the source file (which is renamed and optionally deleted) and the permissions on the enclosing folder to ensure you have suitable permissions to create new files.

Can't do inplace edit without backup   Fatal Error

Some operating systems do not allow you to read from a deleted but still opened file, which is the trick used to do inplace edits without the backup option. You'll need to specify the extension of a backup file so that the file can be renamed and copied from, instead of deleted and copied from.

Can't do inplace edit: %s would not be unique   Severe Warning (inplace edits)

Your filesystem does not support filenames longer than 14 characters, and Perl was unable to create a unique file name during inplace editing with the **-i** switch. The file was ignored.

Can't do inplace edit: %s is not a regular file   Severe Warning (inplace edits)

You tried to use the **-i** switch on a special file, such as a file in **/dev** or a FIFO. The file was ignored.

Can't do setegid!   Internal Error

The **setegid**() call failed for some reason in the **setuid** emulator of **suidperl**.

Can't do seteuid!   Internal Error

The **setuid** emulator of **suidperl** failed for some reason.

Can't do setuid   Fatal Error

This typically means that ordinary Perl tried to **exec suidperl** to do **setuid** emulation, but couldn't **exec** the necessary file. Check that the file exists (it should be called **sperl#####**, where #### is the version number) and that it's readable. In addition, you might want to ensure that there was enough swap and/or real memory.

Can't do waitpid with flags   Fatal Error

The machine on which you are running doesn't have either **waitpid()** or **wait4()**, so only **waitpid()** without flags is emulated. You might want to check the execution status of this function with an **eval**. See Chapter 6.

Can't do {n,m} with n > m   Fatal Error

You've tried to introduce a repetition match range with a lower value (**n**) that is greater than the higher value (**m**).

Can't emulate -%s on #! line   Fatal Error

You've supplied a switch on a shebang (#!) line that doesn't make sense at this point. Check the shebang (#!) line for typographical errors.

Can't exec "%s": %s   Warning (exec)

An **system**, **exec**, or piped **open** call could not execute the named program for the indicated reason. Either the file doesn't have suitable permissions to allow you to execute it; the file wasn't found in your path (as defined by **$ENV{PATH}**), or the executable in question was compiled for another architecture. The same error will be raised if the value in the shebang (#!) line is not valid, or if your system simply doesn't support the shebang (#!) line.

Can't exec %s   Fatal Error

Perl was trying to execute the indicated program for you because that's what the shebang (#!) line said. If that's not what you wanted, you may need to mention **perl** on the shebang (#!) line somewhere.

Can't execute %s   Fatal Error

You used the **-S** switch (to find the script somewhere within **$ENV{PATH}**, but the copies of the script found did not have correct permissions.

Can't find %s on PATH, '.' not in PATH   Fatal Error

You used the **-S** switch, but the script to execute could not be found in your **PATH**. The script exists in the current directory, but **PATH** does not contain '.' to allow the current directory to be used.

Can't find %s on PATH   Fatal Error

You used the **-S** switch, but the script to execute could not be found in the **PATH**.

Can't find label %s   Fatal Error

You said to **goto** a label that isn't mentioned any place where it's possible to go.

Can't find string terminator %s anywhere before EOF   Fatal Error

You started a string somewhere, but haven't supplied a closing terminator—quote, bracket, or otherwise. This causes Perl to use the entire rest of the script as source for the string, but raises an error if it still hasn't found a terminator before the end of the script.

Check the last string your modified, or the last string in the script, and work backwards checking that you've terminated each correctly. Remember that quotes must match both ends; you can't do

```
print 'Hello world!\n";
```

when working with "here" documents. Make sure that you supplied the termination string properly—it shouldn't have any leading whitespace (check indentations). The following will raise an error:

```
print <<EOF
Testing...
    EOF
```

Also remember not to add the semicolon to the termination line.

Can't fork   Fatal Error

A fatal error occurred while trying to **fork** while opening a pipeline.

Can't get filespec - stale stat buffer?   Severe Warning, VMS only

This arises because of the difference between access checks under VMS and under the Unix model Perl assumes is used. Under VMS, access checks are done by file name, rather than by bits in the **stat** buffer, so that ACLs and other protections can be taken into account. Unfortunately, Perl assumes that the **stat** buffer contains all the necessary information and passes it, instead of the filespec, to the access checking routine. It will try to retrieve the filespec using the device name and FID present in the **stat** buffer, but this works only if you haven't made a subsequent call to the CRTL stat() routine, because the device name is overwritten with each call. If this warning appears, the name lookup failed, and the access checking routine gave up and returned FALSE, just to be conservative. (Note: The access checking routine knows about the Perl **stat** operator and file tests, so you shouldn't ever see this warning in response to a Perl command; it arises only if some internal code takes **stat** buffers lightly.)

Can't get pipe mailbox device name   Internal Error, VMS only

After creating a mailbox to act as a pipe, Perl can't retrieve its name for later use.

Can't get SYSGEN parameter value for MAXBUF   Internal Error, VMS only

Perl asked **$GETSYI** how big you want your mailbox buffers to be and didn't get an answer.

Can't goto subroutine outside a subroutine   Fatal Error

The deeply magical **goto** *subroutine* call can only replace one subroutine call for another. It can't manufacture one for you. In general you should be calling it out of only an **AUTOLOAD** routine anyway.

Can't goto subroutine from an eval-string   Fatal Error

The **goto** *subroutine* call can't be used to jump out of an **eval "string"**. It can be used to jump out of an **eval {BLOCK}** however.

Can't ignore signal CHLD, forcing to default   Warning (signal)

Perl has detected that it is being run with the **SIGCHLD** signal (sometimes known as **SIGCLD**) disabled. Since disabling this signal will interfere with proper determination of exit status of child processes, Perl has reset the signal to its default value. This is usually caused by the parent program that is calling Perl not managing its children properly.

Can't localize through a reference77   Fatal Error

You said something like **local $$ref**, which Perl can't currently handle, because when it goes to restore the old value of whatever **$ref** pointed to after the scope of the **local** is finished, it can't be sure that **$ref** will still be a reference.

Can't localize lexical variable %s   Fatal Error

You tried to use **local** on a variable that had been declared using **my**. If you are trying to localize a package variable with the same name you will need to use the fully qualified variable name.

Can't localize pseudo-hash element   Fatal Error

You tried to localize an element of a hash reference using something like this:

```
local $ar-{'key'}
```

You can't do this yet. However, you can localize an array element, which you can use to localize a hash element by accessing the first element of the pseudo array. For example,

```
local $ar-[$ar->[0]{'key'}]
```

Note that this works only because the first element of the array contains a list of the keys mapped against their real array IDs.

Can't locate auto/%s.al in @INC   Fatal Error

You called a function or method that was identified as requiring an autoload, but no autoloading function could be found. Either you've specified the wrong method or there was a problem autosplitting the file.

Can't locate %s   Fatal Error

The file name you supplied to **do**, **require**, or **use** can't be found. Check the name and/or path of the file you specified and that the **@INC** array contains the directory required. You can use the **lib** pragma or modify the **PERL5LIB** and **PERL5OPT** environment variables.

Can't locate object method "%s" via package "%s"   Fatal Error

You called a method that indicated the package that defined the class you required, but the package itself doesn't contain a suitable method definition. The inheritance tree is probably corrupted somewhere. Check the **@ISA** arrays in the packages you are importing.

Can't locate package %s for @%s::ISA   Syntax Warning

The **@ISA** array contains the name of a package that cannot be found. Check the **@INC** array, if you think the name is valid, or the values defined in the **@ISA** array.

Can't make list assignment to \%ENV on this system   Fatal Error

You've attempted to do list assignment with the **%ENV** environment variable, but the operating system (for example, VMS) doesn't support it.

Can't modify %s in %s   Fatal Error

You've tried to modify an entity that can't be modified. The obvious problem is trying to update a literal:

```
'hello'++;
```

Check that you have a valid lvalue or operator on the line mentioned.

Can't modify non-lvalue subroutine call   Fatal Error

You've tried to modify a subroutine call that doesn't support lvalue assignments. Make sure that the subroutine has been properly declared to support lvalues.

Can't modify nonexistent substring   Internal Error

The internal routine that does assignment to a **substr** was handed a **NULL**.

Can't msgrcv to read-only var   Fatal Error

The target of a **msgrcv** must be modifiable to be used as a receive buffer.

Can't open %s: %s   Severe Warning (inplace edits)

The implicit opening of a file through use of the **<>** filehandle, either implicitly (under the **-n** or **-p** command-line switches) or explicitly failed for the indicated reason. Usually this is because you don't have read permission for a file that you named on the command line.

Can't open bidirectional pipe   Warning (pipe)

You can't open a bidirectional pipe using **open**, that is,

```
open(DATA,"|process|")
```

will not work. Try using the **IPC::Open2** module or using a two-stage output/input process.

Can't open error file %s as stderr   Fatal Error, VMS only

Perl does its own command-line redirection and couldn't open the file specified after **2>** or **2>>** on the command line for writing.

Can't open input file %s as stdin   Fatal Error, VMS only

Perl does its own command-line redirection and couldn't open the file specified after **<** on the command line for reading.

Can't open output file %s as stdout   Fatal Error, VMS only

Perl does its own command-line redirection, and couldn't open the file specified after **>** or **>>** on the command line for writing.

Can't open output pipe (name: %s)   Internal Error, VMS only

Perl does its own command-line redirection and couldn't open the pipe into which to send data destined for **stdout**.

Can't open perl script "%s": %s   Fatal Error

The script you specified can't be opened for the indicated reason.

Can't redefine active sort subroutine %s   Fatal Error

You tried to redefine a subroutine used with the **sort** function while it was still active. Try using

```
sort { &func } @x
```

instead of

```
sort func @x.
```

Can't remove %s: %s, skipping file   Severe Warning (inplace edits)

Perl was unable to delete the file being edited in place, and you didn't specify a backup extension, which forces a rename rather than a delete. The file will remain unmodified.

Can't rename %s to %s: %s, skipping file   Severe Warning (inplace edits)

The rename done by the **-i** command line switch to Perl failed—probably because you don't have suitable write permissions.

Can't reopen input pipe (name: %s) in binary mode   Internal Error, VMS only

Perl thought **stdin** was a pipe, and tried to reopen it to accept binary data.

Can't reswap uid and euid   Internal Error

The **setreuid**() call failed for some reason in the **setuid** emulator of **suidperl**.

Can't return outside a subroutine   Fatal Error

You've included a **return** statement somewhere other than within a subroutine, which isn't allowed.

Can't return %s from lvalue subroutine   Fatal Error

You tried to return illegal **lvalues** from a subroutine that is being used as a lvalue. Illegal lvalues include temporary and read-only values, such as literals.

Can't stat script "%s"   Internal Error

For some reason you can't **fstat** the script even though you have it open already.

Can't swap uid and euid   Internal Error

The **setreuid**() call failed for some reason in the **setuid** emulator of **suidperl**.

Can't take log of %g   Fatal Error

You've attempted to calculate the **log** or a negative or zero value, which you can't do. Check the values you are supplying before calling the function or use the **Math::Complex** module.

Can't take sqrt of %g   Fatal Error

You can't get the square root of a negative number without using complex math and imaginary numbers. Check the values you are supplying before calling the function or use the **Math::Complex** module.

Can't undef active subroutine   Fatal Error

You can't undefine a routine that's currently running.

Can't unshift   Fatal Error

You tried to **unshift** an array that couldn't be **unshift**ed.

Can't upgrade that kind of scalar   Internal Error

You cannot convert certain specialized types of scalar, such as code references and **typeglobs**.

Can't upgrade to undef   Internal Error

There's been an internal error trying to upgrade a scalar value to be undefined, when **undef** is actually the lowest possible value of any scalar.

Can't use %%! because Errno.pm is not available   Fatal Error

The **%!** hash, which contains the mappings between error numbers and messages, should be populated by the **Errno** module, which can't be found. Check your installation.

Can't use "my %s" in sort comparison   Fatal Error

You've declared variables called **$a** and/or **$b** using **my** and then tried to use them in a sort. The global **$a** and **$b** are reserved for **sort** comparisons, but the lexical variables will be used first. Rename the lexical variables.

Can't use %s for loop variable   Fatal Error

You can use only a scalar variable as the loop variable. If you want to use a scalar or hash, use a **while** loop and manually extract the information you want for each iteration.

Can't use %s ref as %s ref   Fatal Error

You've tried to de-reference a reference to the wrong type. You've probably tried to de-reference a hash or array as a scalar. Check the reference types you're creating or use **ref** to determine them on the fly.

Can't use \%c to mean $%c in expression Syntax Warning

When extracting data from regular expressions, you can only use the **\x** style of extracting group elements within a substitution. Outside of a substitution you should be using the **$x** format. In fact, you should be using this everywhere, as the use of the **\x** format is now deprecated anyway.

Can't use bareword ("%s") as %s ref while "strict refs" in use Fatal Error

Symbolic or "soft" references are not allowed when the **strict refs** pragma is in force. Either switch off the pragma temporarily or modify your code to use hard references. The most likely time for this to occur is when using dispatch tables, so consider using the following code in place of the normal symbolic references:

```
if (defined($main::{$func}))
{
    *code = \$main::{$func};
    &code($user,$group,$session);
}
```

Can't use string ("%s") as %s ref while "strict refs" in use Fatal Error

Symbolic or "soft" references are not allowed when the **strict refs** pragma is in force.

Can't use an undefined value as %s reference Fatal Error

You tried to use an undefined value as a reference. Check that the variable was populated correctly before continuing.

Can't use global %s in "my" Fatal Error

You cannot declare a global magic variable (such as **$_** or **%ENV**) with **my**. Check the name you've supplied for the variable in question—it may be conflicting with a standard variable.

Can't use subscript on %s Fatal Error

You've tried to specify a subscript on a variable or expression that doesn't support subscript values. If you're using a subscript on a function call, remember to parenthesize the function call in its entirety. For example,

```
@data = localtime()[0..5];
```

should be written as

```
@data = (localtime())[0..5];
```

Can't weaken a nonreference Fatal Error

You attempted to weaken something that was not a reference.

Can't x= to read-only value Fatal Error

You've tried to repeat a constant assignment on a static or read-only value. You've probably missed an operator somewhere, or you need to perform the operation in two stages.

Can't find an opnumber for "%s"   Fatal Error

A string of a form **CORE::word** was given to prototype(), but there is no builtin with the name **word**.

Can't resolve method `%s' overloading `%s' in package `%s'   Fatal Error, Internal Error

There has been an error resolving the overloading specified by a method name (as opposed to a subroutine reference); no such method is callable via the package. If method name is displayed as **???**; **this is an internal error.**

Character class [:%s:] unknown   Fatal Error

The class in the character class [: :] syntax is unknown.

Character class syntax [%s] belongs inside character classes   Warning (unsafe)

The character class constructs [: :], [= =], and [. .] should be defined in their entirety when used inside other character classes.

Character class syntax [. .] is reserved for future extensions   Warning (regular expressions)

Within regular expression character classes ([]), the syntax beginning with [. and ending with .] is reserved for future extensions. If you need to represent those character sequences inside a regular expression character class, quote the square brackets with the backslash: \[. and .\].

Character class syntax [= =] is reserved for future extensions   Warning (regular expressions)

Within regular expression character classes ([]), the syntax beginning with [= and ending with =] is reserved for future extensions. If you need to represent those character sequences inside a regular expression character class, quote the square brackets with the backslash: \[= and =\].

chmod() mode argument is missing initial 0   Warning (chmod)

You've specified the permissions mode to the **chmod** function as something other than an octal number, which must start with a 0. The statement

```
chmod 777, $filename;
```

should be written as

```
chmod 0777, $filename;
```

Close on unopened file <%s>   Warning (unopened)

You've called **close** on a file that had never been opened.

Compilation failed in require   Fatal Error

Perl couldn't compile the file you supplied in a **require** statement. Perl uses this generic message when none of the errors that it encountered were severe enough to halt compilation immediately.

Complex regular subexpression recursion limit (%d) exceeded   Warning (regular expressions)

In order to handle some of the more complex regular expressions that employ backtracking, the regular expression engine is executed over the same subexpression a number times. The limit on the number of times that the expression engine can be called is 32,766 on most architectures, and you've just reached that limit. There are a number of ways of getting around this: Either shorten or split the string into smaller components that can be handled more easily or use **while** or multiple regular expressions. Alternatively, just produce a simpler regular expression.

connect() on closed socket %s   Warning (closed)

You tried to do a connect on a closed socket.

Constant is not %s reference   Fatal Error

You've tried to de-reference a constant value to the wrong type. Check the type you are de-referencing to or that the constant is a proper reference.

Constant subroutine %s redefined   Severe Warning (redefine)

You redefined a subroutine that had previously been eligible for inlining.

Constant subroutine %s undefined   Warning (misc)

You undefined a subroutine that had previously been eligible for inlining.

constant(%s): %s   Fatal Error

The parser found inconsistencies either while attempting to define an overloaded constant or when trying to find the character name specified in the **\N{...}** escape. Check that you've loaded the **overload** or **charnames** pragma correctly.

Copy method did not return a reference   Fatal Error

The internal routine used to copy values during an assignment has discovered an error.

CORE::%s is not a keyword   Fatal Error

You've tried to access/use an entity from the **CORE::** package that doesn't really exists. The **CORE::** package contains only the keywords and functions defined internally by the Perl interpreter.

Corrupt malloc ptr 0x%lx at 0x%lx   Internal Error

The **malloc** package that comes with Perl had an internal failure.

corrupted regexp pointers   Internal Error

The compiled regular expression couldn't be parsed properly by the regular expression engine.

corrupted regexp program   Internal Error

The compiled regular expression couldn't be parsed properly by the regular expression engine.

Deep recursion on subroutine "%s"   Warning (recursion)

You've tried to call a subroutine recursively more than 100 times, which Perl treats as a possible infinite recursion. Check the function and, more importantly, the data on which it is working. If the subroutine is being used to repetitively parse and process a given string, consider using a loop instead of recursion.

defined(@array) is deprecated   Deprecated Feature

The **defined** function checks for an undefined scalar value, which doesn't make sense on an array. If you want to check whether an array is empty, check the scalar value of the array:

```
unless (@array)
```

If you want to check for an undefined value as returned by a function, check the first argument to the array:

```
if (defined($array[0]))
```

defined(%hash) is deprecated   Deprecated Feature

The **defined** function checks for an undefined scalar value, which doesn't make sense on a hash. If you want to check whether a hash is empty, check the hash using **if**:

```
unless (%hash)
```

Although you can check for a defined value within a specific key, you can't check for an undefined key. Also remember that if a function returns a single undefined value to a hash, you'll get the "Odd number of elements in hash list" error.

Delimiter for here document is too long   Fatal Error

You've supplied a label to the "here" document construct that is too long for Perl to handle. It's probably best to keep your labels to less than 32 characters.

Did not produce a valid header   External Error

Not generated by Perl, this is generated by a web browser when you've failed to tell your script to return a suitable MIME header. Try adding

```
print "Content-type: text/html\n\n";
```

to the top of your script.

(Did you mean &%s instead?)   Warning

You've referred to an imported function using something other than the **&** prefix.

(Did you mean *"local"* instead of *"our"*?)   Warning (misc)

You've tried to use **our** to localize a global variable when you should have used **local** instead.

(Did you mean $ or @ instead of %?)   Warning

You've tried to access a key or slice from a hash using the **%** prefix—remember that when accessing a single scalar value the variable should always start with a **$** prefix to indicate a scalar. To access an array use the **@** prefix.

Died   Fatal Error

You called **die** with an empty string, or you called it with no arguments when both $@ and $_ were empty.

(Do you need to predeclare %s?)   Severe Warning

Usually reported in conjunction with "%s found where operator expected". It probably means that a subroutine or module name is being used when it hasn't actually been defined yet. Make sure that you've imported the correct modules and/or functions, or create a forward declaration for the subroutine in question.

Document contains no data   External Error

Your CGI script didn't return any information to the browser but may have returned a suitable HTTP header. Check that your script is returning information correctly.

Don't know how to handle magic of type '%s'   Internal Error

The internal handling of magical variables has been cursed.

do_study: out of memory   Internal Error

This should have been caught by **safemalloc**() instead.

Duplicate free() ignored   (S malloc)

An internal routine called **free**() on something that had already been freed.

elseif should be elsif   Severe Warning

You've used **elseif** instead of **elsif** in an **if** statement.

%s failed—call queue aborted   Fatal Error

An untrapped exception was raised while executing a **CHECK**, **INIT**, or **END** subroutine. Processing of the remainder of the queue of such routines has been prematurely ended.

entering effective %s failed   Fatal Error

While under the **use filetest** pragma, switching the real and effective uids or gids failed.

Error converting file specification %s   Fatal Error, VMS only

Because Perl may have to deal with file specifications in either VMS or Unix syntax, it converts them to a single form when it must operate on them directly. Either you've passed an invalid file specification to Perl, or you've found a case the conversion routines do not handle.

%s: Eval-group in insecure regular expression   Fatal Error

Perl detected tainted data when trying to compile a regular expression that contains the (?{ ... }) zero-width assertion, which is unsafe.

%s: Eval-group not allowed, use re 'eval'   Fatal Error

A regular expression contained the (?{ ... }) zero-width assertion, but that construct is only allowed when the **use re 'eval'** pragma is in effect.

%s: Eval-group not allowed at run time   Fatal Error

Perl tried to compile a regular expression containing the (?{ ... }) zero-width assertion at runtime, as it would when the pattern contains interpolated values. Since that is a security risk, it is not allowed. If you insist, you may still do this by explicitly building the pattern from an interpolated string at runtime and using that in an **eval**.

Excessively long <> operator   Fatal Error

The contents of a <> operator may not exceed the maximum size of a Perl identifier (about 250 characters). If you're just trying to **glob** a long list of file names, try using the **glob** operator or use a directory handle in combination with an array or regular expression.

Execution of %s aborted due to compilation errors   Fatal Error

The final summary message when a Perl compilation fails.

Exiting eval via %s   Warning (exiting)

You are exiting an **eval** by unconventional means, such as a **goto** or a loop control statement.

Exiting format via %s   Warning (exiting)

You are exiting an **eval** by unconventional means, such as a **goto** or a loop control statement.

Exiting pseudo-block via %s   Warning (exiting)

You are exiting a rather special block construct (like a sort block or subroutine) by unconventional means, such as a **goto** or a loop control statement.

Exiting subroutine via %s   Warning (exiting)

You are exiting a subroutine by unconventional means, such as a **goto** or a loop control statement. Use **return** instead.

Exiting substitution via %s   Warning (exiting)

You are exiting a substitution by unconventional means, such as a **return**, a **goto**, or a loop control statement.

Explicit blessing to '' (assuming package main)   Warning (misc)

You tried to bless an object to a class when the class name you supplied was an empty string. This has the effect of blessing the reference into the package **main**. Consider providing a default target package; for example,

```
bless($ref, $p || 'MyPackage');
```

false [] range "%s" in regexp   Warning (regular expressions)

A character class range must start and end at a literal character, not another character class like **\d** or **[:alpha:]**. The "-" in your false range is interpreted as a literal "-". Consider quoting the "-", "\-".

Fatal VMS error at %s, line %d   Internal Error, VMS only

Something happened in a VMS system service or RTL routine; Perl's exit status should provide more details. The file name in at " %s" and the line number in "line %d" tell you which section of the Perl source code is distressed.

fcntl is not implemented   Fatal Error

Your machine apparently doesn't implement **fcntl()**.

Filehandle %s never opened   Warning (unopened)

An I/O operation was attempted on a filehandle that was never initialized. You need to do an **open** or a **socket** call or call a constructor from the **FileHandle** package.

Filehandle %s opened only for input   Warning (io)

You tried to write on a read-only filehandle. Check the format string you supplied to **open**; for opening a read-write filehandle you need to use "+<" or "+>" or "+>>".

Filehandle %s opened only for output   Warning (io)

You tried to read on a write-only filehandle. Check the format string you supplied to **open**; for opening a read-write filehandle you need to use "+<" or "+>" or "+>>".

Final $ should be \$ or $name   Fatal Error

You must now decide whether the final $ in a string was meant to be a literal dollar sign or was meant to introduce a variable name that happens to be missing. Escape the @ using a backslash or supply the variable name.

Final @ shouldR be \@ or @name   Fatal Error

You must now decide whether the final @ in a string was meant to be a literal "at" sign or was meant to introduce a variable name that happens to be missing. Escape the @ using a backslash or supply the variable name.

flock() on closed filehanle %s   Warning (closed)

You called **flock** on a filehandle that was closed. Check the status of the filehandle before making the call.

Format %s redefined   Warning (redefine)

You redefined a format. To suppress this warning, say

```
{
    no warnings;
    eval "format NAME =...";
}
```

Format not terminated   Fatal Error

A format must be terminated by a line with a solitary dot. Perl got to the end of your file without finding such a line.

Found = in conditional, should be ==   Syntax Warning

You said

```
if ($foo = 123)
```

when you meant

```
if ($foo == 123)
```

gdbm store returned %d, errno %d, key "%s"   Severe Warning

A warning from the **GDBM_File** module that a store failed.

gethostent not implemented   Fatal Error

Your C library apparently doesn't implement **gethostent**.

get%sname() on closed socket %s   Warning (closed)

You tried to get a socket or peer socket name on a closed socket. Check the value of the socket before calling the functions.

getpwnam returned invalid UIC %#o for user "%s"   Severe Warning, VMS only

The call to **sys$getuai** underlying the **getpwnam** operator returned an invalid UIC.

glob failed (%s)   Warning (glob)

Something went wrong with the external program used for **glob** and **<*.c>**. Usually, this means that you supplied a **glob** pattern that caused the external program to fail and exit with a non-zero status.

Glob not terminated   Fatal Error

The lexer saw a left angle bracket in a place where it was expecting a term, so it's looking for the corresponding right angle bracket for a **glob** operator and isn't seeing it. Check whether you are not missing another operator or parenthesis or whether you've failed to perform a comparison properly.

Global symbol "%s" requires explicit package name   Fatal Error

You are using the **strict vars** pragma and haven't defined the variable using either **my** or **our** or explicitly with a fully qualified variable name; for example **$MyPackage::myvar**.

goto must have label   Fatal Error

A call to **goto** must have a destination.

Had to create %s unexpectedly   Severe Warning (internal)

A routine asked for a symbol from a symbol table that ought to have existed already, but for some reason it didn't and had to be created on an emergency basis to prevent a core dump.

Hash %%s missing the % in argument %d of %s()   Deprecated Feature

Very old Perl let you omit the % on hash names in some spots.

Hexadecimal number > 0xffffffff non-portable   Warning (portability)

The hexadecimal number you specified is larger than 2**32-1 (4294967295) and therefore non-portable between systems.

Identifier too long   Fatal Error

Perl limits identifiers (names for variables, functions, and so on.) to about 250 characters for simple names and somewhat more for compound names (like **$A::B**). You've exceeded Perl's limits.

Ill-formed CRTL environ value "%s"   Warning (internal), VMS only

Perl tried to read the CRTL's internal environ array, and encountered an element without the = delimiter used to separate keys from values. The element is ignored.

Ill-formed message in prime_env_iter: |%s| Warning (internal), VMS only

Perl tried to read a logical name or CLI symbol definition when preparing to iterate over **%ENV** and didn't see the expected delimiter between key and value, so the line was ignored.

Illegal character %s (carriage return)   Fatal Error

Perl normally treats carriage returns in the program text as it would any other whitespace, which means you should never see this error when Perl was built using standard options. For some reason, your version of Perl appears to have been built without this support.

Illegal division by zero   Fatal Error

You've tried to divide a number by 0. Check the value before performing the calculation. Note that you cannot trap this using **eval**.

Illegal modulus zero   Fatal Error

You tried to divide a number by 0 to get the remainder. Check the value before performing the calculation. Note that you cannot trap this using **eval**.

Illegal binary digit %s   Fatal Error

You used a digit other than 0 or 1 in a binary number.

Illegal octal digit %s   Fatal Error

You used 8 or 9 in a octal number.

Illegal binary digit %s ignored   Warning (digit)

You may have tried to use a digit other than 0 or 1 in a binary number. Interpretation of the binary number stopped before the offending digit.

Illegal octal digit %s ignored   Warning (digit)

You may have tried to use 8 or 9 in a octal number. Interpretation of the octal number stopped before the 8 or 9.

Illegal hexadecimal digit %s ignored   Warning (digit)

You may have tried to use a character other than 0–9, A–F, or a–f in a hexadecimal number. Interpretation of the hexadecimal number stopped before the illegal character.

Illegal number of bits in vec   Fatal Error

The number of bits in **vec** (the third argument) must be a power of two from 1 to 32 (or 64, if your platform supports that).

Illegal switch in PERL5OPT: %s   Very Fatal Error

The **PERL5OPT** environment variable may be used only to set the following switches: -[DIMUdmw].

In string, @%s now must be written as \@%s   Fatal Error

You've used @**word** in an interpolated string, and @**word** is not an actual array, which would normally be interpolated. The most likely reason is that you're using an email address in an interpolated string. If you didn't mean to interpolate an array, you'll need to backslash the @, \@, sign in the string.

Insecure dependency in %s   Fatal Error

You've tried to do something that the tainting mechanism didn't like. The tainting mechanism is turned on when you're running **setuid** or **setgid** or when you specify **-T** to turn it on explicitly. The tainting mechanism labels all data that's derived directly or indirectly from the user, who is considered to be unworthy of your trust. If any such data is used in a "dangerous" operation, you get this error.

Insecure directory in %s   Fatal Error

You can't use **system, exec**, or a piped open in a **setuid** or **setgid** script if $ENV{PATH} contains a directory that is writeable by the world.

Insecure $ENV{%s} while running %s   Fatal Error

You can't use **system, exec**, or a piped open in a **setuid** or **setgid** script if any of $ENV{PATH}, $ENV{IFS}, $ENV{CDPATH}, $ENV{ENV} or $ENV{BASH_ENV} are derived from data supplied (or potentially supplied) by the user. The script must set the path to a known value, using trustworthy data.

Integer overflow in %s number   Warning (overflow)

The hexadecimal, octal, or binary number you have specified either as a literal or as an argument to hex() or oct() is too big for your architecture and has been converted to a floating point number. On 32-bit architecture the largest hexadecimal, octal, or binary number representable without overflow is 0xFFFFFFFF, 037777777777, or 0b11111111111111111111111111111111 respectively. Note that Perl transparently promotes all numbers to a floating point representation internally—subject to loss of precision errors in subsequent operations.

Internal inconsistency in tracking vforks   Severe Warning, VMS only

Perl keeps track of the number of times you've called **fork** and **exec** in order for it to determine whether the current call to **exec** should affect the current script or a subprocess. Somehow this count has become scrambled, so Perl is making a guess and treating this **exec** as a request to terminate the Perl script and execute the specified command.

internal disaster in regexp   Internal Error

Something went badly wrong in the regular expression parser.

internal urp in regexp at /%s/   Internal Error

Something went badly awry in the regular expression parser.

Invalid %s attribute: %s   The indicated attribute for a subroutine or variable was not recognized by Perl or by a user-supplied handler.

Invalid %s attributes: %s   The indicated attributes for a subroutine or variable were not recognized by Perl or by a user-supplied handler.

invalid [] range "%s" in regexp   Fatal Error

The range specified in a character class had a minimum character greater than the maximum character.

Invalid conversion in %s: "%s"   Warning (printf)

Perl does not understand the given format conversion.

Invalid separator character %s in attribute list   Fatal Error

Something other than a colon or whitespace was seen between the elements of an attribute list. If the previous attribute had a parenthesised parameter list, perhaps that list was terminated too soon.

Invalid type in pack: '%s'   Fatal Error

You've used unsupported characters in your **pack** template.

Invalid type in unpack: '%s'   Fatal Error

You've used unsupported characters in your **unpack** template.

ioctl is not implemented   Fatal Error

Your machine apparently doesn't implement **ioctl**().

junk on end of regexp   Internal Error

The regular expression parser is confused.

Label not found for "last %s"   Fatal Error

You called **last** with a named loop argument, but you weren't within a loop of that name.

Label not found for "next %s"   Fatal Error

You called **next** with a named loop argument, but you weren't within a loop of that name.

Label not found for "redo %s"   Fatal Error

You called **redo** with a named loop argument, but you weren't within a loop of that name.

leaving effective %s failed   Fatal Error

While under the **use filetest** pragma, switching the real and effective uids or gids failed.

listen() on closed socket %s   Warning (closed)

You tried to do a **listen** on a closed socket. Check that the socket was created properly in the first place and ensure that it's valid before making a call to **listen**.

Lvalue subs returning %s not implemented yet   Fatal Error

Due to limitations in the current implementation, array and hash values cannot be returned in subroutines used in lvalue context.

Method for operation %s not found in package %s during blessing   Fatal Error

An attempt was made to specify an entry in an overloading table that doesn't resolve to a valid subroutine.

Method %s not permitted   External Error

Usually reported through your browser. Probably points to an invalid HTTP header being returned by your CGI script.

Might be a runaway multi-line %s string starting on line %d   Severe Warning

You've probably missed a delimiter to a string or pattern, and it was trapped only because the string actually terminated in the middle of a subsequent line. Check the previously quoted block and make sure it's terminated in the right place.

Misplaced _ in number   Syntax Warning

An underline in a decimal constant wasn't on a 3-digit boundary. Remember that the 3-digit boundary works from the right to the left. The constant

```
$value = 300_0;
```

should be

```
$value = 3_000;
```

Missing $ on loop variable   Fatal Error
You've forgotten to put the $ in front of the variable you are using as a loop variable. The statement

```
foreach key (keys %hash)
```

should be

```
foreach $key (keys %hash)
```

All scalars should be prefixed with a $ sign.

Missing %sbrace%s on \N{}   Fatal Error
Wrong syntax of character name literal **\N{charname}** within double-quote context.

Missing comma after first argument to %s function   Fatal Error
You've tried to supply a filehandle or other indirect object to a subroutine call when the subroutine doesn't support it. This can be caused either by simply forgetting the comma between the first two arguments or by calling **print** with a filehandle reference that isn't a filehandle reference.

Missing command in piped open   Warning (pipe)
You used the **open(FH, "| command")** or **open(FH, "command |")** but the command was missing or blank.

(Missing operator before %s?)   Severe Warning
Probably reported with the message "%s found where operator expected" as an educated guess to what the problem might be. Check commas, parentheses, and variable/subroutine names.

Missing right curly or square bracket   Fatal Error
Perl found more opening braces or square brackets than closing ones.

Modification of a read-only value attempted   Fatal Error
You attempted to change the value of a read-only value. At the simplest level, you possibly tried

```
'Hello World' = $message;
```

You'll get the same error message if you try to assign a value to a **substr** that goes beyond the end of the string.

Modification of non-creatable array value attempted, subscript %d   Fatal Error
You tried to use an array value that didn't exist—probably because you supplied a negative value—and it couldn't be created either.

Modification of non-creatable hash value attempted, subscript "%s"   Internal Error
You tried to use a hash value that didn't exist, and it couldn't be created automatically either.

Module name must be constant   Fatal Error
You cannot use a variable name as the argument to the **use** statement:

```
my $module = "MyTemplates";
use $module;
```

If you are trying to load modules dynamically, use **require** instead.

msg%s not implemented   Fatal Error
You don't have System V message IPC on your system.

Multidimensional syntax %s not supported   Syntax Warning
Multidimensional arrays aren't written like **$foo[1,2,3]**. They're written like **$foo[1][2][3]**, as in C.

Missing name in "my sub"   Fatal Error
The reserved syntax for lexically scoped subroutines requires that they have a name with which they can be found.

Name "%s::%s" used only once: possible typo   Warning (once)
You've specified a variable only once within a script and used warnings. Perl assumes that this could be a typographical error, since if you are using a variable it must be both assigned to and used to be useful. It's likely that you've accidentally misspelled the name of the variable you wanted. If you did want to use it only once, try using **our** or **my** just so Perl sees the variable in use more than once.

Negative length   Fatal Error
You called **read/write/send** or **recv** with a negative buffer length.

nested *?+ in regexp   Fatal Error
You can't quantify a quantifier without intervening parentheses. So things like ****** or **+*** or **?*** are illegal. Note, however, that the minimal matching quantifiers, ***?**, **+?**, and **??**, appear to be nested quantifiers, but aren't.

No #! line   Fatal Error
The **setuid** emulator requires that scripts have a well-formed shebang (#!) line even on machines that don't support the #! construct.

No %s allowed while running setuid   Fatal Error
Certain operations are deemed to be too insecure to allow a **setuid** or **setgid** script even to attempt.

No -e allowed in setuid scripts   Fatal Error
A **setuid** script can't be specified by the user.

No %s specified for -%c   Fatal Error
The indicated command-line switch needs a mandatory argument, but you haven't specified one.

No comma allowed after %s   Fatal Error
When using **print** and other operators that support indirect objects, you cannot have a comma between the filehandle and the rest of the arguments. For example,

```
print FILE,@data;
```

should be written as:

```
print FILE @data;
```

No command into which to pipe on command line   Fatal Error, VMS only
Perl handles its own command-line redirection and found a | at the end of the command line, so it doesn't know where you want to pipe the output from this command.

No DB::DB routine defined   Fatal Error
You've tried to start the Perl debugger using the **-d** switch, but the **perl5db.pl** script used to support the debugger doesn't define the **DB::DB** routine that should be called at the beginning of each statement. If you have tried to produce your version of the Perl debugger, check that you have defined the **DB::DB** subroutine correctly.

No dbm on this machine   Internal Error
Perl can't find a suitable **dbm** implementation. This shouldn't really happen because Perl comes with its own SDBM implementation of the **dbm** system.

No DBsub routine   Fatal Error
You've tried to start the Perl debugger using the **-d** switch, but the **perl5db.pl** script used to support the debugger doesn't define the **DB::sub** routine that should be called at the beginning of each subroutine call. If you have tried to produce your version of the Perl debugger, check that you have defined the **DB::sub** subroutine correctly.

No error file after 2> or 2>> on command line   Fatal Error, VMS only
Perl handles its own command-line redirection and found a **2>** or a **2>>** on the command line, but can't find the name of the file to which to write data destined for **stderr**.

No input file after < on command line   Fatal Error, VMS only
Perl handles its own command-line redirection and found a < on the command line, but can't find the name of the file from which to read data for **stdin**.

No output file after > on command line   Fatal Error, VMS only
Perl handles its own command-line redirection and found a lone > at the end of the command line, so it doesn't know where you wanted to redirect **stdout**.

No output file after > or >> on command line   Fatal Error, VMS only

Perl handles its own command-line redirection and found a **>** or a **>>** on the command line, but can't find the name of the file to which to write data destined for **stdout**.

No package name allowed for variable %s in "our"   Fatal Error

Fully qualified variable names are not allowed in **our** declarations.

No Perl script found in input   Fatal Error

You called **perl -x**, but no line was found in the file beginning with **#!** and containing the word "perl."

No setregid available   Fatal Error

Configure didn't find anything resembling the **setregid()** call for your system.

No setreuid available   Fatal Error

Configure didn't find anything resembling the **setreuid()** call for your system.

No space allowed after -%c   Fatal Error

The argument to the indicated command-line switch must follow immediately after the switch, without intervening spaces.

No such pseudo-hash field "%s"   Fatal Error

You tried to access an array as a hash, but the field name used is not defined. The hash at index 0 should map all valid field names to array indices for that to work.

No such pseudo-hash field "%s" in variable %s of type %s   Fatal Error

You tried to access a field from a typed variable where the type does not know about the field name. The field names are looked up in the **%FIELDS** hash in the type package at compile time, which is in turn usually created using the **field** pragma.

No such pipe open   Internal Error, VMS only

The internal routine **my_pclose()** tried to close a pipe that hadn't been opened. This should have been caught earlier as an attempt to close an unopened filehandle.

No such signal: SIG%s   Warning (signal)

You tried to access a signal that Perl couldn't find in the **%SIG** hash. Check the keys of the **%SIG** hash or use **kill -l** in your shell to get a list of signals supported by your system.

no UTC offset information; assuming local time is UTC   Severe Warning, VMS only

Perl was unable to find the local timezone offset, so it's assuming that local system time is equivalent to UTC. If it's not, define the logical name **SYS$TIMEZONE_DIFFERENTIAL** to translate to the number of seconds which need to be added to UTC to get local time.

Not a CODE reference   Fatal Error

Perl was trying to evaluate a reference to a subroutine, but it didn't find a subroutine. Check that the subroutine exists and that the reference was populated correctly. Try using the **ref** function to determine the reference type.

The same error can also be seen if you are using dispatch tables and you fail to check, using **exists**, that the subroutine actually exists before execution.

Not a format reference   Fatal Error

You tried to access a reference to a format (which isn't possible!), but it wasn't a format.

Not a GLOB reference   Fatal Error

You tried to access a reference to a **typeglob**, but the reference wasn't a **typeglob**. Try using **ref** to determine the reference type and check that the reference was produced properly in the first place.

Not a HASH reference   Fatal Error

You've tried to access a reference as a hash when the reference doesn't refer to a hash value. Try using **ref** to determine the reference type and check that the reference was produced properly in the first place.

Not a perl script   Fatal Error

The **setuid** emulator requires that scripts have a well-formed shebang (#!) line, even on machines that don't support the #! construct. The line must mention "Perl."

Not a SCALAR reference   Fatal Error

Perl was trying to evaluate a reference to a scalar value, but it found a reference to something else instead. Try using the **ref** function to determine the reference type.

Not a subroutine reference   Fatal Error

Perl was trying to evaluate a reference to a subroutine, but it didn't find a subroutine. Check that the subroutine exists and that the reference was populated correctly. Try using the **ref** function to determine the reference type.

The same error may also be seen if you are using dispatch tables and you fail to check, using **exists**, that the subroutine actually exists before execution.

Not a subroutine reference in overload table   Fatal Error

An attempt was made to specify an entry in an overload table that doesn't somehow point to a valid subroutine.

Not an ARRAY reference   Fatal Error

You're trying to evaluate a reference as an array when the reference isn't an array value. This probably means that your reference hasn't been created properly or is possibly even empty. Alternatively, you're just de-referencing the value incorrectly. Remember that it should be @{**$ref**}, not ${$ref} or %{$ref}. Check your logic to ensure that the reference is being created properly, or use the **ref** function to determine the reference type.

Not enough arguments for %s   Fatal Error

The function requires more arguments than you specified.

Not enough format arguments   Syntax Warning

A format specified more picture fields than the next line supplied.

Null filename used   Fatal Error

You can't require the null file name, especially because on many machines that means the current directory!

Null picture in formline   Fatal Error

The first argument to formline must be a valid format picture specification. It was found to be empty, which probably means you supplied it with an uninitialized value.

NULL OP IN RUN   Internal Error (debugging)

An internal routine called **run**() with a null opcode pointer.

Null realloc   Internal Error

An attempt was made to **realloc** NULL.

NULL regexp argument   Internal Error

The internal pattern matching routines have failed.

NULL regexp parameter   Internal Error

The internal pattern matching routines are corrupted.

Number too long   Fatal Error

Perl limits the representation of decimal numbers in programs to about 250 characters. You've exceeded that length. Try using scientific notation.

Octal number > 037777777777 non-portable   Warning (portability)

The octal number you specified is larger than $2**32-1$ (4294967295) and therefore non-portable between systems.

Octal number in vector unsupported   Fatal Error

Numbers with a leading **0** are not currently allowed in vectors.

Odd number of elements in hash assignment   Warning (misc)

You tried to assign an odd number of elements when initializing a hash, which must have an even number of matching keys and values.

Offset outside string   Fatal Error

You've specified an offset to the **read/write/send** or **recv** functions that actually points to a location outside of the buffer. The only place where this is allowed is with the **sysread** function, where defining a value past the size of the buffer simply increases the buffer size.

oops: oopsAV   Severe warning (internal)

The grammar has become corrupted.

oops: oopsHV   Severe Warning (internal)

The grammar has become corrupted.

Operation `%s': no method found, %s   Fatal Error

You've tried to perform an overloaded operation when there was no handler defined for that operation. While some handlers can be autogenerated in terms of other handlers, there is no default handler for any operation, unless the **fallback** overloading key is specified to be true.

Operator or semicolon missing before %s   Severe Warning (ambiguous)

You've supplied a variable of subroutine call when the parser was expecting an operator. Check the line for missing or bad operators, missing/additional characters, and words for variables and functions. It's probably due to a typographical error.

Out of memory!   Very Fatal Error

The **malloc()** function returned 0, indicating there was insufficient remaining memory (or virtual memory) to satisfy the request. Check your array definitions and any files or data structures that you are importing from the outside world. See the tricks in Chapter 11 for more information on reducing the memory footprint of your scripts.

Out of memory for yacc stack   Fatal Error

The **yacc** parser wanted to grow its stack so it could continue parsing, but **realloc()** wouldn't give it more memory.

Out of memory during request for %s   Very Fatal Error, Fatal Error

The **malloc()** function returned 0, indicating there was insufficient remaining memory (or virtual memory) to satisfy the request. The request was judged to be small, so the possibility to trap it depends on the way Perl was compiled. By default it is not trappable.

However, if Perl was compiled using the **-DPERL_EMERGENCY_SBRK**, it's possible to use the contents of **$^M** as an emergency pool after **die**ing with this message. Note, though, that you can only trap this error once.

Out of memory during "large" request for %s   Fatal Error

The **malloc()** function returned 0, indicating there was insufficient remaining memory (or virtual memory) to satisfy the request. However, the request was judged large enough (compile-time default is 64K), so a possibility to shut down by trapping this error is granted.

Out of memory during ridiculously large request   Fatal Error

You've asked Perl to allocate more than 2^{31} bytes. You've probably supplied a bad value when creating an array such as **$array[time]** instead of **$array[$time]**.

page overflow   Warning (io)

A single call to **write** when using Perl formats produced more lines than can fit onto a single page as defined by the **$=** variable.

panic: ck_grep   Internal Error

Failed an internal consistency check trying to compile a **grep**.

panic: ck_split   Internal Error

Failed an internal consistency check trying to compile a **split**.

panic: corrupt saved stack index   Internal Error

The savestack was requested to restore more localized values than there are in the savestack.

panic: del_backref   Internal Error

Failed an internal consistency check while trying to reset a weak reference.

panic: die %s   Internal Error

We've popped the context stack to an **eval** context and then discovered it wasn't an **eval** context.

panic: do_match   Internal Error

The internal **pp_match()** routine was called with invalid operational data.

panic: do_split   Internal Error

Something terrible went wrong in setting up for the **split**.

panic: do_subst   Internal Error

The internal **pp_subst()** routine was called with invalid operational data.

panic: do_trans   Internal Error

The internal **do_trans()** routine was called with invalid operational data.

panic: frexp   Internal Error

The library function **frexp()** failed, making **printf("%f")** impossible.

panic: goto   Internal Error

We've popped the context stack to a context with the specified label, and then discovered it wasn't a context we know how to do a **goto** in.

panic: INTERPCASEMOD   Internal Error

The lexer got into a bad state at a case modifier.

panic: INTERPCONCAT   Internal Error
The lexer got into a bad state parsing a string with brackets.

panic: kid popen errno read   Fatal Error
A forked child returned an incomprehensible message about its error number.

panic: last   Internal Error
We've popped the context stack to a block context, and then discovered it wasn't a block context.

panic: leave_scope clearsv   Internal Error
A writeable lexical variable became read-only somehow within the scope.

panic: leave_scope inconsistency   Internal Error
The savestack probably got out of sync. At least, there was an invalid **enum** on the top of it.

panic: malloc   Internal Error
Something requested a negative number of bytes of **malloc**.

panic: magic_killbackrefs   Internal Error
Failed an internal consistency check while trying to reset all weak references to an object.

panic: mapstart   Internal Error
The compiler is screwed up with respect to the **map()** function.

panic: null array   Internal Error
One of the internal array routines was passed a null AV pointer.

panic: pad_alloc   Internal Error
The compiler got confused about which scratch pad it was allocating and freeing temporaries and lexicals from.

panic: pad_free curpad   Internal Error
The compiler got confused about which scratch pad it was allocating and freeing temporaries and lexicals from.

panic: pad_free po   Internal Error
An invalid scratch pad offset was detected internally.

panic: pad_reset curpad   Internal Error
The compiler got confused about which scratch pad it was allocating and freeing temporaries and lexicals from.

panic: pad_sv po   Internal Error
An invalid scratch pad offset was detected internally.

panic: pad_swipe curpad   Internal Error
The compiler got confused about which scratch pad it was allocating and freeing temporaries and lexicals from.

panic: pad_swipe po   Internal Error
An invalid scratch pad offset was detected internally.

panic: pp_iter   Internal Error
The **foreach** iterator got called in a non-loop context frame.

panic: realloc   Internal Error
Something requested a negative number of bytes of **realloc**.

panic: restartop   Internal Error
Some internal routine requested a **goto** (or something like it) and didn't supply the destination.

panic: return   Internal Error
We've popped the context stack to a subroutine or **eval** context, and then discovered it wasn't a subroutine or **eval** context.

panic: scan_num   Internal Error
scan_num() got called on something that wasn't a number.

panic: sv_insert   Internal Error
The **sv_insert()** routine was told to remove more string than there was string.

panic: top_env   Internal Error
The compiler attempted to do a **goto**, or something weird like that.

panic: yylex   Internal Error
The lexer got into a bad state while processing a case modifier.

panic: %s   Internal Error
An internal error.

Parentheses missing around "%s" list   Warning (parenthesis)
You said something like this:

```
my $foo, $bar = @_;
```

when you meant

```
my ($foo, $bar) = @_;
```

Remember that **my**, **our**, and **local** bind tighter than comma.

Perl %3.3f required—this is only version %s, stopped   Fatal Error

The module in question uses features of a version of Perl more recent than the currently running version.

Permission denied   Fatal Error

The **setuid** emulator in **suidperl** decided you were up to no good.

pid %x not a child   Warning (exec), VMS only

The **waitpid**() was asked to wait for a process that isn't a subprocess of the current process. While this is fine from a VMS perspective, it's probably not what you intended.

POSIX getpgrp can't take an argument   Fatal Error

Your system has POSIX **getpgrp**(), which takes no argument, unlike the BSD version, which takes a pid.

Possible Y2K bug: %s   Warning (Y2K)

You've concatenated a number—probably from a **localtime** or **gmtime** call—to the number 19, which is probably a Y2K error. Remember that the year figure returned by **localtime** and **gmtime** is expressed as the number of years since 1900, and not just the last two digits of the year.

Possible attempt to put comments in qw() list   Warning (qw)

You've tried to introduce comments into the lines you are using to define the elements of an array defined using the **qw** operator. The **qw** operator treats all the information as literal data, so you'll end up with the comments inserted into the array. If you want comments while building the array, consider building it manually.

Possible attempt to separate words with commas   Warning (qw)

When using the **qw**() operator, words should be separated by spaces, newlines, or other whitespace—not commas. If you're trying to introduce commas into the array elements, consider quoting them individually instead of using **qw**.

Possible memory corruption: %s overflowed 3rd argument   Fatal Error

An **ioctl** or **fcntl** function call returned more data than Perl was bargaining for. Perl guesses a reasonable buffer size, but puts a sentinel byte at the end of the buffer just in case. This sentinel byte got clobbered, and Perl assumes that memory is now corrupted.

pragma "attrs" is deprecated, use "sub NAME : ATTRS" instead   Warning (deprecated)

The old **attrs** pragma has now been replaced by using the new attribute declaration syntax. The code

```
sub doit
{
    use attrs qw(locked);
}
```

should use the new declaration syntax instead.

```
sub doit : locked
{
. . .
```

Precedence problem: open %s should be open(%s)   (S precedence)

You've tried to open a filehandle using **die** as an error trap, which now causes a problem for the precedence rules. The statement

```
open FOO || die;
```

is misinterpreted as

```
open(FOO || die);
```

Try placing parentheses around the filehandle, or use **or** instead of || to handle the error.

Premature end of script headers   External Error

Generated by a CGI script, probably because your script is generating errors or warnings, which in turn is confusing the server about what information it should be returning to the browser. Try running your script from the command line to determine if any errors are being reported and, if so, fix them. If the script is running fine on the command line, try putting

```
BEGIN { print "Content-type: text/html"; }
```

at the top of your script to try and get more information about the problem. See Chapter 7 for more examples of ways to trace CGI errors.

print() on closed filehandle %s   Warning (closed)

The filehandle you're printing on got itself closed sometime before now. Check that the file opened correctly.

printf() on closed filehandle %s   Warning (closed)

The filehandle you're writing to got itself closed sometime before now. Check that the file opened correctly.

Prototype mismatch: %s vs %s   Severe Warning (unsafe)

You've probably forward-declared a subroutine with a given prototype, and then used a different prototype when you actually defined the subroutine. Check the forward and real declarations to make sure they match.

Range iterator outside integer range   Fatal Error

One (or both) of the numeric arguments to the range operator ".." is outside the range that can be represented by integers internally. One possible workaround is to force Perl to use magical string increment by prepending "0" to your numbers.

readline() on closed filehandle %s   Warning (closed)
The filehandle you're reading from got itself closed sometime before now. Check that the file opened correctly and perhaps check the status of the filehandle before it reaches this point to ensure the file is still open.

realloc() of freed memory ignored   Severe Warning (malloc)
An internal routine called **realloc()** on something that had already been freed.

Reallocation too large: %lx   Fatal Error
You can't allocate more than 64K on an MS-DOS machine.

Recompile perl with -DDEBUGGING to use -D switch   Fatal Error (debugging)
You must have compiled Perl with the **-DDEBUGGING** flag in order to use the **-D** command-line switches.

Recursive inheritance detected in package '%s'   Fatal Error
More than 100 levels of inheritance were used. This probably indicates an unintended loop in your inheritance hierarchy.

Recursive inheritance detected while looking for method '%s' in package '%s'   Fatal Error
More than 100 levels of inheritance were encountered while invoking a method. This probably indicates an unintended loop in your inheritance hierarchy.

Reference found where even-sized list expected   Warning (misc)
You've supplied a single element reference to a hash when it was expecting an even number of values to use as the keys and values of the hash. You've probably used braces or square brackets instead of parentheses to populate your hash.

```
%hash = { one => 1, two => 2, };      # WRONG
%hash = [ qw/ an anon array / ];      # WRONG
%hash = ( one => 1, two => 2, );      # Right
%hash = qw( one 1 two 2 );            # Right
```

Reference is already weak   Warning (misc)
You have attempted to weaken a reference that is already weak. Doing so has no effect.

Reference miscount in sv_replace()   Warning (internal)
The internal **sv_replace()** function was handed a new SV with a reference count of other than 1.

regexp *+ operand could be empty   Fatal Error
The part of the **regexp** subject to either the * or + quantifier could match an empty string.

regexp memory corruption   Internal Error
The regular expression engine got confused by what the regular expression compiler gave it.

regexp out of space   Internal Error

A "can't happen" error, because **safemalloc()** should have caught it earlier.

Repeat count in pack overflows   Fatal Error

You can't specify a repeat count in a **pack** template so large that it overflows your signed integers.

Repeat count in unpack overflows   Fatal Error

You can't specify a repeat count in an **unpack** template so large that it overflows your signed integers.

Reversed %s= operator   Syntax Warning

When using an assignment operating such as +=, the = should be last. Either you forgot a value or you added an operator when one wasn't needed.

Runaway format   Fatal Error

You've supplied a format that contained the ~~ repeat-until-blank sequence, but it produced 200 lines of identical output, which probably means it'll continue doing so. Check your logic and format to ensure that you're pulling the right amount of data off the array or scalar each time, and remember to use **shift** or **pop** on an array value so that you don't end up iterating over the same value in a loop.

Scalar value @%s[%s] better written as $%s[%s]   Syntax Warning

You referred to a single array element using slice, rather than scalar notation. If you are expecting to receive only one value, you should use the scalar rather than slice format.

Scalar value @%s{%s} better written as $%s{%s}   Syntax Warning

You've referred to a single hash element using slice, rather than scalar notation. If you are only expecting to receive one value, you should use the scalar rather than slice format.

Script is not setuid/setgid in suidperl   Fatal Error

You tried to use the **suidperl** program on a script that didn't have the **setuid** or **setgid** permission bit set.

Search pattern not terminated   Fatal Error

The lexer couldn't find the final delimiter of a // or **m{}** construct. Remember that bracketing delimiters count nesting level. Missing the leading $ from a variable **$m** may cause this error.

%sseek() on unopened file   Warning (unopened)

You tried to use the **seek** or **sysseek** function on a filehandle that was either never opened or had since been closed.

select not implemented   Fatal Error

This machine doesn't implement the **select()** system call. You'll need to use a round-robin approach to check the status of all of the filehandles you are talking to.

sem%s not implemented   Fatal Error

You don't have System V semaphore IPC on your system.

semi-panic: attempt to dup freed string   Severe Warning (internal)

The internal **newSVsv()** routine was called to duplicate a scalar that had previously been marked as free.

Semicolon seems to be missing   Warning (semicolon)

A nearby syntax error was probably caused by a missing semicolon or possibly by some other missing operator, such as a comma.

send() on closed socket %s   Warning (closed)

You've tried to **send** some data to a socket that was actually closed, either because it didn't open properly or because the socket has already been opened and closed before this statement was reached. Check the status of the socket when opening or before you make this call.

Sequence (? incomplete   Fatal Error

A regular expression ended with an incomplete extension (**?**.

Sequence (?#... not terminated   Fatal Error

A regular expression comment must be terminated by a closing parenthesis. Embedded parentheses aren't allowed.

Sequence (?%s...) not implemented   Fatal Error

A proposed regular expression extension has the character reserved but has not yet been written.

Sequence (?%s...) not recognized   Fatal Error

You used a regular expression extension that doesn't make sense.

Server error   External Error

This is generated in your browser window when trying to run a CGI script. Check that you're script returns suitable headers; for example,

```
print "Content-type: text/html\n\n";
```

Also check that your script returns some information. It may also indicate a more general error with your script, such as a serious fault, or just that the script is generating warning messages (because you switched warnings on). Check the server error log to see if Perl generated any output. You might also want to check the executable permissions on your script and verify that the shebang (#!) line points to the proper Perl application. It may be found either in **/usr/bin/perl** or in **/usr/local/bin/perl**.

Finally, if you are using a hosting service to hold your website and Perl scripts, check that the directory holding the scripts is only writeable by you—some hosting services prevent scripts from executing if they are contained within an "unsafe" directory.

setegid() not implemented   Fatal Error

You've tried to assign to **$)**, and your operating system doesn't support the **setegid()** system call (or equivalent)—at least Configure didn't think so.

seteuid() not implemented   Fatal Error

You tried to assign to **$>**, and your operating system doesn't support the **seteuid()** system call (or equivalent).

setpgrp can't take arguments   Fatal Error

Your system has the **setpgrp()** from BSD 4.2, which takes no arguments, unlike POSIX **setpgid()**, which takes a process ID and process group ID.

setrgid() not implemented   Fatal Error

You've tried to assign to **$(**, and your operating system doesn't support the **setrgid()** system call (or equivalent).

setruid() not implemented   Fatal Error

You've tried to assign to **$<**, and your operating system doesn't support the **setruid()** system call (or equivalent).

Setuid/gid script is writable by world   Fatal Error

The **setuid** script has permissions that allow anybody to write to it—which defeats the object of a **setuid** script. The **setuid** emulator will fail just in case somebody already has written to it.

shm%s not implemented   Fatal Error

You don't have System V shared memory IPC on your system.

shutdown() on closed socket %s   Warning (closed)

You've called **shutdown** on a socket that had already been closed. Check you're logic.

SIG%s handler "%s" not defined   Warning (signal)

The signal handler you are trying to use does not exist. Check the name of the function you supplied to the signal handler hash.

sort is now a reserved word   Fatal Error

You've probably tried to create a filehandle using the word **sort**, which is obviously now a function.

Sort subroutine didn't return a numeric value   Fatal Error

The subroutine you are using with **sort** should return a number. Check that you are doing a comparison on the two values using **<=>** or **cmp**.

Sort subroutine didn't return single value   Fatal Error

When using **sort** with an implied or external subroutine, the subroutine should return only one value—the one that should be promoted up the list. Check the subroutine to make sure that you are doing a proper comparison and returning only one possible value. Also remember that a **sort** routine should return a comparison between the two values it was supplied; errors and/or additional information that you may try to build during the sort process should be handled either using a global variable, or by using a separate loop.

Split loop   Internal Error
A call to **split** had been iterating more times than there were characters in the original source. This probably highlights a problem in your regular expression or in a data structure that is also being updated elsewhere.

Stat on unopened file <%s>   Warning (unopened)
You called **stat** using a filehandle that had never been opened or had since been closed. Try using the file name instead, or check your logic to ensure that the filehandle is valid before you call **stat**.

Statement unlikely to be reached   Warning (exec)
When calling **exec** you really can't put anything after it except a **die**. This is because a call to **exec** will never return (if it succeeds, the Perl interpreter will be replaced), except on failure. This message probably means you've inserted the **exec** function in your program, or you've mistakenly tried to trap the call using something other than **die. Alternatively, you might have just been trying to run an external program, in which case you should've used system** or backticks instead.

Strange *+?{} on zero-length expression   Warning (regular expressions)
You applied a regular expression quantifier in a place where it makes no sense, such as on a zero-width assertion. Try putting the quantifier inside the assertion instead. For example, the way to match "abc," provided that it is followed by three repetitions of "xyz," is **/abc(?=(?:xyz){3})/**, not **/abc(?=xyz){3}/**.

Stub found while resolving method `%s' overloading `%s' in package `%s'   Internal Error
Overloading resolution through the **@ISA** tree may be broken by importation stubs. Stubs should never be implicitly created, but explicit calls to the **can** method may break this.

Subroutine %s redefined   Warning (redefine)
You've tried to define a subroutine that you had already previously defined.

Substitution loop   Internal Error
The substitution was looping infinitely.

Substitution pattern not terminated   Fatal Error
The lexer couldn't find the interior delimiter of a **s///** or **s{}{}** construct. Remember that bracketing delimiters count nesting level. Missing the leading **$** from variable **$s** may cause this error.

Substitution replacement not terminated   Fatal Error
The lexer couldn't find the final delimiter of a **s///** or **s{}{}** construct. Remember that bracketing delimiters count nesting level. Missing the leading **$** from variable **$s** may cause this error.

substr outside of string   Warning (substr), Fatal Error

You've tried to reference a **substr** that pointed outside of a string. That is, the absolute value of the offset was larger than the length of the string. The warning is fatal if **substr** is used in an lvalue context.

suidperl is no longer needed since %s   Fatal Error

Your Perl was compiled with **-DSETUID_SCRIPTS_ARE_SECURE_NOW**, but a version of the **setuid** emulator somehow got run anyway.

switching effective %s is not implemented   Fatal Error

While under the **use filetest** pragma, we cannot switch the real and effective uids or gids.

syntax error   Fatal Error

Probably means you had a typographical error in your script that upset the syntax parser. Common reasons include

- A keyword is misspelled
- A semicolon is missing
- A comma is missing
- An opening or closing parenthesis is missing
- An opening or closing brace is missing
- A closing quote is missing

Often there will be another error message associated with the syntax error giving more information.

syntax error at line %d: `%s' unexpected   External Error

You've accidentally run your script through the Bourne shell instead of Perl. Check the shebang (#!) line, or manually feed your script into Perl yourself.

System V %s is not implemented on this machine   Fatal Error

You've tried to use one of the System V IPC functions on a machine that doesn't support them.

syswrite() on closed filehandle %s   Warning (closed)

You're trying to write to a closed filehandle. Try checking the filehandle's suitability before starting.

Target of goto is too deeply nested   Fatal Error

You've tried to use **goto** to reach a label that was too deeply nested for Perl to reach.

tell() on unopened file   Warning (unopened)

You've tried to use the **tell** function on a filehandle that was either never opened or had since been closed.

Test on unopened file <%s>   Warning (unopened)

You tried to invoke a file test operator on a filehandle that isn't open.

That use of $[is unsupported   Fatal Error

The use of $[as a way of changing the first element of an array has been discontinued. You can now only assign a value of zero or one to the variable:

```
$[ = 0;
$[ = 1;
...
local $[ = 0;
local $[ = 1;
...
```

The %s function is unimplemented   Fatal Error

The function indicated isn't implemented on this architecture.

The crypt() function is unimplemented due to excessive paranoia   Fatal Error

Configure couldn't find the **crypt**() function on your machine.

The stat preceding -l _ wasn't an lstat   Fatal Error

You've tried to check the symbolic link status of the _ **stat** buffer when the _ buffer doesn't point to a symbolic link. Try using the filename rather than the _ buffer.

This Perl can't reset CRTL environ elements (%s)   You've tried to change or delete an element of the CRTL's internal environ array, but your copy of Perl wasn't built with a CRTL that contained the **setenv** function. You'll need to rebuild Perl with a CRTL that does, or redefine **PERL_ENV_TABLES** so that the environ array isn't the target of the change to **%ENV** that produced the warning.

This Perl can't set CRTL environ elements (%s=%s)   Warning (internal), VMS only

You've tried to change or delete an element of the CRTL's internal environ array, but your copy of Perl wasn't built with a CRTL that contained the **setenv** function. You'll need to rebuild Perl with a CRTL that does, or redefine **PERL_ENV_TABLES** so that the environ array isn't the target of the change to **%ENV** that produced the warning.

times not implemented   Fatal Error

Your version of the C library apparently doesn't support the **times**().

Too few args to syscall   Fatal Error

You need to supply at least one argument to the **syscall** function—the system call that you want to call.

Too late for "-T" option   Very Fatal Error

The **-T** command-line option was seen too late by the Perl interpreter, which means that it can't guarantee to taint all the data extracted from the environment. If you're using a script with a shebang

(#!) line, put **-T** as the first option. If you're running a script on the command line, put the **-T** as the first argument.

Too late for "-%s" option   Very Fatal Error

You've tried to include the **-M** or **-m** command line options to import a module within a script, which Perl doesn't support. Change the shebang (#!) line and then employ a **use** statement instead.

Too late to run %s block   Warning (void)

A **CHECK** or **INIT** block is being defined during runtime proper, when the opportunity to run them has already passed. Perhaps you are loading a file with **require** or **do** when you should be using **use** instead. Or perhaps you should put the **require** or **do** inside a **BEGIN** block.

Too many ('s   External Error

You've accidentally run your script through **csh** instead of Perl. Check the shebang (#!) line or manually feed your script into Perl yourself.

Too many)'s   External Error

You've accidentally run your script through **csh** instead of Perl. Check the shebang (#!) line or manually feed your script into Perl yourself.

Too many args to syscall   Fatal Error

Perl supports a maximum of only 14 args to **syscall**.

Too many arguments for %s   Fatal Error

The function requires fewer arguments than you specified.

trailing \ in regexp   Fatal Error

The regular expression ends with a backslash—try escaping the backslash with another backslash.

Transliteration pattern not terminated   Fatal Error

The lexer couldn't find the interior delimiter of a **tr///** or **tr[][]** or **y///** or **y[][]** construct. Omitting the leading $ from variables **$tr** or **$y** may cause this error.

Transliteration replacement not terminated   Fatal Error

The lexer couldn't find the final delimiter of a **tr///** or **tr[][]** construct.

truncate not implemented   Fatal Error

Your operating system doesn't support file truncation. Try deleting the file first and then recreating it.

Type of arg %d to %s must be %s (not %s)   Fatal Error

You've supplied the wrong type of variable to a function or operator. On a built-in function it probably means you've supplied a scalar or array value to **keys** or similar, or you've supplied a scalar or hash to the **push** or other array expecting functions. The same error message will also be raised for your own subroutines if you are using prototypes.

Remember that you can de-reference a reference to an array or hash using the block notation:

```
$hash = {hello => 'world'};
print keys %{$hash};
```

umask: argument is missing initial 0   Warning (umask)
   The **umask** function should be supplied with an octal, not decimal, value. You probably called

```
umask 222;
```

when you meant

```
umask 0222;
```

umask not implemented   Fatal Error
   Your machine doesn't implement the **umask** function.

Unable to create sub named "%s"   Fatal Error
   You attempted to create or access a subroutine with an illegal name.

Unbalanced context: %d more PUSHes than POPs   Warning (internal)
   The exit code detected an internal inconsistency in how many execution contexts were entered and left.

Unbalanced saves: %d more saves than restores   Warning (internal)
   The exit code detected an internal inconsistency in how many values were temporarily localized.

Unbalanced scopes: %d more ENTERs than LEAVEs   Warning (internal)
   The exit code detected an internal inconsistency in how many blocks were entered and left.

Unbalanced tmps: %d more allocs than frees   Warning (internal)
   The exit code detected an internal inconsistency in how many mortal scalars were allocated and freed.

Undefined format "%s" called   Fatal Error
   The format indicated doesn't seem to exist.

Undefined sort subroutine "%s" called   Fatal Error
   The sort comparison routine specified doesn't seem to exist.

Undefined subroutine &%s called   Fatal Error
   The subroutine indicated hasn't been defined, or, if it was, it has since been undefined.

Undefined subroutine called   Fatal Error
   The anonymous subroutine you're trying to call hasn't been defined, or, if it was, it has since been undefined.

Undefined subroutine in sort   Fatal Error

The sort comparison routine specified is declared but doesn't seem to have been defined yet.

Undefined top format "%s" called   Fatal Error

The format indicated doesn't seem to exist.

Undefined value assigned to typeglob   Warning (misc)

An undefined value was assigned to a **typeglob**. You probably tried

```
*foo = undef;
```

when you meant

```
undef *foo;
```

unexec of %s into %s failed!   Fatal Error

The **unexec** routine failed for some reason.

Unknown BYTEORDER   Fatal Error

There are no byte-swapping functions for a machine with this byte order.

Unknown open() mode '%s'   Fatal Error

The second argument of three-argument **open** is not among the list of valid modes: <, >, >>, +<, +>, +>>, - |, | -.

Unknown process %x sent message to prime_env_iter: %s   Internal Error, VMS only

Perl was reading values for **%ENV** before iterating over it, and someone else stuck a message in the stream of data Perl expected.

unmatched () in regexp   Fatal Error

Unbackslashed parentheses must always be balanced in regular expressions.

Unmatched right %s bracket   Fatal Error

The lexer counted more closing curly or square brackets than opening ones, so you're probably missing a matching opening bracket.

unmatched [] in regexp   Fatal Error

The brackets around a character class must match. If you want to include a closing bracket in a character class, backslash it or put it first.

Unquoted string "%s" may clash with future reserved word   Warning (reserved)

You used a bareword that might someday be claimed as a reserved word. Either change the name—so it's in something other than lowercase or contains an underscore character—or predefine a subroutine.

Unrecognized character %s   Fatal Error

The Perl parser has no idea what to do with the specified character in your Perl script (or **eval**). Perhaps you've tried to run a compressed script, a binary program, or a directory as a Perl program.

Unrecognized escape \\%c passed through   Warning (misc)

You've used a backslash-character combination that is not recognized by Perl.

Unrecognized signal name "%s"   Fatal Error

You've specified a signal name to the **kill** function that was not recognized. Check the **%SIG** hash for a list of valid signal names, or call **kill -l** within your shell.

Unrecognized switch: -%s (-h will show valid options)   Fatal Error

You supplied an invalid command-line option to Perl.

Unsuccessful %s on filename containing newline   Warning (newline)

A file operation was attempted on a file name, and that operation failed because the file name included a newline character—check that you've used **chop** or **chomp** on the value you're using.

Unsupported directory function "%s" called   Fatal Error

Your machine doesn't support **opendir** and **readdir**.

Unsupported function fork   Fatal Error

Your operating system, or the currently executing version of Perl, does not support the **fork** function.

Unsupported function %s   Fatal Error

This machine doesn't implement the indicated function, apparently.

Unsupported socket function "%s" called   Fatal Error

Your machine doesn't support the Berkeley socket mechanism.

Unterminated <> operator   Fatal Error

The lexer saw a left angle bracket in a place where it was expecting a term, so it's looking for the corresponding right angle bracket and not finding it. Check the parentheses in your statement to ensure that you're not introducing a <> operator in place of a simple less-than comparison statement.

Unterminated attribute parameter in attribute list   Fatal Error

The lexer saw an opening (left) parenthesis character while parsing an attribute list, but the matching closing (right) parenthesis character was not found. You may need to add (or remove) a backslash character to get your parentheses to balance.

Unterminated attribute list   Fatal Error

The lexer found something other than a simple identifier at the start of an attribute, and it wasn't a semicolon or the start of a block. Check the termination of the attribute list.

Use of $# is deprecated   Deprecated Feature

You should be using **printf** or **sprintf** to format numbers instead of the $# variable.

Use of $* is deprecated   Deprecated Feature

The use of the $* variable, which switched on multi-line pattern matching in regular expressions, should be replaced by using the **//m** and **//s** modifiers on an expression-by-expression basis.

Use of %s in printf format not supported   Fatal Error

You attempted to use a feature of **printf** that is accessible only from C.

Use of bare << to mean <<"" is deprecated   Deprecated Feature

You should supply a real string to the "here" document operator << instead of using the implied empty string when you want to use a blank line as the "here" document terminator. For example, change

```
print <<
Hello
```

to

```
print <<""
Hello
```

Use of implicit split to @_ is deprecated   Deprecated Feature

The implied placement of individual elements into @_ from the **split** function is deprecated, especially within a separate subroutine that has its own @_ array to handle. Assign the results of **split** to a proper array or list.

Use of inherited AUTOLOAD for non-method %s() is deprecated   Deprecated Feature

As an (*ahem*) accidental feature, **AUTOLOAD** subroutines are looked up as methods (using the @**ISA** hierarchy), even when the subroutines to be autoloaded were called as plain functions (**Foo::bar()**), not as methods (**Foo->bar()** or **$obj->bar()**). This bug will be rectified in Perl 5.005, which will use method lookup only for method **AUTOLOAD**s. However, there is a significant base of existing code that may be using the old behavior. So, as an interim step, Perl 5.004 issues an optional warning when non-methods use inherited **AUTOLOAD**s.

The simple rule is that inheritance will not work when autoloading non-methods. The simple fix for old code is that in any module that used to depend on inheriting **AUTOLOAD** for non-methods from a base class named **BaseClass**, execute *AUTOLOAD = \&BaseClass::AUTOLOAD during startup. In code that currently says **use AutoLoader**; **@ISA = qw(AutoLoader)**;, you should remove AutoLoader from @ISA and change **use AutoLoader**; to **use AutoLoader 'AUTOLOAD'**;.

Use of reserved word "%s" is deprecated   Deprecated Feature

The indicated bareword is a reserved word. Future versions of Perl may use it as a keyword, so you're better off either explicitly quoting the word in a manner appropriate for its context of use or using a different name altogether. The warning can be suppressed for subroutine names by either adding a **&** prefix or using a package qualifier, for example, **&our()**, or **Foo::our()**.

Use of %s is deprecated   Deprecated Feature

The construct indicated is no longer recommended for use.

Use of uninitialized value%s   Warning (uninitialized)

An undefined value was used as if it were already defined. It was interpreted as an empty string or a 0, but maybe it was a mistake. To suppress this warning assign a defined value to your variables.

Useless use of "re" pragma   Warning

You did **use re;** without any arguments.

Useless use of %s in void context   Warning (void)

You did something without a side effect in a context that does nothing with the return value, such as a statement that doesn't return a value from a block or the left side of a scalar comma operator. Very often this points not to stupidity on your part, but to a failure of Perl to parse your program the way you thought it would. For example, you'd get this if you mixed up your C precedence with Python precedence and said

```
$one, $two = 1, 2;
```

when you meant to say

```
($one, $two) = (1, 2);
```

Another common error is to use ordinary parentheses to construct a list reference when you should be using square or curly brackets; for example, if you say

```
$array = (1,2);
```

when you should have said

```
$array = [1,2];
```

The square brackets explicitly turn a list value into a scalar value, while parentheses do not. So, when a parenthesized list is evaluated in a scalar context, the comma is treated like C's comma operator, which throws away the left argument—not what you want.

untie attempted while %d inner references still exist   Warning (untie)

A copy of the object returned from **tie** (or **tied**) was still valid when **untie** was called.

Value of %s can be "0"; test with defined()   Warning (misc)

In a conditional expression, you used **<HANDLE>**, **<*>** (as **glob**), **each**, or **readdir** as a boolean value. Each of these constructs can return a value of "0"; that would make the conditional expression false, which is probably not what you intended. When using these constructs in conditional expressions, test their values with the **defined** operator.

Value of CLI symbol "%s" too long   Warning (misc), VMS only

Perl tried to read the value of a **%ENV** element from a CLI symbol table and found a resultant string longer than 1,024 characters. The return value has been truncated to 1,024 characters.

Variable "%s" is not imported%s   Fatal Error

There are two possible problems here. Either you've tried to use a variable as a function call—for example,

```
$function();
```

You've probably got the wrong parentheses—or you've forgotten to de-reference the variable as a function. Alternatively, it could just be a typo.

When the **strict** pragma is in effect, it probably means that you've tried to use a global variable that you thought was imported from elsewhere.

Variable "%s" may be unavailable   Warning (closure)

An inner (nested) *anonymous* subroutine is inside a *named* subroutine, and outside that is another subroutine; and the anonymous (innermost) subroutine is referencing a lexical variable defined in the outermost subroutine. For example,

```
sub outermost
{
    my $a;
    sub middle
    {
        sub { $a }
    }
}
```

If the anonymous subroutine is called or referenced (directly or indirectly) from the outermost subroutine, it will share the variable as you would expect. But if the anonymous subroutine is called or referenced when the outermost subroutine is not active, it will see the value of the shared variable as it was before and during the *first* call to the outermost subroutine, which is probably not what you want. In these circumstances, it is usually best to make the middle subroutine anonymous, using the

sub {} syntax. Perl has specific support for shared variables in nested anonymous subroutines; a named subroutine in between interferes with this feature.

Variable "%s" will not stay shared   Warning (closure)

An inner (nested) *named* subroutine is referencing a lexical variable defined in an outer subroutine. When the inner subroutine is called, it will probably see the value of the outer subroutine's variable as it was before and during the *first* call to the outer subroutine; in such case, after the first call to the outer subroutine is complete, the inner and outer subroutines will no longer share a common value for the variable. In other words, the variable will no longer be shared. Further, if the outer subroutine is anonymous and references a lexical variable outside itself, then the outer and inner subroutines will *never* share the given variable. This is easily demonstrated by

```
sub outer
{
    ($num) = @_;
    my $var = 'first';
    print "Outer($num): $var\n";
    sub inner
    {
        print "Inner($num): $var\n";
        $var = "third\n";
    }
    inner();
    $var = 'second';
}

outer(1);
outer(2);
outer(3);
```

which generates

```
Outer(1): first
Inner(1): first
Outer(2): first
Inner(2): second
Outer(3): first
Inner(3): third
```

The **$var** in the **inner** and **outer** subroutines are now separate variables instead of being shared.

This problem can usually be solved by making the inner subroutine anonymous, using the **sub {}** syntax. When inner anonymous subs that reference variables in outer subroutines are called or referenced, they are automatically re-bound to the current values of such variables.

Variable syntax   External Error

You've accidentally run your script through **csh** instead of Perl. Check the shebang (**#!**) line or manually feed your script into Perl yourself.

Version number must be a constant number   Internal Error

The attempt to translate a **use Module n.n LIST** statement into its equivalent **BEGIN** block found an internal inconsistency with the version number. You've probably tried to supply a variable instead of a constant for the version number.

perl: warning: Setting locale failed   Severe Warning

The whole warning message will look something like this:

```
perl: warning: Setting locale failed.
perl: warning: Please check that your locale settings:
LC_ALL = "En_US",
LANG = (unset)
are supported and installed on your system.
perl: warning: Falling back to the standard locale ("C").
```

Exactly what were the failed locale settings varies. In the above, the settings were that the LC_ALL was "En_US" and that the LANG had no value. This error means that Perl detected that you and/or your system administrator have set up the so-called variable system but Perl could not use those settings. This is not dead serious, fortunately: there is a "default locale" called "C" that Perl can and will use—the script will be run. Before you really fix the problem, however, you will get the same error message each time you run Perl. How to really fix the problem is described in the **LOCALE PROBLEMS** section of the **perllocale** manual page.

Warning: something's wrong   Warning

You called **warn** with an empty string or without any arguments when **$_** was empty.

Warning: unable to close filehandle %s properly   Severe Warning

When calling **open** on an active filehandle, the previous file is closed first. The **close** operation in this case failed. This is probably due to a disk space problem but can also be caused by other processes deleting the file before your script has finished using it.

Warning: Use of "%s" without parentheses is ambiguous   Severe Warning (ambiguous)

You wrote a unary operator followed by something that looks like a binary operator that could also have been interpreted as a term or unary operator. For instance, if you know that the rand function has a default argument of 1.0, and you write

```
rand + 5;
```

you may *think* you wrote the same thing as

```
rand() + 5;
```

but in actual fact, you got

```
rand(+5);
```

put in parentheses to say what you really mean.

write() on closed filehandle %s   Warning (closed)

You're trying to **close** a filehandle that has already been closed. Check the logic to see if you're calling **close** twice. You might also want to check the variable used to hold the filehandle in case it's going out of scope before you try close the file.

X outside of string   Fatal Error

You've supplied a pack template that gives a relative position that is before the start of the string you are unpacking. If you're using a dynamic pack template, consider checking the string length before compiling the template. If you're using a static template, check the data you are importing either so you can make changes to the pack template or dynamically before you call pack.

x outside of string   Fatal Error

You've supplied a pack template that gives a relative position that is beyond the confines of the string you are unpacking. If you're using a dynamic pack template, consider checking the string length before compiling the template. If you're using a static template, check the data you are importing either so you can make changes to the pack template or dynamically before you call pack.

Xsub "%s" called in sort   Fatal Error

The use of an external subroutine as a sort comparison is not yet supported.

Xsub called in sort   Fatal Error

The use of an external subroutine as a sort comparison is not yet supported.

You can't use -l on a filehandle   Fatal Error

You can't use the **-l** stat operator to get the link information from a filehandle because the original file name will have already been resolved. Use the file name instead.

YOU HAVEN'T DISABLED SET-ID SCRIPTS IN THE KERNEL YET!   Fatal Error

Use the **wrapsuid** script to place a wrapper around the script that you want to execute **setuid**.

You need to quote "%s"   Syntax Warning

When assigning a signal handler you should specify a reference the function name instead of using a bareword. Otherwise, Perl will call the function and return the assignment value as the signal handler. For example,

```
$SIG{ALRM} = alarmcall;
```

should be written as

```
$SIG{ALRM} = \&alarmcall;
```

%cetsockopt() on closed socket %s   Warning (closed)

You tried to get or set a socket option on a closed socket. Make sure that the **socket** is open before calling the functions.

\1 better written as $1   Syntax Warning

The use of **\x** to refer to matching groups in a regular expression is now deprecated—use the **$x** form instead.

'|' and '<' may not both be specified on command line   Fatal Error, VMS only

Perl does its own command-line redirection, and it found that **STDIN** was a pipe and that you also tried to redirect **STDIN** using <. Only one **STDIN** stream to a customer, please.

'|' and '>' may not both be specified on command line   Fatal Error, VMS only

Perl does its own command-line redirection, and it thinks you tried to redirect **stdout** both to a file and into a pipe to another command. You need to choose one or the other, though nothing's stopping you from piping into a program or Perl script that "splits" output into two streams, such as

```
open(OUT,">$ARGV[0]") or die "Can't write to $ARGV[0]: $!";
while (<STDIN>) {
print;
print OUT;
}
close OUT;
```

Got an error from DosAllocMem   Internal Error, OS/2 only

Most probably you're using an obsolete version of Perl, and this should not happen anyway.

Malformed PERLLIB_PREFIX   Fatal Error, OS/2 only

PERLLIB_PREFIX should be of the form

```
prefix1;prefix2
```

or

```
prefix1 prefix2
```

with non-empty **prefix1** and **prefix2**. If **prefix1** is indeed a prefix of a builtin library search path, **prefix2** is substituted. The error may appear if components are not found or are too long.

PERL_SH_DIR too long   Fatal Error, OS/2 only

The value contained in the **PERL_SH_DIR** (which should refer to the **sh** shell) is too long.

Process terminated by SIG%s   Warning

Raised in OS/2 when a Perl script was terminated by a signal without a suitable signal handler.

Index

I

J